TEXT AND TASK

'I confess I approach *Festchrifts* with some trepidation. They often appear to be a ragbag of articles in which busy writers have offloaded pieces not wanted elsewhere. But this volume is scintillating. The more I read, the more I wanted to. It never loses sight of the twin focus on Bible and Mission. Though the articles are diverse there is a clear coherence about them. Here is good biblical and theological scholarship, yet wonderfully applied. Depth is not sacrificed on the altar of missionary pragmatism. But nor is application sacrificed on the altar of scholarly obscurantism. Never once did I feel that a chapter was a tired repetition of well-known debates. The volume had the touch of originality about it without being novel for the sake of it. Here are chapters to savour, that will lead us into the Bible and out into mission. It is a fitting tribute to John Olley's life work.'

Derek Tidball, Principal, London School of Theology

'This is a rich collection of essays united by a recognition that the Bible – yes, including the Hebrew Bible – pulsates with God's outgoing love. The unity of scripture and mission is illustrated again and again in a wide variety of contributions that are scholarly and yet passionate. This book, both biblically focused and contextually stimulating, is a fitting tribute to John Olley, who is a significant Australian biblical scholar and missiologist.

'These essays grapple with many of the central missiological issues of the Hebrew Bible such as the dynamic relationship between God and the world, the missional reasons for Israel's existence and the tension between universalism versus particularism. Other essays engage – still biblically – with the twenty-first century context. I found them to be meaty and yet engaged. They illustrate the best of current broadly Evangelical scholarship. Some chapters and ground-breaking in my judgement and none are second-rate.

'This is a wonderful collection which shows that amongst his other qualities, John Olley keeps very good company.'

Dr Ross Langmead, Professor of Missiology and Director, School of World Mission, Whitley College, Australia

TEXT AND TASK

SCRIPTURE AND MISSION

Editor

MICHAEL PARSONS

WIPF & STOCK · Eugene, Oregon

Wipf and Stock Publishers
199 W 8th Ave, Suite 3
Eugene, OR 97401

Text and Task
Scripture and Mission
By Parsons, Michael
Copyright©2006 by Parsons, Michael
ISBN 13: 978-1-62032-316-8
Publication date 5/15/2012
Previously published by Paternoster, 2006

CONTENTS

Dedication   *vii*
Foreword by Walter Brueggemann   *ix*
Preface   *xi*
Contributors   *xiii*
Abbreviations   *xv*

1. The Loss and Retrieval of Ancestral Religion
   – in Ancient Israel and in Australia   *1*
   MARK G. BRETT

2. 'That the World May Know.' Narrative Poetics
   in 1 Samuel 16 – 17   *20*
   DAVID G. FIRTH

3. Solomon and the Building of the Temple   *33*
   ASHLEY CRANE

4. Getting to the Heart of the Matter – a Lamentable Situation   *50*
   DAVID J. COHEN

5. Luther on Isaiah 40: the Gospel and Mission   *64*
   MICHAEL PARSONS

6. Second Isaiah and the Greek Islands   *79*
   MARJO C.A. KORPEL

7. The Significance of the Old Testament for Paul's
   Missionary Calling   *91*
   RICHARD K. MOORE

8. Paul's 'Cloak' and the Completion of the Tanakh   *106*
   DUANE CHRISTENSEN

9. Paul's Gospel to the Gentiles and its Implications
   for Christian Mission to Chinese   *121*
   LUNG-KWONG LO

10. Truth with a Mission – Reading All Scripture Missiologically *140*
    CHRISTOPHER J.H. WRIGHT

11. A Trinitarian Perspective on the Destiny of the Unevangelized *157*
    HAYDN D. NELSON

12. Communities of Witness. The Concept of Election in the Old
    Testament and in the Theology of Karl Barth   *172*
    MICHAEL O'NEIL

13. Repristination. The Recovery of the Gospel in
    Post-Secular Australia   *187*
    STUART DEVENISH

14. From 'Behave, Believe, Belong' to 'Belong, Believe, Behave' – A
    Missional Journey for the 21st Century   *204*
    BRIAN S. HARRIS

15. Prophetic Preaching for a Missional Church   *218*
    MICHAEL J. QUICKE

Indexes   *234*

To John Olley
Scholar, missionary, colleague and friend

FOREWORD

Something of immense importance is happening in the world church that is much to be celebrated, namely, that the church is rediscovering the Bible as a gift for faith. Now that may sound strange since we keep reading the Bible through thick and thin. We have, however, found ways of reading the Bible without hearing it in its urgency. It has been the case in recent generations that the church has strayed in important ways from the liveliness of the Bible – in scholastic dogmatism on the right and in excessive critical perspective on the left. The more it has strayed from the address of the word, the more the church has found things about which to quarrel and consequently has been deterred from its missional witness.

The current recovery of the Bible is happening throughout the church. It is happening in the First World church, because we are being driven back to basics in the face of secularization. In the world beyond Euro-development the recovery is led by the fresh guidance of the Spirit. Wherever that rediscovery is under way, the church is permitted to refocus its energy, to reclaim its sense of vocation, and to appreciate in new ways its buoyancy in joy and its true reason for being, namely, glad obedient testimony to the gospel.

It is clear that the church will not have energy and courage for its true life except with an imaginative embrace of Scripture. It is equally clear, moreover, that an imaginative embrace of Scripture is possible only because of hard, attentive work on the detail of Scripture that requires the most alert and sustained kind of scholarship.

For that reason, I am pleased to welcome and celebrate this present volume that attests to such alert and sustained scholarship, and to celebrate the long career of faithful Scripture study of Dr. John Olley in whose name the volume is offered. Dr John Olley is well known among the contributors to this volume, and surely among many of its potential readers, as a distinctive, passionate and treasured embodiment of scholarship in the service of the church.

It is of course the case that careful, meticulous scholarship is not immediately transposed into missional reality. Rather, such scholarship is a long-term enterprise that creates, maintains, and nourishes a culture of attentiveness that in turn authorizes and nourishes an evangelical imagination. It is that evangelical imagination that makes a new life imaginable and therefore liveable outside the scope of dominant culture. My own sense is that the capacity for life outside the matrix of dominant culture is not only a gift from God to the faithful, but is also an urgent need for the world culture that is now emerging that threatens to be void of the dimension of the Spirit.

The long-term purpose of biblical scholarship in the church is to nurture, form, and reform a 'holy people', a people devoted singularly to the things of

God. There is no doubt that such nurture is now urgent in a world culture given over to greed, fear, and violence, in which many young people have lost their way.

John Olley and his colleagues in this volume are to be commended for staying at the task of probing and attesting to 'a more excellent way', a way made by holy responsiveness to God and by generous justice toward neighbour. 'The two great commandments' that stand at the centre of an evangelical ethic are indeed urgent; they are, however, credible and sustainable only in a culture of faith that is sustained by faithful imagination. For this publication, John Olley is to be especially feted, the writers are to be thanked, and readers are to be welcomed to a rich offer of fresh, obedient thinking.

Walter Brueggemann
Emeritus Professor of Old Testament
The William Marcellus McPheeters Chair
Columbia Theological Seminary
Decatur, Georgia
April, 2005

PREFACE

The present volume has come together as an appreciation of the work and friendship of John Olley who retired at the end of 2003 after a lifetime of theological teaching, research and scholarship, and missionary practice. John is quietly and meticulously passionate in all his pursuits – Old Testament exegesis, mission, the teaching of Hebrew – as well as in pastoral concern for others. It seems to me that John knows something *significant* about everything on which he speaks or writes – from Old Testament to the Sermon on the Mount, from missiology to ecology. He has a wealth of knowledge, but what characterizes him is his Christian humility. At the time of his retirement John was the Principal of the College in which I presently teach Systematic Theology. Often, I would be in conversation with him about an area of my own subject and would simply be amazed at the profound knowledge and understanding that he evidenced in an area (supposedly) 'outside' of his own competence. Always, he would want to tease out the practical implications for church and mission in today's world.

I am immensely grateful to the contributors to this volume who without exception see the importance of the connection between the biblical text and our response to it in mission. The essays are exceptional responses and the quality of them has made my life, as editor, very easy indeed. I am also grateful to Walter Brueggemann, Emeritus Professor of Old Testament, Columbia Theological Seminary, for generously writing the foreword to this book. It was John Olley who introduced me to Brueggemann's exciting and helpful work.

I am also grateful to Derek Tidball, Principal of London School of Theology, and to Ross Langmead, Professor of Missiology and Director, School of World Mission, Whitley College, Melbourne, for reading the whole manuscript and making helpful comments.

My hope is that the volume makes a thoughtful, biblical and theological contribution to the church's sense and practice of mission today and that the Lord will further that mission through its use.

Michael Parsons
The Baptist Theological College
Perth, Western Australia

CONTRIBUTORS
In alphabetical order

Mark G. Brett is Professor of Old Testament, Whitley College; Dean of the Evangelical Theological Association, Melbourne, Australia.

Duane Christensen is retired Professor of Old Testament Languages and Literature, Graduate Theological Union, Berkeley, California, USA.

David J. Cohen is Head of Biblical Studies, The Baptist Theological College, Perth, Western Australia.

Ashley Crane is Principal of Harvest West Bible College, Perth, Western Australia.

Stuart Devenish is Lecturer in Biblical and Mission Studies, Australian College of Ministries, Sydney, Australia.

David G. Firth is Old Testament Tutor at Cliff College, Calver, UK.

Brian S. Harris is Principal of The Baptist Theological College, Perth, Western Australia.

Marjo C.A. Korpel is Lecturer in Old Testament, Theology Faculty, Utrecht University, the Netherlands.

Lung-Kwong Lo is Director of the Divinity School of Chung Chi College, the Chinese University of Hong Kong, Shatin, Hong Kong.

Richard K. Moore is retired Head of New Testament, The Baptist Theological College, Perth, Western Australia.

Haydn D. Nelson is Principal of The Bible College of Western Australia, Perth, Western Australia.

Michael O'Neil is Senior Pastor of Lesmurdie Baptist Church, Perth, Western Australia.

Michael Parsons is Head of Christian Thought, The Baptist Theological College, Perth, Western Australia.

Michael J. Quicke is Koller Professor of Preaching and Communication, Northern Baptist Theological Seminary, Lombard, Illinois, USA.

Christopher J.H. Wright is International Ministries Director, Langham Partnership International, London.

ABBREVIATIONS

ACR	*Australian Catholic Record*
ATA	*Asia Theological*
ATh	*Acta Theologica*
BAR	*Biblical Archaeology Review*
BibInt	*Biblical Interpretation*
BibSt	*Biblische Studien*
BRev	*Bible Review*
BSac	*Bibliotheca Sacra*
CBQ	*Catholic Biblical Quarterly*
CD	Karl Barth, *Church Dogmatics* (Edinburgh: T. & T. Clark, 1956–75).
CH	*Church History*
CT	*Christianity Today*
EQ	*Evangelical Quarterly*
HTR	*Harvard Theological Review*
HUCA	*Hebrew Union College Annual*
Int	*Interpretation*
JBL	Journal of Biblical Literature
JETS	*Journal of the Evangelical Theological Society*
JNSL	*Journal of Northwest Semitic Languages*
JPS	*Jewish Publication Society*
JR	*Journal of Religion*
JSNT	*Journal for the Study of the New Testament*
JSOT	*Journal for the Study of the Old Testament*
JTS	*Journal of Theological Studies*
LW	Luther's Works *['American Edition']* (St. Louis: Concordia / Philadelphia: Fortress Press, 1955–1986).
NTS	*New Testament Studies*
NZSTR	*Neue Zeitschrift Für Systematische Theologie und Religionsphilosophie*
RRR	*Review of Religious Research*
SJT	*Scottish Journal of Theology*
SWC	*Studies in World Christianity*
TB	*Tyndale Bulletin*
TToday	*Theology Today*
VR	*Vox Reformata*
VT	*Vetus Testamentum*
WA	D. Martin Luthers Werke: Kritische Gesamtausgabe (Weimar: Herman Böhlaus Nachfolger, 1883–1987).

WA Br.	*D. Martin Luthers Werke: Briewechsel* (Weimar: Herman Böhlaus Nachfolger, 1930–1948).
ZAW	*Zeitschrift für die alttestamentliche Wissenschaft*

CHAPTER 1

The Loss and Retrieval of Ancestral Religion
– in Ancient Israel and in Australia

MARK G. BRETT

Introduction

'Do not move an everlasting boundary stone, set up by your ancestors (*'avot*)'
(Prov. 22:28).

'Do not move your neighbour's boundary stone, set up by your predecessors in the inheritance you receive in the land YHWH your *'elohim* is giving to you to possess'
(Deut. 19:14).

John Olley has brought together in his life a rare combination of passions: mission and biblical scholarship. If a similar combination were sought amongst his Baptist forbears, perhaps H.H. Rowley might be an appropriate comparison. Rowley was a missionary in China in the 1920s and John taught at Chung Chi College in Hong Kong from 1968–78. Rowley struggled with one of the key questions that will concern us in this chapter: How is Christian mission to be related to the religious practices that preceded it? He argued that mission often takes what is familiar in experience and builds on it a fresh revelation of the character and activity of God.[1] For example, in a significant conversation in Genesis 14:18–22, an indigenous priest names the Creator as 'El Elyon', and Abram replies by calling God 'YHWH, El Elyon', assimilating the Israelite

---

[1] H.H. Rowley, *The Missionary Message of the Old Testament* (London, 1944), 15–16. Rowley proposed an analogy between the way that God was re-named in Israel and the way in which biblical translation in China adopted a traditional name for God 'Shang Ti'. He defended this translation on the grounds that Moses brought a new name for God, but linked this name with the ancestors in Exodus 6:2. 'God also said to Moses, "I am the LORD [YHWH]. I appeared to Abraham, to Isaac and to Jacob as God Almighty [El Shaddai], but by my name YHWH I did not make myself known to them.' We have ample evidence that El was the high god of Canaan, and this is one of several biblical traditions that establish the link with YHWH.

name of God to the indigenous name.² The purpose of this essay is to reexamine the place of ancestral religion in ancient Israel, and to explore its significance for indigenous mission today, especially in Australia.

This task is crucial, I would argue, to the formulation of a postcolonial missiology. The issues today are somewhat different from those that Rowley faced. The transformation of traditional religion, which he proposed, can itself be seen as a form of 'assimilationism' – a more subtle form of colonialism. Deborah Bird Rose has recently described a local example of the more blatant expression of religious conflict in which 'culture way' and 'church way' are diametrically and tragically opposed in a particular indigenous community in Northern Australia. Rose's social description takes its starting point from Marcel Gauchet's thesis in *The Disenchantment of the World* that 'primitive religions', free of the influence of states, represent the pinnacle of religious connectivity, whereas Christianity is the fulfillment of 'disenchantment', a fracturing of the connections with kin and country.³ The irony in Rose's account is that the Christian missionaries in this case were themselves indigenous, reflecting the fact that Aboriginal Christians have differing attitudes towards the indigenization of Christian faith and practice.

It is perhaps a sign of the times that two other recent works by non-indigenous authors have been concerned to articulate some reversals of this process of 'disenchantment' and social fracturing. David Tacey's *ReEnchantment: the New Australian Spirituality* engages in cultural criticism on a grand scale, linking ecospirituality to Aboriginal reconciliation. Ivan Jordan's *Their Way: Towards an Indigenous Warlpiri Christianity* offers self-critical reflections on two decades of missionary work amongst the Warlpiri people in central Australia, who now have adapted traditional corroborees, art, and music for use in Christian worship.⁴ In some respects, these recent books are simply echoing arguments advanced by many indigenous Christians over the last decades, as indicated by the collection of essays edited by Anne Pattel-Gray, *Aboriginal Spirituality: Past, Present, Future.*⁵

---

² See also Sanneh's discussion of the process by which Zulu biblical translations came to adopt the traditional name for God, *uNkulunkulu* – L. Sanneh, *Translating the Message* (Maryknoll, 1989), 171–172.

³ D.B. Rose, 'Pentecostal Missionaries and the Exit from Religion', paper delivered at the Bible and Critical Theory Seminar, Melbourne, June 2004, drawing on M. Gauchet, *The Disenchantment of the World: A Political History of Religion* (Princeton, 1999). A different version of Rose's argument appears in her recent book, *Reports from a Wild Country: Ethics for Decolonisation* (Sydney, 2004), 149–162.

⁴ D. Tacey, *ReEnchantment: The New Australian Spirituality* (Sydney, 2000); I. Jordan, *Their Way. Towards an Indigenous Warlpiri Christianity* (Darwin, 2003).

⁵ Rose's argument may be compared with Djiniyini Gondarra's representation of 'spiritual genocide' in his essay, 'Aboriginal Spirituality and the Gospel' in A. Pattel-Gray (ed.), *Aboriginal Spirituality: Past, Present, Future* (Melbourne, 1996), 42. Cf. also the reference to 'cultural genocide' in Rainbow Spirit Elders, *Rainbow Spirit*

In this chapter, however, I want to examine some biblical resources that might bear on these recent discussions, focusing to begin with on the loss and retrieval of ancestral religion in ancient Israel and Judah. Admittedly, this is an area of research that is fraught with conflicting hypotheses, and even if we could achieve a measure of consensus, many Christian scholars would draw a sharp methodological distinction between the history of Israelite religion and biblical theology of the canonical texts.[6] Nevertheless, there are striking parallels between the recent accounts of disenchantment within indigenous communities and, in particular, the rise of Deuteronomic theology in ancient Judah, and these parallels may provide a fresh perspective both on biblical theology and on missiology.

Ancestor Cults and Deuteronomic Innovations

A number of recent studies have indicated that Sennacherib's invasion in 701 resulted in the mass deportation of the greater part of Judah's rural population, leaving the society dependant upon initiatives from Jerusalem.[7] The Assyrian invasion apparently demolished the old clan system that was the matrix of social identity, legal judgement, land tenure and local forms of religious practice. Sennacherib's deportations were interpreted by Jerusalem theologians as YHWH's judgment on the rural cultic practices, and religion was therefore centralized under the one central cult of YHWH, which had already assimilated El as a divine name but which now interpreted the rural cults as the 'foreign' practice of Aboriginal Amorites.[8] Halpern describes this as a process of

---

Theology (Melbourne, 1997), 51. For similar arguments from Native American Christians, see G.E. Tinker, *Missionary Conquest: The Gospel and Native American Cultural Genocide* (Minneapolis, 1993); J. Treat (ed.), *Native and Christian: Indigenous Voices on Religious Identity in the United States and Canada* (New York, 1996).

[6] See M.G. Brett, 'Canonical Criticism and Old Testament Theology' in A.D.H. Mayes (ed.), *Text in Context* (Oxford, 2000), 63–85.

[7] This argument has been advanced especially by Baruch Halpern in many publications, but see especially his essay, 'Jerusalem and the Lineages in the Seventh Century BCE' in B. Halpern and D.W. Hobson (eds.), *Law and Ideology in Monarchic Israel* (Sheffield, 1991), 11–107. Halpern's work has been affirmed, e.g. by M.S. Smith, *The Origins of Biblical Monotheism: Israel's Polytheistic Background and the Ugaritic Texts* (New York, 2001), 163, 286n.106; E. Otto, 'Human Rights: The Influence of the Hebrew Bible', *JNSL* 25 (1999), 13–14; B.M. Levinson, *Deuteronomy and the Hermeneutics of Legal Innovation* (New York, 1997), 148–149.

[8] Halpern, 'Jerusalem and the Lineages', 78, 81, 86, 91; idem., 'The Baal (and the Asherah) in Seventh-Century Judah: YHWH's Retainers Retired' in R. Bartelmus, et al (eds.), *Konsequente Traditionsgeschichte: Festschrift für Klaus Baltzer* (Göttingen, 1993), 115–154; so also, Levinson, *Deuteronomy and the Hermeneutics of Legal Innovation,* 148–149.

alienation from land, gods, kin and tradition. 'Hezekiah deconsecrated the land' and 'assaulted the resonance of its timeless ancestral associations'.[9]

> For Hezekiah's purposes, it had been essential to amputate the ancestors, those responsible for the bestowal of rural property to their descendants: they, and they alone, consecrated the possession of land.[10]

Assyrian imperial aggression had dislodged the ancestral ties, with the result that communal solidarity and land tenure could be re-constructed around a more centralized theology. Land is henceforth seen as a gift from the national God YHWH, rather than from localized ancestors. Several analogies might be suggested between this hypothesis about seventh-century Judah and the 'disenchantment' process in Australian mission history, an issue to which we shall return below.

The over-riding of ancestral religion may be discerned particularly in the traditions of Deuteronomy. Recent studies have convincingly benchmarked the dating of the Deuteronomic Code in relation to Assyrian material from the seventh century. In particular, Deuteronomy 13 and 28 seem to be based on models derived from the vassal treaties of Sennacherib's successor, king Esarhaddon.[11] In one of the most comprehensive analyses of these comparisons, Eckart Otto argues for a quite specific dating of core Deuteronomic texts between 672 and 612, which had the specific purpose of subversively opposing Assyrian hegemony.[12] The adaptation of Assyrian treaty and loyalty oaths was a bold strategy, asserting YHWH's authority above the obvious power of the Assyrian empire, but in the process demanding the strictest loyalty to YHWH and over-riding even the loyalty due to an individual's family (Deut. 13:7–10).[13]

---

[9] Halpern, 'Jerusalem and the Lineages', 82, cf. 84.

[10] Halpern, 'Jerusalem and the Lineages', 74.

[11] Influential work from this perspective includes W. Moran, 'The Ancient Near Eastern Background to the Love of God in Deuteronomy', *CBQ* 25 (1963), 77–87; M. Weinfeld, *Deuteronomy and the Deuteronomic School* (Oxford, 1972), 81–126. Deuteronomy 28:20–44 appropriates, in particular, the list of curses in VTE §56. See S. Parpolo and K. Watanabe (eds.), *Neo-Assyrian Treaties and Loyalty Oaths* (Helsinki, 1988), 49, and the discussion in H.U. Steymans, *Deuteronomium 28 und die* adê *zur thronfolgeregelung Asarhaddons: Segen und Fluch im Alten Orient und in Israel* (Göttingen, 1995), 119–141; E. Otto, *Das Deuteronomium: Politische Theologie und Rechtsreform in Juda und Assyrian* (Berlin, 1999). Parallels with the earlier Hittite treaties pale into insignificance by comparison.

[12] Otto, *Das Deuteronomium*, 14. The dates frame the period between Esarhaddon's treaties and the fall of Nineveh, marking the end of Assyrian imperial influence.

[13] See, e.g. B.M. Levinson, 'Textual Criticism, Assyriology, and the History of Interpretation: Deuteronomy 13:7 as a Test Case in Method', *JBL* 120 (2001), 238–41.

The removal of the ancestor cults was apparently just one aspect of the Deuteronomic programme. The overall strategy was not so much to revoke the previous traditions but to assert a new elaboration of older Israelite identity and law, claiming continuity within change. Thus, for example, the old festivals were re-established with the new principle of centralization, celebrating not 'in any town' but at a single site, '*the* place YHWH will choose as a dwelling for his name' (Deut 16:5–6). In contrast, Exodus 20:24–25 suggested that an altar of earth could be built 'in *every* place' where YHWH's name is 'remembered', and if the altar is made of stone, then it should be unhewn. The early festival calendar accordingly contains no hint of restriction to one site (Ex. 23:14–17),[14] and we read in 1 Samuel 20:6 of a sacrifice taking place in Bethlehem for David's clan without any suggestion from the narrator that this is unorthodox.[15] Similarly, Samuel happily presides at a sacrifice at the 'high place' (*bamah*) near Ramah (1 Sam. 9:12–13), although from a Deuteronomic point of view such 'high places' should not exist, and they are accordingly destroyed in the reforms of Hezekiah and Josiah (2 Kgs. 18:4; 23:5–9). The Deuteronomic movement brought religion under central organization, and the exclusion of all rival gods and 'names' included a prohibition of the *matsebah* (sacred pillar, e.g. Deut. 16:22) – a feature of ancestor cults, as many recent studies have argued.[16]

Genesis 35:20, for example, says that Jacob set up a pillar (*matsebah*) marking Rachel's tomb, and this tomb of Rachel is also referred to in 1 Samuel 10:2, although the potentially offensive terminology of *matsebah* has apparently been avoided in the latter case. 2 Samuel 18:18 does use the term *matsebah* to refer to a pillar that Absolom sets up so that his name may be remembered. As Karel van der Toorn has argued, this verse may well echo a practice known from neighboring Ugarit and Sam'al, where it was the duty of a son to set up a pillar at which to 'remember' or to 'invoke the name' of his father, and the poignancy of 2 Samuel 18:18 is that Absolom has no son to perform these rites. These examples might well reflect the traces of older forms of family religion.

Studies of vocabulary associated with ancestor cults have thrown new light on some old problems, such as the plural form *'elohim* – customarily translated

---

[14] The Holiness Code also allows that the festivals take place 'in all your settlements' (Lev. 23:14,21,31; cf. Lev. 26:31). See J. Milgrom, *Leviticus 17 – 22* (New York, 2000), 1503–1514.

[15] See further, K. van der Toorn, *Family Religion in Babylonia, Syria and Israel* (Leiden, 1996), 211–218.

[16] T.J. Lewis, *Cults of the Dead in Ancient Israel and Ugarit* (Atlanta, 1989), 118–20; E. Bloch-Smith, *Judahite Burial Practices and Beliefs about the Dead* (Sheffield, 1992), 113–14, 122–26; A. Cooper and B.R. Goldstein, 'The Cult of the Dead and the Theme of Entry in the Land,' *BibInt* 1 (1993), 285–303; van der Toorn, *Family Religion,* 206–235; Smith, *Origins of Monotheism,* 68–70.

'God' or 'gods' depending on the context. It seems that the term *'elohim* might in some cases also refer to divinized ancestors of the underworld, a usage that explains peculiar references to the 'holy ones who are in the earth' (Ps. 16:2), and to the dead Samuel in the context of 'gods [*'elohim*] coming up from the earth' (1 Sam. 28:14).[17] Bloch-Smith argues, for example, that the *'elohim* in Genesis 28:22; 31:52-54 and 46:1 refer to ancestral deities,[18] and this is quite clearly the case in Laban's speech in Genesis 31:30, although the *'elohim* in that chapter are also called *teraphim* in v. 19. Van der Toorn notes that Josiah destroys *teraphim* in 2 Kings 23:4, probably motivated by the warrant in Deuteronomy 18:11, pointing to an understanding of *teraphim* as ancestral icons.[19]

The dead were often seen in family religion as benefactors of their descendants, particularly in the bequest of ancestral land. When Naboth refers to 'the inheritance of my fathers' in 1 Kings 21:3, he is referring to his ancestral estate, and his reluctance to sell the land to the king may be illuminated by the parallel expression in 2 Samuel 14:16 'the inheritance of *'elohim*'. This 'inheritance' can be seen as traditional land which is inalienable because it is a gift of divinized ancestors. Such an interpretation conforms to the paradigm of research which links kin groups, local cults and traditional forms of land tenure.[20] Cultic practices for the dead may well have served the welfare of the ancestors who originally owned the land but, at the same time, these practices would also have re-asserted the descendants' moral rights to the inheritance. In line with this understanding, Alan Cooper and Bernard Goldstein have discerned a literary pattern behind ten different biblical narratives, linking deified ancestors (*'elohim*), the possession of land, and the setting up of a

---

[17] It is possible that these *'elohim* of the earth do not include Samuel himself, and we should note that supernatural beings of the underworld need not be thought of as powerful, like Baal or Asherah. At least, in Isaiah 14:9, they are represented as 'weak'. Isaiah 8:19 refers to consulting the ancestors (*'ovot*) in the context of necromancy; cf. the 'ancestor spirits' (*'ovot*) in 1 Samuel 28:3 and van der Toorn's interpretation in, *Family Religion*, 221–22, 318. See also, B.B. Schmidt, 'Memory as Immortality' in A.J. Avery-Peck and J. Neusner (eds.), *Judaism in Late Antiquity: Part 4, Death, Life-After-Death, Resurrection and the World-to-Come in the Judaisms of Antiquity* (Leiden, 2000), 87–100.

[18] Bloch-Smith, *Burial Practices*, 122–123.

[19] Van der Toorn, *Family Religion*, 224. Traces of ancestral religion have also been found in personal names, such as 'Ammiel' which has been interpreted as 'my ancestor is god', and 'Eliam', meaning 'my god, the ancestor'. See Van der Toorn, *Family Religion*, 228–230.

[20] See H.C. Brichto, 'Kin, Cult, Land, and Afterlife', *HUCA* 44 (1973), 1–54; C.J.H. Wright, *God's People in God's Land: Family, Land and Property in the Old Testament* (Grand Rapids, 1990), 151–59; T.J. Lewis, 'The Ancestral Estate in 2 Samuel 14:16', *JBL* 110 (1991), 597–612; van der Toorn, *Family Religion*, 210–11; Bloch-Smith, *Burial Practices*, 146; Halpern, 'Jerusalem and the Lineages', 57–59.

matsebah, stele or altar. Their argument suggests that the presence of these stones or pillars established the 'real or symbolic presence of deified ancestors', which in turn 'manifests an assertion of ownership in perpetuity'.[21]

The narratives of Joshua 24 and Exodus 23:20 – 24:11, which share this pattern, assert that foreign *'elohim* must not be venerated; their *matsebot* should be broken down (Ex. 23:24), and Joshua sets up a 'large stone' instead (Josh. 24:26–27). It seems that the pattern of ancestral religion – to set up a pillar as a reflection of land tenure – is in Joshua supplanted by a new pillar for YHWH, established in opposition to the other *'elohim* who were worshipped by the ancestors (Josh. 24:14–15). According to Cooper and Goldstein, the gift of land from YHWH supersedes the gifts from the ancestors. This perspective may also be reflected in Psalm 16:2–6,

> I have said to YHWH: You are my Lord. I have nothing of value beside you.
> As for the holy ones who are in the underworld, the mighty ones ...
> I shall not bring their libation of blood, nor take their names on my lips.
> YHWH is my allotted portion and my cup; you hold my lot.
> The lines have fallen for me in pleasant places, yea, my inheritance pleases me.[22]

We should recognize, however, that Joshua 24 and Exodus 23:20 – 24:11 do not share all of Deuteronomy's perspectives on the worship of YHWH, since Joshua establishes his *own* cultic site and writes his own 'law of *'elohim*' in 24:25–26, rather than defer to Mosaic law as elsewhere in the book of Joshua.

Several studies have pointed out that Exodus 23 envisages only the destruction of indigenous cults, not the 'holy war' on indigenous peoples that we find in Deuteronomy 20:16-18. In Exodus, the prior inhabitants are said to be dispossessed by YHWH *alone*, not by Israelite wars, a perspective on land possession that Exodus shares with the Holiness Code (Lev. 18:28; 19:23).[23] In view of such differences, it would be reasonable to conclude that YHWH's control of land tenure was a feature of Israelite religion before Deuteronomy's picture of conquest and centralization was actually created. In other words,

---

[21] Cooper and Goldstein, 'Cult of the Dead', 294, 297. The ten narratives are Gen. 12:1–9; 28:10–22; 31:1 – 32.3; 33:18–20; 35:1–20; Ex. 23:20 – 24:11; Deut. 27; Josh. 3:5 – 5.12; 8:30–35; 24.

[22] The translation follows van der Toorn, *Family Religion*, 210.

[23] M. Fishbane, *Biblical Interpretation in Ancient Israel* (Oxford, 1985), 199–209; B.J. Schwartz, 'Reexamining the Fate of the "Canaanites" in the Torah Traditions' in C. Cohen, A. Hurvitz and S.M. Paul (eds.), *Sefer Moshe: The Moshe Weinfeld Jubilee Volume* (Winona Lake, 2004), 151–70. See further, M.G. Brett, 'Genocide in Deuteronomy: Postcolonial Variations on Mimetic Desire' in M. O'Brien and H. Wallace (eds.), *Seeing Signals, Reading Signs* (London, 2005), 76–90.

Cooper and Goldstein's group of ten texts reflects the assimilation of indigenous rites to the worship of YHWH in a process that was probably independent of Deuteronomy.

Canonical Perspectives

The recent research on ancestral religion has provided some plausible and illuminating reconstructions of the beliefs and practices behind the canonical texts. In Christopher Wright's discussion of these issues, he accepts this point and then follows H.H. Rowley's missiological paradigm by concluding that YHWH religion had a habit of 'taking over established culture patterns and then transforming them into vehicles of its own distinctive theology and ethics'.[24] My own view, mindful of postcolonial studies, would put this argument slightly differently. I would want to emphasize the aspects of cultural transformation that include resistance to abuses of political and economic power.[25] And it seems to me that Wright's work provides some important clues in this regard, especially when we consider the broader scope of canonical perspectives found in Genesis and the Holiness Code (Lev. 17–26).

Even within the historical narratives influenced by Deuteronomy, however, we find significant theological defenses against the abuse of monarchic power. The famous example of Naboth's vineyard demonstrates that a refusal to part with ancestral inheritance was given divine sanction by the narrators (1 Kgs. 21:17–24; 2 Kgs. 9:30 – 10.11). If the idea of national unity under YHWH was simply an ideological mask of centralized monarchic interests, then this story would surely not exist in scripture. If YHWH was seen as the national God who over-rode all local forms of ancestral piety, then the transfer of land between Israelites would have been consistent with the program of nationalization. What is notable about the canonical form of the Naboth incident is that the stubborn maintenance of ancestral land was seen to be sanctioned precisely by YHWH. Naboth says to the king, '*YHWH forbid* me, that I should give the inheritance of my ancestors to you' (1 Kgs. 21:3).[26] The prohibition on moving the boundary stones of the 'predecessors' (*rishonim*) in Deuteronomy 19:14 avoids using the potentially sensitive term 'fathers' (*'avot*), but this verse clearly supports land rights bequeathed by the ancestors, nonetheless.

Following Brichto, Wright emphasizes that rites on behalf of the dead are only forbidden in connection with 'foreign' families and deities, citing the following texts as evidence: Exodus 34:11–16; Numbers 25:1ff.; Psalm 106:28; Deuteronomy 7:1–4. In other words, ancestral traditions within 'Israelite' families were tolerated, and for example, the law directed against the use of tithes in gifts for the dead proscribes exactly that – the use of tithes, not all gifts

---

[24] Wright, *God's Land*, 156.
[25] See B. Ashcroft, *Postcolonial Transformation* (London, 2001), 1–44.
[26] Cf. Brichto, 'Kin, Cult, Land', 31–32; Wright, *God's Land*, 158–159.

for the dead (Deut. 26:14). Thus, Wright concludes, along with Brichto, that there is no apparent rejection of ritual practices for the dead, or the use of *teraphim*, 'provided there was no question of the involvement of other gods than YHWH'. They agree that 'veneration is not worship'.[27] On this interpretation, the national profile of YHWH accommodated ancestral cultural practices, and it is quite possible to claim that YHWH's gifts of land still allowed both for veneration of a clan's ancestors and for an understanding of ancestral land tenure.

This conclusion is reinforced from a quite different perspective in the Holiness Code. Leviticus 25:23–24 prohibits the permanent sale of land on the grounds that it belongs solely to YHWH. A skeptical reader might take this as an ideological strategy for reinforcing monarchic interests over against clan authority, but the requirement in these verses that 'You must provide redemption for the land' affirms the right of return in the Jubilee year for families wishing to reclaim precisely their *traditional* land (25:13). Although the Holiness Code rejects ancestor worship, and cultic practices involving the dead (Lev. 19:28,31; 20:6,27),[28] it nowhere suggests that YHWH's ownership endorses monarchic authority over land. On the contrary, the theology of 'redemption' in the Holiness Code focuses on the restoration of 'kin and country'. In the fiftieth year, when liberty (*dror*)[29] was proclaimed, everyone was to return to their family and land (Lev. 25:10).

The book of Genesis also preserves a pattern of religious practice that is demonstrably different from Mosaic traditions, and many scholars discussed in the previous section argue that this distinctive pattern reflects family cults, rather than the official religion of the state.[30] Without attempting to describe the historical developments of Israelite religion, Walter Moberly sets out the distinctiveness of ancestral religion over against the ethos of Exodus and Deuteronomy in *The Old Testament of the Old Testament: Patriarchal*

---

[27] Brichto, 'Kin, Cult, Land', 28–9, 46–7; Wright, *God's Land*, 156–7. A distinction between veneration and worship is also recognized by evangelical missiologists, e.g. C. Kraft, *Anthropology for Christian Witness* (Maryknoll, 1996), 233–4. The theological argument for the legitimacy of *teraphim* might perhaps be applied to Aboriginal ancestral icons, such as the *tjurunga* of the Aranda. See B. Hill, *Broken Song: T.G.H. Strehlow and Aboriginal Possession* (Sydney, 2002), 158–62.

[28] Lewis, *Cults of the Dead*, 175. See further, J. Milgrom, *Leviticus 23 – 27* (New York, 2000), 1283–91.

[29] The terminology is probably related to the Akkadian term *anduraru*, meaning literally 'return to the mother'. See Weinfeld, *Deuteronomy and the Deuteronomic School*, 153.

[30] An earlier exponent of this view emphasizes that the patterns in Genesis reflect not so much 'a preliminary stage' as a 'substratum' of YHWH religion, a family religion which demonstrates notable similarities with other ancient Near Eastern religious practices. R. Albertz, *A History of Israelite Religion in the Old Testament Period* (London, 1994), 1.29, building on his pioneering work in *Persönliche Frömigkeit und offizielle Religion* (Stuttgart, 1978).

Narratives and Mosaic Yahwism. Noting, for example, that Abram builds altars in two places where it seems that sacred trees already exist (Gen. 12:6–7; 13:18),[31] Moberly emphasizes that ancestral religion is open and inclusive, with virtually no evidence of antagonism with the indigenous people.[32] There is no specialized priesthood, and no distinctive customs like Sabbath or food laws. The Canaanite divine name El Elyon is shared, in Genesis 14:18–20, with the indigenous priest of Salem. Patriarchal 'election' does not have exclusivist emphases, and it lacks the language of holiness, which arises with the Yahwism of Exodus. Both Moberly and Wenham summarize the spirit of Genesis in terms of 'ecumenical bonhomie'.[33]

Whatever the historical relationship between family-based religion and Mosaic Yahwism might have been, there is a sense in which ancestral religion has been partially 'retrieved' in Genesis. And, what is most significant for our purposes, Moberly finds in the canonical texts a model for the relationship between Christianity and Judaism.

> Mosaic Yahwism respected and preserved the distinctiveness of patriarchal religion, saw it as the foundation for its own existence, and recognized the continuing validity of God's dealings with the patriarchs. In a similar way, therefore, the Christian should respect and recognize both the content of Mosaic Yahwism as its own antecedent of continuing validity and also the religious system of Judaism that in its own different way develops from it.[34]

This does not imply the absence of critical responses to preceding traditions, but it does imply a basic attitude of respect, rather than denigration. A key question arising for missiology in Australia is, How does Moberly's thesis relate to the experience of ancestral religion amongst indigenous Australian Christians, particularly bearing in mind the respect given to ancestral land tenure by the biblical theologies already discussed?

---

[31] Deuteronomy 16:21 prohibits the juxtaposition of altars and trees, reflecting anxiety about the tree symbolism of Asherah, but the narrators of Genesis express no such anxiety.

[32] The only exception perhaps is Genesis 35:2,4 which Moberly takes to be evidence of Yahwist influence, yet even this does not attribute the idolatry to Canaanite influence. See R.W.L. Moberly, *The Old Testament of the Old Testament* (Minneapolis, 1992), 88–89.

[33] Moberly, *The Old Testament*, 104; G. Wenham, 'The Religion of the Patriarchs' in A. Millard and D.J. Wiseman (eds.), *Essays on the Patriarchal Narratives* (Leicester, 1980), 157–88. Cf. C. Westermann, *Genesis 12 – 36* (Minneapolis, 1985), 68, 'There is not so much as a single sentence which rejects Canaanite religion or morality'. Also, N. Habel, *The Land is Mine* (Minneapolis, 1995), 115–33.

[34] Moberly, *The Old Testament*, 164.

Implications for Missiology

Genesis, Leviticus and Deuteronomy all pay respect to the ancestors, even though the monotheizing tendency of these books has absorbed the diversity of ancestral religion in very different ways. The ancestors of individual clans have been consolidated into the larger narrative, extending eventually back to Abraham. Within this process, the land rights of the clans have been preserved, and there is an important sense in which 'redemption' in the Torah is unthinkable without the 'connectivity of kin and country', to use Rose's words.[35] Any version of Christian mission that breaks the connections of kin and country actually seems to invert the Torah's logic of redemption.

Genesis articulates the land promises to Abraham, Isaac and Jacob, and Deuteronomy makes these promises the basis of its thinking about divine grace (7:7–8; 8:17–18; 9:5). Leviticus presents a distinct theology of land, along with a system of ethics that can be distinguished from Deuteronomy's.[36] In the canonical form of these books, it is YHWH who is the ultimate land-giver and owner, yet this theology is nowhere interpreted in the Torah in nationalist terms that would over-ride the land rights of the clans. Christopher Wright even feels justified in saying that the ancestral properties were held by 'divine right', although one would need to clarify what this means in the context of the Torah. Deuteronomy and Leviticus enumerate more responsibilities than rights, and Leviticus severely qualifies the idea of ownership by speaking of land 'possession' (*ahuzzah*) – in distinction from the Deuteronomic idea of 'inheritance' (*nahalah*)[37] – stressing that Israelites have the same theological status as resident strangers (Lev. 25:23). But none of this is used to justify the overturning of land allotments given to Israelite ancestors. Even in the prophetic literature that envisages life after the exile in Babylon, the people are redeemed *in the land* (e.g. Is. 35, 54; Ezek. 36 – 37). In short, the biblical ideas of redemption cluster around the restoration of 'kin and country', and to suggest that indigenous Australians need to forsake their kin and country in order to be redeemed, would bend this biblical language to breaking point.

In the history of colonialism, there has often been an assumption that indigenous peoples are configured by the biblical story as 'Canaanites', rather than as 'Israelites', and this has been a convenient weapon in the hands of colonizing Christians – especially amongst the Boers, Conquistadors and Puritans – who imagined that they possessed an 'Israelite' right of conquest.[38]

---

[35] See above, n.3; A. Stock, 'The Development of the Concept of Redemption' in D. Durken (ed.), *Sin, Salvation and the Spirit* (Collegeville, 1979), 49–64.

[36] See, e.g. Weinfeld, *Deuteronomic School*, 225–32; J. Joosten, *People and Land in the Holiness Code* (Leiden, 1996), 137–92, Milgrom, *Leviticus 17 - 22*, 1404–1405.

[37] Milgrom, *Leviticus 17 - 22*, 1404–1405.

[38] See, e.g. F. Deist, 'The Dangers of Deuteronomy: A Page from the Reception History of the Book' in F.G. Martinez, et al (eds.), *Studies in Deuteronomy* (Leiden, 1994), 13–29; S. Niditch, *War in the Hebrew Bible* (Oxford, 1993), 3–5; P. Richard, 'Biblical

This conquest discourse is less in evidence in Australian history,[39] but a similar assumption has often been expressed through the view that indigenous Australian culture is subject to the same exclusion as the pagan Canaanite culture. Thus, missionaries often sought to dismantle Aboriginal marriage customs, or endorsed the removal of indigenous children, imagining that they acted with divine sanction.[40] But in terms suggested by biblical theology, indigenous people are in the same position as Australians of European descent. Insofar as we are Christians, we are all gentiles consolidated under our eponymous ancestor, Jesus Christ, through whom we entered the lineage system of Abraham and were enabled to receive the inheritance he bequeathed (Gal. 3:28-29; Eph. 3:6).

Being configured by biblical narrative in this way means that no gentile culture has a right to over-ride any other. And this is a crucial missiological point in cultural contexts where veneration of ancestors is constitutive of social identity. Thus, for example, Khiok-Khng Yeo can write, 'To advise the Chinese not to offer food and not to eat the food in ancestor worship may be implicitly advising them not to love their parents, not to practice love, and ultimately not to be Chinese.'[41] Wherever veneration of ancestors is constitutive of a culture, the way in which these practices are absorbed into Christian faith will present complex theological issues. As the apostle Paul argues in 1 Corinthians 8, there will be differing views on such issues, and they will need to be considered carefully within the affected communities, without one side claiming superiority over the other.[42]

One thing is clear, however. Christian faith does not mean the erasure of cultural identity altogether. Insofar as the church lives in the spirit of Christ, it

---

Interpretation from the Perspective of Indigenous Cultures of Latin America (Mayas, Kunas, and Quechuas)' in M.G. Brett (ed.), *Ethnicity and the Bible* (Leiden, 1996), 297–314. Rabbinic tradition prohibited this kind of colonialist hermeneutic of war. See, e.g. G. Wilkes, 'Judaism and the Justice of War' in P. Robinson (ed.), *Just War in Comparative Perspective* (Aldershot, 2003), 9–23.

[39] D.B. Rose, 'Rupture and the Ethics of Care in Colonized Space' in T. Bonyhady and T. Griffiths (eds.), *Prehistory to Politics* (Melbourne, 1996), 205.

[40] Pat Dodson, 'Vatican II or Mission Control' Radio National, *Encounter*, 29.6.2003; J. Jacobs, C. Laurence and F. Thomas, 'Pearls from the Deep: Re-evaluating the Early History of Colebrook Home for Aboriginal Children' in T. Swain and D.B. Rose (eds.), *Aboriginal Australians and Christian Missions: Ethnographic and Historical Studies* (Bedford Park, 1988), 140–55; D. Mellor and A. Haebich (eds.), *Many Voices: Reflections on Experiences of Indigenous Child Separation* (Canberra, 2002).

[41] K.K. Yeo, '1 Corinthians 8 and Chinese Ancestor Worship', *BibInt* 2 (1994), 308. For African theologies of the ancestors, see especially T. Mafico, 'The Biblical God of the Fathers and the African Ancestors' in G. West and M. Dube (eds.), *The Bible in Africa: Transactions, Trajectories and Trends* (Leiden, 2000), 481–89; K. Bediako, *Christianity in Africa* (Maryknoll, 1995), 216–33.

[42] Jordan, *Their Way*, 28–33.

will seek in every place to overcome the distortions of colonial power that has subjugated weaker cultures. As the Pauline scholar Sze-kar Wan has argued, the body of Christ constitutes a peoplehood 'not by erasing ethnic and cultural differences but by *combining these differences into a hybrid existence'*.[43] Thus, Paul was able to circumcise Timothy in recognition of his Jewish identity, without imposing this practice on gentiles (Acts 16:1–3). According to Wan, 'In Christ there is neither Jew nor Greek' implies a limiting of powerful ethnicities and affirmation for the weak. The body of Christ is a catholic community of interrelated bodies, making space for diverse ethnicities, without projecting a final reconciliation that amounts to the denial of actual bodies.[44]

These approaches to Christian theology lend weight to Aboriginal debates about the ways in which indigenous law, ritual, veneration and sacred topography can be retrieved as part of the exercise of Aboriginal Christian faith. Djiniyini Gondarra has suggested that the way to proceed with this question is to compare the particularity of Aboriginal identity with the faith of Israel.[45] Gondarrra sees no incompatibility between his Christian faith and either set of laws – Aboriginal or Israelite – since all Christians must combine their faith with the laws or principles of their own cultural identity. He also draws analogies between sacred sites in his own culture and the significance of sites like Bethel and Sinai for the construction of Jewish identity. His allusion to Bethel is especially relevant in light of the references to the Bethel *matsebot* in Genesis 35:14,20, reflecting local forms of ancestral religion. On this view, there is no 'final reconciliation' in which Aboriginal or Jewish identities are entirely erased, but rather, the specificities of social identity are given dignity within the larger body of Christ.

The Choctaw theologian Steve Charleston observes that every indigenous people group has a *unique* covenant with the Creator, although many of the basic themes in these covenants are comparable with Israel's story – land, law, sacred places and rituals.[46] The anthropologist David Turner similarly describes Aboriginal Australia as being made up of a plurality of 'promised lands', each

---

[43] Sze-kar Wan, 'Does Diaspora Identity imply some sort of Universality? An Asian-American Reading of Galatians' in F. Segovia (ed.), *Interpreting Beyond Borders* (Sheffield, 2000), 126–27; cf. J. Barclay, 'Neither Jew nor Greek: Multiculturalism and the New Perspective on Paul' in Brett (ed.), *Ethnicity and the Bible,* 209–14; M. Volf, *Exclusion and Embrace* (Nashville, 1996), 47–48.

[44] Miroslav Volf accordingly rejects any model of reconciliation that neglects cultural differences, *Exclusion and Embrace*, 43, 51–52, 109–110.

[45] D. Gondarra, *Series of Reflections on Aboriginal Religion* (Darwin, 1996).

[46] S. Charleston, 'The Old Testament of Native America' in S.B. Thistlethwaite and M.B. Engel (eds.), *Lift Every Voice: Constructing Christian Theologies from the Underside* (San Francisco, 1990), 49–61; cf. M.G. Brett, '*Canto Ergo Sum*: Indigenous Peoples and Postcolonial Theology', *Pacifica* 16 (2003), 247–256.

with its own chosen people.⁴⁷ Indigenous Christians, according to Charleston, are therefore the bearers of three 'Testaments' – the New Testament of Christian scripture, the Hebrew Bible of Israel, and the 'Old Testament' of their own indigenous tradition.

Charleston has no difficulty saying that God became incarnate within the people of Israel, and consequently their story is of primary importance within the making of Christian identity. Jesus was a Jew, but as the risen Christ, he is Choctaw and Navajo and Kiowa, and so on, in relation to all of their 'Old Testaments'. Although the very name 'Christ' (*christos* translating *mashiach*) derives from a set of messianic expectations generated within the particular cultural mix of ancient Israel, the life of the historical Jesus, a Jew, transformed the old messianic expectations about the advent of justice. To say that Jesus is 'the Christ' is to interpret the meaning of his life within the contested cultural terms of the first century.⁴⁸ The life of Jesus still has to be made intelligible from within subsequent cultural traditions, including indigenous ones. This is an essential feature of 'Christian' identity: the risen Christ participates in each indigenous tradition, re-interpreting each 'Old Testament', and not just Israel's.⁴⁹

Translations of the Bible which seek 'dynamic equivalence' have elicited these issues as well, e.g. when the Pitjantjatjara New Testament interprets the *logos* of John 1 as *tjukurpa* – a term encompassing a range of possible meanings, including the Aboriginal Dreaming or Law.⁵⁰ As Kwame Bediako

---

⁴⁷ D.H. Turner, *Life before Genesis, a Conclusion: An Understanding of the Significance of Australian Aboriginal Culture* (New York, 1987); idem., 'The Incarnation of Nambirrirrma' in Swain and Rose (eds.), *Aboriginal Australians and Christian Missions*, 479. An analogy between Israel's Testament and the Warlpiri Testament is reflected in the Warlpiri translation of Galatians 3.28, which Tony Swain renders in English as 'with or without *kuruwarri*, we are nonetheless one in God'. *Kuruwarri* are both the tracks of Dreaming ancestors preserved in the land as well as the designs used to symbolize these tracks. 'Jew' in Galatians 3.28 is translated as 'with *kuruwarri*'. T. Swain, 'The Ghost of Space: Reflections on Warlpiri Christian Iconography and Ritual' in Swain and Rose (eds.), *Aboriginal Australians and Christian Missions*, 452–69, 465–66.

⁴⁸ See, e.g. J. Charlesworth, 'From Jewish Messianology to Christian Christology: Some Caveats and Perspectives' in J. Neusner, et al (eds.), *Judaisms and their Messiahs at the Turn of the Christian Era* (Cambridge, 1987), 225–264.

⁴⁹ Charleston, 'Native America', 59. Cf. J. Wilcken, 'Christology and Aboriginal Religious Traditions', *ACR* 75 (1998), 184–94, who relates this issue to the idea of the 'pre-existent Christ' behind the Jesus of history; Sanneh, *Translating the Message*, 182–84, who describes an example linking kinship language of the Yoruba to the 'cosmic Christ'.

⁵⁰ See the wide-ranging discussion in R. Boer, *Last Stop to Antarctica: The Bible and Postcolonialism in Australia* (Sheffield, 2001), 150–79, along with my critical review in *St Mark's Review* 192 (2003), 43–44. The term has now expanded in use to encompass

puts it, 'indigeneity does not lie at the *end* of a quest. Rather it is presumed within the very translatability of the Christian religion.'[51] Vernacular translation of the Bible generates a cultural hybridity that the translator cannot control, a point which is discussed at length by Lamin Sanneh in his remarkable study of the cultural impact of Christian missions.[52]

In Australia, we would need to say that the risen Christ is Pitjantjatjara, Warlpiri, Kulin, and so on, but non-indigenous people cannot prescribe the ways in which Christ is embodied and named in these contexts. And non-indigenous Christians need to confess that by moving the 'boundary stones' of the ancestors in Australia – denying the land rights of their descendants – we have rendered the biblical concepts of 'redemption' largely unintelligible.[53] Expectations of redemption in the Hebrew Bible concerned the restoration of family and land, and these expectations can hardly be 'fulfilled' by the fracturing of kin and country. Manifest injustices are, in the end, not compatible with any messianic theology. Christians may disagree about how the recuperation of families and land may be related to national politics, but the Church has its own 'sorry business' to undertake,[54] and the intelligibility of the gospel will depend upon its coherence with the biblical practices of redemption.

Bibliography

Albertz, R., *A History of Israelite Religion in the Old Testament Period*, vol. 1 (London: SCM, 1994).

Ashcroft, B., *Postcolonial Transformation* (London: Routledge, 2001).

---

the whole Bible, 'old and new', in the Bible Society translation by P. and A. Eckert, *Tjukurpa Palya: Irititja Munu Kuwaritja* (Canberra, 1997); W. Edwards, '*Tjukurpa Palya* – The Good Word: Pitjantjatjara Responses to Christianity' (forthcoming). For a parallel argument linking the *logos* of John 1 with a Native American Christology, see C.S. Kidwell, H. Noley and G. Tinker, *A Native American Theology* (Markyknoll, 2001), 76–84.

[51] Bediako, *Christianity in Africa*, 123.

[52] Sanneh, *Translating the Message*, especially 157–210. On cultural hybridity in theology, see R.J. Schreiter, *The New Catholicity* (Maryknoll, 1997), 63–83 and Brett, '*Canto Ergo Sum*'.

[53] Anthony Thiselton rightly argues that Christian language about salvation needs the 'public criteria of meaning' established by Israel's tradition, since a disembodied spiritual discourse would lapse into unintelligibility. A.C. Thiselton, *The Two Horizons* (Grand Rapids, 1980), 233. Cf. Wright, *God's Land*, 110–114.

[54] See, e.g. Jordan's discussion of the meeting of representatives from the Baptist Union of Australia and the Warlpiri people at Brooks Soak in 1999, to remember the Coniston Massacre of 1928 (*Their Way*, 26–7). Significantly, the meeting included a Eucharistic sharing of bread and billy tea, with Warlpiri elder Jerry Jangala invoking the eponymous ancestor, Jesus Christ, who also died an unjust death. On the analogy between the Christian Eucharist and the indigenous invocation of ancestors, see also B. Hill, *Broken Song*, 49, 437.

Barclay, J., 'Neither Jew nor Greek: Multiculturalism and the New Perspective on Paul' in M.G. Brett (ed.), *Ethnicity and the Bible,* (Leiden: Brill, 1996), 209–14.

Bediako, K., *Christianity in Africa* (Maryknoll: Orbis, 1995).

Bloch-Smith, E., *Judahite Burial Practices and Beliefs about the Dead* (Sheffield: Sheffield Academic Press, 1992).

Boer, R., *Last Stop to Antarctica: The Bible and Postcolonialism in Australia* (Sheffield: Sheffield Academic Press, 2001).

Brett, M.G., 'Canonical Criticism and Old Testament Theology' in A.D.H. Mayes (ed.), *Text in Context* (Oxford: Oxford University Press, 2000), 63–65.

— 'Canto Ergo Sum: Indigenous Peoples and Postcolonial Theology', *Pacifica* 16 (2003), 247–256.

— 'Genocide in Deuteronomy: Postcolonial Variations on Mimetic Desire' in M. O'Brien and H. Wallace (eds.), *Seeing Signals, Reading Signs– Festschrift for Antony F. Campbell* (London: Continuum, 2005), 76–90.

Brichto, H.C., 'Kin, Cult, Land, and Afterlife', *HUCA* 44 (1973), 1–54.

Charleston, S., 'The Old Testament of Native America' in S.B. Thistlethwaite and M.B. Engel (eds.), *Lift Every Voice: Constructing Christian Theologies from the Underside* (San Francisco: HarperCollins, 1990), 49–61.

Charlesworth, J., 'From Jewish Messianology to Christian Christology: Some Caveats and Perspectives' in J. Neusner, et al (eds.), *Judaisms and their Messiahs at the Turn of the Christian Era* (Cambridge: Cambridge University Press, 1987), 225–264.

Cooper, A. and B.R. Goldstein, 'The Cult of the Dead and the Theme of Entry in the Land,' *Biblical Interpretation* 1 (1993), 285–303.

Deist, F., 'The Dangers of Deuteronomy: A Page from the Reception History of the Book' in F.G. Martinez, *et al* (eds.), *Studies in Deuteronomy* (Leiden: Brill, 1994), 13–29.

Dodson, P., 'Vatican II or Mission Control' Radio National, *Encounter*, 29.6.2003.

Eckert, P. and A., *Tjukurpa Palya: Irititja Munu Kuwaritja* (Canberra: Bible Society in Australia, 1997).

Edwards, B., *'Tjukurpa Palya* – The Good Word: Pitjantjatjara Responses to Christianity' (forthcoming).

Fishbane, M., *Biblical Interpretation in Ancient Israel* (Oxford: Clarendon, 1985).

Gauchet, M., *The Disenchantment of the World: A Political History of Religion* (Princeton: Princeton University Press, 1999).

Gondarra, D., *Series of Reflections on Aboriginal Religion* (Darwin: Bethel Presbytery, Uniting Church in Australia, 1996).

Habel, N., *The Land is Mine* (Minneapolis: Fortress, 1995).

Halpern, B., 'Jerusalem and the Lineages in the Seventh Century BCE' in B. Halpern and D.W. Hobson (eds.), *Law and Ideology in Monarchic Israel* (Sheffield: Sheffield Academic Press, 1991), 11–107.

— 'The Baal (and the Asherah) in Seventh-Century Judah: YHWH's Retainers Retired' in R. Bartelmus, et al (eds.), *Konsequente Traditionsgeschichte: Festschrift für Klaus Baltzer* (Göttingen: Vandenhoeck & Ruprecht, 1993), 115–54.

Hill, B., *Broken Song: T.G.H. Strehlow and Aboriginal Possession* (Sydney: Vintage, 2002).

Jacobs, J., C. Laurence and F. Thomas, 'Pearls from the Deep: Re-evaluating the Early History of Colebrook Home for Aboriginal Children' in T. Swain and D.B. Rose (eds.), *Aboriginal Australians and Christian Missions: Ethnographic and Historical*

Studies (Bedford Park: Australian Association for the Study of Religions, 1988), 140–55.

Joosten, J., *People and Land in the Holiness Code* (Leiden: Brill, 1996).

Jordan, I., *Their Way: Towards an Indigenous Warlpiri Christianity* (Darwin: Charles Darwin University, 2003).

Kidwell, C.S., H. Noley and G.E. Tinker, *A Native American Theology* (Maryknoll, New York: Orbis, 2001).

Kraft, C.H., *Anthropology for Christian Witness* (Maryknoll, New York: Orbis, 1996).

Levinson, B.M., *Deuteronomy and the Hermeneutics of Legal Innovation* (New York: Oxford University Press, 1997).

— 'Textual Criticism, Assyriology, and the History of Interpretation: Deuteronomy 13:7 as a Test Case in Method', *Journal of Biblical Literature* 120 (2001), 238–241.

Lewis, T.J., *Cults of the Dead in Ancient Israel and Ugarit* (Atlanta: Scholars Press, 1989).

— 'The Ancestral Estate in 2 Samuel 14:16', *Journal of Biblical Literature* 110 (1991), 597–612.

Mafico, T., 'The Biblical God of the Fathers and the African Ancestors' in G. West and M. Dube (eds.), *The Bible in Africa: Transactions, Trajectories and Trends* (Leiden: Brill, 2000), 481–489.

Mellor, D. and A. Haebich (eds.), *Many Voices: Reflections on Experiences of Indigenous Child Separation* (Canberra: National Library of Australia, 2002).

Milgrom, J., *Leviticus 17 – 22* (New York: Doubleday, 2000).

— *Leviticus 23 – 27* (New York: Doubleday, 2000).

Moberly, R.W.L., *The Old Testament of the Old Testament* (Minneapolis: Fortress, 1992).

Moran, W., 'The Ancient Near Eastern Background to the Love of God in Deuteronomy', *Catholic Biblical Quarterly* 25 (1963), 77–87.

Niditch, S., *War in the Hebrew Bible* (Oxford: Oxford University Press, 1993).

Otto, E., 'Human Rights: The Influence of the Hebrew Bible', *Journal of Northwest Semitic Languages* 25 (1999), 1–20.

— *Das Deuteronomium: Politische Theologie und Rechtsreform in Juda und Assyrian* (Berlin: de Gruyter, 1999).

Parpolo, S. and K. Watanabe (eds.), *Neo-Assyrian Treaties and Loyalty Oaths* (Helsinki: Helsinki University Press, 1988).

Pattel-Gray, A. (ed.), *Aboriginal Spirituality: Past, Present, Future* (Melbourne: HarperCollins, 1996).

Rainbow Spirit Elders, *Rainbow Spirit Theology* (Melbourne: HarperCollins, 1997).

Richard, P., 'Biblical Interpretation from the Perspective of Indigenous Cultures of Latin America (Mayas, Kunas, and Quechuas)' in M.G. Brett (ed.), *Ethnicity and the Bible* (Leiden: Brill, 1996), 297–314.

Rose, D.B., 'Rupture and the Ethics of Care in Colonized Space' in T. Bonyhady and T. Griffiths (eds.), *Prehistory to Politics* (Melbourne: Melbourne University Press, 1996), 190–215.

— 'Pentecostal Missionaries and the Exit from Religion', paper delivered at the Bible and Critical Theory Seminar, Melbourne, June 2004.

— *Reports from a Wild Country: Ethics for Decolonisation* (Sydney: University of New South Wales Press, 2004).

Rowley, H.H., *The Missionary Message of the Old Testament* (London: Carey Press, 1944).
Sanneh, L., *Translating the Message* (Maryknoll, New York: Orbis, 1989).
Schmidt, B.B., 'Memory as Immortality' in A.J. Avery-Peck and J. Neusner (eds.), *Judaism in Late Antiquity. Part 4, Death, Life-After-Death, Resurrection and the World-to-Come in the Judaisms of Antiquity* (Leiden: Brill, 2000), 87–100.
Schreiter, R.J., *The New Catholicity* (Maryknoll, New York: Orbis, 1997).
Schwartz, B.J., 'Re-examining the Fate of the "Canaanites" in the Torah Traditions' in C. Cohen, A. Hurvitz and S.M. Paul (eds.), *Sefer Moshe: The Moshe Weinfeld Jubilee Volume* (Winona Lake: Eisenbrauns, 2004), 151–170.
Smith, M.S., *The Origins of Biblical Monotheism: Israel's Polytheistic Background and the Ugaritic Texts* (New York: Oxford University Press, 2001).
Steymans, H.U., *Deuteronomium 28 und die adê zur thronfolgeregelung Asarhaddons: Segen und Fluch im Alten Orient und in Israel* (Göttingen: Vandenhoeck & Ruprecht, 1995).
Stock, A., 'The Development of the Concept of Redemption' in D. Durken (ed.), *Sin, Salvation and the Spirit* (Collegeville: Liturgical Press, 1979), 49–64.
Swain, T., 'The Ghost of Space: Reflections on Warlpiri Christian Iconography and Ritual' in T. Swain and D.B. Rose (eds.), *Aboriginal Australians and Christian Missions: Ethnographic and Historical Studies* (Bedford Park: Australian Association for the Study of Religions, 1988), 452–469.
Tacey, D., *ReEnchantment* (Sydney: HarperCollins, 2000).
Thiselton, A.C., *The Two Horizons* (Grand Rapids, Michigan: Eerdmans, 1980).
Tinker, G.E., *Missionary Conquest: The Gospel and Native American Cultural Genocide* (Minneapolis: Fortress, 1993).
Toorn, K. van der, *Family Religion in Babylonia, Syria and Israel* (Leiden: Brill, 1996).
Treat, J. (ed.), *Native and Christian: Indigenous Voices on Religious Identity in the United States and Canada* (New York: Routledge, 1996).
Turner, D.H., *Life before Genesis, a Conclusion: An Understanding of the Significance of Australian Aboriginal Culture* (New York: Lang, 1987).
– 'The Incarnation of Nambirrirrma' in T. Swain and D.B. Rose (eds.), *Aboriginal Australians and Christian Missions* (Bedford Park: Australian Association for the Study of Religions, 1988), 470–483.
Volf, M., *Exclusion and Embrace* (Nashville: Abingdon Press, 1996).
Wan, S., 'Does Diaspora Identity imply some sort of Universality? An Asian-American Reading of Galatians' in F. Segovia (ed.), *Interpreting Beyond Borders* (Sheffield: Sheffield Academic Press, 2000), 126–127.
Weinfeld, M., *Deuteronomy and the Deuteronomic School* (Oxford: Clarendon Press, 1972).
Wenham, G., 'The Religion of the Patriarchs' in A. Millard and D.J. Wiseman (eds.), *Essays on the Patriarchal Narratives* (Leicester: Inter-Varsity Press, 1980), 157–188.
Westermann, C., *Genesis 12 – 36* (Minneapolis: Augsburg, 1985).
Wilkes, G., 'Judaism and the Justice of War' in P. Robinson (ed.), *Just War in Comparative Perspective* (Aldershot: Ashgate, 2003), 9–23.
Wilcken, J., 'Christology and Aboriginal Religious Traditions', *Australian Catholic Record* 75 (1998), 184–194.

Wright, C.J.H., *God's People in God's Land: Family, Land and Property in the Old Testament* (Grand Rapids, Michigan: Eerdmans, 1990).

Yeo, K.K. '1 Corinthians 8 and Chinese Ancestor Worship', *Biblical Interpretation* 2 (1994), 294–311

CHAPTER 2

'That the World May Know.'
Narrative Poetics in 1 Samuel 16 – 17

DAVID G. FIRTH

Introduction

It is a pleasure for me to dedicate this essay to John Olley. I first met John when he was chairman of the Australian Baptist Missionary Society (now Global InterAction). John and his wife Elaine visited us in Zimbabwe, where I was an ABMS missionary teaching Old Testament at the Theological College of Zimbabwe. Since then, our paths have crossed at a number of points, including the discovery that we both spent some time as the pastor of the St Ives Baptist Church in Sydney. Of more importance is our mutual interest in mission (especially the work of ABMS / Global InterAction) and in Old Testament studies. John has always modelled a passionate commitment to both of these areas, and it is my hope that this essay can further that work.

The account of David and Goliath is so well-known that it has come to have proverbial status within western culture. Nevertheless, the popular perception of the story is one that fits poorly with its dominant scholarly reading. The reasons for this are not hard to find. Popular usage of the story tends to focus on the bravery and resourcefulness of the shepherd boy David who overcomes the giant Goliath. While this reading is romantically attractive, it fails to attend to the internal dynamics of the narrative in which bravery and resourcefulness are not the dominant issues. Moreover, there are a myriad of textual issues that raise questions as to the nature of the text that is to be interpreted and the relationship of this chapter to the events that surround it. These elements have a profound effect on the story's own dynamics.

The purpose of this contribution is to argue that an examination of the poetics employed within the narrative move in a very different direction to that of both popular perception and scholarly orthodoxy. The narrative itself climaxes with David's speech to Goliath before the battle, a speech which concludes the process by which David's own speech patterns seek to recast the understanding of events that have been promulgated by Goliath (and which have formed the basis of Saul's actions so far). Moreover, it is also intended as the high point in the series of introductions to David that occur through chapters 16 – 17. That is to say, rather than being a confused text of uncertain dynamics, chapters 16 – 17 are intentionally structured to show that it is David who understands that Israel exists to proclaim and demonstrate the reality of Yahweh to the world. The various themes that run through both chapters find their demonstration in the encounter with Goliath, which is in effect a power encounter that announces the authority of Yahweh to the world. It is this understanding of the authority and power of Yahweh that marks out David as the one who has appropriately been chosen by Yahweh to succeed Saul to the throne.

Narrative Sequence and Order in 1 Samuel 16 – 17

The relationship between chapter 16 and chapter 17 is a matter that has proved particularly difficult to untangle.[1] When read as a chronologically sequential set of narratives, the account raises a number of significant issues – problems that are apparent from the outset of the story of David's anointing in 16:1–13. This is evident from the fact that Samuel is nervous about journeying to the family of Jesse to anoint one of his sons, the narrative importance of which can be seen from the fact that references to 'Jesse the Bethlehemite' function as an inclusion for the whole of chapters 16 – 17.[2] What is not clear is why it is that a journey to the household of Jesse should provide a problem for Samuel, a problem that can only be resolved by Yahweh pointing out that it is still possible for him to go there for reasons that Saul might regard as legitimate. Yet, to judge by the response of the town's elders, this was not a plan that they were altogether confident that Saul would accept, which suggests that there were wider tensions between Saul and the town that they also recognized, even if they did not associate them with the house of Jesse. The difficulty that we have is that there has been nothing in the narrative so far that would suggest that a member of the house of Jesse should pose a problem to Saul. Indeed, since Jesse has to be consecrated apart from the town's elders (16:5) it would seem that Jesse is not a particularly prominent person within the town.[3] However, the narrative suggests that Jesse's family has already come to prominence as one that posed a threat to Saul, even though nothing has so far been recounted.

A further problem is generated by the account of David's move to the household of Saul in 16:14–23. Although David is summoned as a musician who will play the harp to calm Saul when the 'baleful spirit from Yahweh' comes upon him, the importance of this role is somewhat undercut by the

---

[1] See the excellent summary of scholarship on these issues in A.F. Campbell, S.J., *1 Samuel* (Grand Rapids, 2003), 167–193.

[2] The use of the same title at 16:18 has a different function in that it is embedded within the account of David's move to Saul's court, though it still serves to bind these stories together in that the title appears nowhere else in the Bible.

[3] Against S.L. McKenzie, *King David: A Biography* (New York, 2000), 52.

introduction that is given to him by Saul's lad, whose outline of David's résumé suggests considerably more about his skill as a warrior than as a musician, even though it does not minimize the latter (16:18). David is clearly known as an effective warrior already, though nothing has so far been related about this. Moreover, his more important role within Saul's household is to become Saul's kit-bearer, which the earlier stories of Jonathan in 1 Samuel 13 – 14 have already indicated is a position of considerable military importance. We are even told that Saul came to love David in this role,[4] though this sits ill at ease with the dominant reading of David as a young shepherd boy. Indeed, it indicates that David was not only personally known to Saul and loved by him, but that he had already been introduced to him specifically as a son of Jesse.

Where the accounts of David's anointing and movement to Saul's court become more obviously problematic is when we turn to chapter 17. Here, David has to be introduced to Saul (17:32–37), having only come over to the army's camp to deliver supplies to his brothers and their commander (17:17f.). That is to say, instead of being Saul's kit-bearer, he is once again portrayed as the young shepherd, and in particular one who is probably too young to be involved in the battle since only his three eldest brothers, and not all seven, are present with Saul. At this point, he betrays no knowledge of formal military skill, although he does believe that his experiences in tending his father's sheep will have provided him with the ability to deal with the Philistine. This sits awkwardly with the statements of 16:18,23. Further, after the defeat of Goliath, Saul needed to inquire of Abner, his army commander, as to the family to which David belonged (17:55), presumably because he had promised special status to the family of the soldier who killed the giant. Yet, David was loved by Saul and known to him as a member of Jesse's family.

Not surprisingly, these difficulties have led scholars to postulate a number of source critical theories in which the historical kernel is located in 16:14–23, to which the anointing story has later been added.[5] This account is generally held to be the beginning of a source known as the History of David's Rise (HDR), though the Goliath story may not belong to this source,[6] which accounts for its significant points of conflict. Defenses of the sequence have tended to

---

[4] The MT is actually ambiguous as to who was loved. G.C.I. Wong, 'Who Loved Whom? A Note on 1 Samuel xvi 21', *VT* 47 (1997), 554–6, has argued that it was David who loved Saul. Not only would this go against every other occurrence of *'Ahb* involving David since he is elsewhere always the object of the verb, but it seems to fit the narrative structure of verses 14–23 awkwardly. Saul's love of David, understood as a commitment to him rather than anything emotional, explains his promotion of him.

[5] So P.K. McCarter, Jr., *1 Samuel: A New Translation with Introduction, Notes & Commentary* (Garden City, 1980), 30.

[6] The decision as to the place of the Goliath story in the HDR is often influenced by the decision made as to whether or not one follows the text of the MT or LXX^B for 1 Samuel 17, since LXX^B has very few narrative difficulties. See below, 'The Text of 1 Samuel 17'.

depend upon a psychological reading of Saul's motivation in 17:55–58,[7] though the absence of any direct clues in this regard should lead one to be very cautious about following this approach. Fokkelmann's rigorous defense of the textual structure of 1 Samuel 16 – 17 has established the literary possibility of the integrity of the narrative.[8] However, this does not explain why it was necessary to construct the narrative in this form. Alter is surely correct to suggest that something is gained through the combination of these texts,[9] but the concept of composite artistry, which essentially says we should accept the contradictions as part of the art, seems to make a virtue of necessity.

What will be argued, however, is that attention to the *theological goal* of 1 Samuel 17 in relationship to chapter 16 actually provides an explanation of the current form of the narrative. To achieve this, however, we need to attend to the poetics of narrative sequencing so as to demonstrate that the integrity of the narrative is not found in a supposed chronological sequence, but rather in a series of introductory elements that need to be presented in a particular order so as to demonstrate the justice of David's claim to the throne. That is to say, the problems that are generally highlighted derive from the perception that the narrative is to be read chronologically. An examination of other texts within Samuel indicates, however, that chronological sequencing is not necessarily a priority, and that there are segments where the narrative is deliberately dischronologized in order to emphasize certain key theological themes.

A dischronologized narrative is one within a set of discrete episodic narratives (rather than a serial narrative where each episode builds directly on its predecessor) in which the episodes are placed outside of their chronological sequence in order to highlight a theme or issue.[10] Good examples of this technique within the books of Samuel occur in 2 Samuel, chapters 5 – 8 and 21 – 24.[11] Each of the narrative units within these chapters has its own internal chronology, but an examination of them indicates that they are not in a chronological relationship to one another.[12] Thus, although the general

---

[7] E.g. R. Polzin, *Samuel and the Deuteronomist: A Literary Interpretation of the Deuteronomic History. Part 2: 1 Samuel* (Bloomington, 1989), 171–6; R.D. Bergen, *1, 2 Samuel* (Nashville, 1996), 198f.. However, Bergen does regard 17:55–58 as a flashback too.

[8] J.P. Fokkelmann, *Narrative Art and Poetry in the Books of Samuel: A Complete Interpretation Based on Stylistic and Structural Analyses* (Assen, 1986), 2.144f., 201–208.

[9] R. Alter, *The Art of Biblical Narrative* (New York, 1981), 146–152.

[10] This needs to be distinguished from the distinction between *recit* and *historie* in which the variation in chronology is internal to a specific narrative.

[11] D.G. Firth, 'Shining the Lamp: The Rhetoric of 2 Samuel 5 – 24', *TB* 52 (2002), 209–220.

[12] One might also note the presence of this mode of narration in the book of Judges. Although the Samson narrative is placed at the end of the cycle of judges, it is clear that Samson must have been quite early since he comes from a period in which Dan was still

movement of the books of Samuel is chronological, there is no need for each story to be later than its predecessor within the overarching narrative. However, it is characteristic of these narratives that they retain information that points to their approximate historical situation. For example, the association of David with Hiram in 2 Samuel 5:11f. might be thought to be directly associated with David's capture of Jerusalem (2 Sam. 5:6–10), and thus to come from the beginning of David's reign. But Hiram was active only at the very end of David's reign,[13] so these events (and possibly even the capture of Jerusalem itself) were also near the end. This is not evidence that the narrator was confused. 2 Samuel 5 – 8 is clearly a carefully structured whole. Rather, it was necessary to present the material in a dischronologized form in order to highlight certain key themes, but to retain the chronological pointers in order to inform readers that this process was being followed. In 2 Samuel 5:17 – 8:14 and in chapters 21 – 24 dischronologization enables the material to be presented within a chiasm, though this is not the only way in which this technique can be applied.[14] In this case, it is likely that the narrative order is the reverse of their actual order, although one cannot be absolutely precise on this point. What matters is that the markers of dischronologization are left in the text in order to alert readers that there is a thematic arrangement of the material, a process that ends with the beginning of chapter 18.

The Text of 1 Samuel 17

Before turning to consider the poetics of the text it is essential that we determine the text that we are to examine. As is well known, the text of 1 – 2 Samuel is one that is subject to considerable debate, with the differences between the MT and LXX greater here than for any book other than Jeremiah. Complicating this process further is the presence of the fragments from Qumran, of which 4QSam[a] is by far the most important. For our purposes, though, the question will be related only to the relationship between the MT and

---

trying to settle on the coastal plain. Similarly, although chapters 17 – 21 must post-date Samson, it is not possible to determine exactly where they fit into the chronology of the period. The reason, of course, is that the material in chapters 2 – 16 and 17 – 21 needed to be presented in a specific form, and chronology was not the key issue.

[13] J. Bright, *A History of Israel* (London, 1980), 204, reckons David reigned from ca. 1000–961 BC and Hiram ca. 969–936 BC.

[14] Both H.H. Klement, *II Samuel 21 – 24. Context, Structure and Meaning in the Samuel Conclusion* (Frankfurt, 2000), 157–59, and H.J. Koorevaar, 'De Macrostructuur van het Boek Samuël', *ATh* 17 (1997), 56–86, point to evidence for significant portions of 1 and 2 Samuel being structured as chiasms. Even if one does not accept all of their conclusions, their work points to the fact that chronological concerns were not always dominant in the final form of the books of Samuel.

LXX since the Qumran manuscripts do not cover this story in a manner sufficient to influence the principal text-critical questions.[15]

Our most important text-critical questions cluster around the relationship between MT and LXX^B since it is LXX^B that provides the most probable LXX text and is significantly shorter than MT. It is generally agreed that LXX^A has been conformed to MT since it includes all of the text omitted by LXX^B, but does so with a considerable variance in translation style. For this reason, we can reasonably assume that LXX^B represents the most probable LXX text. The difficulties that this throws up are quite significant. Although there are a number of minor disagreements between LXX and MT, the most important are that 17:12–32,50,55–58 are absent from LXX.[16] The importance of the LXX text for the structure of the narrative is that it then becomes possible to construct a coherent narrative from 16:14. David has, according to this text, entered Saul's service as his kit-bearer and can therefore be presumed to have already been present with the army when Goliath issued his challenge (17:1–11). Following the challenge, David went to Saul and indicated that he would fight Goliath, with the account ending with Goliath's death rather than the embarrassing question about David's identity that Saul put to Abner in MT. Pointing to this more coherent narrative, Campbell therefore argues that the additional material in MT represents a second tale that has been subsequently woven into the original story that is now preserved in LXX.[17] This argument is further buttressed by Tov[18] who argues that the translator of LXX^B is so clearly faithful to the *Vorlage* that it could not have been the LXX which brought about the modifications.

Although superficially persuasive, these arguments are not finally compelling. Tov's argument fails in that it merely demonstrates that the LXX^B translator was faithful to the *Vorlage*, but the argument cannot be resolved in terms of identifying who actually made the changes to the text. The translator may well have been faithful to the *Vorlage*, but all this would prove is that the text translated was shorter than the MT, and that the differences precede the LXX. It does not help with a decision about the more likely text. The narrative

---

[15] 4QSam^a covers only 17:4–6. In doing so, however, it does support the LXX's reading of Goliath's height as four cubits and a span (roughly two metres) as opposed to the MT's six cubits and a span (roughly three metres). Cf. E.C. Ulrich, Jr., *The Qumran Text of Samuel and Josephus* (Missoula, 1979), 79; A. Fincke, *The Samuel Scroll from Qumran: 4QSam^a Restored and Compared to the Septuagint and 4QSam^c* (Leiden, 2001), 93.

[16] The omission from 17:58 actually continues to 18:5, but the double reference to 'Jesse the Bethlehemite' (16:1; 17:58) seems to provide an *inclusio* for the whole of 16 – 17. So, also, R.F. Youngblood, '1 & 2 Samuel' in F.E. Gaebelein (ed.), *The Expositor's Bible Commentary* (Grand Rapids, 1990), 3.682f..

[17] Campbell, *1 Samuel*, 171–83. Similar positions are taken by McCarter, *I Samuel*, 307; H.J. Stoebe, *Das erste Buch Samuelis*, (Gütersloh, 1973), 313f..

[18] E. Tov, 'The David and Goliath Saga', *BRev* 2 (1986), 34–41.

arguments raised by Campbell are more compelling, although in fact they do not resolve all of the difficulties – why would Saul deny that David has military experience if in fact it is already well known to him that he has (17:33)? Narrative conflicts remain, even if they are reduced.

However, although textual critics normally prefer a shorter text, the very fact that the LXX resolves so many of the difficulties could also be seen as making it suspect. Moreover, the conflicts with 16:1–13 remain in that there has still been no reason why it should specifically be a journey to the house of Jesse that troubles Samuel. Thus, a probable interpretation of the evidence is that the LXX text represents an early recognition of the difficulties that the MT of 1 Samuel 17 posed in relation to 16:14–23 and sought to omit those details (which do not really comprise a story in their own right) which appeared to conflict with it. The complete blocks of text that could be removed were, but there were some points where this was not possible for the narrative to continue to develop. Therefore, on the principle that only complete scenes were omitted, some difficulties needed to be left in. If this is correct, then we should retain the MT for the overall structure of the narrative as representing the more difficult text. It is this text that we need to examine in more detail.

Structural Repetitions in the Saul and David Stories

If 1 Samuel 16 – 17 does represent a dischronologized narrative, then we ought to be able to provide reasons for it. That this is possible becomes apparent when we recognize that both Saul and David are given three introductions within 1 Samuel, and the form of these introductions shows considerable overlap. The exact chronological arrangement of the Saul stories is also difficult to untangle, thankfully not an issue that need detain us here, though the fact that there are three introductions to Saul has generally been felt to represent a problem in its own right. It may be that there has been deliberate patterning both ways, with a specific goal being that the elevation narratives for both David and Saul mirror one another while also providing further justification for David's elevation above Saul beyond that which is required by the account of Saul's rejection in chapters 13 – 15.

Edelman has proposed that the account of Saul's rise was shaped by the need to work through three key stages that would have been expected from the cultic ceremony associated with coronation – designation, testing and coronation.[19] Although not following Edelman's structure precisely, we can note the parallels between David and Saul in the following table.

---

[19] D.V. Edelman, *King Saul in the Historiography of Judah* (Sheffield, 1991), 31. A not dissimilar proposal was made by W.L. Humphreys, 'The Tragedy of King Saul: A Study in the Structure of 1 Samuel 9 – 31', *JSOT* 6 (1978), 18–27.

	Saul	David
Private Anointing	1 Sam. 10:1ff.	1 Sam. 16:1ff.
Public Acceptance	1 Sam. 10:17ff.	2 Sam. 5:1ff.
Military Demonstration	1 Sam. 11	1 Sam. 17

The order of events between the two is different, though in part this is necessitated by the fact that David will not initiate direct action against Saul while he is still king. Thus, David's public acceptance as king cannot be formalized until 2 Samuel 5:1, though in fact there are already clear hints of this as early as 1 Samuel 18:6–9 when Saul recognized in the popular acclamation given to David that the kingdom is all that remained to be claimed by him. Both accounts need to begin with an anointing narrative in order to provide readers with an important insight as to how they are to read the accounts that follow.

The parallels, however, can also mask some important distinctions, so it is essential to note the ways in which variations on the themes are presented. In particular, there are already hints about Saul's unsuitability for the longer-term role of king in the account of how he came to be anointed in 1 Samuel 9. The narrative itself is highly satirical in that it is Saul's lad who knows more about seeking lost donkeys and the ways of prophets than does Saul. In effect, it shows Saul as someone who is not particularly competent at coping with donkeys whereas David is shown in each of his three introduction stories as a highly competent shepherd, climaxing in the ways in which this motif is developed in the encounter with Goliath (1 Sam. 16:11,19; 17:15, 20,34–36).[20] This contrast provides background against which the comparative competence of both David and Saul can be judged.[21]

What is particularly important is that it was a commonplace assertion of ANE monarchs that they were the shepherds of their people, so the ways in which the shepherd motif for David is gradually brought to prominence through the narrative structure from background information about his identity (16:11,19; 17:15,20) through to the element that fundamentally shapes his understanding of the ways in which Yahweh works (17:34–36) is an essential element in the way in which the narrator is shaping our understanding of David's suitability as a future king. Indeed, that David's understanding of Yahweh has come through his work as a shepherd is further confirmation that he is indeed the man after Yahweh's own heart (1 Sam. 13:14).[22]

---

[20] Though note Eliab's misunderstanding of David's activities in 17:28.
[21] D. Rudman, 'The Commissioning Stories of Saul and David as Theological Allegory', *VT* 50 (2000), 525f..
[22] This remains true in terms of the intent of the text even if one were to accept McKenzie's assertion in *King David*, 50, that it is unlikely that David was a shepherd. The probability of a youngest son taking on this role seems to me to be very high, so I

The use of these structural repetitions, even with the variations employed within them, does not require that each panel follows its predecessor exactly. Thus, it will be noted that 16:14–23 has no equivalent in the account of Saul's rise. However, the narrator is still constrained by certain features of the account, most notably the fact that there was no king before Saul, whereas David will have to negotiate the process of a change in the ruling family. David's final acceptance and accession therefore needs to be delayed, though it is still remarkable to note just how long it does take.

Having noted that, we should still give some attention to 16:14–23 as the element that is peculiar to the account of David's rise. The heart of this passage is found in the words of Saul's lad in 16:18, in which David's various skills are laid out – providing a list well in excess of the stated need of providing Saul with a musician to deal with the 'baleful spirit from Yahweh'. Instead, it is David's military prowess that is highlighted, though Saul's immediate qualification of David as being with Jesse's sheep is thus doubly ironic – in the development of chapters 16 – 17 it is the shepherd motif that gradually points to David as the more obvious king, whereas for Saul it is a mechanism for lowering David's status in comparison with the glowing terms in which his lad has described him. Saul is lowering David's status from warrior to shepherd, but in the encounter between David and Saul in 17:32–36 it is precisely the fact that David is a shepherd that makes him an effective warrior, in spite of his lack of training and equipment.

What is important for our purposes is that just as there were three introduction stories for Saul, so also 1 Samuel 16 – 17 provides three introduction stories for David. The pattern of repetition, and then the variations within the repetitions, points to those features about David that set him apart from Saul as a more suitable monarch. In particular, the account of David's introduction provides three separate accounts to parallel the three accounts given for Saul's rise. The repetitions thus suggest that we need to read these accounts in the light of each other. The variations that then arise are structured to point to David as the superior candidate, especially through the development of the shepherd motif, a process that requires that 1 Samuel 17 be presented after 1 Samuel 16 rather than within its chronological sequence.

Poetics and Speech in 1 Samuel 17

But if 1 Samuel 17 needed to be presented after 1 Samuel 16, we need also to attend to the elements within it that highlight what it is to assert that David is the shepherd that the nation needs, and not Saul. Although there are a number of elements present within 1 Samuel 17, it is the element of speech that is of crucial importance because it is through it that David is able to announce his

---

don't share his historical skepticism on this point, but the exegetical point about the intent of the text is not affected either way.

understanding of the ways of Yahweh, and also show the significance of his defeat of Goliath. What matters is not so much the fact that he kills Goliath but rather the interpretation that is to be placed upon it, which is that this victory is a testimony to the whole world of the reality of Yahweh.

The importance of speech within 1 Samuel 17 is apparent from the fact that twenty-five of its fifty-eight verses contain speech, whilst speech is indicated but not reported directly in verses 23, 30 and 52. That is to say, roughly 40 per cent of the narrative is made up of speech, though the proportion increases significantly once David arrives at the camp until the point where he has defeated Goliath. Although chapter 17 is usually treated as a battle account, the battle itself occupies very little space, with the defeat of Goliath taking only one verse (17:49 – though the characteristic use of repetitions means that there is more time spent on the summary in 17:50–51), whilst the defeat of the whole of the Philistine army is narrated in 17:52–53. That is, actual battle accounts represent less than 10 per cent of the narrative.

It is noteworthy that no Israelite speaks at the scene of battle until David arrives, and when they do they simply repeat the view that Goliath himself has sought to generate. In fact, the narrator has sought to foreground Goliath's claims in the opening section (17:1–11) by providing a lengthy description of him in a way that stresses his seemingly impregnable status as one who is both huge and equipped with the latest in military technology, though carefully not mentioning his lack of mobility. This is important because the soldiers (and, explicitly, Saul in 17:11) will all accept Goliath's claim to superiority, which is why none of them will fight in spite of the lengthy period over which Goliath speaks disdainfully of Israel.[23] That is why Goliath's initial speech can only be provided after this description, a speech in which he displays considerable rhetorical subtlety by playing off Israel's current status as Saul's 'servants' and their supposedly better option of serving the Philistines (17:8–10). Goliath's speech thus serves to confirm the perspective that the narrator has already developed of someone with immense power and before whom Saul and Israel can only quake with fear.

The only speech in the next section (17:12–23) is Jesse's set of directions for David when he sent him to the battle zone with supplies for his brothers and their unit commander (17:17–18). This serves to provide a reason as to why David was present at the battle since as the youngest brother his proper function was to remain at home with the sheep. It also provides the narrator with an opportunity to show that David had, in fact, followed his father's instructions precisely. However, at the end of this section we encounter the first piece of non-reported speech in verse 23. Although Goliath's speech at this point could have been reported, the narrator actually muffles him slightly by stating only that he repeated his earlier speech. Yet, it is this piece of non-reported speech

---

[23] The verb μ *rap* is used throughout, suggesting a disdainful contempt, though M.K. George, 'Constructing Identity in 1 Samuel 17', *BibInt* 7 (1999), 398, prefers 'shame'.

that will now shape the whole of David's activity, a fact made clear by the closing comment that David heard him.

In verses 24–30 we have a record of responses to the presence of Goliath in which the soldier's fear is expressed verbally (v.25), though they also mention some other speech that has not been reported so far – that Saul will enrich and offer special status to the one who kills Goliath.[24] This speech from the soldiers not only serves to describe their own fear, it also indicates that Saul is not willing actually to lead the men in the battle, in spite of the fact that 8:20 indicates that this is precisely why Israel needed a king. This in turn prepares us for David's first recorded words in which he not only asks for clarification as to Saul's message, but also introduces the first reference to God among the Israelites by insisting that Goliath is in fact defying the armies of the living God. David's speech introduces a theological note to the narrative; a note that subverts Goliath's opening speech in which the outcome was purely a matter of military force. David's theme will then be the point that he expounds in his encounter with Saul – it is the presence of God with Israel that makes the difference. David the shepherd is also David the prophet, the one who can announce Yahweh's intent.[25] Saul cannot fully grasp this, as is evident from his attempt to clothe David in his own armour, equipment that neatly mirrors that of Goliath. David's speeches to the soldiers and then to Saul gradually clarify the fact that Goliath is defying God, and it is God who will deliver him from the power of the Philistine.

Speech becomes even more important from this point. We expect as the combatants face each other that we will have the report of the battle. But before this happens there are further speeches from Goliath (vv. 43–44) and David (vv. 45–47). Goliath's speech unwittingly draws on the animal theme that David introduced in his shepherd speech to Saul – if Yahweh has given David victory over lions and bears, then a dog may not seem to be too much of a problem! Moreover, only now does Goliath introduce a theological theme, cursing David by his gods. In response, we have David's most carefully constructed speech in what is the theological heart of the chapter.[26] Goliath has raised the issue of his own gods, even though the account of Dagon in 5:1–4 may not inspire too much confidence. David's response is to announce before the battle takes place that Yahweh will give David the victory and he will cut off Goliath's head. But this is not because David is Yahweh's anointed – the chapter does not betray any knowledge of this. It is because the victory will be

---

[24] The exact sense of *jopv'* is uncertain, though it appears to mean that the person's family would gain tax-free status. See Youngblood, '1 & 2 Samuel', 698.

[25] A.R. Ceresko, 'A Rhetorical Analysis of David's "Boast" (1 Sam. 17:34–37)', *CBQ* 47 (1985), 58–74, provides a fine rhetorical analysis of David's speech, though labeling it as a boast provides an unnecessarily negative assessment of it.

[26] Cf. W. Dietrich, 'Die Erzälungen von David und Goliat in 1 Sam. 17', *ZAW* 108 (1996), 190.

a declaration to the whole world of the reality of Yahweh and only then a testimony to those gathered of Yahweh's power. In short, it is a statement that places David's coming victory in a specific missiological framework,[27] so that the end of his sequence of introductions climaxes with this point. The victory, which can then be briefly announced, simply demonstrates the truth of David's claim. David is the shepherd the nation needs, the one who can lead them in their battles, but he can do this because he knows that Israel's existence is missiologically significant, that Israel's existence is a witness to the reality of Yahweh to all the clans of the earth (Gen. 12:3).

Conclusion

That the account of David's introduction is confusing if one seeks to read it as a chronologically arranged text is clear. But when one attends to the poetics of these chapters within the larger structure of 1 Samuel then it is possible to realize that the narrative is presented in precisely this order for a specific purpose. That purpose is to demonstrate that David is the shepherd that the nation of Israel needs as king, and he is the shepherd that the nation needs as king precisely because he understands the fact that Israel is to exist as a testimony to the nations of the reality of Yahweh. It is that knowledge that shapes his actions, and provides a reason for the present arrangement of the text. In turn, it was this same knowledge that was intended to shape Israel's continued missional existence.

Bibliography

Alter, R., *The Art of Biblical Narrative* (New York: Basic Books, 1981).
Bergen, R.D., *1, 2 Samuel* (Nashville: Broadman and Holman, 1996).
Bright, J., *A History of Israel* (London: SCM, 1980³).
Brueggemann, W., *First and Second Samuel* (Louisville: John Knox, 1990).
Campbell, A.F., *1 Samuel* (Grand Rapids, Michigan: Eerdmans, 2003).
Ceresko, A.R., 'A Rhetorical Analysis of David's "Boast" (1 Sam. 17:34–37)', *Catholic Biblical Quarterly* 47 (1985), 58–74.
Dietrich, W., 'Die Erzälungen von David und Goliat in 1 Sam. 17', *Zeitschrift für die Alttestamentliche Wissenschaft* 108 (1996), 172–191.
Edelman, D.V., *King Saul in the Historiography of Judah* (Sheffield: Sheffield Academic Press, 1991).
Fincke, A., *4QSam^a Reconstructed* (Leiden: E.J. Brill, 2000).
Firth, D.G., 'Shining the Lamp: The Rhetoric of 2 Samuel 5 – 24', *Tyndale Bulletin* 52 (2002), 203–224.
Fokkelmann, J.P., *Narrative Art and Poetry in the Books of Samuel: A Complete Interpretation Based on Stylistic and Structural Analyses*, vol. 2, (Assen, the Netherlands, van Gorcum 1986).

---

[27] W. Brueggemann, *First and Second Samuel* (Louisville, 1990), 132, is one of the few commentators to recognize the missiological significance of David's speech.

George, M.K., 'Constructing Identity in 1 Samuel 17', *Biblical Interpretation* 7 (1999), 389–412.
Humphreys, W.L., 'The Tragedy of King Saul: A Study in the Structure of 1 Samuel 9 – 31', *Journal for the Study of the Old Testament* 6 (1978), 18–27.
Klement, H.H., *II Samuel 21 – 24. Context, Structure and Meaning in the Samuel Conclusion* (Frankfurt am Maim: Peter Lang, 2000).
Koorevaar, H.J., 'De Macrostructuur van het Boek Samuël', *Acta Theologica* 17 (1997), 56–86.
McCarter, P.K. Jr., *1 Samuel: A New Translation with Introduction, Notes & Commentary* (Garden City: Doubleday, 1980).
McKenzie, S.L., *King David: A Biography* (New York: Oxford University Press, 2000).
Polzin, R., *Samuel and the Deuteronomist: A Literary Interpretation of the Deuteronomic History. Part 2: 1 Samuel* (Bloomington: University of Indiana Press, 1989).
Rudman, D., 'The Commissioning Stories of Saul and David as Theological Allegory', *Vetus Testamentum* 50 (2000), 519–530.
Stoebe, H.J., *Das erste Buch Samuelis* (Gütersloh: Gerd Mohn, 1973).
Tov, E., 'The David and Goliath Saga', *Bible Review* 2 (1986), 34–41.
Ulrich, E.C. Jr., *The Qumran Text of Samuel and Josephus* (Missoula: Scholars Press, 1979).
Wong, G.C.I., 'Who Loved Whom? A Note on 1 Samuel xvi 21', *Vetus Testamentum* 47 (1997), 554–556.
Youngblood, R.F., '1 & 2 Samuel' in F.E. Gaebelein (ed.), *The Expositor's Bible Commentary*, vol. 3 (Grand Rapids, Michigan: Zondervan, 1990), 553–1104.

CHAPTER 3

Solomon and the Building of the Temple

ASHLEY CRANE

Introduction

The choice to focus this contribution for John Olley's *Festschrift* was based on a number of personal interactions over the years with John regarding how Solomon built the Temple, and especially the implicit role of Pharaoh's daughter in the structure of the text. John himself recently wrote on this very topic, and his work will be taken into account in this essay.[1] Unfortunately, with the possible exception of the current Temple retaining wall, nothing remains of Solomon's Temple[2] except this brief description in 1 Kings, and later in Chronicles.[3] Thus, the focus of this essay will be upon the text of 1 Kings 1 – 11 in an attempt to uncover what can be discerned in the text and its structure regarding Solomon and his Temple. We will then briefly examine possible contemporary implications arising from our findings.

With an initial cursory reading of the salient chapters in 1 Kings one can come away feeling that they have read an in-depth view of Solomon and his Temple.[4] However, a careful reading will reveal a very selective description of Solomon and his Temple. The text lacks any detailed description of the building of the Temple, and the narrator(s)[5] 'leaves out those very points that

---

[1] J. Olley, 'Pharaoh's Daughter, Solomon's Palace, and the Temple: Another Look at the Structure of 1 Kings 1 – 11', *JSOT* 27 (2003), 355–369.
[2] See E.M. Laperrousaz, 'King Solomon's Wall Still Supports the Temple Mount', *BAR* (1987), 34–44.
[3] However, many believe that 'the Chronicler distorted the picture by merging the Temple and the desert Tabernacle' – V. Hurowitz, 'Inside Solomon's Temple', *BRev* (1994), 25. However, this essay will not enter into a comparison between Kings and Chronicles.
[4] While 'Temple' is commonly used in English versions, the Hebrew typically says 'house'. We will use both phrases in this essay.
[5] While we acknowledge the work of scholarship seeking to recover the authorship of Kings, the various Deuteronomistic authors and the possible later editing work by the

would be necessary for the reader to reconstruct the building,[6] and the architectural terminology[7] is obscure'.[8] Hurowitz says that when 'compared with other descriptions of temples in ancient Near Eastern literature, this account is exceptional in its detail and realism'.[9] However, we will find that this 'detail and realism' mentioned by Hurowitz is focused on the ornateness and splendour of the Temple, and not on aspects which one might expect (i.e. those having cultic value). This reveals the narrator's intent wherein the narrator has structurally interwoven a number of implicit rebukes towards Solomon, revealing Solomon's focus to be on his own house, his fame, his pleasure, and upon Pharaoh's daughter, and not upon fully walking in the ways of the Lord.

What the Text Reveals about the Temple

One may ask if the narrator of 1 Kings, chapters 1 – 11 is describing the overall architectural design of the Temple, or just drawing our attention to special or particular features. The narrator's intent may be discerned by the stressing of some features (especially the ornate), and the omission of others (especially those cultic and those one would expect when describing the construction of Israel's Temple). We can observe an example of this selective information in the initial description of the Temple's construction in 1 Kings 6:1–10.[10]

- There is no mention in 1 Kings of the site upon which the Temple is built.[11]

Priestly school, for clarity we will simplify and just use 'narrator'. For more on authorship issues see e.g. S.J. DeVries, *1 Kings* (Waco, 1985). This essay will not enter the exhaustive discussion of the composition of Kings. Rather we will deal with the text as we have received it.

[6] In fact it is difficult to establish clearly from the text what the Temple may have looked like in its finished state. This can be seen by the many artistic designs that have been suggested. However, Hurowitz, 'Inside Solomon's Temple', 25, curiously believes that 'a careful reader can pick up pencil and essay and begin to sketch the architecture!'

[7] Hurowitz, 'Inside Solomon's Temple', 25, correctly states that 'the description includes technical terms we barely understand'. For a list of these terms see DeVries, *1 Kings*, 94–95.

[8] W.J. Dumbrell, '2121 *hekhal*' in W.A. VanGemeren (ed.), *New International Dictionary of Old Testament Theology and Exegesis* (Grand Rapids, 1997), 1.1029.

[9] Hurowitz, 'Inside Solomon's Temple', 25.

[10] See DeVries, *1 Kings*, 94–95, for a breakdown of the Hebrew architectural terms used in 1 Kings 6 – 7.

[11] It is significant that the narrator does not state the site of the Temple, whereas the Chronicler takes lengths to establish the location as the threshing floor of Araunah the Jebusite (1 Chron. 21, 22; cf. 2 Sam. 24:25), which is later tied to the site of the binding of Isaac on Mount Moriah (2 Chron. 3:1). If the Chronicler is correct on these two points of location, as most conclude, then it is doubly surprising that the narrator did not state

- Only a brief description is given of the overall dimensions of the 'house' (6:2).
- A brief description is given of the portico extending from the 'Main Hall' [*hekhal*] (6:3). However, there is no mention of any other rooms. The Holy of Holies is not mentioned until 6:19 – then just stating its size and that it was lined with gold.
- The next feature mentioned is the windows, yet without any indication of their positioning in the structure (6:4).
- There is no mention here of specific doorways, either how many or their location. A doorway and stairs are mentioned, but these appear to be associated with the external chambers and not the Temple proper (6:8). The double door to the Holy of Holies is mentioned later, but the focus there is on the ornateness of the doors (6:31).
- Although a structure of three chambers surrounding the Temple is described (6:5–6,8,10), there is no indication of how these external chambers affected the final shape of the Temple, especially as the uppermost chamber is described as wider than the lowest.[12]
- Interrupting the description of the chambers, the narrator mentions Solomon's decree that no noise from 'quarry' tools was to be heard in the construction of the Temple (6:7). However, the text does not give a specific reason for this rule.[13] This verse, however, reveals the Temple's stone construction.
- There is a general statement that Solomon finished the Temple, and panelled it with cedar (6:9). This again refers to the ornateness of the Temple.
- An 'inner court' is mentioned without any comment on a corresponding 'outer court' (6:36). It might be that Perhaps the 'great court' in 1 Kings 7:9–12 is that court. Again, its mention serves to describe the ornateness rather than the existence of the court.

---

the site. One of the reasons given is that the focus of the narrator was in accordance with Deuteronomy 12:5, that the Temple's location was to be given by God and not any person, thus 'it was impossible, then, to use an historical event [to explain this (in Kings)], since it would have detracted from the Deuteronomistic conception of divine selection' – I. Kalimi, 'The Land of Moriah, Mount Moriah, and The Site of Solomon's Temple in Biblical Historiography', *HTR* 83 (1990), 350.

[12] This essay lacks the space for the many suggestions offered regarding the appearance of the Temple, or for the similarities between Solomon's Temple and other contemporary temples. See Hurowitz, 'Inside Solomon's Temple', 26; V. Fritz, 'Temple Architecture', *BAR* 13 (1987), 42.

[13] Perhaps the rule derives from the prohibition in Torah against using iron tools on an altar (Ex. 20:28; Deut. 27:5). Rupprecht suggests that Solomon 'modified an existing Jebusite Temple' and the prohibition was 'that the Temple was already in use' – cited in R. Tomes, 'Our Holy and Beautiful House', *JSOT* 70 (1996), 42. Yet, the text does not imply this at any point, and it directly refers to construction, not inhabitation.

Thus, this initial account gives an incredibly brief thumbnail sketch of the Temple, while leaving out many important items that one would expect to encounter. It is noticeable the external chambers receive greater attention than any other part. Although the remainder of 1 Kings 6 and 7:15–51 give a more detailed view of the Temple and furnishings, it is with the same selective focus upon the splendour rather than upon the cultic function of the Temple. Significantly, while the ornate design of the Temple architecture is mentioned throughout, little attention is given to the cultic furnishings. For example, the altar of sacrifice is not mentioned.[14]

Fritz correctly points out that scholars are divided as to whether the 'central building [of the Temple] consisted of one, two, or three rooms' as the text is rather vague and talks only about 'a portico or porch (*ulam*) in front of the main hall (*hekhal*) of the House (*bayit*) (1 Kgs. 6:3)'.[15] The two pillars, Jachin and Boaz (7:15–22), are usually seen as holding up the roof of the portico and not the Temple proper. Another example of vagueness is the description of the Holy of Holies. It is supposed to be equal in dimension at thirty feet height,[16] but as Hoerth[17] correctly observes, '[T]he Temple building stood forty-five feet tall. The Bible is silent as to how the remaining fifteen feet of height were accounted for' [1 Kgs. 6:2,20].[18]

In 1 Kings 7:15–51 the focus is upon the two pillars (7:15–22), the bronze sea (7:23–26), the bronze carts (7:27–37), the bronze lavers (7:38–39), and then on various furnishings of the Temple (7:40–51). Some of these are described in detail (e.g. the carts), yet there is no cultic reason evident for this detail other than to show again the wealth and splendour of these furnishings.

Overall, the narrator's emphasis on the Temple's construction is on the magnificence and ornateness of the Temple rather than on providing a detailed construction plan. The narrator gives as much attention to the gold and cedar used as upon anything else, showing that gold and/or cedar covered everything, even as an encasement for the Temple itself. The narrator mentions items and furnishings as much for their splendid features as for any cultic reason. We are informed of the many carved ornamental items (buds and flowers – 6:18), and

---

[14] This stands in stark contrast to the detailed descriptions of the cultic furnishings in Exodus.

[15] Fritz, 'Temple Architecture', 39. Fritz holds to the Temple proper being only one long room.

[16] The overall dimensions are also unclear as 'the Portico appears to have been 10 cubits deep' (1 Kgs. 6:3). The Main Sanctuary was 40 cubits (1 Kgs. 6:17). The Inner Sanctuary was 20 cubits (1 Kgs. 6:20). This adds up to 70 cubits, not 60' – Fritz, 'Temple Architecture', 39.

[17] A.J. Hoerth, *Archaeology and the Old Testament* (Grand Rapids, 1998), 281.

[18] Fritz, 'Temple Architecture', 39, says, 'Perhaps the Inner Sanctuary (*debir*) was only a kind of olive wood structure placed within the Main Sanctuary. Above the Inner Sanctuary was probably an empty space 10 cubits high.' This is an example of the speculation that must take place to reconstruct the Temple from the text as we have it.

the doors to the Inner Sanctuary that were made of olive wood and carved with cherubim, palm trees and flowers, and then overlaid with gold (6:31–32).[19] Inside the Inner Sanctuary was an altar overlaid with gold, and two cherubim of olive wood overlaid with gold (6:21–28).

Therefore, we may question if the narrator's selective account has the implicit purpose of stating that Solomon's focus was on building an ornate and magnificent Temple, and not on the cultic reason to construct the Temple. Interestingly, this may also be seen in Solomon's prayer of dedication (1 Kgs. 8:22–53).

PAGAN INFLUENCE AND ARTISANS

Most scholars see the Temple as a 'long-room Temple' with similarities to other temples of that time, such as in the nearly contemporary sanctuary found at Tell Tayinat in Syria.[20] Much of the architecture and furnishings described in 1 Kings 7 have their roots in the surrounding nations of which Endres says, '[I]f our stance is critical we will speak of Solomonic syncretism. If, on the contrary, we incline towards an appreciation of wisdom, we may speak of recovering a deeper meaning in non-Israelite symbols.'[21] Yet, there is evidence of Solomonic syncretism, especially with the use of Phoenician craftsman causing a strong Phoenician influence (7:13,14).[22]

The use of pagan craftsmen and temple plans caused a departure from the simple tabernacle plan provided by God in Exodus as the way to worship him. Instead they constructed an ornate Temple that attracted praise for its design rather than praise for the Lord of the Temple. Endres claims that this was part of the slippery slope Solomon was on, as seen for example with his pagan wives, as he 'allowed foreign elements into the Temple, through the doorway from his harem'.[23]

However, it is significant that the text itself does not imply any criticism for this Phoenician influence, nor does it appear from the text that the Lord was concerned about the structure of the Temple. The Lord's four encounters with

---

[19] This is quite a feat considering how difficult olive wood is to work with!

[20] Hoerth, *Archaeology and the Old Testament*, 281. For detailed examinations of Solomon's Temple in comparison to other temples see Fritz, 'Temple Architecture'; C.J. Davey 'Temples of the Levant and the Building of Solomon', *TB* 31 (1980), 107–146; V. Hurowitz, *I Have Built You an Exalted House: Temple Building in the Bible in Light of Mesopotamian and Northwest Semitic Writings* (Sheffield, 1992).

[21] J. Endres, *Temple, Monarchy and Word of God* (Wilmington, 1988), 119. Endres goes on to say, 'We find here an unusual development in Israel: contrary to their history of rejecting every aspect of worship of other gods, this new moment is characterized by willingness to revalue and transform a multitude of alien symbols' (119).

[22] Fritz, 'Temple Architecture', 45, sees the Phoenician temples as the inspiration for Solomon's Temple. These Phoenician temples were influenced by the 'long-room temples in northern Syria and eventually back to the *megaron* house in Anatolia' (49).

[23] Endres, *Temple, Monarchy and Word of God*, 119.

Solomon lack reference to any features of the Temple. While the text does not indicate any request or even desire by the Lord for this Temple, the text reveals that he is content to inhabit the Temple (1 Kgs. 8:10–11). We may even suggest that 1 Kings 8:10–11 is a deliberate echo of Exodus 40:34–35, showing indeed that the Lord accepted the Temple. But we notice, too, that his primary desire is for Solomon's heart, not the work of his hands (cf. 1 Kgs. 3:10–14; 6:11–13; 9:3–9; 11:11–13).

Solomon's Focus

Although Solomon features as the builder of the Temple (6:6,14),[24] as the one to whom the Lord spoke, and as the one who offered the prayer of dedication for the Temple (8:22–66). With the building of the Temple, he is nevertheless portrayed in a way that is almost ambiguous. For instance, it takes Solomon four years to start the construction of the Temple (6:1),[25] perhaps even at the prompting of Hiram, as it is not until Hiram approaches Solomon that the construction begins (5:1).[26] This is a significant length of time as David had already prepared materials for the construction and charged Solomon to build (2 Chron. 22).[27] Once Solomon started he built with zeal, sparing no expense. But, as noted above, the narrator portrays Solomon's focus as upon the splendour and not necessarily upon the cultic purpose of the Temple.

Then, in a significant interruption of the Temple construction the narrator gives an account of Solomon's own house, showing its cost and splendour, along with his other building projects (1 Kgs. 7).[28] Significantly, the narrator gives few details of Solomon's palace (7:1,8), primarily noting that Solomon took twice as long to build his own house as he did to build YHWH's house (6:38; 7:1).[29] This point is often overlooked by the modern reader due to the

---

[24] This is also seen in the verb structure in 1 Kings 6 – he built, made, carved, overlaid, set up, and so on.

[25] However, Hurowitz, *I Have Built You An Exalted House*, 227, calculates that 'the narrator assumes the period of co-regency to have lasted precisely (or typologically?) three years, and that Solomon started to build the Temple during his first year as king in his own right'. But this is reading into the text in an attempt to harmonize it. The other dating point given is the exodus, a motif for the narrator (1 Kgs. 6:1).

[26] However, we note the Chronicler shows Solomon as approaching Hiram (2 Chron. 2:3). This again is an example of each narrator/author writing from their individual theological viewpoint.

[27] It is possible that David had spoken to Hiram about cedars for the Temple when Hiram supplied the cedars for David's house (2 Sam. 5:11), especially as David had arranged for cedars for the Temple (2 Chron. 22:4).

[28] In Solomon's defense, 1 Kings 9:10 suggests that the Temple and palace were built consecutively.

[29] Solomon's house took thirteen years to complete compared to the Temple's seven. The buildings attached to the palace compound were of significant size, for example the House of the Forest of Lebanon was much larger than the Temple (cf. 6:2; 7:2).

chapter division between these verses, and because most English translations use 'Temple' in 6:37–38 and 'house/palace' in 7:1 when the Hebrew uses the same word ('house') for both. If we read quickly across the chapter division, as the original reader would have, then we can catch the narrator's implicit rebuke that Solomon was more focused upon his own 'house' than he was upon the Lord's 'house'. In addition, the narrator shows Solomon's house as being far larger than the Lord's house (6:2, cf. 7:2,6). Furthermore, placed in the middle of describing Solomon's ornate house and buildings is the narrator's comment that Solomon made a house like the Portico of Judgement for Pharaoh's daughter (7:7–8).[30] Thus we find Solomon giving Pharaoh's daughter not only a place of prominence in the Temple/palace compound, but also a possible 'voice' in Israel.

This may be a statement in itself regarding the importance that the narrator placed upon Solomon's house. It is, at the same time, an implicit criticism by the narrator of the fact that Solomon was more interested in building his own house than he was in building the 'house' of the Lord, and that he built a house for Pharaoh's daughter in this compound.[31] We also note that following the account of the Temple's construction are the details of Solomon building other cities using the same labour force (9:15–19).[32]

The narrator lists Solomon's reasons for building the Temple as follows: to fulfil the vision of his father David (5:3; cf. 8:24–26), because God had given rest (5:4a, cf. 8:56; Deut. 12:9–10), and as a place for the name of the Lord (5:5). We may observe that there is no mention of Solomon's desire to worship the Lord (as compared to David's desire). However, Solomon's prayer of dedication and his blessing of the congregation of Israel indicates his heart was for God at the time of that dedication (1 Kgs. 8).

Interestingly, the cloud, signifying the presence of the Lord (as in the wilderness journeys and the Tabernacle dedication – Ex. 40:34–35), filled the

---

[30] The Hebrew makes it difficult to determine if the mention of 'like *this* portico' [*ulam*] refers to that of Solomon's house or the Portico of Judgement (7:7–8). On one hand, we acknowledge that the narrator may have been just saying that the same construction materials were used for all three buildings, and so may have been mentioning technical details relating to construction. Yet, a number of English versions (NRSV; JPS Tanakh; NIV) interpret it as suggesting that the house for Pharaoh's daughter was like the Portico of Judgement. This appears to be the narrator's intent, and as such can be seen as another implicit criticism against Solomon establishing Pharaoh's daughter in a house built similarly to the place from where he would judge Israel.

[31] Even Jeremiah criticized king Jehoiakim for his palace building project (Jer. 22:13–17). For the narrator the Temple was the important building, but for Solomon it appears to be his own house and palace compound.

[32] Is this to show that the narrator considered Solomon a 'builder', and the Temple was another project to Solomon? It is only after the Temple is built and dedicated that the narrator places any attention upon the other buildings of Solomon, perhaps showing that the Temple is the focus of the text and of the narrator.

Temple when the Ark of the Covenant was placed in the Inner Sanctuary, and, noticeably, not in response to Solomon's prayer of dedication (1 Kgs. 8:9–11). In further significance, we observe that Solomon responded to this manifest presence of the Lord by drawing the attention of the congregation to himself and the 'magnificence' or ornateness of the Temple and the fact that he built it, rather than calling the people to worship the Lord (8:13).[33] His prayer of dedication was focused on what the worshippers obtain from facing the Temple rather than their duty to worship the same God who manifest himself in a cloud as in the times of Moses (8:22f.).

This also suggests a divided heart for Solomon. It may suggest that he enjoyed his ornate building achievements as much, if not more, than the presence of the Lord. It may also be pointed out again that the Lord did not directly respond to Solomon's grand speech and prayer of dedication. The Lord did not speak to Solomon out of the cloud as he did to Moses (cf. Ex. 33:9–11). Thus, Solomon is not shown by the narrator as having the same relationship with the Lord that Moses had had before him.

THE STRUCTURE OF THE TEXT

One of the ways we can identify the narrator's implicit theological intentions in the text is to examine the structure of the text itself. A number of suggestions regarding the structure of the text have recently arisen,[34] but most interact with Frisch's seminal work, either agreeing or disagreeing with his proposal.[35] Frisch's structure shows the building of the Temple as the central focus for the narrator in 1 Kings 1 – 11. Solomon is the primary figure in the surrounding frames, showing his move from the heights at the beginning of his reign to the lows at the end. This is almost demonstrated as the rise and fall of Solomon. According to Frisch, the central part is the building and dedication of the Temple.

It will be noticed that on the following page I have changed Frisch's formatting to a more traditional chiastic structure. This is in order to aid further comments that follow.

---

[33] In his prayer of dedication, Solomon frequently mentions that he built the Temple (8:13,20,27,44,48). We may ask if this was Solomon boasting of his efforts rather than giving glory to the Lord?

[34] These include K.I. Parker, 'The Limits to Solomon's Reign: A Response to Amos Frisch', *JSOT* 51 (1991), 15–21; idem., 'Solomon as Philosopher King? The Nexus of Law and Wisdom in 1 Kings 1 – 11', *JSOT* 53 (1992), 75–91; D.S. Williams, 'Once Again: The Structure of the Narrative of Solomon's Reign', *JSOT* 86 (1999), 49–66; Olley, 'Pharoah's Daughter', 355–369.

[35] A. Frisch, 'Structure and its Significance', *JSOT* 51 (1991), 10.

Solomon and the Building of the Temple

The beginning of Solomon's reign: from Adonijah's proclamation of himself as king until the establishment of Solomon's reign (1:1 – 2:46).
    Solomon and the Lord: loyalty and the promise of reward (3:1–15).
        The glory of Solomon's reign: wisdom, rule, riches and honour (3:1–16 – 5:14).
            Towards building the Temple: collaborations with Hiram, and the Corvée for the Temple (5:15–32).
            ⟶ The building and dedication of the Temple (6:1 – 9:9).
            In the wake of building the Temple: trade with Hiram, and the Corvée for building projects (9:10–25).
        The glory of Solomon's reign: trade, riches, wisdom and honour (9:26 – 10:29).
    Solomon and the Lord: disloyalty and the announcement of punishment (11:1–13).
The end of Solomon's reign: rebellions against Solomon and the division of the kingdom (11:14 – 12:24).

However, we may suggest a modification to Frisch by noting several implicit aspects of the text. First, as noted above, the structure of the text appears to indicate that Solomon's focus may have been as much, if not more, upon the splendour of his own palace, possessions, and power.[36] As Fritz correctly observes, 'Basically, King Solomon wanted a palace .... the Temple was to be part of the palace compound.'[37] Second, we also note three significant times that the narrator mentions Pharaoh's daughter, forming a frame of its own within the overall structure. The two outer frames for Pharaoh's daughter note that Solomon originally had her housed in the City of David (3:1–3; 9:24). Parker, with later support from Williams, presents a linguistic case linking 3:1–3 with 9:1–9, rather than to 11:1–13 as did Frisch. However, we find greater agreement with Olley who builds on this but links 3:1 to 9:24–25 due to the linguistic similarities of both.[38]

The central point of the frame for Pharaoh's daughter (7:8–9) implies that her house was designed like the 'Portico of Judgement', with the construction

---

[36] Included in the word 'power' is political power which Solomon obtained by treatises with the surrounding nations that required political marriages. These wives, under the cultural ways of the times, had the right to worship their own gods. Instead of Solomon demanding that they worship the Lord God of Israel he made provision for their pagan worship and entered into that worship with them (1 Kgs. 11:1–8).

[37] Fritz, 'Temple Architecture', 44.

[38] These include the mention of Pharaoh's daughter, the City of David, the building of the 'house' of the Lord, Solomon's house, and his house for Pharaoh's daughter, as well as the offering of sacrifices and incense – Olley, 'Pharaoh's Daughter', 356f..

of her house as the central point in the account of Solomon's house, and seemingly as part of the overall palace compound. This also may be seen as an implicit criticism by the narrator regarding Solomon's marriage and the establishment of Pharaoh's daughter in two such prominent places in Israel (i.e., the City of David, and the Temple/palace compound).

Olley also notes the links between 3:1–3 and 9:24–25, and proposed a modification of Frisch's structure to represent the chiastic centrality of Solomon's house and his house for Pharaoh's daughter.[39] Olley correctly points out that 'One effect of the new structure is the placing of less emphasis on the Temple and more on "walking in YHWH's ways".'[40] Frisch curiously says that in 3:1-3 'it is stressed that his marriage to the daughter of Pharaoh does not interfere with his devotion to the Lord'.[41]

However, in 3:1–3 the narrator ties the mention of Pharaoh's daughter to the construction of the Temple, showing her placement in the City of David and awaiting the completion of the Temple and palace compound. This can still be seen as an implicit criticism, and paves the way for the subsequent passages regarding her, such as 1 Kings 11 which explicitly criticizes Solomon for his many wives, who 'turned his heart' – specifically mentioning Pharaoh's daughter.[42]

I therefore modify Frisch's structure, based on the comments above, and building on John Olley's work. This will allow me to reflect thematically Solomon's focus on the splendour of his reign, on the splendour of his buildings – including the Temple, and especially his own house which took twice as long to build – on his marriage to Pharaoh's daughter and also on the establishment of Pharaoh's daughter's house as part of the overall Temple and palace compound.

---

[39] Olley, 'Pharaoh's Daughter', 358, 354.
[40] Olley, 'Pharaoh's Daughter', 367.
[41] Frisch, 'Structure and its Significance', 11.
[42] Frisch, 'Structure and its Significance', 5, correctly notes that in 3:1-3 Solomon walked in the ways of the Lord as did his father, but this is all part of the overall structure to demonstrate the rise and fall of Solomon. Thus, placing the comment about Pharaoh's daughter directly before this statement of Solomon walking after the Lord was part of the narrator's structural outline to show that the problem that would cause Solomon to walk away from the Lord was there in the beginning. Solomon did not go after Pharaoh's daughter because he fell away; she was the one who began to turn his heart. Our point that criticism regarding Solomon can be found in 3:1-3 can be supported by mentioning that Solomon worshipped at the high places, which again can be paralleled with 11:7. That text has explicit criticism of Solomon worshipping at high places.

Solomon and the Building of the Temple

The beginning of Solomon's reign: from Adonijah's proclamation of himself as king until the establishment of Solomon's reign (1:1 – 2:46).
    Solomon takes Pharaoh's daughter as wife (in the City of David) (3:1–3).
        The glory of Solomon's reign: wisdom, rule, riches and honour (3:4 – 4:34).
            The magnificent building of the house of YHWH (5:1 – 6:38).
⟶   Solomon's ornate house, including Pharaoh's daughter's house (7:1–12 [cf. v. 8]).
            The magnificent building of the house of YHWH (7:13 – 9:9).
        The glory of Solomon's reign: trade, riches, cities, wisdom, honour (9:10–23).
    Solomon brings Pharaoh's daughter into her house in the compound (9:24).
The end of Solomon's reign: his wealth, Pharaoh's daughter and other wives 'turn his heart', pagan worship, opposition, Solomon's death (9:26 – 11:43 [cf. 11:1]).

Solomon's Encounters with the Lord

Another important area in the 1 Kings passage are the four encounters that Solomon had with the Lord (3:5–14; 6:11–13; 9:1–9; 11:11–13). Olley has carefully laid these out showing the 'charge/judgement' given to Solomon, the 'stated consequence' for Solomon's response, and also that the text focuses upon Solomon 'walking in the ways of the Lord'.[43] Frisch draws attention to two of these encounters that occur in the midst of Solomon's building projects and presents them in the following structure.[44]

Vision 1 (6.11–13)		*Vision 2* (9.1–9)	
vv. 1–11	(Introduction)	vv. 1–2	(Introduction)
v. 12a	The building of the Temple	v. 3	The building of the Temple
v. 12b	Fidelity to the covenant	vv. 4–5	Fidelity and its reward
vv. 12c–13	The reward of fidelity	vv. 6–9	Disloyalty and its punishment

---

[43] Olley, 'Pharaoh's Daughter', 361–63, correctly outlines these as 'two visions' (3:5–14; 9:1–9) and 'two sayings' (6:11–13; 11:9–13). Parker also refers to all four and says that 'a more internally consistent alternative might be to parallel Solomon's two dreams and to parallel Yahweh's two speeches to Solomon' – Parker, 'The Limits to Solomon's Reign', 19.

[44] Frisch, 'Structure and its Significance', 12.

We may observe that when the Lord spoke to Solomon these two times, as in the initial encounter in 3:5–14, he is not concerned about the Temple, but about Solomon's heart and that he should follow him as David his father had done, and for Solomon to live his life according to the principles that the Temple represented.[45] Significance can also be found in the Lord speaking to Solomon in the midst of the Temple's construction, as if to warn Solomon that the Lord's abiding presence will not result from this Temple but rather from his continued obedience (6:11–13). Significantly, nowhere does the narrator record the Lord directly instructing Solomon to build the Temple, nor how to build. Interestingly, Solomon is not recorded as consulting with God regarding the structure.[46] This stands in stark contrast to God's involvement with Moses and the Tabernacle. From all this we may suggest that the Temple was not necessary for God's presence amongst his people, as the existing Tabernacle was sufficient. Moreover, as I have intimated already, obedience to God's commandments is what ensures his continued presence.

With the second vision during the Temple's construction (9:1–9) there comes a strong predictive warning not to turn from the worship of God. Olley correctly links the use of 'a *second* time' for the vision in 9:2 to the vision of 3:5 (and not to 6:11 as Frisch does) pointing out that 6:11 was a 'saying' that should be linked to the other 'saying' in 11:9–13.[47] Thus, 1 Kings 3:5 reflects the original vision God spoke to Solomon in a dream granting beyond Solomon's request for 'an understanding heart', but tempered with the warning to follow God as did his father David. Thus these two visions frame Solomon's Temple/palace building programme.

The narrator textually placed this 'second time' vision encounter sandwiched between two significant episodes. It is preceded by the Lord's presence in the cloud and Solomon's dedication (1 Kgs. 8), then succeeded by Solomon's continued building programme culminating in Pharaoh's daughter being brought to her 'house' in the Temple/palace compound (9:24). Thus, what is underlined in the flow of this textual structure is that Solomon had the opportunity for obedience by *not* bringing Pharaoh's daughter into her house in the Temple/palace compound.[48]

---

[45] The Temple is only effective while the presence of the Lord is in it, and he is only there if his servants are loyal to him alone and do not go after other gods.

[46] There are only two other times in 1 Kings that the Lord speaks to Solomon. First, at Gibeon (3:5,11–14), and then finally to remove the kingdom from him (11:11).

[47] Olley, 'Pharaoh's Daughter', 359. Olley notes that the introductory statement in 6:11 also distances this encounter as being the one alluded to by the statement of 'second time' in 9:2. Olley also notes other linguistic parallels linking 3:1–15 to 9:1–9. Williams, 'Once Again', 49–66, also evidences the linguistic link between these two passages.

[48] Likewise, Solomon had the opportunity *not* to include Pharaoh's daughter in any plans after the initial vision in 3:5f..

It is also significant that the statement 'So he finished the Temple' (9:25) comes *after* Pharaoh's daughter was established in her house, and the statement that Solomon offered sacrifices three times a year, again implicitly indicates Solomon's divided heart, torn between serving the Lord and the attention and prominence he gives to Pharaoh's daughter. Unfortunately, Solomon did not heed these visionary warnings, his heart turned from the Lord and he built high places to Chemosh and Molech, and for the gods of all his foreign wives (11:7–9; cf. Deut. 17:1–7; Neh. 13:26).[49] The Lord's final appearance to Solomon was a direct consequence of Solomon's heart turning away, and this time the monologue was one of final judgement for Solomon and for his kingdom (11:9–13).

We also note that the narrator shows Solomon breaking the four prohibitions regarding Israel's kings, given in Deuteronomy 17:16–17. In this regard the texts of 1 Kings are most likely another implicit rebuke towards Solomon.

- He imports horses from Egypt (1 Kgs. 10:28 [cf. Deut. 12]).
- He has numerous foreign wives, notably Pharaoh's daughter (1 Kgs. 11:3).
- He multiplies gold (1 Kgs. 10:14,25).
- He makes 'silver as common in Jerusalem as stone' (1 Kgs. 10:27).

In the first two Solomon can be seen as returning the people to Egypt. In the same way, Solomon's use of slave labour to accomplish his additional building projects also caused Israel to return to the conditions of Egypt (9:20–22). The wealth therefore appears to benefit just Solomon and not the common Israelite, thus showing that his pursuit was for personal pleasure and not for the people. Thus, Solomon departed from being the ideal king.[50]

Reflections on the Text

Some may say that the narrator's ambiguous description of the Temple is because it was no longer standing and thus he did not know what it actually looked like. Yet, although the narrator would have most likely completed the compilation and final editing after the last event mentioned in Kings, most believe that the narrator used original sources from the days when the Temple stood.[51] As Tomes says, '[T]here seems to be a *prima facie* case that the Deuteronomistic account has incorporated an earlier account, written while the

---

[49] Earlier he burned incense at the high places (3:3), which is mentioned as a rebuke although the Lord appeared to him at that high place!

[50] For further comments on this see Parker, 'Solomon as Philosopher King?', 85.

[51] The use of 'they are still there to this day' (1 Kgs. 8:8) suggests that this section was written at a later time, but when the Temple was still standing.

Temple was still standing, which may or may not have formed part of the Books of the Acts of Solomon.'[52] Thus we may find theological reasons for the selective account, wherein the narrator wanted to draw attention to Solomon's focus to make a magnificent Temple rather than just a dedicated place of cultic worship. As Frisch correctly observes, the narrator 'sees the other side of the splendour, the injury to religious ideals which has accompanied these achievements'.[53] As noted above, I have suggested that the narrator was implicitly criticizing Solomon, showing him to be focused as much, and perhaps more so, on building his own palace and cities as building the Temple. We also find implicit criticism in the strategically placed accounts of Pharaoh's daughter, and by the equally strategically placed encounters of Solomon with God.

Hurowitz says that rather than focusing on the building details the narrator 'was more interested in portraying Solomon as a great king who built a fabulous building'.[54] While we have observed above that the narrator may not have been presenting Solomon as such 'a great king' as Hurowitz finds, I agree that the Temple is portrayed as 'fabulous'. The account of the construction of the Temple serves to show the splendour of the Temple and to impress everyone who saw or read about the Temple (1 Kgs. 8:13). As well as providing an implicit rebuke for Solomon as noted above, this would also have shown those in exile what they had had and lost, causing them to reflect on their ways. It showed them that the Jerusalem Temple could match the Babylonian temples in splendour. It may also have encouraged them to pursue the construction of a new Temple, but with the focus on worship and walking in the ways of the Lord.

The Temple is very important to the narrator, and to us, as it is the building that 'represents God's exalted heavenly abode, from which God acts in mercy towards his people'.[55] This was the place for the Lord to dwell on earth and, as Davey states, 'the building itself was an expression of his character'.[56] Yet, we have seen above that the Temple was largely Phoenician, not Israelite, in design.

Parker is fairly positive about the situation. We can observe that under Solomon, now the worship of Israel is centralized and at the dedication of the Temple (1 Kgs. 8) 'for at least one brief moment in Israel's history, the entire nation is united under its ideal king'.[57] The bringing of the ark into the Temple right before the dedication, and the Ark's installation in the innermost

---

[52] R. Tomes, 'Our Holy and Beautiful House', *JSOT* 70 (1996), 35.
[53] Frisch, 'Structure and its Significance', 13.
[54] Hurowitz, 'Inside Solomon's Temple', 30.
[55] G.V. Smith, '2290 *zbl*' in W.A. VanGemeren (ed.), *New International Dictionary of Old Testament Theology and Exegesis* (Grand Rapids, 1997), 1.1074.
[56] Davey, 'Temples of the Levant', 143.
[57] Parker, 'Solomon as Philosopher King?', 82.

sanctuary of the Temple imply 'that the ark and the law become the heart of Solomon's kingship'.[58] While Parker seeks to portray Solomon as not just the successor of David but as 'the new Moses'[59] [cf. 1 Kgs. 8:53,56], we may point out that Solomon's encounters with the Lord do not reflect those of Moses, nor is Solomon instructed to build a house for the Lord, and unlike Moses he is not given any instructions for this house, nor does Solomon seek God for direction as did Moses. However, later generations up to the present moment, can see the ideal of YHWH filling the Temple in response to the Ark bearing the law being set up in the Holy of Holies.

As for Solomon, he may have loved the Lord (3:3), but he seems to have loved other things (wealth, fame, and wives) more than the Lord (11:6). We find this especially with Pharaoh's daughter whom he set up in the Temple/palace compound. This was Solomon's failure. Thus, the narrator shows the Temple as magnificent, but Solomon weighted down with his humanity.[60]

Reflections from the Text

We may ask how these findings might be applied to us today in our world. First, we may observe that God is not overly interested in the buildings in which we worship him. God was not shown to be impressed with the 'magnificent' Temple, or concerned about who built it or how ornate it was. God was content to dwell in a tent that would not have impressed anyone from the surrounding nations. The Queen of Sheba would hardly have come to see the Tabernacle (1 Kgs. 10).[61] Certainly, the narrator does not indicate that God displayed his presence any more than when he filled the Temple in the cloud after the Ark of the Covenant containing his law was brought into the Holy of Holies. The narrator makes it clear that the Lord's next appearance to Solomon came after the finish of the building and 'all Solomon's desire which he wanted to do' (9:1). At that point it was to challenge Solomon 'to walk before me' (9:4).[62]

---

[58] Parker, 'Solomon as Philosopher King?', 81.
[59] Parker, 'Solomon as Philosopher King?', 81.
[60] Endres, *Temple, Monarchy and Word of God*, 120, correctly notes that 'the enthusiasm about Solomon's Temple and the largely submerged voice of social criticism [against Solomon] detected within this text presents us with one of the thorniest problems of biblical spirituality'.
[61] I would also suggest that God was not impressed over the size of the sacrifice offered during the dedication.
[62] We note that the narrator does record the Lord saying he has consecrated the Temple, but the focus of the Lord's speech was to challenge Solomon to 'walk in my ways' and then to lay out the consequences of not walking in his ways (1 Kgs. 9:1–9).

This indicates that God does not care about the building in which we gather to worship him, nor about how plain or ornate it is, nor who was involved in the construction, nor its architectural design. God will fill a tent or mud hut in a third world country with his cloud of presence in the same way that he filled the ostentatious Temple. These things are temporal and God has eternal things in mind, such as we, his people, walking in his ways, showing the reality of YAHWEH to the world around us.

Olley claims that the 'second effect' of his rearranged structure is that 'the narrator's intertwining of Solomon's glory and his failings ... can be of significance to a people in exile, lamenting the loss of material glory'.[63] We need to realize in this age of materialism, that wealth does not bring us any favour with God, nor does lack of wealth lose us any favour. Only walking in God's ways brings favour. Olley correctly concludes on this point that 'Wisdom and wealth are to be used for the benefit of the whole community, not for oneself and one's colleagues.'[64] So often today the 'wealth' of a church is used on buildings rather than on the body of Christ attending those buildings, or on the surrounding community they endeavour to reach with the gospel. We must not 'enslave' those who we have been commissioned to reach. We should not seek for people to come and admire our ornate buildings, but rather come in response to God's presence in our midst and 'fall and worship God, saying "God is really among you"' (1 Cor. 14:25).

The Lord is concerned about the heart of the worshipper, not buildings or possessions. Olley correctly points out that 'the story of Solomon's failure, despite his having built the Temple and offering sacrifices (9:25), becomes also a warning to the people not to rely on the Temple and participation in its worship'.[65] Solomon's heart appears to have been one of pride focused more on his achievements than on worshipping God. Solomon perhaps thought the work of his hands was sufficient to impress both people and God, and because he had done so much work for God he could then be exempt from following every detail of Torah. His proud achievements appear to have been more important to him than humble worship.

Each time God appeared to Solomon he challenged him regarding his heart and covenantal obedience to live as his father David had done. David was chosen because God does not look on the outside but on the inside (1 Sam. 16:7). Solomon had the example but chose not to follow it. He allowed things of this world to turn his heart away from God and not to walk in his ways. Thus the narrator now provides us two examples. We can walk in God's ways as David, or with a divided heart as Solomon.

---

[63] Olley, 'Pharaoh's Daughter', 368.
[64] Olley, 'Pharaoh's Daughter', 368.
[65] Olley, 'Pharaoh's Daughter', 367.

Bibliography

Brettler, M., 'The Structure of 1 Kings 1 – 11', *Journal for the Study of the Old Testament* 49 (1991), 87–97.

Davey, C.J., 'Temples of the Levant and The Buildings of Solomon', *Tyndale Bulletin* 31 (1980), 107–146.

DeVries, S.J., *1 Kings* (Waco: Word, 1985).

Dumbrell, W.J., '2121 *hekhal*' in W.A. VanGemeren (ed.), *New International Dictionary of Old Testament Theology and Exegesis*, vol. 1 (Grand Rapids, Michigan: Zondervan, 1997), 1026–1031.

Endres, J., *Temple, Monarchy and Word of God* (Wilmington: Michael Glazier, 1988).

Frisch, A., 'Structure and its Significance: The Narrative of Solomon's Reign (1 Kings 1 – 12.24)', *Journal for the Study of the Old Testament* 51 (1991), 3–14.

Fritz, V., 'Temple Architecture: What can Archaeology Tell Us About Solomon's Temple?', *Biblical Archaeology Review* 13 (1987), 38–49.

Hoerth, A.J., *Archaeology and the Old Testament* (Grand Rapids, Michigan: Baker, 1998).

Hurowitz, V., *I Have Built You An Exalted House: Temple Building in the Bible in Light of Mesopotamian and Northwest Semitic Writings* (Sheffield: Sheffield Academic Press, 1992).

— 'Inside Solomon's Temple', *Bible Review* (1994), 25–37.

Kalimi, I., 'The Land of Moriah, Mount Moriah, and The Site of Solomon's Temple in Biblical Historiography', *Harvard Theological Review* 83 (1990), 345–362.

Laperrousaz, E.M., 'King Solomon's Wall Still Supports the Temple Mount', *Biblical Archaeology Review* (1987), 34–44.

Olley, J., 'Pharaoh's Daughter, Solomon's Palace, and the Temple: Another Look at the Structure of 1 Kings 1 – 11', *Journal for the Study of the Old Testament* 27 (2003), 355–369.

Parker, K.I., 'Solomon as Philosopher King? The Nexus of Law and Wisdom in 1 Kings 1 – 11', *Journal for the Study of the Old Testament* 53 (1992), 75–91.

— 'The Limits to Solomon's Reign: A Response to Amos Frisch', *Journal for the Study of the Old Testament* 51 (1991), 15–21.

Smith, G.V., '2290 *zbl*' in W.A. VanGemeren (ed.), *New International Dictionary of Old Testament Theology and Exegesis*, vol. 1 (Grand Rapids, Michigan: Zondervan, 1997), 1074–1075.

Stigers, H.G., 'Temple, Jerusalem' in M.C. Tenney (ed.), *The Zondervan Pictorial Encyclopedia of the Bible*, vol. 5 (Grand Rapids, Michigan: Zondervan, 1976), 622–656.

Tomes, R., '"Our Holy and Beautiful House": When and Why was 1 Kings 6 – 8 Written?', *Journal for the Study of the Old Testament* 70 (1996), 33–50.

Williams, D.S., 'Once Again: The Structure of the Narrative of Solomon's Reign', *Journal for the Study of the Old Testament* 86 (1999), 49–66.

CHAPTER 4

Getting to the Heart of the Matter – A Lamentable Situation

DAVID J. COHEN

Introduction

My intense interest in the Psalms began when learning Hebrew language with John Olley and then through his subsequent willingness to assist me in my early research on the Psalter. John's love of Hebrew language and the Hebrew Bible continues to be an inspiration to me as I have pursued my own studies. I consider it a privilege to know John as a scholar of great passion and knowledge and as a personal friend.

The Psalter has always maintained a prominent place in Judeo-Christian history as an indispensable and efficacious means of self-expression towards God. For people of faith, both gathered and scattered, the Psalms provide a richly diverse body of literature which emanates from the crucible of everyday life. Those who authored and those who use the Psalms share in these common experiences of life. This connection between author and reader, together with the aesthetic qualities of psalms, have provided a significant resource for the articulation of deep emotion and thinking about God, self and others through the ages. The Psalms possess a clear connection with reality but also maintain a unique sense of timelessness.

In more recent times the Psalms have been analysed and elucidated in a plethora of ways. In part this endeavour has been an attempt to identify what makes the Psalms so unique and to develop a greater awareness of the reasons for their place in religious practice. Lament psalms, as a distinct type of psalm, deserve particular attention as they seem to have all but vanished from the worship landscape of many Christian communities of faith. The non-liturgical church setting, of which I am a part, has experienced a gradual decrease in regular Scripture reading in both corporate worship and personal devotion. Psalms tend to be used sparingly, if at all, and one consequence of this is a decreasing engagement with lament psalms.

Given the prevalence of lament in the Psalter and its presence in the cultic experience of people of faith for generations, we are obligated to re-discover its place and power in worship and devotion. This re-discovery would provide a response to people in today's world who are, without doubt, experiencing distress and seeking ways of dealing with distress. To re-capture a sense of the lament's importance as a significant mode of self-expression a number of foundational issues in research on the Psalms must first be considered. These issues provide signposts to gain our bearings. From there we can embark on a fresh exploration, encountering some additional signposts, which will provide a broader perspective on the power of lament and its practical uses in dealing with distress.

Signposts in the Landscape of Lament

SIGNPOST ONE: CULTIC FUNCTION

The first signpost encountered in exploring the landscape of lament is the cult-functional approach. A number of thoughtful and creative proposals have been proffered to identify the original *Sitz im Leben* of the Psalms. Despite a lack of historical information these attempts have undoubtedly brought into sharper focus the fact that psalms emerged from the experiences of real people as responses to real events. Psalms also facilitated the expression of thoughts and emotions emanating from such events. Lament psalms, as a significant part of cultic practice, provided an inherent validation of people's experience of distress.

There is little doubt as to the perennial place of psalms as a way of connecting faith and experience through liturgy. In short it can be concluded that laments, along with the rest of the Psalms, were intentionally utilized as the basis of devotion for individuals and communities of faith. This reality is highlighted by the recognition of the Psalter as the hymnbook of the Second Temple and its continued usage throughout history by both Jews and Christians. An acknowledgement of the unique nature of lament as an expression of real-life experience alongside the consistent use of these psalms in the Judeo-Christian cultic context suggests that lament psalms are unique in quality, integral to the expression of worship and essential to the ongoing devotion and spiritual formation of individuals and communities of faith.

SIGNPOST TWO: FORM

The form of lament psalms offers another signpost on the landscape of lament. Form provides the space within which expression can most effectively take place. A key development in twentieth century psalms' research was the identification of numerous discrete forms within the Psalter of which individual lament and communal lament are two examples. This identification of a distinctive lament form gave rise to various attempts to describe what constitutes a lament. A fresh possibility emerges from this. Historical usage of lament and the form of lament suggest that the content is both descriptive (and to some degree prescriptive) of a process which reflects a way of dealing with distress.

The nature of lament form could be characterized as a matrix made up of four response collections.[1] They are as follows

- Expressing
- Asserting
- Investing
- Imagining

Each of these response collections can be articulated using a diversity of language. Essentially they highlight four key responsive actions to phenomenological distress.

SIGNPOST THREE: POETRY

Poetry is the chosen language of lament and it provides a third signpost. Alter helpfully describes this kind of poetry as 'an instrument for conveying densely patterned meaning and sometimes contradictory meaning'.[2] Kugel adds to this by emphasizing the prominence of patterns and regularity within Hebrew poetry.[3] For example, the presence of parallelism serves to enhance, contrast, re-emphasize or re-phrase the concepts being expressed. Poetic features are not simply germane to a discussion of the composition of laments but also to the performative nature of laments.[4] This poetry cannot simply be heard. Rather, it must to be engaged with through performance.[5] Throughout history the coupling of this poetry with various musical forms has further enhanced the performative impact of the Psalms.

In lament psalms the reader/performer is invited to utilize confronting words and imagery which provoke powerful images. In addition to this, the emotive qualities of the experiences are also brought to the foreground. This poetic language provides an incomparable medium for the articulation of

---

[1] The exact nature of the matrix and the response collections is addressed in detail in a subsequent section.
[2] R. Alter, *The Art of Biblical Poetry* (New York, 1985), 112.
[3] J. Kugel, *The Idea of Biblical Poetry: Parallelism and its History* (New Haven, 1981), 69–70. While Kugel's comments describe poetry in the Hebrew Bible generally they obviously include the material of Psalter as significant examples of this.
[4] The language itself used in Psalms indicates the intended usage which would necessarily include singing, chanting and reading aloud rather than exclusively silent contemplation.
[5] E.S. Gestenberger, *Psalms*, Part 1, vol. XIV, 'The Forms of Old Testament Literature' (Grand Rapids, 1988), 14. He suggests the presence of a five-syllable stress feature which he identifies as a 'dirge rhythm' in the lament psalms.

distress. While powerful in its ability to carry emotion and image, it is not restrictive to expression but, rather, facilitates freedom of expression and offers safety in using a mode familiar to the community. The fusion of poetic language, musical accompaniment and performance contributes to the forging of a powerful form of articulation. This fusion produces material which cannot be simply examined, analysed or explained from an objective standpoint. It must in fact be experienced in order to fully engage with distress and thereby create a favourable environment for spiritual formation.

SIGNPOST FOUR: NARRATIVE

The fourth signpost is narrative. While scholars have tended to view poetry and narrative as distinct literary modes, in reality lament psalms are a kind of poetic narrative. They tell stories of distress in a poetic style. This telling of stories is not limited in scope to a complaint. Rather, they often reflect a more wholistic view of distress. This narrative, couched in poetic language, provides the linguistic vehicle for externalizing distress, facilitating freedom of emotional expression and shaping the experience of distress. As a result of this, lament psalms demonstrate a strong sense of movement through the presenting distress.[6] This movement often appears to gain impetus by reflecting on the past[7] and engaging in a kind of re-authoring which culminates in the imagining of a new future.

The power of this poetic narrative style is its effectiveness in expressing both mythic and parabolic thinking.[8] A mythic narrative unfolds where successful resolution of distress is viewed as a realistic possibility. However, in contradistinction to this, a parabolic narrative is also present acknowledging a lack of immediate resolution and the associated ambiguities. The matrix of lament is a mould in which these two facets of thinking can be expressed and shaped.

Another characteristic of this poetic narrative is its dialectic quality which provides the impetus for authentic expression of both mythic and parabolic thinking about distress.[9] The dialectic draws together the person, God and perceived enemies in an intense engagement. Evidence in lament psalms themselves suggests that this dialectic contributes in part to a movement from the expression of distress to the expression of praise.[10] In addition to this, a

---

[6] E.g. Ps. 22.

[7] E.g. Ps. 44.

[8] E.G. D'Aquili, 'The Myth-Ritual Complex: A Biogenetic Structural Analysis', *Zygon* 18 (1983), 247–82, discusses the usage of terms in greater detail.

[9] C. Westermann, *Praise and Lament in the Psalms* (Edinburgh, 1981), 193–194. Dialectic, as identified by Westermann, refers to the communication which is implied between self, God and the enemy. It is deliberately provocative and, at times, argumentative.

[10] In this sense praise and lament are viewed as two sides of the one coin.

broad movement from dis-orientation to re-orientation is present in most lament psalms.[11] This highlights the relational shifts which can also occur in lament. Taking these two concepts together, dialectic and orientation, alerts us to the dynamic power of lament in narrating distress. It highlights the possibility of engagement with and transitioning through distress.

SIGNPOST FIVE: INTRAPSYCHIC DYNAMICS

Exploring the intrapsychic dynamics of lament continues the journey into some largely unchartered territory. It is a signpost which points us to newer frontiers. The work of Westermann in highlighting the dialectic nature of lament provides a helpful departure point. Clearly, from the text, a tripartite relationship is evident. Not only is the person present in the situation of distress but so are God and an enemy or enemies. Only the dialectic between the person and God is literally articulated in the lament psalms. However, it is not unreasonable to conclude that the person is also engaged in a dialectic with self and the enemy. These key intrapsychic dynamics are best discussed in terms of relationship and control.

Person and God

The first line of communication evident in the tripartite dialectic is between the person and God. God is the significant other in relationship with the person. A profound question such as 'My God, my God, why have you abandoned me?'[12] is a paradoxical expression of both relationship *and* alienation where the person is attempting to make sense of relationship with God in the face of distress. This alienation appears to be a common factor in the experience of distress.

While the person may feel alienated and not in control of the situation when confronted with distress, God can somehow be entrusted with control. There is an assertion that God is present and that this presence is efficacious to the person in distress. In contrast to this Broyles highlights the way in which God's disposition is often described in terms of wrath, rejection, forgetting and hiding of the face.[13] A rather confronting example of this is Psalm 17:1–5 where the faithfulness of the person is pitted starkly against the implied unfaithfulness of God. The relationship is no doubt uncomfortable where God is viewed concurrently as the solution and the problem.

Notwithstanding this, the authenticity of relationship between the person and God at this point makes it possible to reach a deep level of honesty. There is not simply a tacit recognition of God's presence in the situation. The person is often asserting a state of innocence and a substantial plea for God's action in

---

[11] See P. Ricoeur, *The Rule of Metaphor, Multidisciplinary Studies in the Creation of Meaning in Language* (London, 1978).
[12] Ps. 22:1 (JPS).
[13] C.C. Broyles, *The Conflict of Faith and Experience in the Psalms: A Form-Critical and Theological Study* (Sheffield, 1989), 62–63.

the hope of God's attentiveness and exercise of power. This assertive position demonstrates great courage and self-assuredness in speaking to God which has its foundation in the freedom to express oneself before God, *about* self and *about* God.

Person and Self

A dialectic between the person and self is also present. Even a cursory reading of laments reveals a person who describes self in a variety of ways. Always as one who is in need[14] and frequently one who is faithful, innocent and upright.[15] Another way of self-description is found in penitential psalms, a sub-category of lament, where the psalmist describes self in terms of sin, recognizing the need to confess and repent. These are all attempts on the part of the person to come to terms with self in the face of distress. It should also be noted that all these thoughts are directed towards God and, hence, are relational by definition.

Psalms of lament also provide an avenue for expressing an intrinsic yearning for the self to grasp control in the face of distress. However, while the person desperately desires this sense of control a different experience of reality is evident. Despite the ambivalence and ambiguity associated with a lack of control there is no attempt to deny or internalize the experience. In lament the struggle for control in one's situation is clearly articulated in the face of intense distress. As Farmer notes, 'They [the psalmists] do not wait passively for God to notice their pain and come to their aid. Rather, they cry out as an act of faith in the steadfast love of the one they confidently trust will not reject them for what they feel or say.'[16]

Person and Enemy

The third line of communication in the tripartite relationship is that which exists between the self and the perceived enemy. Although there does not appear to be physical confrontation or direct conversation between the two a relationship is clearly portrayed. Part of the lament process is recognizing that, at least initially, the enemy is in control. Frequently the thought is expressed in terms of what the enemy has done or may do to the person and the powerlessness that the person feels in the situation. This sense of dis-empowerment can also initially be observed in the person's relationship with God. Neither God nor the enemy is responding in the way desired or perhaps expected.

Much internal evidence describes the source of distress in terms of the enemy's activities. The anonymity of the enemy contributes to the stereotypical

---

[14] J.L. Mays, *The Lord Reigns: A Theological Handbook to the Psalms* (Louisville, 1994), 30. Mays discusses this at length. See Pss. 34:6; 40:17; 69:29 *et passim*.

[15] E.g. Pss. 4:3; 7:10; 10:8.

[16] K.D. Farmer, 'Psalms' in C.A. Newsom and S.H. Ringe (eds.), *The Women's Bible Commentary* (London, 1992), 140.

nature of lament. This portrayal leads Miller to the conclusion that 'the enemies are in fact whoever the enemies are for the singers of the Psalms'.[17] It is possible that the enemy may even be self in some circumstances. Perhaps penitential psalms are the clearest examples of this. It seems that in lament there is an inherent need for an enemy as another direction in which emotion can be vented. The actual identity is a subordinate issue.

It should also be observed that there is some evidence within laments to suggest the presence of others who are actually supportive towards, rather than opposed to, the author. Gerstenberger highlights the presence of the community and also a figure he refers to as a 'ritual expert'.[18] Lament is not something which occurs in isolation for the person, but, rather, it can involve the community in a supportive role.

The Matrix of Lament

These five signposts form an important foundation for any praxis involving lament. The term matrix is intentionally used to describe the content and function of lament psalms. It is a mould in which distress can be cast or shaped. As a result a new perspective on distress can emerge. The co-existence of, and interaction between, the four response-collections found in the matrix of lament (expressing – asserting – investing – imagining) provides the substance for the mould. The figure below represents this in diagrammatic form.

These should not be viewed as stages through which the person necessarily passes sequentially. It is also important to note that the response collections, as discrete elements, can be engaged with more than once as a person deals with a specific experience of distress. The significance is not so much the order in which the response collections are encountered but, rather, that they are all encountered.

The first response collection is that of expressing. It combines the elements of invocation and complaint. This is the articulation of the person's predicament as perceived from a human perspective. It is the raw expression of

---

[17] P.D. Miller, *Interpreting the Psalms* (Philadelphia, 1986), 50.
[18] Gerstenberger, *Psalms*, 14.

deep emotional torment and questioning. Of course the prominence and function of questions in this collection cannot be underestimated. In one sense the questions are rhetorical. They need to be asked even if there is no response. However, in another sense they also implicitly demand some kind of response from God. This forms a natural dialectic between the person and God.

Using Buber's idea of the 'I-Thou' relationship,[19] God can be viewed as the significant other in relationship to the distressed person. However, at this point it could be more precisely enunciated as I *about* Thou. Here the person is free to express feelings about God even though there is a perceived alienation from God. This expression also encompasses feelings and thoughts of I *about* self. Questioning of self and questioning of God are both present. The person is desperately striving to find a position before God within the maelstrom of distress. At this point in the experience control is perceived to be with the enemy, whoever or whatever that entity is. The person is powerless and God appears to be inactive, at best, or, at worst, impotent.

The second response collection is that of asserting. This consists of elements such as confession of sin or innocence and a plea. At this point the matrix is an articulation of I *to* Thou and I *to* self. The nature of this collection suggests that part of dealing with distress for the person is to assert oneself to a significant other (in this case God) perhaps in an attempt to feel justified in requesting action on God's part. It also appears to be an attempt to wrest control from the enemy by asserting that the person can attain some semblance of control over the situation. An assertion is also made that, in fact, God is not impotent and can respond in an effective way to the person. These assertions emphasize both the value of human life and the nature of the dependence of that life on God.

The element of plea, as a part of the asserting collection, marks a significant pivotal point as the person attempts to take control of the situation. It achieves this by asserting the necessity and substance of God's response. In some ways the plea is a personal response to the questions asked of God in the expressing response collection. The plea demonstrates recognition of the potential for the person to re-gain control through a collaborative effort. It is an explicit attempt by the person to motivate God to action and actually moves the person from asserting to investing in God as the one who *will* act on behalf of the person.

The investing response collection marks a significant shift in terms of relationship and control. It articulates a renewed confidence of I *in* Thou and I *in* self. The person invests in God by entrusting God with both the ability and willingness to respond to the situation of distress. This demonstrates a level of trust which enables the person to rest in the confidence that God will act *for* and not *against* the person. At this point the enemy does not appear to hold the same position of power and control in the tripartite relationship. In fact, an explicit attempt by the person to take control is frequently evident with the

---

[19] M. Buber, *I and Thou* (Edinburgh, 1937).

employment of imprecation. Despite this imprecatory language it is significant to note that the person vests God with the power to act violently toward the enemy, not self. While emotions of anger and bitterness are freely expressed through imprecation, violent physical reprisal by the person is apparently not an option. Together with this kind of imprecatory language the investing response collection often includes elements such as an acknowledgement of God's response or an affirmation of confidence in God to respond.

The fourth response collection is that of imagining. This, more than any other part of lament, marks a renewed view of solidarity in the relationship between the person and God. At this point the person imagines a new position of I *with* Thou. Accompanying this is a sense of contentment with self. This response collection can include elements such as a vow or pledge, hymnic blessing or anticipation of thanks, all of which paint a picture of hopeful imagination. The distress has been encountered, engaged with and endured with God and the sense of alienation is no longer present. It is possible that the relationship with God is now stronger and deeper as a result of the lament. It is also significant that this imagining clearly emerges from the relational context of the person confronting the distress *with* God. Control seems to rest jointly with the person and God. There is no suggestion in lament that God is rescuing by taking the matter completely out of the person's hands. Rather, dealing with distress is an experience to be faced cooperatively and collaboratively.

AN EXAMPLE OF THE MATRIX OF LAMENT

We now turn to an example of lament in order to observe how the matrix functions. Psalm 22 is an individual lament of acute contrasts. These contrasts reflect the person's internal experience of distress. Kraus describes this saying, 'What is typical and paradigmatic in the statements of suffering and praise in their recourse to conventional means of speech and conception, catches hold of something that is archetypal and supraindividual.'[20]

The jarring shifts in expression found in this psalm have not passed unnoticed by scholars. As a result some have proposed that the psalm was originally two separate entities which have been fused together.[21] However, the diversity of expression may in fact be a helpful reflection of authentic human response in the face of distress. The juxtaposing of lament and praise in this psalm highlights the intensity of the distress fusing with the possibility of resolution. Davis comments that Psalm 22 is 'exploding the limits' of how people can express their feelings to God.[22] Although the sense of alienation is clear from the start of this psalm, the exact source, or nature, of the distress is not described. The lack of detail in this regard contributes to the psalm's

---

[20] H-J. Kraus, *Psalms 1–59* (Minneapolis, 1988), 301.
[21] E.g. P.C. Craigie, *Psalms* (Waco, 1983), 1.197.
[22] See E.F. Davis, 'Exploding the Limits: Form and Function in Psalm 22', *JSOT* 53 (1992), 93.

stereotypical nature. Psalm 22 brings into sharp focus the paradigmatic function of lament.

Verses 1 and 2 of the psalm form an expressing response collection. In this instance it consists of an invocation which quickly breaks out into a complaint against God. Instantly expression through a dialectic with God is evident in the very moment the person, perhaps surprisingly, speaks *to* God about God's perceived absence from the situation. It is an expression of both doubt and faith. There is an obvious sense of cognitive dissonance where the experience and theology of the person fail to match.

Implied in the imagery of day and night is the protracted nature of the distress. God's absence is also described here in two distinct ways. First, God is perceived as not acting to help the distressed person and, second, God is viewed as having actively abandoned the person in distress. Notwithstanding this, the expressing response collection is still articulated within the context of some form of faith relationship. The person continues to believe that communication with God, as a significant other, is possible. Paradoxically the relationship is evident despite feelings of alienation and isolation being exposed. The questions and statements are expressed *about* God and *about* self in response to this experience.

A dramatic shift occurs within verses 3–5. The affirmation of confidence in God forms part of the investing response collection. Investing is again articulated through dialectic. The person argues that God has the ability to act in the situation by virtue of God's inherent power and pre-eminent position. Remembrance is often prevalent at this juncture which also brings renewed confidence to the person. The investing response collection also functions as an attempt to rouse God out of perceived inactivity. A sense of hope is articulated here as I *in* Thou. In other words the hope for resolution of the distress is placed firmly in God's control. The other feature of note at this point in the psalm is the progression from expressing to investing followed by a return to expressing in verses 6–8. This highlights the vacillation between the response collections which is often characteristic of lament psalms.

The articulation in verses 6–8 is in the form of a complaint. Terse language used here highlights the often chaotic experience of confronting distress. It also juxtaposes the potential potency of God (vv. 3–5) with the impotency of human beings (vv. 6–8). The dialectic at this point is also directed towards the enemy who provides the third aspect to the tripartite relationship in the lament. Although the enemies are not directly addressed they are characterized as a group actively working against the person. Hence, the sense of isolation is heightened.

The expression of complaint found here is simply an outpouring of the emotions associated with persecution, alienation, isolation and self-doubt. The 'worm' image is probably a metaphor describing a sense of lowliness or humiliation of the person. These feelings of isolation and powerlessness combine to produce a further struggle to understand the very nature of self and the relationship of self to God. The person views self as unable to cope alone and no more than fair game for others' ridicule.

Again verses 9–10 mark a dramatic shift. In stark contrast to the previous verses, an affirmation of confidence is now articulated. Investing, at this point, maintains the emphasis on I *in* Thou shifting the focus back to God and God's action. This is clearly a narrative facet of the psalm. The story of the past is framed in terms of total dependence on God and absolute connectedness with God from birth onwards. Thus personal safety and solidarity with God are equally emphasized. Addressing God in the second person reinforces this sense of relational connection as the person re-frames the story in the light of current experience. In addition to this, the phrase 'my God' provides an echo which contrasts with verse 1. The emphasis here is one of intimacy rather than alienation. This remembrance adds weight to the dialectic directed towards God. The person is articulating a confidence in God who cannot fail to deliver in the present on the basis of past experience.

The poetic narrative style of verses 11–18 articulates the story of distress for the person with a complaint and then a protracted description of the situation. The first part of verse 11 is a plea which provides a glimmer of hopeful imagination to the suffering. Yet, despite this, the following movement is then one of deepening complaint about the situation. The focus is firmly fixed on self and the circumstances producing the distress. This again is a case of expressing where the person articulates ideas of I *about* self. The imagery of wild animals surrounding the person is indicative of a sense of physical as well as psychological desolation. The effect of this opposition by enemies in the context of God's perceived inactivity leads the person to express a complaint about the imminence of death (v. 15) and that God is to blame. Paradoxically the complaint towards God and the expectancy that God can and will intervene coexist. A movement from expressing to investing is evident at this point.

Verses 19–21 record the asserting element of lament (I *to* Thou) with a petition directed to God. This is a concerted plea for action on God's part. The divine name is used here for the first time in the psalm and is indicative of greater intimacy, either real or desired. There seems to be a renewed confidence in God's ability to act. In fact the person is asserting that Yahweh is the only hope for resolution in the situation. This asserting reaches a peak of confidence at the close of verse 21 where the person unambiguously states, '[Y]ou have rescued me.' The deliverance is 'completed' in spite of the surrounding circumstances.

In verses 22–26, perhaps rather unexpectedly, a hopeful imagining emerges from this melting pot of thoughts and feelings generated by distress. The concept of I *with* Thou is articulated through a hymn of thanks. The vision here expresses a sense of solidarity, not alienation, between the person and God. The enemies have now faded into the background becoming of little or no consequence. Control is with the person and God. Now the psalmist is praising God and is surrounded by a community with whom solidarity is possible.

Hence, the imagining is ostensibly an existential reality rather than an eschatological ideal.

It is also important to note that the hymn contains two vows, in verses 22 and 26. The first is one of personal commitment to share with others what Yahweh has done and the second describes in more detail the expected response from people who have been satisfied with God's actions. This personal commitment highlights control being with the person and God. This hymn of thanks then broadens into a hymn of praise encompassing the whole of creation in verses 27–31. Again this constitutes a part of the imagining for the person. It provides an altered and expanded perspective on both the present and the future. The culmination of this is an unambiguous, hope-filled pronouncement regarding the future.

In summary then, we see an emerging picture of how distress expressed in lament is, in general, a movement from alienation and lack of control to a position of renewed and perhaps deeper intimacy and a strong sense of self-control. It is important to observe that the experience of distress may not have passed at this point. However, a movement towards integration and resolution of the experience has begun.

The Matrix of Lament and Spiritual Formation

Without doubt, varying degrees of distress are experienced by all people. Communities of faith, such as the church, cannot ignore this reality. Distress must be embraced as a valuable opportunity for reflection and meaning-making. In order to achieve this, an appropriate tool and a conducive environment need to be provided for the task. Lament psalms offer such a tool, a helpful matrix in which experiences of distress can be articulated. In a dynamic way the matrix of lament encompasses the full gamut of normal human reactions to distress. When expressing, asserting, investing and imagining are articulated this matrix provides a mould for cradling and shaping the person. It does this by facilitating an intentional navigation through the difficult terrain of distress.

Usage of poetic narrative in the matrix of lament offers two significant possibilities. First, it provides a flexible language for the expression of emotions and vivid imaginings. Second, the narrative style of the poetry provides a vehicle for telling the story of distress and also allows the possibility of re-authoring the narrative to envision a new future. Thus it incorporates a rich combination of past, present and hopeful future. So lament is not simply a raw complaint about a particular set of circumstances or platitudes with no likely substance.

If these benefits of lament are to be re-discovered as a feature of spiritual formation then it needs to be done in an intentional way. A simple awareness of the laments is insufficient if viewed in isolation from phenomenological distress. Even if we gain a deeper understanding of the benefits of lament we have come up short. Lament psalms are not simply literature. They are to be engaged with through performance. A performative view of lament psalms suggests the presence of ritual. Ritual activity combined with lament psalms provides a powerful combination of language, time and space for the matrix of lament to function. As Brueggemann has observed, 'While the experience certainly shaped the pattern of expression, it is also true that the pattern of expression helped shape the experience, so that it could be received, understood and coped with.'[23] This linking of ritual with the language of lament offers a profound liminal space for reflecting on distress. The ritual itself also offers some level of control for the person by giving shape to the expression of thinking and emotion. It also provides a general direction for lament to take as distress is faced.

If ritualized there may well be times when a person laments while not actually facing a specific distress in life. Notwithstanding this, participation in this kind of ritual can establish and reinforce a helpful and healthy pathway for coping with real distress as it arises. This kind of repetition would in turn contribute to the ongoing spiritual formation of the person. Issues of memory and imagination have already been emphasized as a critical part of dealing with distress and again ritual effectively facilitates both these activities. While nothing can be prescribed as a specific form of ritual it could include a wide variety of actions expressing each of the matrix's four response collections – expressing, asserting, investing, imagining. These would be defined by parameters of time, space, language, movement and symbol.

In conclusion, it is important to note that the lament form, as found in the Psalms, is by no means the beginning and end of what it means to lament. However, the matrix identified in these psalms does provide a valuable starting point for contemporary expressions of lament. The church, as a community of faith, must acknowledge its own experience of distress before a world that is in distress. Beginning with this we can then affirm that the church is a safe place which practices an affirming process where distress can be expressed by people of faith *and* people searching for faith. The matrix of lament provides an entry point for this to take place. At this point people can reflect on their experiences of distress and be meaningfully formed in their spirituality. It is partly in and through our ability to lament that we will engage with God and each other in deeply profound ways. This engagement through lament will change us as individuals and as communities of faith. A hopeful imagination will emerge from the midst of distress.

---

[23] Brueggemann, *Psalms in the Life of Faith*, 69.

Bibliography

Alter, R., *The Art of Biblical Poetry* (New York: Basic Books, 1985).

Anderson, A.A., *Psalms*, vols. 1 and 2 (Grand Rapids, Michigan: Eerdmans, 1972).

Anderson, H. and E. Foley, *Mighty Stories, Dangerous Rituals* (San Francisco: Jossey-Bass, 1998).

Billman, K.D. and D. Migliore, *Rachel's Cry: Prayer of Lament and Rebirth of Hope* (Cleveland, Ohio: United Church Press, 1999).

Reid, S.B., *Listening In: A Multicultural Reading of the Psalms* (Nashville: Abingdon Press, 1997).

— (ed.), *Psalms and Practice* (Collegeville, Minnesota: Liturgical Press, 2001).

Broyles, C.C., *The Conflict of Faith and Experience in the Psalms: A Form-Critical and Theological Study* (Sheffield: JSOT Press, 1989).

Brueggemann, W., *Psalms in the Life of Faith* (Minneapolis: Fortress Press, 1995).

Buber, M., *I and Thou* (R.G. Smith (tr.), Edinburgh: T. & T. Clark, 1937).

Craigie, P.C., *Psalms*, vol.1 (Waco, Texas: Word Books, 1983).

D'Aquili, E.G., 'The Myth-Ritual Complex: A Biogenetic Structural Analysis', *Zygon* 18 (1983), 247–282.

Davis, E.F., 'Exploding the Limits: Form and Function in Psalm 22', *Journal for the Study of the Old Testament* 53 (1992), 93–105.

Driver, T.F., *Liberating Rites: Understanding the Transforming Power of Ritual* (Oxford: Westview Press, 1998).

Endres, J.C. and E. Liebert, *A Retreat with the Psalms* (New York: Paulist Press, 2001).

Farmer, K.D., 'Psalms' in C.A. Newsom and S.H. Ringe (eds.), *The Women's Bible Commentary* (London: SPCK, 1992), 137–44.

Gestenberger, E.S., *Psalms*, Part 1 Vol. XIV, 'The Forms of Old Testament Literature' (Grand Rapids, Michigan: Eerdmans, 1988).

JPS Hebrew-English Tanakh (Philadelphia: Jewish Publication Society, 1999).

Kraus, H-J., *Psalms 1-59* (H.C. Oswald (tr.), Minneapolis: Augsburg, 1988).

Kugel, J., *The Idea of Biblical Poetry: Parallelism and its History* (New Haven: Yale University Press, 1981).

Mays, J.L., *The Lord Reigns: A Theological Handbook to the Psalms* (Louisville, Kentucky: Westminster John Knox Press, 1994).

Miller, P.D., *Interpreting the Psalms* (Philadelphia: Fortress Press, 1986).

Mowinckel, S., *The Psalms in Israel's Worship*, 2 vols. (Oxford: Blackwell, 1962).

Rappaport, R.A., *Ritual and Religion in the Making of Humanity* (Cambridge: Cambridge University Press, 1999).

Ricoeur, P., *The Rule of Metaphor: Multidisciplinary Studies in the Creation of Meaning in Language* (C.E. Kelbley (tr.), London: Routledge & Kegan Paul, 1978).

Westermann, C., *Praise and Lament in the Psalms* (Edinburgh: T. & T. Clark, 1981).

CHAPTER 5

Luther on Isaiah 40: the Gospel and Mission

MICHAEL PARSONS

Introduction

John Olley's passion for both Old Testament exegesis and for mission often comes together in his comments on the prophet Isaiah – whether in academic discussion with students in the classroom or simply in private conversation. Isaiah's own passion that all would one day come to know and worship the holy and living God whom he proclaimed resounded in John's quiet excitement that sprang quite naturally from a reading of the text and translated into contemporary and relevant application. It is appropriate, then, that Isaiah 40 should form the pivotal point of this essay on Martin Luther's vision for the church's task.

In an essay on the subject of mission in the context of sixteenth century theology two things need to be recognized. First, we need to recognize that 'mission' itself is a difficult word to define. Indeed, in what has become a seminal work in the area, David Bosch says that ultimately 'mission remains undefinable; it should never be incarcerated in the narrow confines of our own predilections. The most we can hope for is to formulate some *approximations* of what mission is all about.'[1] His working definition seems to be quite general, 'Christian mission gives expression to the dynamic relationship between God and the world.'[2] For that reason it is best to adopt what appears to be the

---

[1] D.J. Bosch, *Transforming Mission: Paradigm Shifts in the Theology of Mission* (Maryknoll, 1991), 9, emphasis original. Later, he says that 'it remains extraordinarily difficult to determine what mission is' (511).

[2] Bosch, *Transforming Mission*, 9. Later he articulates this: 'Mission is, quite simply, the participation of Christians in the liberating mission of Jesus. It is the good news of God's love, incarnated in the witness of a community, for the sake of the world' (519). See W.A. Dyrness, *Let the Earth Rejoice!* (Pasadena, 1991), 190, for a similar definition.

contemporary scholarly consensus that mission should be widely or holistically understood.[3]

The second thing we notice is that the reformers have had a bad press generally as far as mission goes. They are often seen as indifferent to mission, as too concerned with reforming to be engaged in front-line missionary activity, as too directed towards 'preaching for the renewal of piety'[4] in the context of a Christian Europe. Even Bosch, who accepts the reformers' theology as fundamentally missional, speaks of their ambiguity to missionary *activity*.[5] And it is often this dichotomy between missionary ideal and missionary activity that is the sticking point for scholars in reading the reformers in this area. We find it again, for example, in an essay by H. DeWaard.[6] He claims that Luther's theology was ideally suited to mission, given its emphases on a burden for the lost, on God's redemptive purpose, on the church-word-Spirit structure as somehow redemptive ('a kind of missionary structure'). Though he concedes this much his conclusion is that mission was not adequately expressed by the reformers. DeWaard concludes that the reason for this is because they emphasized apostolic doctrine to the detriment of 'apostolic movement'.[7]

Though this approach to the reformers is in some ways understandable I believe that it is basically mistaken because it is commonly spelled out on the basis of a nineteenth century definition of mission. DeWaard, himself, speaks tellingly of 'the heathen beyond their borders'. Verkuyl, taking a similar perspective, complains that the reformers 'make no noteworthy contribution to missiological study' in the context of his failure to locate in their theology 'a whole view of *world mission*'.[8] Though Bosch himself appears ambivalent about the reformers' contribution he admits that they have often been found

---

[3] See, particularly, Bosch, *Transforming Mission*, 11, 268–511; V. Samuel and C. Sugden (eds.), *Mission as Transformation. A Theology of the Whole Gospel* (Oxford, 1999); H. Peskett and V. Ramachandra, *The Message of Mission. The Glory of Christ in all Time and Place* (Leicester, 2003).

[4] The phrase is from H. Bornkamm, *Luther in Mid-Career 1521–1530* (Philadelphia, 1983), 199. He explains this as Luther's summons *to Christians* to their spiritual responsibility (216–217).

[5] Bosch, *Transforming Mission*, 243, 247, 261.

[6] H. DeWaard, 'The Reformers and Mission', *VR* 37 (1981), 2–10.

[7] N. Blough, 'Messianic Mission and Ethic: Discipleship and the Good News' in W.R. Shenk (ed.), *The Transfiguration of Mission. Biblical, Theological and Historical Foundations* (Scottdale, 1993), 178, argues in a similar way. See also, J. Verkuyl, *Contemporary Missiology. An Introduction* (Grand Rapids, 1978), 18–19; S.B. Bevans and R.P. Schroeder, *Constants in Context. A Theology of Mission for Today* (Maryknoll, 2004), 195–196.

[8] DeWaard, 'The Reformers and Mission', 9; Verkuyl, *Contemporary Missiology*, 19, emphasis added.

guilty 'for not subscribing to a definition of mission which did not even exist in their own time'.[9] But there are other ways of looking at this.

Martin Brecht, for example, is helpful in his delineation of the 'movement' of reformation during Luther's career.[10] He shows clearly that the reformer was concerned to encourage the spread of evangelical preaching wherever possible. It was for him an urgent task. Brecht draws the relationship between divine and human responsibility and activity in reformation. Luther, he says, 'encouraged, supported, or admonished wherever he was approached or when he considered it necessary. In general he let things run their own course, trusting in the power of God's word to triumph.'[11] Later, Brecht says that by 1532 the preaching of the gospel had spread in Germany and beyond, and that 'the new movement possessed a stronger dynamic than Luther himself had realized'.[12] This perspective intimates a more positive conclusion. It has the advantage of allowing for the sixteenth century context and understanding, underlining as it does the intentionality of the reformer in the concrete situation. It also permits a broader definition of mission, though (as far as I am aware) Brecht nowhere defines what Luther means by 'reform' in the context of the liberating gospel of Christ.

Recently, one scholar has brought 'reform' and 'mission' together in the context of Reformation theology in a way that seems to me to do justice to both terms without an inherent anachronism. Scott Hendrix argues that the Reformation was an attempt to re-root the faith, 'to re-christianize Europe'.[13] His argument pivots around the idea that the reformers came to condemn the traditional religion as something *less than Christian*.[14] He says, significantly, that the reformers 'cast the message of the Reformation *in missionary terms*'. Accordingly, '[T]hey went about their task with zeal, planting a new and truer religion and denouncing the obstacles that stood in their way. That true religion was, in their eyes, a purer form of Christianity, and its propagation led to intense polemics against non-Christians.'[15]

He insists that the Reformation understood itself as 'a missionary movement'. Hendrix substantiates this claim by stating that once Luther had

---

[9] Bosch, *Transforming Mission*, 244.
[10] M. Brecht, *Martin Luther. Shaping and Defining the Reformation. 1521–32* (Minneapolis, 1990). See, particularly, 345–349.
[11] Brecht, *Martin Luther*, 346.
[12] Brecht, *Martin Luther*, 459.
[13] S. Hendrix, 'Rerooting the Faith: The Reformation as Re-Christianization', *CH* 69 (2000), 558–77. He spells this out, 'It was the ... effort to plant the faith more authentically and firmly in one place – Europe' (575).
[14] By using the words 'came to condemn' I am seeking to convey the very important point that initially the Reformation began as 'an intra–Catholic debate' as Steinmetz forcefully reminds us. See D.C. Steinmetz, 'The Intellectual Appeal of the Reformation', *TToday* 57 (2001), 459–72, particularly 459.
[15] Hendrix, 'Rerooting the Faith', 561–2, emphasis added.

been 'seized by the urgency' of the situation he chose the apostolic mission as a paradigm for the Wittenberg movement. He cites the reformer's observation that the time in which he ministered was the *kairos* of the coming of the gospel to Germany like a passing shower of rain.[16] The conclusion to which Hendrix comes as it relates to Luther is put in the following words

> It began to form as I realized how frequently Luther used the word Christian and repeatedly called upon his readers and hearers to act in a specifically Christian way. On the one hand, what else should one expect from a Christian reformer? But, on the other, why would a reformer harp on the need to act like a true Christian if that reformer already lived in a Christian culture, which he generally endorsed? Indeed, Luther did not accept his context as authentically Christian with only minor deformities.[17]

This seems not only a viable, but also a realistic assessment on at least two counts. First, it appears to accord with Luther's own writing, as the following examination will demonstrate. Second, Hendrix's thesis is clearly in line with contemporary scholarly emphasis on defining 'mission' concretely rather than theoretically.

A pertinent example of this is found in the work of the Mennonite missiologist Wilbert Shenk. He says the following concerning relevant missiology, '[It] will be one that helps the church embrace its mission fully *through a clear discernment of the times*, together with a vision of what a dynamic missionary response requires. ... It is *not* a set of timeless axioms waiting to be applied to all situations ... the community witnesses to the world of its own experience of being transformed through encounter with Christ.'[18]

According to this statement what Hendrix is asserting about Luther and mission is essentially appropriate. We no longer *need* to look for explicit statements about converting the distant heathen and the like. We discover in Luther's work a clear discernment of the times and a call to the kerygmatic community to share its own transforming encounter with the living God through Christ with the surrounding world. If 'authentic proclamation ... is a witness that takes place in a given social, political and historical context'[19] then

---

[16] Hendrix, 'Rerooting the Faith', 565–6. The observation comes from LW 40.55 (WA 15.32). See also Luther's letter to Melanchthon, 13 July 1521, LW 48.262 (WA Br. 2.359), cited by Hendrix. Hendrix also indicates that 'this missionary awareness shaped much of Reformation theology' (566).

[17] Hendrix, 'Rerooting the Faith', 566. See also, 568–569.

[18] W.R. Shenk, 'The Relevance of a Messianic Missiology for Mission Today' in idem., (ed.), *The Transfiguration of Mission*, 30, 32, emphasis added.

[19] L. Henson, 'Defining Mission: Theological and Procedural Elements in considering "Australian Mission"' in M. Hutchinson and G. Treloar (eds.), *This Gospel Shall be*

we might say that Luther is not only aware of mission (so defined) but also that he is energized with the need to speak God's liberating and justifying grace into the concrete situation.

Following the insightful correctives that Hendrix brings to the subject, and allowing for a broader and more concrete definition of what mission is about I intend to examine Luther's lectures on Isaiah 40 (given around 1529) to show the reformer's discernment of the condition of the surrounding world and his awareness of the church's task of mission. At one point he remarks, 'Comfort means nothing unless there is a malady.'[20] So, quite simply, there are two questions that this short study poses in the context of mission. What is the malady that Luther discerns? What is the comfort he has to offer?

The Condition of the World

Luther, generally, intended his exegesis 'to speak the crucial, liberating Word for his "today"'.[21] It is therefore not surprising that he begins his lectures on Isaiah 40 with the comment that 'the next four chapters prophesy the most joyful things concerning Christ and *the church in our time*'.[22] It is this contemporary nature of the message that he wants to underline to those who listen.

A close reading of these lectures reveals that Luther envisions two categories of people – those who belong to the Lord and those who do not, Christians and the ungodly (that is, quite literally, those *without* God).[23] He speaks quite forcefully of 'we who are the disciples of Christ and his Word' and of the self-righteous who exhibit 'the internal sins of Antichrist', who are 'as completely lost'.[24] As we will see, Luther gives many within the Roman Church, together with fanatics and heretics, as examples of the latter. He illustrates the former with those justified by Christ and, significantly, those who with troubled consciences long for peace with God and who are even now on the way to that peace. This, in itself, seems to go a long way in justifying the conclusions drawn by Hendrix that Luther largely saw the world outside the evangelical Church as ungodly and in need of salvation – that is (to employ a term coined later) as 'a mission field'.

Preached (Sydney, 1997), 34–5. See also, D.J. Bosch, *Witness to the World. The Christian Mission in Theological Perspective* (London, 1980), 200.

[20] LW 17.3 (WA 31^2.261).

[21] S.H. Hendrix, 'Luther against the Background of the History of Biblical Interpretation', *Int* 37 (1983), 239.

[22] LW 17.3 (WA 31^2.261), emphasis added.

[23] See, e.g. LW 17.14, 19 (WA 31^2.271, 274). Notice Luther explicitly says this elsewhere, 'There are two world's, as it were. The one is the devil's, in which men are secure, proud, neglecting God and the Gospel. ... The other is Christ's', *Comm. Ps.* 1, LW 12.92.

[24] LW 17.19, 27 (WA 31^2.274, 281), respectively.

It is important to notice that when the reformer speaks of the problem inherent in the fallen world he does so with universality in mind. That is, though he employs certain specific examples he does so while suggesting that *everyone* outside of Christ is caught up in the same malady, though it will be manifested in different ways. Thus he speaks of human nature generally as attempting 'to achieve things by itself' and having 'no desire for Christ'.[25] On the prophet's words, 'Surely the people are grass,' Luther remarks that there is nothing good in anyone and though the flesh has some knowledge of God (*sensus divinitatis*), ironically, without divine grace that in itself will divert interest *from* God in a search for its own advantage. Luther introduces a perceptive illustration. He pictures a monk saying, 'God must be worshipped.' Here Luther discerns 'a spark of divine worship'. However, soon the monk is concluding, 'I will put on my cowl *so that I may become upright* and worship God.'[26] All reason is 'thoroughly blinded', suggests Luther. God is conceived as nothing more than a man, 'as one who like a beggar needs us'. Perhaps his strongest statement in these particular lectures is that 'it is inborn in us that we want to be gods and we strive for divinity'.[27]

Given this universal basis, how does Luther analyze the malady? According to the reformer, people are fundamentally proud, arrogant and self-glorying. He discerns hypocrisy and presumption that disable men and women from accepting the grace of God offered in Christ.[28] Beneath everything, though, he characteristically pinpoints the self as the major problem (self-reliance, self-righteousness and self-centredness) – implying that unbelievers are basically idolaters. Isaiah 40, with its reflection on idols (vv. 18–20) and its rhetorical depiction of the greatness of God (vv. 21–31) appears to lend support to this, of course.[29]

Self-reliance is extremely difficult to overcome, humanly speaking. When confronted with 'Prepare the way of the Lord', for instance, the ungodly respond with, 'What more am I to do?' indicating their lack of understanding and their orientation to self.[30] Self-centredness, itself, shows in people's trust in themselves. Notice Luther's comment, 'Others, who trust in their own merits,

---

[25] LW 17.7 (WA 31².264). See also, LW 17.27 (WA 31².281–2).
[26] LW 17.12 (WA 31².268–9), emphasis added.
[27] LW 17.21, 20 (WA 31².276), respectively.
[28] See LW 17.9, 11–12, 18 (WA 31².266, 268–9, 273).
[29] D.B. Sandy, *Plowshares and Pruning Hooks. Rethinking the Language of Biblical Prophecy and Apocalyptic* (Downers Grove, 2002) 20, comments on these verses, 'God's towering attributes stand out most vividly on the flat landscape of human helplessness.' This certainly echoes Luther's emphases. See also, K. Holter, *Second Isaiah's Idol-Fabrication Passages* (Frankfurt, 1995), 33–89; M.Z. Brettler, 'Incompatible Metaphors for YHWH in Isaiah 40 – 66', *JSOT* 78 (1998), 97–120; R.F. Melugin, 'Israel and the Nations in Isaiah 40 – 55' in H.T.C. Sun and K.L. Eades (eds.), *Problems in Biblical Theology* (Grand Rapids, 1997), 249–264.
[30] LW 17.9 (WA 31².267). See also, LW 17.31–32 (WA 31².285).

resources, riches, etc., *are not the people of God*.'[31] Clearly, self-centredness makes people resistant to grace. Luther soon describes this in terms of idolatry. He seeks to define its nature. Notice, though, how he moves from universal to specific examples in the following. '[T]he ungodly self-righteous shape God according to their own worship and prescribe for themselves a god according to their own opinion. Thus the heretics prescribe their own worship and their cowled righteousness and say, "Here is God and his work." ... They want to whittle God according to their purpose.'[32]

What is noticeable here is the way that Luther uses the word 'purpose', not 'idea'. This signifies a theme in these lectures. It is not just that the ungodly have a wrong idea about God (though that is evidently the case), but it is as much that their *purpose* is to be gods themselves. 'This is what it means to fashion God,' Luther explains, 'He becomes the creature, and I the creator.'[33] That is central to idolatry as Luther defines it and there is definitely a sense of impudence and disobedience about it. Luther says that it is 'the nature of every ungodly man to mold God for himself and refuse to be molded by God'.[34] Idolatry creates a god who is manageable, one who needs our 'works', one who evaluates us as upright – agreeing with our own estimate, of course. Idolatry denies that God is good and seeks to create a god who might be appeased.[35] We can control such a god, counting 'the divine Majesty for nothing'.[36] In fact it is just as in the beginning when Satan tempted the primal pair to be like God. Luther comments, 'That ambition to be God still inheres in us.'[37] In the context of discussing Luther's phrase *homo incurvatus in se*, Lohse describes sin as 'the desire to set oneself in place of God, not allowing God to be one's God'.[38] The prophet Isaiah speaks against this tendency because 'there is simply no comparison between the greatness of God and our littleness' (in Luther's words).[39] And that, surely, is the sad irony of the world's malady, as Luther sees it.

The reformer picks up on another irony. Perhaps alluding to Christ's words in Matthew 6:2 ('They have received their reward'), Luther emphasizes that the

---

[31] LW 17.3 (WA 31².261), emphasis added.
[32] LW 17.16–17 (WA 31².272–3).
[33] LW 17.17 (WA 31².273).
[34] LW 17.17 (WA 31².273). Later Luther comments cynically, 'Why, then do you want to invent a way in which you want to shape Him [God], *as if He were not already* God?' (LW 17.24, emphasis added).
[35] LW 17.24 (WA 31².279).
[36] LW 17.19 (WA 31².275).
[37] LW 17.19 (WA 31².274). The role of Satan is stressed in Luther's lectures.
[38] B. Lohse, *Martin Luther's Theology. Its Historical and Systematic Development* (Edinburgh, 1999), 250.
[39] LW 17.25 (WA 31².279).

self-righteous have already received all they are going to receive.[40] 'The self-righteous ... have what they may see, what may appear, what may be approved before all, that they lead an outstanding life with so many prayers, so much fasting'.[41] The contrast between the self-righteous (the ungodly) and Christians (the godly) could not be starker. Luther draws this contrast in graphic terms by emphasizing the torment through which the truly righteous live. Though many godly are in prison, many suffer torture, and though all are denounced as heretics and publicly condemned Luther calls for confidence.

> God bids us lift up our head. He sets forth His Word and with it gives Himself to us, so that all things are ours and we, on the other hand, may cast our weakness off on Christ. If I am a sinner, Christ is righteous; if I am poor, Christ is rich; if I am foolish, Christ is wise; if I am a captive, Christ is present to set me free; if I am forsaken, Christ takes me to Himself; if I am cast down, Christ consoles me; if I am weary, Christ refreshes me. Finally, He pours Himself out for me altogether.[42]

In those powerful words Luther's emphasis is clearly that (despite appearances) in Christ believers have everything – God, Christ and 'all things' together with them.

Recently, Susan Schreiner has shown that part of the early modern self-understanding was its concern with 'the disjunction between appearance and reality and the consequent search for the real'.[43] She later comments, that 'to see God is to see all of reality differently. The new perspective of faith raises the mind above the self-enclosed world of idolatry and gives one true access to a reality that is still presently unseen.'[44] Here, in the preceding paragraph, Luther discovers 'the real' in Christ. The problem with the world outside of Christ is that they cannot (or refuse to) see it. They have, says Luther, resisted the grace of God.[45] What does the gospel have to offer to a world like this? And, what is the church to do? What is its mission, given the context?

---

[40] On the self-righteous, see, particularly, LW 17.5, 10, 16–18 (WA 31^2.262–3, 267–8, 272–273).
[41] LW 17.27 (WA 31^2.282).
[42] LW 17.28 (WA 31^2.282).
[43] S.E. Schreiner, 'Appearance and Reality in Luther, Montaigne and Shakespeare', *JR* 83 (2003), 345–80, specifically, 345.
[44] Schreiner, 'Appearance and Reality', 356–7. See also, her earlier essay, 'The Spiritual Man Judges All Things: Calvin and the Exegetical Debate about Certainty in the Reformation' in R.A. Muller and J.L. Thompson (eds.), *Biblical Interpretation in the Era of the Reformation* (Grand Rapids, 1996), 189–215.
[45] LW 17.7 (WA 31^2.264–5).

The Gospel and Mission

The primary point to notice in the context of Luther speaking with a sense of mission, as he does here, is that the mission in which the church is involved is at its core both God-centred and trinitarian. The message preached is about the centrality of God. Lecturing on verse 9, Luther comments that this is the doctrine that should be preached. 'This is the gist of your preaching,' he says, '*Behold your God*! "Promote God alone, His mercy and grace. Preach Me alone".' Preachers are to avoid speaking about rules, works and righteousness. They must 'speak of Christ alone.' He then gives the reason, 'In Him alone rests all our salvation.' This message is the strength of the gospel.[46] This is important, but there is a good deal more to it.

What comes across in these lectures is that in mission the church is involved in the work of God, in the sense of being involved *with* the triune God in *his* work. The text 'Prepare the way of the Lord', for Luther, indicates the Lord's activity in us. God alone can resist the natural inclination for self-glory, 'so that He may reveal His own glory and we may appear empty'.[47] Similarly, Christ is preached,[48] but, also, it is Christ who speaks of himself and who consequently reveals his glory and life in the Christian community.[49] Likewise, the Spirit affects change, convincing of sin.[50] In other words, mission is essentially *missio Dei* in which the church by nature and calling is committed.

Lohse rightly underlines the work of the Spirit in this: 'According to Luther all activity in which God engages with reference to the world and humankind is mediated through the Spirit.' And, again, 'It is the Spirit who brings men to Christ. Without the Spirit it is entirely impossible to come to him.'[51] But, judging by his lectures considered here, it seems appropriate to enlarge on this and speak of the *trinitarian* nature of Luther's thinking. More recently, Jürgen Moltmann has voiced this perspective well, 'It is not the church that has the mission of salvation to fulfill in the world; it is the mission of the Son and the Spirit through the Father that *includes* the church.'[52] Similarly, Luther indicates that mission has its source in, and is carried on in conjunction with, the triune God. This is really the meaning of *missio Dei* in Luther's thought.

---

[46] LW 17.14 (WA 31^2.270–71).
[47] LW 17.10 (WA 31^2.267).
[48] LW 17.4, 10 (WA 31^2.262, 268), respectively.
[49] LW 17.9, 10 (WA 31^2.267, 268), respectively. See also, LW 17.4 (WA 31^2.262).
[50] LW 17.4, 12 (WA 31^2.262, 269), respectively.
[51] Lohse, *Martin Luther's Theology*, 235, 236, respectively.
[52] J. Moltmann, *The Church in the Power of the Spirit* (London, 1975), 64, emphasis added. Shenk, 'The Relevance of a Messianic Missiology', 18, comments, 'The authority for all missionary action is the *missio Dei*. Our efforts and actions must be submitted to the priority of God's missional purpose.' See also, S.J. Grenz, *Renewing the Center* (Grand Rapids, 2000), 322.

The gospel in trinitarian context is primarily a consoling ministry that contrasts with the terrifying nature of the law previously preached.[53] It says to those who sense God as enemy, judge, prosecutor, or even as devil, 'Don't be afraid. ... He is on your side, He is gracious to you.'[54] And, as one would expect, it is the nature of the gospel to extol divine grace. Luther does it enthusiastically. On the text that says, 'She has received from the Lord's hand double,' (v. 2 – which Luther reads as 'double blessing', not punishment[55]) the reformer says, 'We see praise of grace here, that for all our sins we receive double gifts. ... Grace is wonderful. Not only is a single gift given for sins, but doubled and outstanding gifts are given. ... By the pure mercy of God ... by the grace of God alone, not as a result of our merits, *but for our sins.*'[56]

Through the gospel God offers forgiveness of sins, a righteousness that is not our own and faith.[57] Rather than the imperative mood of law (which demands), the declarative gospel announces that our warfare has ended and that we are clothed in Christ.[58] Basically, the gospel reveals God, not as he is in himself (*Gott an sich*), but as he is in Christ, and as he is *for us*. In this revelation human glory is brought to nothing before such a God, we are emptied and humbled.[59]

The question at this point is, What is the church's task? From Luther's perspective the answer is obvious, it is to preach the word! Luther rarely writes or preaches without reference to the importance and centrality of the word. These lectures are no exception. On the phrase, 'the voice crying in the wilderness' (v. 3) Luther comments that this voice, the voice of the consoling gospel of Christ (in contrast to the whispering voice of law), is a 'clear and complete and universal proclamation which purely and joyously and most loudly declares that the warfare is ended and that sins are forgiven'.[60] This voice has power, it is spiritual, it is central to the church's mission. It is the

---

[53] See J.E. Strohl, 'Luther's Spiritual Journey' in D.K. McKim (ed.), *The Cambridge Companion to Martin Luther* (Cambridge, 2003), 152.
[54] LW 17.4 (WA 31^2.261).
[55] On the concept of punishment in this verse, see G.V. Smith, *The Prophets as Preachers* (Nashville, 1994), 143.
[56] LW 17.7 (WA 31^2.265), emphasis added. A little later he adds, 'We have learned this by experience.'
[57] Luther speaks of 'the scandal of righteousness' in this context – LW 17.11 (WA 31^2.268).
[58] LW 17. 4–5 (WA 31^2.262). The terms 'imperative' for law and 'declarative' for gospel are useful here and come from G.O. Forde, 'Law and Gospel in Luther's Hermeneutic', *Int* 37 (1983), 240–52. Similarly, M. Wriedt, 'Luther's Theology' in D.K. McKim (ed.), *Cambridge Companion*, 106, says, 'By law Luther understands all statements of Scripture that uncover the sin of humans and accuse them. In contrast, the gospel includes all statements that promise comfort, redemption, and the grace of God.'
[59] See, particularly, LW 17.20, 27–9 (WA 31^2.276, 281–283).
[60] LW 17.8 (WA 31^2.265).

beginning of all spiritual knowledge and of life itself. It is the voice that gives, rather than demands. Through the Spirit it speaks,

> Do you want a gracious God? ... 'You have a gracious God.' Do you want to be comforted? ... 'You are comforted.' Here, then, you observe God's people. ... To them the Gospel is spoken, to their heart and feeling. .... Let the preacher say, 'I not only preach Christ to you as the One who forgives, but I also give you His righteousness, so that, clothed with Him, you may have all that is His. ... Do you want to be holy? I will make you holy, yes, most holy through Christ.'[61]

The voice of the gospel calls upon those who hear to be humbled before God, to believe and trust in him, to cry for his strength and help. Together with this the gospel seeks to convince, to rebuke and to exhort.[62]

The answer to the question of who should 'preach' the gospel may surprise us. Of course, Luther is adamant that preachers *must* preach the gospel. They are called to that task; it is the preacher's divinely given vocation. That is their responsibility before God (*coram Deo*). However, Luther is just as unambiguous on the fact that both preachers *and* hearers must be involved in what we might term 'evangelism' or 'mission'. On the metaphor of 'wilderness' (v. 3) Luther remarks that in contrast to the law that was spoken in a restrictive context ('like a jail, a wall, and a city'), the gospel is 'open to all, public, and unrestrained like a wilderness'. His point is that the voice of gospel should be proclaimed everywhere, loudly, and he says that this voice is 'sent forth in the wilderness both by the preacher himself *and by the hearers*'.[63]

Later, he is equally as emphatic. On the biblical description of Zion as 'herald of good tidings' (v. 9) Luther says,

> *Every Christian is also an evangelist*, who should teach another and publish the glory and praise of God. ... For since Zion has been well informed and taught, she must proclaim and urge joyful tidings. ... "Make yourself heard! Go forth freely in public, think nothing of the size of the opposition, because you have this great teaching to which the mountains should be subject. Therefore arise above them, that is, be their teacher and master and let them be your disciples."[64]

This comment is significant – though Luther qualifies it by saying that he would *prefer* it to be those called to preach who speak thus to the surrounding world. However, what the reformer says here certainly and clearly implies that it is the responsibility of both preachers *and hearers* (having themselves

---

[61] LW 17.4 (WA 31².262).
[62] See LW 17.4–9, 12, 14, 18 (WA 31².261–7, 269, 270, 273).
[63] LW 17.8 (WA 31².266), emphasis added.
[64] LW 17.13–14 (WA 31².270), emphasis added.

learned the truth) to speak the gospel to those outside of Christ. The expectation is that some, at least, will become disciples.

In an early essay Gerrish demonstrates that in Luther the functions of priesthood belong to *every Christian*, including proclamation of the gospel.[65] More recently, Goertz, in developing the concept of the priestly dignity of each believer, has shown that for Luther concern for the salvation of one's neighbour is inherent to priestly service.[66] Those are clearly Luther's concerns here, but notice that the aim of this missional activity is to proclaim the 'glory and praise of God'.[67]

Luther mentions opposition, and this theme is dominant throughout the latter part of his lectures. Indeed, the lectures become a discourse on God's strength in the face of the church's apparent weakness. Luther speaks to the reality of persecution that threatened evangelical believers, of course. On verse 10 ('Behold, the Lord comes with might') he points out that the apostles themselves appeared weak, in fact 'nothing appeared in the apostles less than the strength of God', but in them the 'power of God moved forward against the power of the world'. Significantly, he concludes that the Lord comes 'hidden under weakness'.[68] Later he speaks of 'the power of God', 'the greatness of God', together with the unlimited wisdom and righteousness of God.[69] The believer is imagined to say, 'Nothing is less apparent', to which God replies emphatically by the questions, 'Have you not heard? Do you want to judge on the basis of your eyes?' Luther concludes that those with genuine faith must lift their heads to 'the God of the promises, not the judgement of our perceptions'.[70] And, characteristically, 'Our boasting remains in the Word. We are foolish, sheep for the slaughter, weak. Our God is wise, a liberator, living and strong.

---

[65] B.A. Gerrish, 'Priesthood and Ministry in the Theology of Luther', *CH* 34 (1965), 404–22. P. Althaus, *The Theology of Martin Luther* (Philadelphia, 1966), 315–16, says, 'Luther recognizes no community which is not a preaching community and no community in which all have not been called to be witnesses.' He quotes LW 27.394 (WA 7.57), all believers 'have the right and duty to confess, to teach, and to spread God's Word'.

[66] For his argument, see H. Goertz, *Allgemeines Priestertum und ordiniertes Amt bei Luther* (Marburg, 1997), chapter 4.

[67] On this concept in contemporary missiology, see J. Piper, *Let the Nations be Glad. The Supremacy of God in Missions* (Grand Rapids, 2003), 17, 43.

[68] LW 17.15 (WA 31^2.271). Similarly, he says that 'in this decade the Gospel ran under weakness'. See also, LW 17.16, 22–5 (WA 31^2.272–3, 277–80). Interestingly, Luther says of the prophet's words, 'He gives power to the faint' (v. 29), 'The emphasis lies on the word "faint", but we look for the stress on the word "power"' – LW 17.31 (WA 31^2.284)

[69] LW 17.26–7 (WA 31^2.280–281).

[70] LW 17.29 (WA 31^2.282).

We are poor and wretched, Christ is rich and cheering. Summary: What we lack He has in ample supply.'[71]

Divine strength comes after we become nothing. Luther remarks in a personal comment, 'This happened to me, Martin Luther, who against my will came up against the whole world and then God helped me.'[72] In the final analysis the reformer's concept of both mission theology and mission activity is to be seen in his idea of reformation in his concrete situation.

Conclusion

In answer to the two questions posed at the beginning of this short essay, we have concluded the following. Luther envisages the world as without God and, basically, as self-seeking and disobedient. The gospel is the only hope of salvation in Christ and of peace with God. We noticed, too, that Hendrix's notion that Luther sees his task as missional has been largely substantiated.

Luther seems to have a clear concept of mission as trinitarian, as *missio Dei*, in which the church is essentially involved with the purpose and in the activity of the triune God. In this the reformer prefers to send out ordained preachers to speak the gospel, though there is clear evidence that *all believers* have that responsibility and privilege.

In itself the church is weak and unable to proclaim the glory of God to the surrounding (and often hostile) world. Therefore, it carries out its missional responsibility, not in its own inherent weakness, but in the gracious and sustaining power of God.

In a recent work Howard Peskett and Vinoth Ramachandra seek to define mission. They write, 'Mission is not primarily about *going*. Nor is mission primarily about *doing* anything. Mission is about *being*. It is about being a distinctive kind of people. ... It is about modeling before a skeptical world what the living God ... really is like.'[73] Earlier, they speak of mission as 'counter-storytelling' in a given situation.[74] This seems to me to resonate with Luther's ideas. If we *are* changing our concept of 'mission' (and that paradigm shift is indicated in much of the literature) then we might do well to look again at the reformers' view of mission.[75] Perhaps it was not as inadequate as we have

---

[71] LW 17.29–30 (WA 31².283).

[72] LW 17.31 (WA 31².285).

[73] Peskett and Ramachandra, *The Message of Mission*, 123, original emphasis. Considering the social and religious location in which Luther found himself Andrew Walker's comments in a different context may still be poignant, 'When you are under siege, the primary *missionary* imperative is not to survive but to preserve the gospel' A. Walker, *Telling the Story. Gospel, Mission and Culture* (London, 1996), 190.

[74] Peskett and Ramachandra, *The Message of Mission*, 33–52.

[75] I comment on 'reformers' view of mission' rather than simply on Luther's view because I have discovered similar teaching in some of Calvin's sermons as well. See, M. Parsons, *Studies in Calvin's Sermons on Micah* (Lewiston, forthcoming), ch. 6.

often been led to believe. If Luther is right in asserting that 'Every kind of world outside of grace is a crooked and rough road'[76] – and I believe he is – then, allowing for the different, concrete situation in which he lived and ministered, he may have something to teach us about reaching those worlds for God.

Bibliography

Althaus, P., *The Theology of Martin Luther* (Philadelphia: Fortress Press, 1966).
Bevans, S.B. and R.P. Schroeder, *Constants in Context. A Theology of Mission for Today* (Maryknoll, New York: Orbis, 2004).
Blough, N., 'Messianic Mission and Ethic: Discipleship and the Good News' in W.R. Shenk (ed.), *The Transfiguration of Mission. Biblical, Theological and Historical Foundations* (Scottdale, Pennsylvania: Herald Press, 1993), 178–198.
Bornkamm, H., *Luther in Mid-Career 1521–1530* (Philadelphia: Fortress Press, 1983).
Bosch, D.J., *Transforming Mission: Paradigm Shifts in the Theology of Mission* (Maryknoll, New York: Orbis, 1991).
— *Witness to the World. The Christian Mission in Theological Perspective* (London: Marshall, Morgan and Scott, 1980).
Brecht, M., *Martin Luther. Shaping and Defining the Reformation. 1521–32* (Minneapolis: Fortress Press, 1990).
Brettler, M.Z., 'Incompatible Metaphors for YHWH in Isaiah 40 – 66', *Journal for the Study of the Old Testament* 78 (1998), 97–120.
DeWaard, H., 'The Reformers and Mission', *Vox Reformata* 37 (1981), 2–10.
Dyrness, W.A., *Let the Earth Rejoice!* (Pasadena, California: Fuller Seminary Press, 1991).
Forde, G.O., 'Law and Gospel in Luther's Hermeneutic', *Interpretation* 37 (1983), 240–252.
Gerrish, B.A., 'Priesthood and Ministry in the Theology of Luther', *Church History* 34 (1965), 404–422.
Goertz, H., *Allgemeines Priestertum und ordiniertes Amt bei Luther* (Marburg: Elwert, 1997).
Grenz, S.J., *Renewing the Center: Evangelical Theology in a Postmodern Era* (Grand Rapids, Michigan: Baker, 2000).
Hendrix, S.H., 'Luther against the Background of the History of Biblical Interpretation', *Interpretation* 37 (1983), 229–239.
— 'Rerooting the Faith: The Reformation as Re-Christianization', *Church History* 69 (2000), 558–577.
Henson, L., 'Defining Mission: Theological and Procedural Elements in considering "Australian Mission"' in M. Hutchinson and G. Treloar (eds.), *This Gospel Shall be Preached* (Sydney: Centre for the Study of Australian Christianity, 1997), 27–48.
Holter, K., *Second Isaiah's Idol-Fabrication Passages* (Frankfurt: Peter Lang, 1995).
Lohse, B., *Martin Luther's Theology. Its Historical and Systematic Development* (Edinburgh: T. & T. Clark, 1999).

---

[76] LW 17.10 (WA 31^2.267).

Luther, M., *Lectures on Isaiah*, chapters 40 – 66 in *Luther's Works*, vol. 17 (H.J.A. Bouman (tr.), St Louis: Concordia Publishing House, 1972 – *D. Martin Luthers Werke: Kritische Gesamtausgabe*, vol. 31² (Weimar: Herman Böhlaus Nachfolger, 1912–22).

Melugin, R.F., 'Israel and the Nations in Isaiah 40 – 55' in H.T.C. Sun and K.L. Eades (eds.), *Problems in Biblical Theology* (Grand Rapids, Michigan: Eerdmans, 1997), 249–264.

Moltmann, J., *The Church in the Power of the Spirit* (London: SCM, 1975).

Parsons, M., *Studies in Calvin's Sermons on Micah* (Lewiston, New York: Edwin Mellen Press, forthcoming).

Peskett, H. and V. Ramachandra, *The Message of Mission. The Glory of Christ in all Time and Place* (Leicester: Inter-Varsity Press, 2003).

Piper, J., *Let the Nations be Glad. The Supremacy of God in Missions* (Grand Rapids, Michigan: Baker, 2003).

Samuel, V. and C. Sugden (eds.), *Mission as Transformation. A Theology of the Whole Gospel* (Oxford: Regnum, 1999).

Sandy, D.B., *Plowshares and Pruning Hooks. Rethinking the Language of Biblical Prophecy and Apocalyptic* (Downers Grove, Illinois: Inter-Varsity Press, 2002).

Schreiner, S.E., 'Appearance and Reality in Luther, Montaigne and Shakespeare', *Journal of Religion* 83 (2003), 345–380.

— 'The Spiritual Man Judges All Things: Calvin and the Exegetical Debate about Certainty in the Reformation' in R.A. Muller and J.L. Thompson (eds.), *Biblical Interpretation in the Era of the Reformation* (Grand Rapids, Michigan: Eerdmans, 1996), 189–215.

Shenk, W.R., 'The Relevance of a Messianic Missiology for Mission Today' in idem. (ed.), *The Transfiguration of Mission. Biblical, Theological and Historical Foundations* (Scottdale, Pennsylvania: Herald Press, 1993), 17–36.

Smith, G.V., *The Prophets as Preachers* (Nashville, Tennessee: Broadman and Holman, 1994).

Steinmetz, D.C., 'The Intellectual Appeal of the Reformation', *Theology Today* 57 (2001), 459–472.

Strohl, J.E., 'Luther's Spiritual Journey' in D.K. McKim (ed.), *The Cambridge Companion to Martin Luther* (Cambridge: Cambridge University Press, 2003), 149–164.

Verkuyl, J., *Contemporary Missiology. An Introduction* (Grand Rapids, Michigan: Eerdmans, 1978).

Walker, A., *Telling the Story. Gospel, Mission and Culture* (London: SPCK, 1996).

Wriedt, M., 'Luther's Theology' in D.K. McKim (ed.), *The Cambridge Companion to Martin Luther* (Cambridge: Cambridge University Press, 2003), 86–119.

CHAPTER 6

Second Isaiah and the Greek Islands[1]

MARJO C.A. KORPEL

Introduction

The Hebrew word *'iyyîm* is found nine times in Isaiah 40 – 55. It is mostly translated as 'coastlands' (Is. 41:1,5; 42:4,10,12; 49:1; 51:5) in RSV, but once we find 'isles' (Is. 40:15) and once 'islands' (Is. 42:15).[2] A person not acquainted with Hebrew would not suspect that the same word is used. In commentaries we find the same kind of confusion. John Oswalt, for example, renders 'islands' in 41:1,5; 42:15; 49:1; 51:5, but 'coastlands' in 40:15; 42:4,10,12.[3] Some scholars prefer 'islands' throughout;[4] others opt for 'coastlands' in all instances.[5]

From early times on it has been a common opinion among scholars that *'iyyîm* designates not only islands, but also coastlands in a rather wide sense of the word. Kampegius Vitringa, for example, included Greece, Asia Minor, Italy, France and Spain, even the whole of Europe as well as Africa.[6] It would

---

[1] Thanks are due to the joint Bible Research Group of the Theological Faculty of Utrecht University and the Catholic Theological University, Utrecht, for various useful comments on a preliminary version of this paper that I presented to them in November 2004.
[2] Apparently this is followed by W. Brueggemann, *Isaiah 40 – 66* (Louisville, 1998).
[3] J.N. Oswalt, *The Book of Isaiah, Chapters 40 – 66* (Grand Rapids, 1998).
[4] E.g. K. Baltzer, *Deutero-Isaiah: A Commentary on Isaiah 40 – 55* (Minneapolis, 2001); J. Blenkinsopp, *Isaiah 40 – 55: A New Translation with Introduction and Commentary* (New York, 2002).
[5] E.g. J.L. Koole, *Isaiah III*, 2 vols. (Kampen / Leuven, 1997–1998). In 42:15 Koole renders 'mud flats', without emending the text.
[6] K. Vitringa, *Uitlegging over het boek der profeetsyen van Jezaias*, deel 2 (Leiden, 1739), 211; deel 4 (Leiden, 1740), 894, 966. The same kind of exposition is found in countless popular expositions, e.g. H.A. Wiersinga, *Zendingsperspectief in het Oude Testament* (Baarn, nd.), 125–37. Obviously Paul's interpretation of Isaiah 49:6 in Acts 13:47 played a role here.

seem fairly obvious that such an interpretation was aimed at a legitimation of missionary activity on a mondial scale. Prophecies like Isaiah 42:4, alluded to in Matthew 12:21, seemed to equate the 'islands' with the heathen world in need of conversion. Is this exegesis still acceptable?

In modern studies about the relation between Israel as the elected people of God and the nations it is usually emphasized that the Old Testament does not contain any adhortation to undertake missionary activity among the foreign nations, not even in Second Isaiah.[7] According to Robert Martin-Achard, Israel has to invite the nations to join in the worship of the LORD simply by its exemplary behaviour. However, even this will not happen in historical times, but belongs to the last chapter of the history of salvation. The nations will serve the LORD only at the end of times; it is an *eschatological* expectation. At the same time the conversion of the Gentiles is a *theocentric* event. Neither the nations themselves, nor Israel will effectuate their recognition of God's unicity and universal power, although Israel does have a role as an intermediary. According to Martin-Achard, it is in the New Testament that the eschatological fulfillment of the Old Testament takes place and this would justify the missionary activity of the church.[8]

The problem with this kind of approach is that it sacrifices the undeniable particularism of the Old Testament to its more universalistic visions and postpones the realization of the latter to a remote future. This is an objectionable method in general,[9] and as far as Second Isaiah is concerned it is definitely wrong. His message was intended for his contemporaries, he spoke of an actual foreign ruler called Cyrus, of actual exiles still living in Babylonia, about definite geographic localities called Zion and Babylon, and so on. For this prophet, the 'later things' were included in the 'former things', so that it would seem unwarranted to make a sharp distinction between past, present and future.[10] I agree with Kenton Sparks that the Book of Second Isaiah contains definite indications that the prophet hoped for a spiritual revival among the nations of his own days as a result of the new acts of salvation he expected

---

[7] R. Martin-Achard, *Israël et les nations: La perspective missionnaire de l'Ancien Testament* (Neuchâtel, 1959), 69–72; A. Wilson, *The Nations in Deutero-Isaiah: A Study on Composition and Structure* (Lewiston, 1986), 329, 'It is inappropriate to speak of a theology of mission in Deutero-Isaiah, and he did not envision proselytes.' See, also, H.D. Preuss, *Theologie des Alten Testaments* (Stuttgart, 1992), 313, 'However, this cannot (yet) be interpreted as an adhortation to undertake missionary activity.'

[8] Martin-Achard, *Israël et les nations*, 69–72. In the same vein, Wilson, *The Nations in Deutero-Isaiah*, 129–92, 320, 323–4; D.H. Odendaal, *The Eschatological Expectation of Isaiah 40 – 66, with special Reference to Israel and the Nations* (Nutley, 1970), 171–176.

[9] See J.D. Levenson, 'The Universal Horizon of Biblical Particularism' in M.G. Brett (ed.), *Ethnicity and the Bible* (Leiden 1996), 143–169.

[10] Cf. H. Leene, *De vroegere en de nieuwe dingen bij Deuterojesaja* (Amsterdam, 1987).

from his God and which the nations would be obliged to witness.[11] But obviously this is not the same as an unconditional promise of universal peace as a result of missionary activity of Israel or the Servant of the LORD.[12]

Particularism and Universalism in the Ancient Near East

It is sometimes thought that universalism was a late development in the religion of Israel, a direct consequence of Second Isaiah's strict monotheism. But claims of universal hegemony of deities occur much earlier in the ancient Near East. The Sumerian god Ninurta, for example, demands that captives of subdued nations be brought before him to worship him.[13] Further on the god decrees that his kingship shall comprise the ends of the cosmos.[14] In a bilingual hymn to Anu we read, 'May the kings of the lands bring you heavy tribute, may humanity daily stand before you with sacrifices and supplication, showing humility. ... Let people from all over the inhabited world send up prayers to you.'[15] In the famous report of Wenamun the Egyptian emissary warns the king of Byblos, 'Now as for Amun-Re, the King of the Gods, it is he who is the lord of life and health! And it is he who was the lord of your fathers. They spent their time of life offering to Amun. You too, you are a servant of Amun!'[16]

It would be easy to multiply such examples. To be sure, in polytheism it is not very complicated to add foreign deities to one's pantheon. Almost all lists of deities of the ancient world comprise foreign gods and goddesses, sometimes at exalted positions in the hierarchy. This made it possible to preserve some of one's own religion and culture in a foreign polytheistic context.[17] We now know that among the Hittites, for example, strangers were granted asylum and

---

[11] K.L. Sparks, *Ethnicity and Identity in Ancient Israel: Prolegomena to the Study of Ethnic Sentiments and Their Expression in the Hebrew Bible* (Winona Lake, 1998), 305–314.

[12] Contrast a fantasy like the following in D. Volz, *Jesaja II* 9/2 (Leipzig, 1932), 167: DtIsa suddenly realized 'that the founding of God's sovereignty on earth would not happen eschatologically, but would be human work, and that he, DtIsa, would be called to do this. ... Thus, he leaves the work to his compatriots ... departs and sails to the islands, to be a light to the nations in accordance with the will of God.'

[13] J.S. Cooper, *The Return of Ninurta to Nippur* (Rome, 1978), lines 158–161.

[14] Cooper, *The Return of Ninurta*, line 168.

[15] After F. Thureau-Dangin, *Rituels accadiens* (Paris, 1921), 71, lines 1–4, 7–8. See also, H.W.F. Saggs, *The Encounter with the Divine in Mesopotamia and Israel* (London: 1978).

[16] *Report of Wenamun*, 2.30–32. Cf. H. Goedicke, *The Report of Wenamun* (Baltimore, 1975), 87.

[17] See the contributions of I. Singer, J. Bottéro, C. Zivie-Coche in I. Alon, et al. (eds.), *Concepts of the Other in Near Eastern Religions* (Leiden 1994).

were admitted to rituals.[18] The same was true in Ugarit. There the *ger* partook in cultic ceremonies in which at the same time other foreign people were castigated because of their supposedly sinful behaviour (KTU 1.40 par.). In Ugarit too even a murderer whose whereabouts was unknown could find asylum in the temple (KTU 1.19:III.46–48). In times of war refugees from many other countries were offered shelter and food in the kingdom of Ugarit.[19] Therefore it is mistaken to attribute a more open attitude towards strangers to Israel than to other peoples of the ancient Near East and certainly it cannot be stated that this openness would be the result of its monotheistic faith.[20] On the contrary, texts like Deuteronomy 23:3, Ezra 9 – 10 and Nehemiah 13:1 deny foreigners access to the temple, whereas at the same time the Book of Ruth accepts a Moabitess as a convert to the God of Israel and even makes her the ancestress of David.[21]

If this is the case, we should be prepared to accept that perhaps *all* civilizations of the ancient world, including Israel, shared the ambiguous attitude to strangers that is so characteristic of our own times.[22] The foreigners were welcome as long as they served the interests of the ruling class, but were harassed if they dared to oppose it. In the case of ancient Israel the monotheistic faith undoubtedly complicated matters because, at least in Second Isaiah's time, the jealous God of Israel did not tolerate any other deity next to him. But the message of this prophet too is that if foreigners comply with God's demand to worship him alone, the foreign nations can be saved, as it is stated clearly in

---

[18] J. Klinger, 'Fremde und Aussenseiter in Hatti' in V. Haas (ed.), *Aussenseiter und Randgruppen: Beiträge zu einer Sozialgeschichte des Alten Orients* (Konstanz, 1992), 197–204.

[19] J.C. De Moor, *The Rise of Yahwism: The Roots of Israelite Monotheism* (Leuven, 1997²), 242.

[20] Contra H. Spieckermann, 'Die Stimme des Fremden im Alten Testament', *Pastoral Theologie* 83 (1994), 52, 'Exactly by experiencing of God in the encounter with the stranger Israel opens up the possibility to value foreignness differently from what the ancient oriental world was accustomed to.' This is echoed by J.E. Ramírez Kidd, *Alterity and Identity in Israel: The* ger *in the Old Testament* (Berlin 1999), 131, '[U]nlike the surrounding cultures, *alterity* in Israel did not necessarily imply *hostility.*' It is also inaccurate to state that the oldest ancient Near Eastern testimony of the right of asylum is found in the Book of the Covenant (Ex. 21:12–14). So C. Houtman, *Het altaar als asielplaats: Beschouwingen over en naar aanleiding van Exodus 21:12–14* (Kampen, 1990), 11.

[21] Cf. M.C.A. Korpel, *The Structure of the Book of Ruth* (Assen, 2001), 88–90, 224–233.

[22] Therefore one should not try to resolve this ambiguity by offering a solution that applies to Israel alone. In any case it is a rather forced approach to interpret the tension between particularism and universalism in Second Isaiah exclusively on the basis of Pentateuchal traditions, as is attempted by R.E. Watts, 'Echoes from the Past: Israel's Ancient Traditions and the Destiny of the Nations in Isaiah 40 – 55', *JSOT* 28 (2004), 481–508.

Isaiah 45:22, 'Turn unto me and be saved, all you ends of the earth.' On the basis of Isaiah 41:5 and 42:10 it may be concluded that the 'ends of the earth' are more or less synonymous with the 'islands' which apparently were located at the prophet's remotest geographical horizon.

The 'Islands' in Second Isaiah

The earliest Semitic occurrence of the word for 'island' is found in Ugaritic where it seems to designate the islands forming the delta of the Nile in Egypt.[23] The word also occurs in Punic and possibly in Phoenician.[24] Ultimately it may prove to be a so-called 'Kulturwort', a word used in many different languages to describe a frequently used item in a polyglot context. It occurs also in non-Semitic languages like Egyptian (*'iw* [*jw*]).[25] If it is a 'Kulturwort' indeed, it may even be related to Dutch 'ei-land', English 'is-land', and so on[26] – land surrounded by or bordered by water.

The Hebrew term *'iy* occurs forty times in the Old Testament, nineteen times of which are in the Book of Isaiah. In general the word denotes 'a land whose boundaries are determined by water'.[27] In many studies the 'islands' are quickly identified with 'coastlands',[28] but it remains to be seen whether this is warranted for Second Isaiah. Apparently the identification is based on parallel terms like 'peoples' or 'nations'. But Hebrew parallelism is not always synonymous. It often balances related, but slightly different concepts.[29]

I do not deny that in some cases the rendering 'coastland' is more likely than 'island', for example in Isaiah 20:6 where 'this *'iy*' evidently designates the coast of Philistea, and Ezekiel 27:6–7 where the coasts of Alashia (Cyprus)

---

[23] J.C. De Moor and K. Spronk, *A Cuneiform Anthology of Religious Texts from Ugarit* (Leiden, 1987), 126; J.C. De Moor, *An Anthology of Religious Texts from Ugarit* (Leiden, 1987), 19n.100. For the irregular plural form *'iht* see J. Tropper, *Ugaritische Grammatik* (Münster, 2000), 163, 296.

[24] J. Hoftijzer and K. Jongeling, *Dictionary of the North-West Semitic Inscriptions* (Leiden, 1995), 1.43–44.

[25] R. Hannig and P. Vomberg, *Kulturhandbuch Ägyptens: Wortschatz der Pharaonen in Sachgruppen* (Mainz, 1999), 279. Cf. *HALAT*, 37; *HAHAT*, 44.

[26] Cf. *Webster's Third New International Unabridged Dictionary*, Version 3.0, Springfield, Massachusetts: Merriam-Webster Inc., 2003, s.v. 'island': 'alteration (influenced by English *isle*) of earlier *iland*, from Middle English, from Old English *igland*; akin to Old Frisian *eiland* island, Old Norse *eyland*; all from a prehistoric North Germanic-West Germanic compound whose first constituent is represented by Old English *ig, ēg* island'.

[27] D. Block, 'Nations/Nationality' in W.A. VanGemeren (ed.), *New International Dictionary of Old Testament Theology and Exegesis* (Carlisle, 1997), 4.967.

[28] See the scholars referred to above, notes 5 and 6.

[29] See e.g. W.G.E. Watson, *Classical Hebrew Poetry: A Guide to its Techniques* (Sheffield, 1984), 114–159.

are mentioned. Also a peninsula might be regarded as an *'iy* (Sidon, Is. 23:2,6). However, in other cases the meaning 'island' is clearly preferable. According to Jerermiah 2:10 the Kittim lived on *'iyyîm* which could only be reached by ship. The island Crete is meant in Jeremiah 47:4 (see, also, 25:22). In Esther 10:1 the *'iyyîm* are differentiated from continental land.

The comparison of the *'iyyîm* with fine dust in Isaiah 40:15 definitely favours an interpretation as 'islands' rather than 'coastlands'. Only a multitude of small islands evokes the image of particles of dust. Also in 41:1–5 the *'iyyîm* are compared to dust that will be scattered by Cyrus. Whereas in 42:4 it is uncertain whether it is the coastlands or the islands that shall wait for the teaching of the servant of the LORD. The latter alternative is more attractive in 42:10 and 42:12, because the parallelism suggests that the *'iyyîm* are situated *in* the sea, like the animals inhabiting the water.

Many scholars have decided to emend the text of 42:12 or render *'iyyîm* in an unusual way because the common meaning does not seem to make sense here. However, since 'rivers' balances 'pools', *'iyyîm* balances 'to dry up' which suggests dry ground in the middle of a mass of water. The strophe parallelism with 'hills' and 'mountains'[30] would seem to indicate that the *'iyyîm* rise up from the sea.

The remaining instances of *'iyyîm* in Second Isaiah (49:1; 51:5) cannot be decided with certainty in my opinion. Both 'coastlands' and 'islands' are acceptable renderings here. However, these texts too suggest that the *'iyyîm* are situated far from the speaker[31] and since in the majority of cases the rendering 'islands' is preferable in Second Isaiah, I am inclined to favour 'islands' here too.

According to Genesis 10:5[32] the island peoples were descendants of Javan – the Hebrew word for Ionia and later Greece. Ionia is attested since the early 12th century BC in two texts from the Canaanite city of Ugarit. It is cited there as a foreign centre of outstanding artistry in the field of decorated bowls (KTU 1.4:I.42).[33] Among the descendants of Javan were Tarshish and Kittim (Gen. 10:4), evidently eponyms of Greek ethnic entities. 'Kittim' is especially interesting, because fresh evidence from Ugarit indicates that the Kittim were among the Sea Peoples that invaded the Levant as early as ca. 1190 BC.[34] So

---

[30] A standard pair, cf. M.C.A. Korpel and J.C. De Moor, *The Structure of Classical Hebrew Poetry: Isaiah 40 – 55* (Leiden, 1998), 686.

[31] Is. 51:5 by antithetical parallelism with 'near', v. 5a.

[32] It is likely that the prophet was acquainted with some version of the primordial history, cf. P.B. Harner, 'Creation Faith in Deutero-Isaiah', *VT* 17 (1967), 298–306; Korpel and De Moor, *The Structure of Classical Hebrew Poetry*, 267, 379.

[33] G. Del Olmo Lete and J. Sanmartín, *A Dictionary of the Ugaritic Language in the Alphabetic Tradition* (Leiden, 2003), 2.966.

[34] De Moor, *The Rise of Yahwism*, 248, with bibliography. See also E.D. Oren (ed.), *The Sea Peoples and Their World: A Reassessment* (Philadelphia, 2000).

the contacts between Israel and the Hellenic world were probably much earlier and more intensive than many scholars are willing to recognize. Many recent studies indicate lively contacts between the various nations involved.[35] Just as David employed the 'Cheretites' (Cretans) and 'Pelethites' (Philistines)[36] as mercenaries, so many other kings in the ancient Near East employed Sea Peoples. The city of Kition on Cyprus probably owed its name to the Kittites. The names of Sardinia and Sicily preserve the names of other Sea Peoples (Sherdanu, Sikiloi) up to our own days. Just as in many modern affluent societies, the contacts with these foreigners were friendly as long as they served their masters well, but rapidly deteriorated as soon as they stood up for themselves.

The Book of Second Isaiah reflects[37] the time of the rise of Persia and Greece, nations that were bound to clash soon afterwards.[38] With explicit references to the impending fall of Babylon and Cyrus's victories, we are apparently still close to the end of the Neo-Babylonian empire. It would be strange, however, if the other upcoming superpower of those days, Greece, would have been neglected in a book envisioning the universal triumph of Israel's God. If Egypt, Ethiopia and Seba in the south are mentioned (Is. 43:4; 45:14) and Cyrus is described as coming from the northeast (Is. 41:25, 46:11), where are the nations from the west? Actually the prophet emphasizes that the children of Israel will be brought back not only from the north, south and east, but also from the west (Is. 43:5–6; 49:12).[39] The frequent association of the

---

[35] See e.g. M.C. Astour, *Hellenosemitica: An Ethnic and Cultural Study in West Semitic Impact on Mycenaean Greece* (Leiden, 1965); W. Helck, *Die Beziehungen Ägyptens und Vorderasiens zur Ägäis bis ins 7.Jahrhundert v.Chr.* (Darmstadt, 1979); C. Lambrou-Phillipson, *Hellenorientalia: The Near Eastern Presence in the Bronze Age Aegean, ca. 3000-1100 B.C.* (Göteborg, 1990); J.P. Brown, *Israel and Hellas*, 3 vols. (Berlin, 1995–2003); idem., *Ancient Israel and Ancient Greece: Religion, Politics, and Culture* (Minneapolis, 2003); S. Alkier and M. Witte (eds.), *Die Griechen und das antike Israel: Interdisziplinäre Studien zur Religions- und Kulturgeschichte des heiligen Landes* (Fribourg, 2004); A.C. Hagedorn, 'Who would invite a stranger from abroad? The Presence of Greeks in Palestine in Old Testament Times' in R.P. Gordon and J.C. De Moor (eds.), *The Old Testament in its World* (Leiden, 2005), 68–93. Of course one should not exaggerate the importance of these contacts. The fact that Second Isaiah appears to be acquainted with important Pentateuchal traditions but has only a vague notion of the Greek isles argues against a far-reaching theory like that of J.-W. Wesselius, *The Origin of the History of Israel: Herodotus's Histories as Blueprint for the First Books of the Bible* (London, 2002).

[36] For the etymological identity see De Moor, *The Rise of Yahwism*, 171n.345.

[37] In the present connection it is irrelevant whether this reflection is prospective or descriptive.

[38] It may well be that the prophet foresees this clash in 41:1–5. Relatively soon after the Persian occupation the Greeks took over Palestine (332 BC).

[39] See also Is. 11:11 and Zech. 8:7, possibly dating from the same period.

'iyyîm with Tarshish (Is. 23:6; 60:9; 66:19; Ps. 72:10) indicates that it was a term describing remote overseas localities west of Israel. This is confirmed by Isaiah 24:15 where the *'iyyîm* 'of the sea' (or, of the west) stand in antithetical parallelism with 'the east'.[40] Greek coins issued during the fifth and fourth centuries BC show that Tarshish (Tarsus)[41] was hellenized early and belonged to the sphere of influence of Greece in the period under discussion.[42] However, since Tarshish is differentiated from the 'islands' (Is. 60:9; 66:19; Ps. 72:10) and according to Is. 66:19 Javan belongs to the faraway *'iyyîm*, the latter must have been situated further to the west.

Interestingly, in this context, the *Encyclopedia Britannica 2004* describes Greece as follows, 'Greece has more than 2,000 islands, of which 170 are inhabited; some of the easternmost Aegean islands lie just a few miles off the Turkish coast. Given this situation, it is no accident that Greece has always had a strong nautical tradition.'

It is my contention that the 'islands' in Second Isaiah are a description of the Hellenic world which, just like Persia and all other nations, is expected to bow to the God of Israel and return the exiled Jews to their homeland. It was the fifth century BC that saw the emergence of intellectual giants like Euripides, Herodotus, Socrates, Sophocles, Thucydides and Xenophon in Greece. Jews did not need to sail as far as the Greek mainland to become acquainted with this explosion of learning and culture. The author of the book of Jonah, which dates

---

[40] Cf. E.J. Young, *The Book of Isaiah* (Grand Rapids, 1996), 2.170.

[41] The common identification of Tarshish with Tartessos in SW Spain is highly unlikely because the geographical horizon of the Assyrians who associated the country and city with Yawan since the 7th century BC hardly extended that far west. Cf. S. Parpola, *Neo-Assyrian Toponyms* (Neukirchen-Vluyn, 1970), 186–87, 349. Esarhaddon lists them among 'kings who dwell in the middle of the sea' which accords well with the biblical testimony. Cf. R. Borger, *Die Inschriften Asarhaddons Königs von Assyrien* (Graz, 1956), 86. 1 Kings 10:22 does not imply that Tarshish was located so far away that its ships had to travel three years to reach the Levant. In the Achaemenid period the Ionian islands were located opposite the west coast of present day Turkey whereas the Lydians inhabited the coast of the mainland there. Biblical Lud is associated with Tarshish, Put (cf. Jer. 46:9) and Javan in Isaiah 66:19. In my opinion Lud should be identified with Lydia. In Ezekiel 30:5 we have two embracing antithetical pairs, so that Ethiopia || Arabia, Put (Pontos?) || Lud (Lydia). In 1 Chronicles 1:7 Tarshish and Kittim appear to be associated with Rodanim, the inhabitants of Rhodos. For the location of Tarsus and all other geographical entities mentioned, see S. Mittmann and G. Schmitt, *Tübinger Bibelatlas* (Stuttgart, 2001), map B.IV.23.

[42] A.H.M. Jones, 'Tarsus' in N.G.L. Hammond and H.H. Scullard (eds.), *The Oxford Classical Dictionary* (Oxford, 1970^2), 1039. In antiquity seagoing ships could reach Tarsus via the river Kydnos and the harbour was important as a station on the route to the Greek islands. Cf. E. Olshausen, 'Tarsos' in K. Ziegler, et al. (eds.), *Der Kleine Pauly: Lexikon der Antike* (München, 1975), 5.529–530.

from the Persian period,[43] could easily imagine an Israelite prophet fleeing to Tarshish (Jon. 1:3). The bold statement that the 'islands' are craving for the teaching of the LORD, mediated by his servant (Is. 42:4; 51:4–5), might well be understood as a first polemical slight against the 'wisdom' of the Greeks which would mark so many subsequent encounters between Jews and Greeks.[44]

It seems likely that after the collapse of the Neo-Babylonian empire some Jews were taken along as slaves by the Persians.[45] Isaiah 60:19–20 speaks of Jewish[46] exiles who will return from many places, among them the 'islands'. According to Isaiah 60:9 ships from Tarshish will bring them back home. So, there did exist Jews in exile in the Hellenic part of the ancient world. True, the number of possibly Jewish personal names in Greek documents dating from the sixth and fifth century BC is very low.[47] But it is to be expected that if Jews were there as resident foreigners, the Greeks employed them in rather low positions, as slaves, mercenaries or handworkers.[48] In the ancient world such people were rarely mentioned by name in official documents, or if they were, it was often under the new names they had got from their masters.[49] These Jews

---

[43] See L.L. Grabbe, *Judaism from Cyrus to Hadrian*, vol. 1: The Persian and Greek Periods (Minneapolis, 1992), 1.46; idem., *Judaic Religion in the Second Temple Period: Belief and Practice from the Exile to Yavneh* (London, 2000), 17–18; E. Ben Zvi, *Signs of Jonah: Reading and Rereading in Ancient Yehud* (London, 2003), especially, 8, 15–18, 116–26.

[44] See about these contacts from the fourth century onwards, L.H. Feldman, *Studies in Hellenistic Judaism* (Leiden, 1996), 487–503.

[45] Cf. S. Schoenberg, {http://www.jewishvirtuallibrary.org/jsource/vjw/Greece.html}.

[46] For the Jewish identity of the 'survivors' in Is. 66:19 see Oswalt, *The Book of Isaiah, Chapters 40 – 66*, 688–689.

[47] The names of Azariah, Hatita, Isaiah, Moses, Obadiah and Simeon might be represented, cf. P.M. Fraser and E. Matthews, *A Lexicon of Greek Personal Names*, vol. 1: The Aegean Islands, Cyprus/Cyrenaica (Oxford, 1987), 15, 237, 407; idem., vol. 2: Attica (M.J. Osborne, S.G. Byrne, eds.), Oxford, 1994), 277, 322, 398–99; M.J. Osborne and S.G. Byrne, *The Foreign Residents of Athens:* An annex to *A Lexicon of Greek Personal Names* (Leuven, 1996), 124.

[48] According to Ezekiel 27:13 Tyre traded human beings with Ionia (Javan) and Joel 4:6 [tr. 3:6] confirms that in the fourth century Judahite slaves were sold to Ionia. Cf. H.W. Wolff, *Dodekapropheton 2: Joel und Amos* (Neukirchen-Vluyn, 1969), 93; A. Weiser, *Das Buch der zwölf Kleinen Propheten*, 1 (1985), 124.

[49] For some examples of renaming of Jewish exiles in Egypt, Babylonia and Palestine in the Persian period see M.C.A. Korpel, 'Disillusion among Jews in the Postexilic Period' in Gordon and De Moor (eds.), *The Old Testament in its World*, 145–57. At least in later times the same practice is attested in Greece and Rome: 'The slave was an outsider, who brought no rights with him from the society he came from. ... The extent of this deracination is symbolized by the fact that he had to accept the religion of his new owner's houshold ... and had no name apart from that which his owner chose to give him' – T.E.J. Wiedemann, *Greek and Roman Slavery* (London, 1981), 33. See, also, 34.

on the faraway Greek islands lost a dear part of their identity, but as the book of Second Isaiah demonstrates, they were certainly not forgotten by their compatriots.

This contribution is a small tribute to John Olley, a fine scholar, well versed in Greek, an exegetical expert on the Book of Isaiah, and an inhabitant of the largest 'island' in the world, the Australian continent. Yet a man whose open-mindedness characterizes him as all but an islander.

Bibliography

Alkier, S. and M. Witte (eds.), *Die Griechen und das antike Israel: Interdisziplinäre Studien zur Religions- und Kulturgeschichte des heiligen Landes* (Fribourg: Academic Press, 2004).

Alon, I. et al. (eds.), *Concepts of the Other in Near Eastern Religions* (Leiden: Brill, 1994).

Astour, M.C., *Hellenosemitica: An Ethnic and Cultural Study in West Semitic Impact on Mycenaean Greece* (Leiden: Brill, 1965).

Baltzer, K., *Deutero-Isaiah: A Commentary on Isaiah 40 – 55* (M. Kohl (tr.), Minneapolis: Fortress Press, 2001).

Ben Zvi, E., *Signs of Jonah: Reading and Rereading in Ancient Yehud* (London: Sheffield Academic Press, 2003).

Blenkinsopp, J., *Isaiah 40 – 55: A New Translation with Introduction and Commentary* (New York: Doubleday, 2002).

Block, D., 'Nations/Nationality' in W.A. VanGemeren (ed.), *New International Dictionary of Old Testament Theology and Exegesis* (Carlisle: Paternoster, 1997), 4.966–972.

Borger, R., *Die Inschriften Asarhaddons Königs von Assyrien* (Graz: Weidner, 1956).

Brown, J.P., *Ancient Israel and Ancient Greece: Religion, Politics, and Culture* (Minneapolis: Fortress Press, 2003).

— *Israel and Hellas*, 3 vols (Berlin: De Gruyter, 1995–2003).

Brueggemann, W., *Isaiah 40 – 66* (Louisville: Westminster John Knox, 1998).

Cooper, J.S., *The Return of Ninurta to Nippur* (Rome: Pont. Inst. Biblicum, 1978).

Del Olmo Lete, G. and J. Sanmartín, *A Dictionary of the Ugaritic Language in the Alphabetic Tradition*, vol. 2 (W.G.E. Watson (tr.), Leiden: Brill, 2003).

Encyclopedia Britannica 2004 (CD-ROM).

De Moor, J.C., *An Anthology of Religious Texts from Ugarit* (Leiden: Brill, 1987).

— *The Rise of Yahwism: The Roots of Israelite Monotheism* (Leuven: Peeters, 1997^2).

— and K. Spronk, *A Cuneiform Anthology of Religious Texts from Ugarit* (Leiden: Brill, 1987).

Feldman, L.H., *Studies in Hellenistic Judaism* (Leiden: Brill, 1996).

Fraser, P.M. and E. Matthews, *A Lexicon of Greek Personal Names*, vol. 1: The Aegean Islands, Cyprus/Cyrenaica (Oxford: Clarendon, 1987).

Also, L.C. Reilly, *Slaves in Ancient Greece: Slaves from Greek Manumission Inscriptions* (Chicago, 1978), IX.

— *A Lexicon of Greek Personal Names*, vol. 2: Attica (M.J. Osborne, S.G. Byrne (eds.), Oxford: Clarendon, 1994).
Goedicke, H., *The Report of Wenamun* (Baltimore: John Hopkins University Press, 1975).
Gordon, R.P. and J.C. De Moor (eds.), *The Old Testament in its World* (Leiden: Brill, 2005).
Grabbe, L.L., *Judaic Religion in the Second Temple Period: Belief and Practice from the Exile to Yavneh* (London: Routledge, 2000).
— *Judaism from Cyrus to Hadrian*, vol. 1: The Persian and Greek Periods (Minneapolis: Augsburg Fortress, 1992).
Hagedorn, A.C., 'Who would invite a stranger from abroad? The Presence of Greeks in Palestine in Old Testament Times' in R.P. Gordon and J.C. De Moor (eds.), *The Old Testament in its World* (Leiden: Brill, 2005), 68–93.
Hannig, R. and P. Vomberg, *Kulturhandbuch Ägyptens: Wortschatz der Pharaonen in Sachgruppen* (Mainz: Von Zabern, 1999).
Harner, P.B., 'Creation Faith in Deutero-Isaiah', *Vetus Testamentum* 17 (1967), 298–306.
Helck, W., *Die Beziehungen Ägyptens und Vorderasiens zur Ägäis bis ins 7.Jahrhundert v.Chr.* (Darmstadt: Wissenschaftliche Buchgesellschaft, 1979).
Hoftijzer, J., and K. Jongeling, *Dictionary of the North-West Semitic Inscriptions*, vol. 1 (Leiden: Brill, 1995).
Houtman, C., *Het altaar als asielplaats: Beschouwingen over en naar aanleiding van Exodus 21:12–14* (Kampen: Kok, 1990).
Jones, A.H.M., 'Tarsus' in N.G.L. Hammond and H.H. Scullard (eds.), *The Oxford Classical Dictionary* (Oxford: Clarendon Press, 1970^2), 1039.
Klinger, J., 'Fremde und Aussenseiter in Hatti' in V. Haas (ed.), *Aussenseiter und Randgruppen: Beiträge zu einer Sozialgeschichte des Alten Orients* (Konstanz: Univ. Verlag, 1992), 197–204.
Koole, J.L., *Isaiah III*, 2 vols. (A.P. Runia (tr.), Kampen: Pharos / Leuven: Peeters, 1997–1998).
Korpel, M.C.A., 'Disillusion among Jews in the Postexilic Period' in R.P. Gordon and J.C. De Moor (eds.), *The Old Testament in its World* (Leiden: Brill, 2005), 145–157.
— *The Structure of the Book of Ruth* (Assen: Van Gorcum, 2001).
— with J.C. De Moor, *The Structure of Classical Hebrew Poetry: Isaiah 40 – 55* (Leiden: Brill, 1998).
Lambrou-Phillipson, C., *Hellenorientalia: The Near Eastern Presence in the Bronze Age Aegean, ca. 3000–1100 BC* (Göteborg: Åström Förlag, 1990).
Leene, H., *De vroegere en de nieuwe dingen bij Deuterojesaja* (Amsterdam: VU Uitgeverij, 1987).
Levenson, J.D., 'The Universal Horizon of Biblical Particularism' in M.G. Brett (ed.), *Ethnicity and the Bible* (Leiden: Brill, 1996), 143–169.
Martin-Achard, R., *Israël et les nations: La perspective missionnaire de l'Ancien Testament* (Neuchâtel: Delachaux, 1959).
Merriam-Webster, *Webster's Third New International Unabridged Dictionary* (Springfield, Massachusetts – electronic edition Version 3.0, 2003).
Mittmann, S. and G. Schmitt, *Tübinger Bibelatlas* (Stuttgart: Deutsche Bibelgesellschaft, 2001).

Odendaal, D.H., *The Eschatological Expectation of Isaiah 40 – 66, with special Reference to Israel and the Nations* (Nutley: Presbyterian and Reformed, 1970).
Oren, E.D. (ed.), *The Sea Peoples and Their World: A Reassessment* (Philadelphia: University Museum, 2000.)
Olshausen, E., 'Tarsos' in K. Ziegler, et al. (eds.), *Der Kleine Pauly: Lexikon der Antike*, Bd. 5 (München: Druckenmüller, 1975), 529–530.
Osborne, M.J. and S.G. Byrne, *The Foreign Residents of Athens. An Annex to A Lexicon of Greek Personal Names* (Leuven: Peeters, 1996).
Oswalt, J.N., *The Book of Isaiah, Chapters 40 – 66* (Grand Rapids: Eerdmans, 1998).
Parpola, S., *Neo-Assyrian Toponyms* (Neukirchen-Vluyn: Neukirchener Verlag, 1970).
Preuss, H.D., *Theologie des Alten Testaments*, Bd. 2 (Stuttgart: Kohlhammer, 1992).
Ramírez Kidd, J.E., *Alterity and Identity in Israel: The ger in the Old Testament* (Berlin: De Gruyter, 1999).
Reilly, L.C., *Slaves in Ancient Greece: Slaves from Greek Manumission Inscriptions* (Chicago: Ares, 1978).
Saggs, H.W.F., *The Encounter with the Divine in Mesopotamia and Israel* (London: Athlone, 1978).
Sparks, K.L., *Ethnicity and Identity in Ancient Israel: Prolegomena to the Study of Ethnic Sentiments and Their Expression in the Hebrew Bible* (Winona Lake: Eisenbrauns, 1998).
Spieckermann, H., 'Die Stimme des Fremden im Alten Testament', *Pastoral Theologie* 83 (1994), 38–51, 52–57.
Thureau-Dangin, F., *Rituels accadiens* (Paris: University of France, 1921).
Tropper, J., *Ugaritische Grammatik* (Münster: Ugarit-Verlag, 2000).
Vitringa, K., *Uitlegging over het boek der profeetsyen van Jezaias*, deel 2 (Leiden: Van der Deyster, 1739)
— *Uitlegging over het boek der profeetsyen van Jezaias*, deel 4 (Leiden: Van der Deyster, 1740).
Volz, D., *Jesaja II* (Leipzig: Deichert, 1932).
Watson, W.G.E., *Classical Hebrew Poetry: A Guide to its Techniques* (Sheffield: JSOT Press, 1984).
Weiser, A., *Das Buch der zwölf Kleinen Propheten*, 1 (1985[8]).
Wesselius, J.-W., *The Origin of the History of Israel: Herodotus's Histories as Blueprint for the First Books of the Bible* (London: Sheffield University Press, 2002).
Wiedemann, T.E.J., *Greek and Roman Slavery* (London: Croom Helm, 1981).
Wiersinga, H.A., *Zendingsperspectief in het Oude Testament* (Baarn: Bosch & Keuning,, nd.).
Wilson, A., *The Nations in Deutero-Isaiah: A Study on Composition and Structure* (Lewiston: Edwin Mellen Press, 1986).
Wolff, H.W., *Dodekapropheton 2: Joel und Amos* (Neukirchen-Vluyn, Neukirchener-Verlag, 1969).
Young, E.J., *The Book of Isaiah*, vol. 2 (Grand Rapids, Michigan: Eerdmans, 1996).

CHAPTER 7

The Significance of the Old Testament for Paul's Missionary Calling

RICHARD K. MOORE

Introduction

It was my privilege to teach with John Olley for quarter of a century (1979–2003). Throughout that time we were colleagues at the Baptist Theological College of Western Australia, where John had responsibility for Old Testament and was Principal from 1991–2003, while my area was New Testament. When we first met, in October 1978, we had both done extensive research involving the Septuagint and the *dikaiosune* word family. In the ensuing years I was to gain further insights from John, particularly in the latter field. Indeed, for me personally our relationship has been very enriching.

John's major interests in theological teaching, Old Testament and Mission (informed and enriched by his decade as a missionary in Hong Kong) are the areas which come together in the present essay. I am grateful for the opportunity this *Festschrift* offers for exploring the way the Old Testament functioned for Paul as he explained and defended his view of the role non-Jewish peoples have in God's saving purpose in his letter to the Christians of Rome, especially as he understood his own calling primarily as that of proclaiming the good news to non-Jews.

Paul's Self-Perception

In his earlier letter to the churches of Galatia, Paul had referred explicitly and at length to his calling to proclaim the good news to those who are not Jews. There he recounted how his upbringing and training led him to be a staunch advocate of orthodox Judaism, even to the point of persecuting the young Christian churches (Gal. 1:13–14). It was a 'revelation from Jesus Christ' (Gal. 1:12) that turned his life about, involving God's gracious call to him to proclaim God's Son among non-Jewish people. While there is only one authentic good news (Gal. 1:6–9), it is beamed to two different groups, and the

Christian leadership in Jerusalem recognized that Paul had been divinely commissioned to work among non-Jews, just as they had been commissioned to work among their fellow Jews (Gal. 2:7–9). For a Jew, of course, the good news and to whom it was beamed carried social implications, specifically in regard to table fellowship. And on this point Paul regarded Peter's behaviour at Antioch (the centre of the beginning of outreach to non-Jews, according to Acts) as inconsistent with the truth of the good news (Gal. 2:11–14).

But in Romans, too, Paul described himself to his addressees, most of whom he had not met, as 'an apostle to non-Jews' (Rom. 11:13); as one given the priestly duty of proclaiming God's good news to the non-Jews, so that the offering of the non-Jews might become acceptable to God (Rom. 15:16); and as one through whom Christ had led non-Jews to obey God by what he did and said (Rom. 15:18).

There is evidence that the turn-around in Paul's life, consequent upon what he described as 'a revelation from Jesus Christ' (Gal. 1:12), was followed by a considerable period in which we must presume his world-view underwent extensive and appropriate transformation. By the time he emerged and his amanuenses were putting pen to papyrus from the late 40s, Paul was able to write in defense of his now Christian perspective while still using the same scriptures of his upbringing and training. Now, however, to use his own language (2 Cor. 3:13–18) the 'veil' covering those scriptures had been lifted. Now he saw in those scriptures aspects to which he had earlier been impervious. Yes, the Israelites were God's children; yes, the glory, the covenants, the giving of the Torah, the divine service, the promises, the patriarchs, do belong to them; and yes, even the Messiah came from their stock (Rom. 9:1–5). But Paul now detected other notes in the scriptures as well, God's concern not only for his own people but also for *all* the world's peoples. Such a concept lay at the very heart of the divine calling he personally perceived for his own life. In his writings he now used the scriptures with which he had grown up in defense of his Christian world-view.

Old Testament Passages in Romans cited in Support of Paul's Calling to be an Apostle to Non-Jews

The notion that God's salvation is offered universally, that is, to Jews as well as non-Jews, is a major theme of Romans. Data contributing to it occurs in some forty-eight verses found in nine of the sixteen chapters comprising Romans.[1] In five of these chapters (that is, Romans 4, 9 – 11, and 15) Paul supports his argumentation with quotations from the Old Testament.[2] While Romans 4 contains only four such quotations, there is a heavy concentration of them in

---

[1] See Appendix A.
[2] See Appendix B.

both Romans 9 – 11 (twenty-nine quotations)³ and Romans 15:7–21 (five quotations). Behind these thirty-six quotations, the Nestle-Aland *Novum Testamentum Graece* (on which this data is based) identifies forty-five Old Testament sources.⁴ This indicates that Paul drew upon no less than thirteen Old Testament writings. Prominent among them are Isaiah (15x), Psalms (7x), Deuteronomy (6x), and Genesis (6x). Exodus and Hosea are each drawn upon twice, while Leviticus, 1 Samuel, 2 Samuel, I Kings, Joel, Nahum, and Malachi are used once each.

Romans 4, 9 – 11 and 15:7–21 may be considered conscious expansions on Paul's part of a corollary he had enunciated at Romans 3:29–30, 'Or is God only the God of Jews? Is he not the God of non-Jews as well? Yes, of non-Jews as well. After all, God is one, and just as he will bring a circumcised person into a right relationship as a consequence of faith, so he will an uncircumcised person through faith.' This is one of three corollaries found in Romans 3:27–31. They follow on immediately after Paul's fullest and most concentrated exposition of how one comes into a right relationship with God (Rom. 3:21–26). Here *dikaiosune theou* occurs twice. In Romans the phrase functions as shorthand for the action by which God *rectifies* people or *brings them into a right relationship with himself.*

This whole section, Romans 3:21–31, had been anticipated in the opening words of the body of Romans (1:16–17),

> For I am not ashamed of the good news; after all, it is God's powerful means of bringing about salvation for every person who has come to faith, for the Jew in the first instance, and for the Greek. For in the good news the way to a right relationship with God [*dikaiosune theou*] is revealed as a consequence of faith for a life of faith, just as it stands on record, "It is the person who is in a right relationship as a consequence of faith who will live."⁵

Here we have not only *dikaiosune theou* as the focus of the good news Paul proclaims, but a significant statement about the universal availability of God's salvation – 'salvation for every person who has come to faith, for the Jew in the first instance, and for the Greek'.⁶ In the most detailed exposition of how we enter into a right relationship with God, Romans 3:21–26, the universal availability of *dikaiosune theou* is also clearly affirmed, 'It is a way of right

---

³ I have not taken into account the two quotations incorporated in Paul's paeon of praise (Rom. 11:40, c. Is. 40:13 LXX; Rom. 11:35, c. Job 41:3) since they fall outside the scope of this essay.
⁴ See Appendix B.
⁵ Unless otherwise indicated, the English version used in this article is *Under the Southern Cross: an Australian translation of the New Testament* (publication pending).
⁶ It is evident that 'Greek' here is the full equivalent of *ethnos* ('non-Jew'). Many English versions render it 'gentile'.

relationship with God [*dikaiosune theou*] through faith in Jesus Christ for *all* who have faith. For there is no difference since *all* have sinned and miss out on God's glory, they are brought into a right relationship freely, by his grace, through the redemption which is in Christ Jesus.'

The three passages under review do contain 'proof-texts' from the Old Testament, but Paul goes far beyond the mere quoting of them as proofs that the non-Jews are part of God's saving purposes. His quotations of the Old Testament are incorporated in the intricate argumentation he develops in these passages, in which they anchor home the series of points being made.

ROMANS 4

Romans 4 follows on immediately after the three corollaries Paul had identified in Romans 3:27–31. In it he addresses all three corollaries: (1) the principle of faith as the means of coming into a right relationship with God (Rom. 3:27–28); (2) the universal availability of salvation (Rom. 3:29–30); and (3) the need to uphold the Law (Rom. 3:31). In light of his concluding assertion 'we uphold the Law' (Rom. 3:31) he turns immediately to Abraham (4:1). Appealing to the Law (Torah) his initial concern is to show that Abraham's relationship with God was established on the basis of faith, not works. To do so he quotes Genesis 15:6 (Rom. 4:3), 'Abraham put his faith in God, and that was regarded as the basis for his right relationship.'

Together with Habakkuk 2:4, Genesis 15:6 is one of only two Old Testament texts containing both a word from the *dikai-* family and a word from the *pist-* family (faith/to have faith/believe) which Paul quotes in support of his doctrine of God's rectification ['justification'] of the ungodly. Both are quoted in the two letters where he develops this doctrine in greatest detail, namely, Galatians and Romans.

From Genesis 15:6 Paul extrapolates and illustrates the general principle that God rectifies the ungodly on the basis of faith, not works (Rom. 4:4–5), 'Now for the working person wages are not considered to be a favour, but an obligation. However, for the person who doesn't do any work but who puts their faith in the one who brings the ungodly into a right relationship, that person's faith is regarded as the basis for a right relationship.'

Paul finds that David's experience corroborates the point he is making (Rom. 4:6), and quotes Psalm 32:1–2 [Ps. 31:1–2 LXX] in support of his point (Rom. 4:7–8), 'How blessed are those whose crimes are forgiven and whose sins are covered over. How blessed is the man whose sin the Lord does not take into account.' In the Psalm David refers to himself obliquely in the third person as 'the man whose sin the Lord does not take into account'. As he is referring to himself, he uses *aner* (man) here, rather than *anthropos* (person). Nevertheless, David's statement has a 'whosoever' ring to it (see below); it is capable of being applied to *anyone* who enjoys forgiveness of sins, the blessing of not having one's sins taken into account.

At 4:9 Paul returns to Abraham and explores the context in which Genesis 15:6 is set. His leading question is, 'Well then, is this blessing for the circumcised person or for the person who is not circumcised?' (Rom. 4:9) – that is, is it for the Jew only or also for the non-Jew? Paul points out that when the statement of Genesis 15:6 was applied to him, Abraham was still uncircumcised (Rom. 4:10–11a). From this he deduces that Abraham is 'the ancestor of all who have faith while in the uncircumcised state, so that they too might be regarded as being in a right relationship' (Rom. 4:11b) and that for those who have been circumcised he is an ancestor only if they are 'not merely circumcised but also follow in the footsteps of the faith our ancestor Abraham had while still in the uncircumcised state' (Rom. 4:12).

Paul goes on to argue that the promise Abraham and his descendants received to inherit the world came not through the Law, but through his faith (Rom. 4:13–15). After all, there was no Mosaic Law in Abraham's day, and so Paul's statement that 'in situations where there is no Law neither is there any breaking of the Law' (Rom. 4:15) the first clause clearly is applicable to Abraham. The underlying principle is that of grace, which is accessed by faith (Rom. 4:16). It enables not only people with the Law (Abraham's physical descendants), but also people with a faith like Abraham's (his spiritual descendants) to benefit from the promise. Consequently, Abraham is 'the ancestor of all of us' (Rom. 4:16).

At this point Paul introduces the first of two quotations from the Law (Torah) in support of his contention that God's rectifying purposes extend beyond the Jews. 'I have appointed you ancestor of many nations' (Rom. 4:17, c. Gen. 17:5 LXX). He does so by alluding to the Genesis context in which Abraham, still childless through Sarah, put his faith in the God who (1) 'brings the dead to life' and (2) 'addresses things not yet in existence as if they already existed' – an allusion, firstly, to his great age (his body 'had already died, being about a hundred years old', Rom. 4:19) and, secondly, to unborn generations. It is quickly followed by a second quotation from Genesis 15:5, 'That is what your descendants will be like' (Rom. 4:18). In the Genesis context the referent is the multitude of stars in the night sky. The verse Paul quotes here immediately precedes Genesis 15:6[7] which he had cited at Romans 4:3 and whose phraseology permeates Romans 4 as a whole.

The apostle has construed an intricate argument here. It rests on these four texts in support of his contention that the *dikaiosune* God offers is universally available to all who have the kind of faith with which Abraham responded to God's revelation.

---

[7] That is, 'Abraham put his faith in God, and that was regarded as the basis for his right relationship.'

ROMANS 9–11

The function of Romans 9 – 11 within the overall argument of Romans continues to be debated among scholars. While some treat it as an excursus, assuming and amplifying aspects of the preceding presentation, others regard it as the central section and pinnacle of Paul's argumentation. The issue is not unrelated to the role *dikaiosune theou* plays in Paul's overall argument. A number of discussions downplay the prominence of Paul's doctrine of rectification in this block, yet *dikaiosune* occurs no less than eleven times between Romans 9:30 and 10:10.

It has been claimed that Jewish-gentile relationships are at the heart of these chapters. That is certainly true for Romans 11:13–32, where Paul is explicitly addressing non-Jews, but does not appear to characterize the entire block. I have argued elsewhere for the view that this section has the character of an excursus and for the following structure.

Excursus: *dikaiosune theou* in historical perspective: Israel's role in salvation-history

   a. Israel in the *past*, and God's purpose of election   Ch 9
   b. Israel in the *present*, and right relationship based on faith   Ch 10
   c. Israel in the *future*, and the restoration of a remnant   Ch 11

Accepting the value of the chapter divisions in this instance, we can identify at the beginning of each chapter a section in which Paul makes it clear that as a Christian he continues to identify closely with his own people: 9:1–5; 10:1–4; 11:1–6. As noted above, Paul quotes from the Old Testament no less than thirty-one times in this block, and each quotation makes a contribution to his case that non-Jewish peoples have a place in God's saving, rectifying, purposes. The quotations are used in conjunction with several Old Testament constructs as well as concepts developed by the apostle himself.

The construct of Election

The problem motivating Paul as he launches into this section is the apparent failure of Israel to live up to its potential (9:6–13). Can it be that God's communication has failed (9:6)? In denying such a suggestion, Paul appeals to the construct of *election* (mentioned explicitly at 9:11). The fundamental premise is that mere descent from the ancestors (he specifies Abraham and Israel, 9:6–7) is no guarantee that a person will benefit from the ancestral promises. The three quotations from Genesis (Rom. 9:7,9,12) and that from Malachi (Rom. 9:13) are used to illustrate divine election at work.

- 'it is your descendents through Isaac who will take your name' (Gen. 21:12 LXX, c. Rom. 9:7);

- 'I will come at this time and Sarah will have a son' (Gen. 18:10,14 c. Rom. 9:9);
- 'the greater will be a slave to the lesser' (Gen. 25:3, c. Rom. 9:12);
- 'I loved Jacob, but I hated Esau' (Mal. 1:2 LXX, c. Rom 9.13).

The concept of the Divine Prerogative

Paul recognizes that the concept of election may well convey the impression that God is not acting in a way that is just; hence the rhetorical question at 9:14, 'Well then, how shall we express it? Surely there is no injustice on God's part, is there?' At this point he introduces the notion of the *divine prerogative* – God, as God, has the right to show mercy or compassion on anyone he desires. Paul supports this by God's words to Moses in Exodus 33:19 LXX (cited Rom. 9:15), 'I will have mercy on the person on whom I have mercy and I will show compassion to the person to whom I show compassion.' He concludes that the operative factor is not human desire or human effort, but divine mercy (9:16). Further, God not only takes the initiative in showing mercy, but also in hardening people (9:18). The example Paul adduces in support of this is that of the words Yahweh addressed to Pharaoh through Moses, 'It was for this very purpose that I raised you up, that I might demonstrate my power in you and so that my name might be proclaimed throughout the earth' (Ex. 9:16, c. Rom. 9:17). The apostle sums up the notion of divine prerogative in 9:18, 'It follows, then, that he has mercy on whoever he decides to, but he also hardens whoever he decides to.'

Paul continues to tease out the concept of the divine prerogative in 9:19–21 with his illustration (drawn from Isaiah) of the right of the potter to choose how he uses any given piece of clay (Is. 29:16; 45:9, cited Rom. 9:20). Again, it is introduced by a rhetorical question in diatribe style, 'Why then does he still find fault? For who is in a position to resist his wishes?'

In the discussion which follows (Rom. 9:22–24) the power God wished to show in the case of Pharaoh is also expressed as anger, and the 'hardening' of the earlier passage has as its equivalent destruction. Having introduced the positive aspect of the recipients of God's mercy (9:23) Paul goes on to assert that God called such not only from among the Jews, but also from among non-Jews (9:24). Four quotations, each introduced with the briefest of connectors, follow immediately. The first two are drawn from Hosea (Hos. 2:23, c. Rom. 9:25; Hos. 1:10, c. Rom. 9:26) where Yahweh asserts that those denied a relationship with him in the past will come to be known as his people, his children. The two remaining quotations, both from Isaiah and attributed to him, do not mention or imply non-Jews, but focus on Israel's shortcomings. The first (Is. 10:22–23 / Hos. 2:1 LXX, c. Rom. 9:27–28) implies a decimation of Israel. Even though they are as numerous as the sand of the seashore, the Lord's execution of his sentence on earth will reduce them to a mere remnant. The second (Is. 1:9 LXX, c. Rom. 9:29) points out that only the Lord, acting in his power, has ensured his chosen people have descendants; otherwise, they would have suffered the fate of Sodom and Gomorrah.

Drawing this section together (Rom. 9:30–33), Paul returns to the language of *dikaiosune* to explain that while non-Jews were not even seeking a right relationship with God, nevertheless they obtained it, a right relationship associated with faith. Israel, on the other hand, seeking a right relationship based on the Law, failed to attain to Law. Pursuing their objective as if it were attainable through good behaviour rather than through faith, they missed out. Paul characterizes their failure in terms of the stumbling stone imagery he draws from Isaiah 28:16; 8:14 (c. Romans 9:33), 'Take note! I am laying in Zion a stumbling-stone and a rock causing offense, yet the person who puts their faith in him will have no reason to be ashamed.' While the first line is negative, the second is positive. In terms of Paul's argumentation here, the first line applies to Israel, the last to the non-Jews.

The Law/Faith contrast

Following the affirmation of Paul's desire for the salvation of his fellow-Israelites and his analysis of their present state as due to both ignorance and lack of submission to God's way of establishing a right relationship, the apostle points to Christ (the stumbling-stone for Jews, Rom. 9:32–33) through whom the Law's purpose has been fulfilled 'resulting in a right relationship for everyone who has faith' (Rom. 10:4). He then draws a contrast between the aspiration to right standing by Law and that by faith. He takes as his scriptural basis Deuteronomy 30 and several related texts. Moses provides the model for Law-Rightness (Rom. 10:5, c. Lev. 18:5) while the notion of Faith-Rightness is based on Deuteronomy 30:12–14. There Moses is pointing out to the Israelites that what he is commanding them is not beyond their reach – it is not inaccessible by being in heaven or across the sea, but it is to hand, on their lips and in their hearts. In the form of text that Paul utilizes here the sea (the 'deep') has become the abyss, or underworld to which Christ descended between his death and resurrection. So he quotes and applies these texts as follows,

> But the right relationship based on faith speaks in this way, 'Do not say in your heart, "Who will ascend to heaven?" (that is, to bring Christ down) or, "Who will descend to the deep?" (that is, to bring Christ back from among the dead).' Then what does it say? 'The message is near you; it is on your lips and in your heart', that is, it is the message about faith which we proclaim publicly.

In Paul's hands the Mosaic context is thoroughly Christianized; not only are the ascent and descent movements interpreted Christologically, but the Law of Moses in the original setting has now become the good news about Christ which Paul proclaims.

'Whosoever' texts

The next two Old Testament quotations follow a significant statement by Paul in which *dikaiosune* and salvation are linked (as also at 1:16–17, and frequently in Isaiah). He says, 'For if you acknowledge the Lord Jesus with your lips and believe in your heart that God raised him from among the dead, you will be saved. For through the heart there is faith, resulting in a right relationship, through the lips there is acknowledgment, resulting in salvation.'

It follows the section just discussed immediately and is supported by two Old Testament citations which may be characterized as 'whosoever' texts. This quaint and old-fashioned term, made familiar through the Authorized Version, has the advantage of suggesting that they have universal applicability, and that is just how they function in Paul's argument here as he defends his conviction that the good news is not only for Jews but for non-Jews. 'No-one who puts their faith in him will be disappointed' (Rom. 10:11, c. Is. 28:16). 'Every one, whoever they may be, who calls on the Lord's name, will be saved' (Rom. 10:13, c. Joel 3:5 LXX).

The 'mechanics' of salvation

The quotations just discussed are followed by a brief passage (Rom. 10:14–15) in which Paul explains the 'mechanics' of salvation. Although the apostle presents the points in reverse order, his case may be summed up as follows:

1. God sends preachers of the good news about Christ.
2. Their public proclamation makes it possible for people to listen to that good news.
3. Listening to the good news is the context in which faith is able to arise (see Rom. 10:17).
4. That faith is directed towards Christ. It is experienced as the inner conviction that God raised Jesus from death and expressed in the profession of Jesus as Lord (Rom. 10:9-10).

He then anchors this defense of proclamation as the instrument of salvation by the following affirming text, 'How beautiful are the feet of those who bring the good news of good events!' (Rom. 10:15b, c. Is. 52:7; Nah. 2:1).

Proclamation is no guarantee of a faith response

With an eye on Israel, Paul now points out that proclamation of the good news in itself is no guarantee of a faith response. For listening to the good news does not ensure that *obedience* follows (Rom. 10:16). The primary context of Isaiah's complaint was proclamation to Israel / Judah. 'Lord, who has believed what we report?' (Rom. 10:16b, c. Is. 53:1 LXX). The following quotation is admittedly more general. 'Their sound has gone out into all the earth, their communications have reached even the extremities of the inhabited world' (Rom. 10:18, c. Ps. 19:4). However, the apostle immediately focuses on Israel again, although his next two Old Testament quotations refer explicitly to non-Jews, 'I will arouse you to jealousy with those who are not even a nation, I will arouse you to anger with a stupid nation' (Rom. 10:19, c. Deut. 32:21). 'I was found by those who were not even looking for me, I appeared to those who were not even asking for me' (Rom. 10:20, c. Is. 65:1).

However, his sustained critique of Israel is again evident in the final quotation with which this section concludes. 'Throughout the day I have been imploring with outstretched hands a people disobedient and obstinate' (Rom. 10:21, c. Is. 65:2). Noticeably, this is introduced with the words, 'By contrast, he says to Israel.'

The construct of a Remnant: Elijah

The construct Paul utilizes here is one drawn from the Old Testament – that of a remnant (Rom. 11:5).

The response to the question with which he opens this section ('Surely God has not rejected his own people, has he?' Rom. 11:1) appears to be given in the words of scripture ('God has not rejected his own people', Rom. 11:2, c. 1 Sam. 12:22) although he gives no indication that he is quoting here.

Paul illustrates his argument by the case of Elijah. The quotations Paul introduces from the Elijah narrative (1 Kgs. 19:10,14,18, c. Rom. 11:3–4) are designed to demonstrate the presence of a remnant in Israel, even when it is hidden from the eyes of one of Yahweh's most prominent servants in the Old Testament, Elijah. 'Why, aren't you aware of what the Scripture text says through Elijah, how he appeals to God against Israel? "Lord, they have killed your prophets; they have demolished your altars; only I am left, and they are trying to take my life as well." But what was the divine response? "I have reserved for myself seven thousand men who have not bowed their knees to Baal."' From this data Paul concludes, 'So too, then, at the present time a remnant has come into being through grace, in accordance with election' (Rom. 11:5).

The fate of the non-elect in Israel

It is clear from Paul's statement below that for Paul the 'remnant' in Israel coincides with the elect in Israel (although the elect are not, of course, confined to Israel). 'Then what conclusion are we to draw? That Israel failed to obtain what it was searching for – although the elect obtained it; the rest, however, were hardened' (Rom. 11:7). He goes on immediately to quote as follows, 'God rendered them semi-conscious, with eyes incapable of seeing and ears incapable of hearing right to this very day' (Rom. 11:8, c. Deut. 29:4; Is. 29:10). 'May their table become their snare and their trap, their downfall and their retribution. May their eyes become dark so that they can't see and their backs be permanently bent' (Rom. 11:9–10, c. Ps. 69:22–23).

A mystery: all Israel will be saved

Still addressing the non-Jews among God's people in Rome, Paul introduces the final Old Testament quotation in our review of Romans 11 in the context of a mystery (Rom. 11:25). By the term 'mystery' Paul appears to be referring to Israel's experience vis-à-vis the good news. For from his discussion above it is obvious that for Paul Israel falls into two groups, the elect and 'the rest' (Rom. 11:7). Outside Israel, consistent with the divine prerogative, some non-Jews also are numbered among the elect. Consequently, there is a 'partial hardening' of Israel until the full complement of non-Jews comes in (Rom. 11:25). Paul goes on to explain (almost as if it were self-evident) that by this means 'all Israel will be saved' (Rom. 11:26). In this latter statement elect non-Jews seem to be included in the concept of Israel, perhaps a 'spiritual Israel' or the like is in mind, rather like Abraham's fatherhood being extended to non-Jews (Rom. 4:11b–12). To clinch his argument Paul cites Isaiah 59:20–21 / Isaiah 17:9 as a demonstration from the scriptures that 'All Israel will be saved' (Rom. 11:26), 'The Deliverer will emerge from Zion, he will deflect ungodliness from Jacob. And this is the covenant I will enter into with them when I take away their sins.'

The apostle asserts that in the experience of Jewish/non-Jewish relationships in his time, Israelites appear to non-Jews as their enemies, though from the perspective of election and the promises made to their ancestors they are 'dearly loved' (Rom. 11:28). He gives as the reason for this God's complete consistency. 'God does not change his mind about the gifts he gives people or the vocation to which he calls them' (Rom. 11:29). Paul further argues for a 'leveling' of the ground on which Jew and non-Jew stand. On the one hand the disobedience of non-Jews had not prevented them from experiencing God's mercy; in a similar way the present disobedience of Israel is to the end that they too might experience divine mercy (Rom. 11:31). This 'leveling' is also evident in the statement with which Paul concludes this section, 'For God has subsumed all people under the category of disobedience, so that he may treat all with mercy' (Rom. 11:32).

ROMANS 15:7–21

The final passage to be considered consists of two distinct parts, 15:7–13 and 15:14–21. The first part, 15:7–13, is actually the concluding subsection of a larger unit, Romans 14:1 – 15:13. It coheres through the notion of 'acceptance' (*proslambanomai*, used four times). Fellow-Christians are to accept one another (Rom. 14:1; 15:7a) on the grounds that God has accepted them (Rom. 14:3), and that Christ has accepted them (Rom. 15:7b). In this extensive section Paul discusses matters of conscience over which Christians divide, giving three examples: (1) whether or not to eat meat (Rom. 14:2–3,6b,14–15,17,20–21,23); (2) whether or not to observe special ceremonial days (Rom. 14:5–6a); (3) whether or not to drink wine (Rom. 14:21). The appeal to these specific issues to justify the view that 14:1 – 15:13 is primarily concerned with Jewish/gentile relationships is weak, but Paul's return to the issue of God's mercy being extended to non-Jews in 15:7–13 (with the appeal to accept one another repeated at 15:7) strongly suggests it continued to be a divisive issue in Christian congregations of the mid first century.

The second part, 15:14–21, belongs with the larger unit 15:14–33. As the apostle comes to the end of his letter, he returns to the personalia that characterized 1:8–15. Consequently, his references to non-Jews here, and his invocation of a quotation from Isaiah 52:15 at Romans 15:21, have a much more personal character.

It is in the Old Testament quotations in the first part (Rom. 15:7–13) that Paul comes closest to 'proof-texting' in the traditional sense. The four quotations follow one after the other and are only loosely joined by brief connective phrases. By its character each quotation is self-contained as a 'proof' that the non-Jews have a place in God's saving purposes.

> For this reason I will acknowledge you among non-Jewish
> people and I will sing praise to your name.
> (Rom. 15:9, c. Ps. 17:50 LXX; 2 Sam. 22:50)
>
> Be glad, you non-Jewish people, with his people.
> (Rom. 15:10, c. Deut. 32:43 LXX)
>
> Praise the Lord, all you non-Jewish people and let all the peoples
> praise him.
> (Rom. 15:11, c. Ps. 117:1)
>
> There will be a root from Jesse and he who rises up to rule non-
> Jewish people; non-Jewish people will place their hopes in him.
> (Rom. 15:12, c. Is. 11:10 LXX)

In the second part (Rom. 15:14–21) there is but one Old Testament quotation, 'Those to whom the announcement about him has not been made will see, and those who have not heard will understand' (Rom. 15:21, c. Is. 52:15 LXX). Paul invokes it in justification of his policy of taking the good news to places and peoples to whom Christ had not yet been proclaimed (Rom. 15:20).

Conclusion

We have seen that Paul defends one of the major themes of Romans, namely, that God's salvation and *dikaiosune* are available on a universal basis, in three sections of Romans, chapters 4, 9 – 11, 15). In these passages he quotes the Old Testament frequently, no less than thirty-eight times. In a few places, especially Romans 15, his quotations serve as 'proof texts', but the vast majority of quotations are incorporated into his intricate argumentation.

In my detailed work on Paul's doctrine of rectification ('justification') I noted that of all the potential Old Testament texts Paul may have drawn upon for 'righteousness' and cognates, especially in Isaiah, he quotes *not one of them*, but takes as his Old Testament basis Genesis 15:6 and Habakkuk 2:4, using each in both Galatians and Romans. I am suggesting that a similar phenomenon operates here. For the present investigation we may take Isaiah 49:6 as one example (of many) Old Testament passages which would have suited Paul's purpose ideally. 'It is too small a thing for you to be my servant to restore the tribes of Jacob and bring back those of Israel I have kept. I will also make you a light for the Gentiles, that you may bring my salvation to the ends of the earth.'

Yet he makes no use of this passage, even though his familiarity with this chapter of Isaiah is evident from his use of it at 2 Corinthians 6:2 (Is. 49:8) and Romans 14:11 (Is. 49:18). A major reason for his particular selection of passages seems to be their value for the detailed argumentation into which they are incorporated. His method goes far beyond mere 'proof-texting' to embrace various constructs already established in the Old Testament tradition as well as fresh arguments of his own. At stake was not simply the issue of how widely God's mercy extended, important though that is, but his own sense of vocation as 'apostle to the non-Jews'.

Bibliography

Aland, K., et al. Nestle-Aland *Novum Testamentum Graece* (Stuttgart: Deutsche Bibelgesllschaft, 1993^{27}).

Archer, G.L. and G. Chirichigno *Old Testament Quotations in the New Testament* (Chicago: Moody, 1983).

Hübner, H., *Vetus Testamentum in Novo 2: Corpus Paulinum* (Göttingen: Vandenhoeck & Ruprecht, 1997).

Moore, R.K., *Rectification ('Justification') in Paul, in historical perspective, and in the English Bible*, 3 vols (New York: Edwin Mellen, 2002–2003).

Moore, R.K., *Under the Southern Cross: an Australian Translation of the New Testament* (in preparation).

Appendix A

Data in Romans contributing to Paul's contention that the good news is universally available

$_1$5.13.14.16	$_2$9.10.14.26	$_3$9.22.29.30	$_4$10.11.16.17.18	$_9$17.24.25.26.30
$_{10}$4.11.12.12.13.19.20	$_{11}$11.12.13.15.25.32	$_{15}$9.9.10.11.12.12.16.16.18.21.27	$_{16}$4.26	

Appendix B

Old Testament quotations in Romans which Paul uses to support his contention that the good news is universally available

No.	Romans reference	Old Testament reference	No.	Romans reference	Old Testament reference
Romans 4					
1	4:3	Gen. 15:6	3	4:17	Gen. 17:5
2	4:7–8	Ps. 31.1–2 LXX	4	4:18	Gen. 15:5
Romans 9—11					
5	9:7	Gen. 21:12 LXX	21	10:11	Is. 28:16
6	9:9	Gen. 18:10,14	22	10:13	Joel 3:5 LXX
7	9:12	Gen. 25:23 LXX	23	10:15	Is. 52:7
8	9:13	Mal. 1:2–3 LXX			Nah. 2:1
9	9:15	Ex. 33:19 LXX	24	10:16	Is. 53:1 LXX
10	9:17	Ex. 9:16	25	10:18	Ps. 19:4
11	9:20	Is. 29:16 LXX	26	10:19	Deut. 32:21
12	9:25	Hos. 2:23	27	10:20	Is. 65:1
13	9:26	Hos. 1:10	28	10:21	Is. 65:2
14	9:27–28	Is. 10:22–23	29	11:2	1 Sam. 12:22
15	9:29	Is. 1:9			Ps. 94:14
16	9:33	Is. 8:14	30	11:3–4	1 Kgs. 19:10,14,18
		Is. 28:16	31	11:8	Deut. 29:4
17	10:5	Lev. 18:5			Is. 29:10
18	10:6	Deut. 9:4	32	11:9–10	Ps. 69:22–23
		Deut. 30:12	33	11:26–27	Is. 59:20–21
19	10:7	Ps. 107:26			Is. 27:9
20	10:8	Deut. 30:14			
Romans 15					
34	15:9	2 Sam. 22:50	36	15:11	Ps. 117:1
		Ps. 18:49	37	15:12	Is. 11:10 LXX
35	15:10	Deut. 32:43 LXX	38	15:21	Is. 52:15 LXX

Appendix C

Range and Distribution of Old Testament scriptures quoted
in support of Paul's contention that the good news is universally available

Old Testament Scripture	Romans 4	Romans 9	Romans 10	Romans 11	Romans 15	Total
Genesis	3	3				6
Exodus		2				2
Leviticus			1			1
Deuteronomy			4	1	1	6
1 Samuel				1		1
2 Samuel					1	1
1 Kings				1		1
Psalms	1		2	2	2	7
Isaiah		5	5	3	2	15
Hosea		2				2
Joel			1			1
Nahum			1			1
Malachi		1				1
TOTAL	**4**	**13**	**14**	**8**	**6**	**45**

CHAPTER 8

Paul's 'Cloak' and the Completion of the Tanakh

DUANE CHRISTENSEN

Introduction

The study of the canon of sacred scripture in both the Tanakh (Hebrew Old Testament) and the Greek New Testament has produced sharp dispute within the academic community.[1] Our purpose here is not to resolve differences of opinion on this issue, but rather to explore implications of current research in the so-called Word Count Project,[2] as it relates to the theme of this *Festschrift* – and to the life work of John Olley, who exemplifies the successful bridging of the world of academia and ministry within the Christian faith community. The thesis explored here is that the primary stimulus in the formation of the canon of both the Tanakh of Jewish tradition and the Greek New Testament in the Christian Bible takes place within the context of mission – and that it takes place primarily at the beginning of the historical process, rather than in the latter stages, in both instances. In particular, we posit the concept of 'master editors' for both the Hebrew Old Testament and the Greek New Testament.

Formation of the Tanakh (Hebrew Bible) in Nascent Judaism

It is often assumed that the Tanakh achieved canonical acceptance among the Jews in a three-fold historical process: beginning ca. 400 BCE with the Torah (Pentateuch), followed by the Prophets by ca. 200 BCE, and completed with the addition of the Writings by ca. 90–100 CE. The acronym *TaNaKh* reflects the popular understanding of this three stage canonical process.[3] In short, the early Christians received a closed Old Testament canon consisting of twenty-two books, as described by Josephus who mentions five books by Moses, thirteen

---

[1] For a thorough discussion of the issues, see L.M. McDonald and J.A. Sanders (eds.), *The Canon Debate* (Peabody, 2002).
[2] See our website, {www.bibal.net}.
[3] The word *TaNaKh* is an acronym, formed from the initial letters of its three parts: Pentateuch (*Torah*), Prophets (*Nevi'im*) and Writings (*Kethuvim*).

by the prophets, and four other books of hymns and wisdom.[4] Josephus does not list the twenty-two books of the Tanakh (Hebrew Bible) by name, however, and there is no consensus within the scholarly community as to which four books constitute his third category.[5] The most convincing identification of the books within each of the three divisions he describes is found in Lightstone's discussion of the tripartite rabbinic Masoretic Bible of the medieval period.[6]

1 The Pentateuch (*Torah* [of Moses]) – 5 books

    Genesis
    Exodus
    Leviticus
    Numbers
    Deuteronomy

2 The Prophets (*Nevi'im*) – 10 books (8 in the older 22-book canon)

   The Former Prophets: 6 books (4 in the older 22-book canon)

    Joshua
    Judges
    1 Samuel   {combined with 2 Samuel as a single book}
    2 Samuel
    1 Kings   {combined with 2 Kings as a single book}
    2 Kings

   The Latter Prophets: 4 books

    Isaiah
    Jeremiah
    Ezekiel
    'The Twelve' [Minor Prophets]   {as a single book}

---

[4] See Josephus' description of the canon in *Against Apion* 1.8, 'We have not a countless number of books, discordant and arrayed, against each other; but only two and twenty books ... and of these, five belong to Moses, which contain both the laws and the history of the generations of men until his death. ... From the death of Moses, moreover, until the reign of Artaxerxes king of the Persians after Xerxes, the prophets who followed Moses have described the things which were done during the age of each one respectively, in thirteen books. The remaining four contain hymns to God, and rules of life for men.'

[5] See D.L. Christensen, 'Josephus and the Twenty-Two-Book Canon of Sacred Scripture', *JETS* 29 (1986), 37–46.

[6] J.N. Lightstone, 'The Rabbis' Bible: The Canon of the Hebrew Bible and the Early Rabbinic Guild' in McDonald and Sanders (eds.), *The Canon Debate*, 171.

3   The Writings (*Kethuvim*) – 9 books

    Psalms
    Proverbs
    Job
    'Five Scrolls' (*Megilloth*)   {as a single book}
    Daniel
    Ezra
    Nehemiah
    1 Chronicles
    2 Chronicles

The four books in Josephus' third category are Psalms, Proverbs, Job and the 'Five Scrolls' (*Megilloth* – i.e. Song of Songs, Ruth, Lamentations, Ecclesiastes and Esther). The five 'Festal Scrolls' are thus a single canonical category, much the same as the twelve 'Minor Prophets'. The 'thirteen prophets' in Josephus' second category are three groups of four arranged around the book of Daniel.

Joshua	Judges		Isaiah	Jeremiah
1 – 2 Samuel	1 – 2 Kings		Ezekiel	'The Twelve'
		Daniel		
	Ezra		Nehemiah	
	1 Chronicles		2 Chronicles	

Daniel is thus presented as a prophet who functions as a 'bridge' connecting three groups of four books – the Former Prophets, the Latter Prophets, and the still 'Later Prophets' (i.e. the 'Work of the Chronicler').

David Noel Freedman makes a strong case for a 'master editor' responsible for writing what he calls the 'Primary History' – the Torah plus the Former Prophets.[7] It is likely, however, that this 'master editor' was responsible for the entire seventeen-book 'Deuteronomic Canon' within a four-part literary structure, which may be outlined in the form of a simple chiasm.

Torah	Former Prophets
Latter Prophets	'Hagiographa'

---

[7] D.N. Freedman, *The Nine Commandments: Uncovering the Hidden Pattern of Crime and Punishment in the Hebrew Bible* (New York, 2000).

The term 'Hagiographa' refers to the four books in the Tanakh, which, according to Josephus, 'contain hymns to God, and precepts for the conduct of human life' (*Against Apion* 1.8).

> Psalms   Proverbs
>
> Job   '*Megilloth*'

Evidence for Freedman's conclusion is found in a series of episodes, which are distributed book by book through eight successive books in the Tanakh. This series of episodes chart the violation of the first nine of the ten commandments one by one, starting with the sin of national apostasy (the worship of the golden calf, Ex. 32), which violates the first and second commandments. The series concludes with the sin of bearing false witness (the ninth commandment) on the part of Jezebel in the story of Naboth's vineyard in 1 Kings 21. Because covetousness lies behind all the crimes committed, each act implicitly breaks the tenth commandment as well.

The ten commandments constitute the essence of the covenant relationship established between God and the people of Israel at Mount Sinai. The pattern of defiance of that covenant led inexorably to the downfall of the nation, the destruction of their Temple in Jerusalem, and the banishment of survivors from the promised land. The message is clear to a community in the Babylonian Exile that their fate is not the result of God's abandoning them. It is the consequence of their abandonment of God. The true people of God are those who maintain their covenant commitment by observing the ten commandments.

Genesis does not include an episode in this series because the covenant at Mount Sinai, in which the stone tablets with the ten commandments were given to Moses, takes place later – in the book of Exodus. Freedman identifies the 'master editor' as the scribe Baruch, working together with his brother Seraiah, in the sixth century BCE (see Jer. 32:12; 45:1–5; 51:59–64).

I would add two items to Freedman's discovery about the canonical process. In the first place, the work of the 'master editor' included the Latter Prophets as well as the Former Prophets, and also the 'Hagiographa' (Psalms, Proverbs, Job and the *Megilloth*). This 'Hagiographa' was subsequently expanded into the fourth and concluding section of the Tanakh – the Writings (*Kethuvim*), which took place in the formation of the twenty-two-book 'Pentateuchal Canon' in the time of Ezra and Nehemiah. Moreover, the scribe Ezra takes his place within the list of 'master editors' in the canonical process that produced the Tanakh of Jewish tradition (ca. 400 BCE).

Second, I posit the nature of the editing process, which transformed sacred story into canonical scripture, for Baruch and his brother Seraiah stand within a scribal family in ancient Israel that had mastered the ancient principles of numerical composition. Ezra, the scribe *par excellence* in ancient Israel, who was second only to Moses in importance among the Jews of antiquity, continued this same ancient practice.

The phenomenon of numerical composition is the determining factor in producing 'canonical' (authoritative) texts in ancient Israel.[8] By weaving the numerical value of the ineffable name YHWH into the fabric of the text, these works became symbolically the 'word of God'. The scribes of ancient Israel were trained in this method of literary composition, which survived well into the Common Era. And, as we will see below, Luke (working together with the apostle Paul) was a 'master editor' within a modification of this same scribal tradition, in the composition of the *Completed Tanakh* – i.e. the Jewish Tanakh (Hebrew Bible) plus the Greek New Testament.

Completion of the Tanakh: The Addition of the Greek New Testament

Though there is virtual consensus among biblical scholars on the translation of the Greek word *phailonen* in 2 Timothy 4:13 with the meaning 'cloak' (i.e. a 'thick, upper garment' of some sort), truth is not measured by majority opinion. This term is a *hapax legomenon* – it appears only here in the Greek New Testament. In the great uncial texts of antiquity the term is spelled *phelones*. The common interpretation of the word as 'cloak' in various translations of the New Testament (ancient and modern), which is taken from the Greek word *phainoles* ('cloak'), presumes a metathesis. The fact that such a metathesis did take place is demonstrated by the fact that the word *pheloni* means 'cloak' in modern Greek. The diminutive form *phailonion*, with a similar meaning, appears in Greek papyri of the second and third centuries CE.[9] In modern Greek, the word *phailonion* refers to the main outer vestment of an eastern orthodox priest.

Liddell and Scott do not list the word *phailones* as such; but under the word *phainoles* they cite the New Testament (presumably 2 Tim. 4:13) with a note that 'the forms *phailones* and *phelones* are dubious'.[10] The use of the word *pheloni* in modern Greek with the meaning 'cloak' is not persuasive in terms of determining the meaning of the word in antiquity; for this usage can be explained from the common interpretation of the word *phailonen* (or *pheloni*) in the Greek New Testament. Moreover, the discussion of whether the term *phainoles* is a Latin loanword form *paenula* (Hahn, Fraenkel, and Schwyzer), or whether the Latin *paenula* is borrowed from an original Greek *phainola*

---

[8] See D.L. Christensen, 'The Numerical Composition of the Tanakh' in idem., *Explosion of the Canon: The Greek New Testament in Early Church History* (North Richland Hills, 2004), 20–24.

[9] See Oxyrhynchus Papyri [933, 30]; Griech. Pap. zu Giessen [12,4]; and in *Aegyptische Urkunden aus den Museen zu Berlin* [816, 24].

[10] Liddell and Scott, *Greek-English Lexicon* (New York, 1874), 1589.

(Moulton and Milligan) is not relevant to our discussion here, for we are dealing with the word *phailonen* and not the word *phainolen*.

It appears that *phailonen* in 2 Timothy 4:13 is a technical term that was not widely understood by those responsible for transmitting and translating the Greek New Testament, ancient and modern. Thus the fact that the Syriac Peshitta translates the term as 'book-carrier' deserves a closer look, particularly when the second half of that verse describes its contents, namely 'papyrus scrolls' (*ta biblia*) and 'parchment leaves' (*tas membranas*). What we have here may be likened to the word 'jacket' in English, which in addition to its primary meaning of 'a short coat' designed to be placed around the upper part of the human body, is also used for purposes other than clothing, such as a life *jacket*, or even a book *jacket* – which is even used in reference to recordings, audio tapes, compact disks, and DVDs in the music industry.

When we encounter an unfamiliar word in any language, our first recourse in determining its meaning is its literary context. And here we encounter a problem so far as the traditional interpretation of the word *phailonen* is concerned. In Acts 28:30 we read that Paul 'lived (in Rome) two whole years *at his own expense* and welcomed all who came to him'. Paul had the means to purchase a cloak in Rome to deal with the cold of winter, if he needed one. Why then would he send a message all the way to Asia Minor to obtain his cloak for the approaching winter season? And why did he not fetch this cloak earlier, when he was imprisoned for two years in Caesarea? Moreover, Paul had friends with him who would gladly have made that purchase for him locally in either instance. Paul's request that Timothy do his 'best to come before winter' (2 Tim. 4:21) need not be interpreted as fear of the discomfort he would face shortly in a cold Roman prison. It is more likely that Paul's concern here reflects his personal knowledge of the changing weather, which would make a sea voyage on Timothy's part dangerous and cause him to delay his journey from Asia Minor to Rome. Paul's recent experience in his sea voyage off the coast of Crete as the ship departed from Fair Havens on route to a better harbour at Phoenix, where they intended to wait out the winter weather, was fresh in his mind (see Acts 27). The adverse winds of the approaching winter season made that journey from Sidon, past Cyprus, and on to the island of Crete difficult. It was an early winter storm that drove the ship across the Mediterranean Sea to shipwreck on Malta where Paul and Luke almost lost their lives. Paul knew that if Timothy did not come to Rome before winter, it would be a lengthy wait before Timothy and Mark could join Paul and Luke in their "canonical ministry" in Rome, which appears to have been focused on the formation of the Greek New Testament as a numerical composition.

In their study of the codex in antiquity, Roberts and Skeat reached the conclusion that the word *membranas* in 2 Timothy 4:13 refers to parchment leaves with writing on both sides.[11] This particular text is apparently the oldest reference to a codex in antiquity. Every fragment of the Greek New Testament recovered from antiquity is written on a leaf from the pages of a codex. There are no surviving fragments of the Greek New Testament from scrolls; for from the very beginning, the New Testament as canonical scripture was written in the form of a codex. Moreover, it is possible that Paul and others in early Christianity are responsible for inventing the codex, in which pages were sewn together to form the first 'books' in the way we think of them today. They did this to gain ready access to the content of the scriptures in their apologetic activity as evangelists, for it is much easier to locate a specific text by turning the pages of a codex than by unrolling a ponderous scroll.

At the time 2 Timothy 4:13 was written, there was no Greek word for a 'book' in the way that word is used today. Our text suggests that the word *biblion* refers specifically to a papyrus scroll, whereas the word *membrana* refers to the pages of a codex. On the other hand, the English word Bible, which is derived from the Greek word *biblos*, refers exclusively to a 'codex-form' of a book; whereas in antiquity the *biblia* were in fact scrolls. It is easy to see the source of confusion here and to understand why the translation of a technical term from the nascent book-making industry of antiquity as 'cloak' gained wide credence on the part of interpreters and translators of the Greek New Testament through the centuries.

The consequences are profound when the Greek text of 2 Timothy 4:13 is properly interpreted; for it is a bit like putting on a new pair of glasses with the right prescription, which enable us to see more clearly at a glance what before was blurred and consequently misinterpreted. The Greek text of 2 Timothy 4:10 can be read quite differently from the interpretation of the NRSV, 'for Demas, in love with this present world, has deserted me and gone to Thessalonica'. If Demas deserted Paul at this point in time, how does one explain other references that present him as a loyal colleague of Paul? If these other texts refer to points in time prior to the presumed desertion of 2 Timothy 4:10, there is no problem; but a close reading suggests that such is not the case.

In Colossians 4:14, Demas appears in association with Luke, Aristarchus *and Mark* (4:10), Jesus Justus (4:11), and Epaphras (4:12). From this passage, it appears that Mark, Aristarchus, and Jesus Justus were Jews (cf. 4:11); but Demas, Epaphras, and Luke were gentiles. Demas is also mentioned in Philemon 24, in company with Epaphras, Aristarchus, Luke – and *once again Mark* – among those present with Paul during his imprisonment in Rome. In 2 Timothy 4:9–13, Demas has parted company with Paul – *before the arrival of Mark*; for Demas departed for Thessalonica and Luke alone remained with Paul in Rome (4:11). In other words, Aristarchus, Epaphras, and the others

---

[11] See C.H. Roberts and T.C. Skeat, *The Birth of the Codex* (London, 1983); and T.C. Skeat, '"Especially the Parchments": A Note on 2 Timothy iv. 13', *JTS* 30 (1979), 173–177.

(*including Mark*) have not yet arrived in Rome. Timothy is instructed to *bring Mark* with him when he comes to join forces with Paul and Luke (2 Tim. 4:11), and Mark is present with Demas in both of these references. If the supposed 'desertion' of Demas took place before Mark's arrival in Rome, it was resolved rather quickly; for Demas is present in Rome with Paul, Mark, and the others at the time the letters to the Colossians and to Philemon were written. Both of these letters were written while Paul was in prison in Rome, *in the company of Mark*.

Numerous scholars call attention to the fact that the description of Demas as 'in love with this present world' is eschatological language. Moreover, it should be noted that Demas went to Thessalonica; and the subject of 2 Thessalonians, in particular, is the matter of eschatology. 1 Thessalonians presents the 'second coming' of Jesus as imminent, and the author's concern is to prepare the church for this approaching day of the Lord (1 Thes. 4:13 – 5:11). In sharp contrast, the author of 2 Thessalonians is taking pains to refute the idea that Jesus' return is near, by reminding the church of a number of events that must precede it (2:1–12). The author draws on a rich reservoir of apocalyptic tradition to show that the church's present affliction will be reversed on the day of the Lord (1:5–10). Since that climactic day has not yet arrived (2:1–12), actions in the present circumstances continue to be important (2:15 – 3:16).

Though many scholars conclude that Paul is not the author of 2 Thessalonians, it is possible to read this letter as an attempt on Paul's part to clarify his earlier discussion on matters of eschatology. The content of this letter may also be interpreted as an attempt on Paul's part to restore Demas as a colleague, after his departure for Thessalonica, when he was not yet ready to accept Paul's teaching on the subject of eschatology that projected certain events into the more distant future.

In the middle of the first century CE there was widespread belief in the approaching dawn of a new age among both Christians and Jews throughout the Roman Empire. And for many, including Paul, the year 63 CE was a cardinal year in prophetic expectation. According to Wacholder, a new sabbatical cycle of seven years in the Jewish calendar commenced in the fall of that year.[12] For Jews, the sabbatical cycles were important prophetic indicators. The book of Daniel posits seventy sabbatical cycles of seven years until the kingdom of God would arrive on earth. Daniel divided those four hundred and ninety years into a period of forty-nine years (seven times the seven-year sabbatical cycle), another four hundred and thirty-four years (62 x 7 sabbatical cycles), and a final seven-year period that is divided into two parts of three and a half years each. Regardless of what the author of Daniel may have originally meant, many in the first century believed that the 'seventieth week of years' in Daniel's prophecy was near at hand. They specifically thought that it would coincide

---

[12] B.Z. Wacholder, 'The Calendar of Sabbatical Cycles During the Second Temple and the Early Rabbinic Period', *HUCA* 44 (1973), 153–196.

with the sabbatical cycle scheduled to begin in 63 CE and to end in 70 CE. These final seven years of Daniel's prophecy were thought to embrace a period of great trouble for Israel, the city of Jerusalem, and the Temple. The conclusion of the seven years was expected to witness the advent of the messianic kingdom of God. For Paul and others, this meant that Jesus would return at this time to begin his millennial reign as king in Jerusalem.

Paul believed that the glorious return of Christ would be an occasion when 'the Lord himself, with a cry of command, with the archangel's call and with the sound of God's trumpet, will descend from heaven, and the dead in Christ will rise first. Then we who are alive, who are left, will be caught up in the clouds together with them to meet the Lord in the air; and so we will be with the Lord forever' (1 Thes. 4:16–17). These words were written around 50 CE. Some years later Paul elaborated on his eschatological beliefs in greater detail to the church at Corinth.

> But each in his own order. Christ the first fruits, then at his coming those who belong to Christ. Then comes the end, when (Christ) hands over the kingdom of God the Father, after he has destroyed every ruler and every authority and power. For he must reign until he has put all his enemies under his feet. The last enemy to be destroyed is death. ... When all things are subjected to him, then the Son himself will also be subjected to the one who put all things in subjection under him, so that God may be all in all (1 Cor. 15:23–28).

Paul was so certain of the soon arrival of God's kingdom that he told the Romans that 'Satan would be crushed under their feet very soon' (Rom. 16:20).

The Epistle to the Hebrews and the Letter of James express similar belief in the imminence of Christ's return. Hebrews speaks of 'these last days' (1:2), 'the end of the age' (9:26), the day of reckoning is 'approaching' (10:25), for 'in a very little while, the one who is coming will come and will not delay' (10:37). James, the brother of Jesus, was martyred in the spring of 62 CE in Jerusalem. In his letter, he told his readers that it was 'the last days' and that they should be patient 'until the coming of the Lord ... for the coming of the Lord is near' (Jas. 5:3,7,8). The apostle John was no less urgent in his appeal that the end of the age was near, 'Children, it is the last hour! As you have heard that antichrist is coming, so now many antichrists have come. From this we know that it is the last hour' (1 Jn. 2:18). The return of Christ in that generation seemed an assured thing because Jesus himself was thought to have taught it, 'Truly I tell you, this generation will not pass away until all these things have taken place' (Mt. 24:34). Jesus told his disciples that some of them would not die before they would 'see the Son of Man coming in his Kingdom' (Mt. 15:27–28).

In popular belief, however, two important events had to take place before the last sabbatical period of Daniel's prophecy could begin. Jerusalem and the Temple would be destroyed first, according to Daniel 8:26–27. Moreover, the

Roman Empire had to be overthrown; for there was hardly a prophetic interpreter at that time who did not consider the Roman Empire to be the 'iron legs' of the Babylonian image in Daniel 2. The 'iron legs' would break into ten divisions, some strong as iron and others weak as miry clay. In 63 CE, when the new sabbatical cycle began, those 'iron legs' were as strong as ever.

Instead of a world war starting between East and West in 63 CE, followed by a revolt of the various kingdoms within the Roman dominion, to fulfil what Christians thought to be Christ's prophecies (Mt. 24:6–7), the opposite occurred. Rome was stronger than ever. With the passing of that year, Paul concluded that the 'iron legs' of Rome were going to remain in power for a long time to come. Paul realized that the prophesied ten kings, and the 'little horn', were not going to appear at that time in the first century. Not long afterwards, Peter also became convinced that much time was still left in world history before the second coming of Jesus would take place. That's what Peter has in mind when he says that a day with the Lord is as a thousand years.

By the end of the year 63 CE (if not earlier), it was obvious to Paul (and soon to Peter and John as well) that it was necessary to establish an authoritative body of sacred writings for use in the Christian community until those end-time events would actually take place. It is reasonable to assume that Paul and Luke took a significant step to that end some years earlier by editing eight of Paul's letters, together with the Gospel of Luke, in a form that parallels the Writings of the Tanakh (Hebrew Bible), as a fifth and concluding segment of the canon of sacred scripture.

Torah – 5 books of Moses	Genesis, Exodus, Leviticus, Numbers, Deuteronomy
Former Prophets – 4 books	Joshua, Judges, 1 – 2 Samuel, 1 – 2 Kings
Latter Prophets – 4 books	Isaiah, Jeremiah, Ezekiel, 'The Twelve' (Minor Prophets)
Former (Hebrew) Writings	9 books (in a 4 + 1 + 4 pattern)
Latter (Greek) Writings	9 books (in a 4 + 1 + 4 pattern)

The first edition of the Latter (Apostolic) Writings, which were intended to be canonical scripture from the outset, were structured in a 4 + 1 + 4 pattern as follows.

Romans	1 Corinthians	Timothy	1 Thessalonians
	Gospel of Luke		
2 Corinthians	Galatians	2 Thessalonians	Titus

Eight letters of Paul are arranged in two groups of four, with the Gospel of Luke in the centre. Each of these sub-groups is structured in the form of a simple chiasm.

The arrangement of the 'Latter (Apostolic) Greek Writings' in the first stage of the canonical process that ultimately produced the 'Completed Tanakh' reflects the structure of the 'Former (Hebrew) Writings', which may be outlined as follows.

Psalms	Job	Ezra	Nehemiah
	Daniel		
Proverbs	*Megilloth*	1 Chronicles	2 Chronicles

The term *Megilloth* refers to the five 'Festal Scrolls' (Song of Songs, Ruth, Ecclesiastes, Lamentation and Esther). In this structure, Daniel is a connecting bridge between two groups of four books, each of which appears in the form of a simple chiasm.

Paul was already at work in the canonical process before he made his fateful journey to Jerusalem (ca. 58 CE); for he states that he left his 'book-carrier' (*phailonen*) and its contents with Carpus at Troas (2 Tim. 4:11–13; cf. Acts 20:5). Luke apparently first met Paul in Troas on an earlier occasion before they sailed from Asia Minor to Neapolis, the port city of Philippi in Macedonia (Acts 16:11–12). Luke is apparently the 'man from Macedonia' that Paul saw in a vision (Acts 16:8–9), as C. Peter Wagner argues;[13] for the account in Acts 16:11–12 marks the beginning of the 'we-sections' in the book of Acts, which indicate the sections of that book where Luke himself was actually present in the narrative he has written.

Luke, who resided in Philippi, was already working with Paul on canonical matters before the two of them set sail for Troas on route to Jerusalem in ca. 58 CE (Acts 20:5). They left their manuscripts with Carpus in Troas for safe-keeping. Together, Luke and Paul produced what we call here the 'Latter (Apostolic) Writings', which were conceived from the outset as a fifth and concluding section of the Tanakh.

The Gospel of Luke played a central role in the second stage of the canonical process that produced the 'Completed Tanakh' as well, this time as the central book in what eventually becomes a 'New Torah' – the four Gospels and Acts of the Apostles. This second stage in the canonical process took place in Jerusalem (ca. 58–60), while Paul was a prisoner in Caesarea, with Luke at

---

[13] C.P. Wagner, *Blazing the Way*: Book 3, 'Acts 15 – 28' (Ventura, 1995), 55–58.

work in the Church of Jerusalem. That work continued two years later in Rome where Paul was a prisoner and Luke was with him (ca. 60–62 CE).[14]

The third stage in the canonical process that produced the Greek New Testament was apparently launched by Luke when he 'edited' a copy of the Epistle to the Hebrews, which he then sent to Paul in Rome, as he waited for Timothy to join him (Heb. 13:22–23). Timothy did not come in time and Luke went on to Rome alone – to continue his canonical activity with Paul (ca. 61–62 CE). In the meantime, Paul invited Timothy to join him and Luke and to bring the manuscripts Paul and Luke had left in Troas (cf. Acts 20:5); and, perhaps more importantly, to bring Mark with him (2 Tim. 4:11–13). When Mark and Timothy arrived in Rome, the Gospel of Mark became the centre around which the Gospel of Matthew and a revised edition of the Gospel of Luke were edited in what we now call the Synoptic Gospels (Matthew, Mark and Luke). This three-part literary work was conceived from the outset as an integral part of a 'New Torah', which was made up of four Gospels (including John) and Acts of the Apostles (written by Luke). At this point in time (ca. 62 CE), the 'New Testament' of the *Completed Tanakh* was conceived as a twenty-two book counterpart to the twenty-two book canon of the Tanakh, as subsequently described by Josephus (*Against Apion* 1.8).

The martyrdom of James, the brother of Jesus and head of the church in Jerusalem, in the spring of 62 CE served as a catalyst to speed up the canonical activity in Rome. Peter joined Mark, Luke and the others. The subsequent martyrdom of both Paul and Peter in Rome some time after the great fire of 64 CE left only the apostle John among the four original 'pillars' of the early Christian church (Peter, John, James the brother of Jesus, and Paul). John lived on through the Jewish Revolt and destruction of Jerusalem (66–70 CE), and beyond to the end of the reign of Domitian (81–96 CE).

It was John and his followers who produced a forty-nine book canon of the 'Completed Tanakh', in which the four Gospels and Acts of the Apostles function as a 'New Torah' connecting the two testaments, each of which is made up of twenty-two books. Though the nature of the conceptual design of forty-nine books structured around a 'New Torah' was forgotten in the subsequent life of the expanding Christian church in a non-Jewish environment within the Roman Empire, the design itself survives in popular tradition. It is seen in the traditional order of the twenty-two (or twenty-four) books in the Tanakh (Hebrew Bible) within Jewish tradition, and in the popular order of the twenty-seven books of the New Testament as we now have it.

---

[14] For a detailed discussion of this stage in the canonical process, see Christensen, *Explosion of the Canon*, 57–76.

Conclusion: The Concept of a 'Master Editor' of Each Testament

Labuschagne has shown that the Hebrew Scriptures are numerical compositions in the sense that the numbers 17 and 26, which are associated with the divine name YHWH, are consciously woven into the fabric of the Hebrew text so as to make it symbolically the 'Word of God'.[15] The book of Deuteronomy illustrates this phenomenon.[16] In terms of word-count, multiples of the numbers 17 and 26 appear in ten of the eleven *Parashot* (weekly portions in the lectionary cycle), and in various larger combinations of these literary units.[17] The total number of words in Deuteronomy was carefully contrived to be exactly 14,300 words (i.e. 26 x 10 x 55). The central core of Deuteronomy (chs. 12–25) is an expansion of the ten commandments, which are called the 'ten words' and the name of the book itself in Hebrew is 'These are the words'. The number 55 is triangular 10 (i.e. the sum of the digits one through ten). The total word-count is thus a theological statement about the book itself, declaring that these words, which are based on the ten commandments, are the words of YHWH.

Something similar is found in the book of 'The Twelve' (the Minor Prophets), where the total word-count of 14,352 (i.e. 26 x 12 x 23) underscores the nature of this composite work, suggesting that the weaving together of these twelve parts into a single book bears witness to the glory of YHWH.[18] Though study of word-count in the Greek New Testament has scarcely begun, it is already clear that Paul's Letter to the Galatians displays a similar phenomenon with a total word-count of 2210 (i.e. 26 x 17 x 5).[19]

It is too early to explain in detail the nature of the numerical composition of the Hebrew Bible and the Greek New Testament. From the outset, God appointed the people of Israel to be a 'light to the nations'. As the book of Jonah suggests, Israel accepted her missionary role only with great reluctance. Within the context of the Babylonian Exile, the brothers Baruch and Seraiah appear to have played the role of 'master editors' of at least the Torah and the Former Prophets, as David Noel Freedman has shown. It is my personal opinion that their role in the 'editing' process of the Tanakh included the whole

---

[15] C.J. Labuschagne, *Numerical Secrets of the Bible: Rediscovering the Bible Codes* (North Richland Hills, 2000). See also his website, {www.labuschagne.net}.

[16] See D.L. Christensen, 'Deuteronomy as a Numerical Composition' in idem., *Deuteronomy 1:1 – 21:9* (Nashville, 2001), ci–cvii.

[17] Christensen, 'Deuteronomy as a Numerical Composition', cv–cvi.

[18] The numbers 23 and 32 are associated with the Hebrew word for 'glory', as shown by C.J. Labuschagne, *Numerical Secrets* (North Richland Hills, 2000), 121–27. The details of this numerical structure of the Book of the Twelve will appear in my commentary on Nahum in the Anchor Bible Commentary. A preliminary study of the numerical structure of Nahum, Habakkuk, Zephaniah and Haggai will appear shortly in my commentary in the NIBCOT series. See 'Word-Count in the Book of the Twelve – Progress Report' on the website {www.bibal.net}.

[19] *Explosion of the Canon*, 137–140.

of the so-called 'Deuteronomic Canon' (the seventeen-book canon of the 6th century BCE).[20] Ezra subsequently expanded this work to form the 'Pentateuchal Canon' of twenty-two books, which remains the official canon of sacred scripture within Judaism. The memory of the numerical composition of the Tanakh survived into the Common Era. The apostle Paul understood that sacred literature is symbolically transformed into canonical scripture by weaving the divine name into the fabric of the text in terms of word-count in the time-honoured principles of numerical composition. Within the context of Paul's missionary journeys, Luke emerged as Paul's compatriot, and ultimately the successor of Baruch, Seraiah and Ezra before him in the distant past – as 'master editor' of the Greek New Testament, which constitutes the fifth and concluding section of the *Completed Tanakh*.

Bibliography

Attridge, H.W., 'Christianity from the Destruction of Jerusalem to Constantine's Adoption of the New Religion' in J.H. Charlesworth and C.A. Evans (eds.), *Christianity and Judaism: A Parallel History of Their Origins and Early Development* (Sheffield: JSOT Press, 1993), 151–194.

Barton, J., *Holy Writings, Sacred Texts: The Canon in Early Christianity* (Louisville, Kentucky: Westminster John Knox, 1997).

Beckwith, R.T. *The Old Testament Canon of the New Testament Church* (Grand Rapids, Michigan: Eerdmans, 1985).

Blenkinsopp, J., *Prophecy and Canon: A Contribution to the Study of Jewish Origins* (Notre Dame, Indiana: University of Notre Dame Press, 1977).

Bruce, F.F., 'Some Thoughts on the Beginning of the New Testament Canon', *Bulletin of the John Rylands University Library, Manchester* 65 (1983), 37–60.

Christensen, D.L., 'Deuteronomy as a Numerical Composition' in idem., *Deuteronomy 1:1 – 21:9* (Nashville: Thomas Nelson, 2001), ci–cvii.

— 'Josephus and the Twenty-Two-Book Canon of Sacred Scripture', *Journal of the Evangelical Theological Society* 29 (1986), 37–46.

— *Minor Prophets II: Nahum, Habakkuk, Zephaniah and Haggai* (Peabody, Massachusetts: Hendrickson, forthcoming).

— *The Explosion of the Canon: The Greek New Testament in Early Church History* (North Richland Hills: BIBAL Press, 2004).

Cross, F.M., *From Epic to Canon: History and Literature in Ancient Israel* (Baltimore: Johns Hopkins University Press, 1998).

Elliott, J.K., 'Manuscripts, the Codex, and the Canon', *Journal for the Study of the New Testament* 63 (1996), 105–123.

Ellis, E.E., 'The Old Testament Canon in the Early Church' and 'Biblical Interpretation in the New Testament Church' in M.J. Mulder (ed.), *Mikra: Text, Reading and Interpretation of the Hebrew Bible in Ancient Judaism and Early Christianity* (Philadelphia: Fortress, 1988), 653–726.

---

[20] Christensen, *Explosion of the Canon*, 14–17.

Freedman, D.N., *The Nine Commandments: Uncovering the Hidden Pattern of Crime and Punishment in the Hebrew Bible* (New York: Doubleday, 2002).

Thackeray, H. St. J. and R. Marcus (trans.), *Josephus' Works*, vol. 1, *The Life. Against Apion* (Cambridge, Massachusetts: Harvard University Press, 1934).

Labuschagne, C.J., *Numerical Secrets of the Bible: Rediscovering the Bible Codes* (North Richland Hills: BIBAL Press, 2000).

Leiman, S.Z., *The Canon and Masorah of the Hebrew Bible* (New York: Ktav, 1974).

Lightstone, J.N., 'The Rabbis' Bible: The Canon of the Hebrew Bible and the Early Rabbinic Guild' in L.M. McDonald and J.A. Sanders (eds.), *The Canon Debate* (Peabody, Massachusetts: Hendrickson, 2002), 163–84.

McDonald, L.M., *The Formation of the Christian Biblical Canon* (Peabody, Massachusetts: Hendrickson, 1995^2).

— 'The Origins of the Christian Biblical Canon', *Bulletin for Biblical Research* 6 (1996), 95–132.

— and J.A. Sanders (eds.), *The Canon Debate* (Peabody, Massachusetts: Hendrickson, 2002).

Roberts, C.H., *The Birth of the Codex* (London: Oxford University Press, 1983).

Skeat, T.C. '"Especially the Parchments": A Note on 2 Timothy iv. 13', *Journal of Theological Studies* 30 (1979), 173–177.

Stuart, M., *A Critical History of the Old Testament Canon* (London: George Routledge, 1849).

Wacholder, B.Z., 'The Calendar of Sabbatical Cycles During the Second Temple and the Early Rabbinic Period', *Hebrew Union College Annual* 44 (1973), 153–196.

Wagner, C.P., *Blazing the Way*, Book 3, 'Acts 15 – 28' (Ventura, Regal, 1995).

CHAPTER 9

Paul's Gospel to the Gentiles and its Implications for Christian Mission to Chinese

LUNG-KWONG LO

Introduction

Paul is proud of his identity as the apostle to the gentiles (Rom. 1:5; 11:13; 15:16; Gal. 1:16; 2:7–9; cf. Eph. 3:1–13; Col. 1:25–27).[1] He has brought the gospel of Jesus Christ from the Jews to the gentiles.[2] For this calling, he has been accused of being an apostate of the Jews.[3] The gospel that Paul preached to the gentiles has been generally known as the law-free gospel.[4] Since the Reformation, understanding of Paul's gospel has been focused on 'justification by faith' which is regarded as the core of Pauline theology.[5] From this understanding developed the Protestant doctrine of justification which has been

---

[1] See, e.g. D.J-S. Chae, *Paul as Apostle to the Gentiles* (Carlisle, 1997), 1. Concerning the issue of Paul's commissioning to go to the gentiles, see P.T. O'Brien, *Gospel and Mission in the Writings of Paul: An Exegetical and Theological Analysis* (Carlisle, 1993), 22–25.
[2] See S. Westerholm, *Perspectives Old and New on Paul: The 'Lutheran' Paul and His Critics* (Grand Rapids: 2004), 440.
[3] See P. Stuhlmacher, 'Paul: Apostate or Apostle?' in P. Lapide and P. Stuhlmacher (eds.), *Paul: Rabbi and Apostle* (Minneapolis: 1984), 11–30.
[4] E.g. J. Becker, *Paul: Apostle to the Gentiles* (Louisville: 1993), 57.
[5] See G. Stanton, 'Paul's Gospel' in J.D.G. Dunn (ed.), *The Cambridge Companion to St. Paul* (Cambridge: 2003), 179. For a survey of the modern debate of this doctrine in Paul's thought, see R.Y.K. Fung, 'The Status of Justification by Faith in Paul's Thought: A Brief Survey of a Modern Debate', *Themelios* 6 (1980–81), 4–11. This Lutheran understanding has been criticized by many scholars. See K. Stendahl, 'The Apostle Paul and the Introspective Conscience of the West', *HTR* 56 (1963), 199–215; F. Watson, *Paul, Judaism and the Gentiles: A Sociological Approach* (Cambridge: 1986), 2–10; J.D.G. Dunn, 'A Fresh Look at the Biblical Emphases' in idem. and A.M. Suggate (eds.), *The Justice of God: A Fresh Look at the Old Doctrine of Justification by Faith* (Carlisle: 1993), 5–29.

described as 'the real centre of the theological system of the Christian church'.[6] However, the importance of this doctrine has always been seen from a dogmatic perspective, the significance of social, national and cultural implications of his gospel to the gentiles has not attracted much attention.[7] Dahl, an exception to this, points out that

> The doctrine of justification proves that Christian Gentiles need not and should not ... become Jews, not even in part, in order to become full members of the church. ... As Christians, Gentiles should remain part of the ethnic group from which they came. ... It is not by accident that we find the quotation: 'There ... is neither Jew nor Greek, there is neither slave nor free, there is neither male nor female; for you are all one in Christ Jesus' (Gal. 3: 28; cf. 5:6. 6:15; Rom. 3:29f.; 10:12f.) in the context of a discussion of the doctrine of justification. ... The doctrine of justification ... which Paul so emphatically asserts has practical social consequences.[8]

Dahl's understanding has been substantiated by a recent development in Pauline studies – 'a new perspective on Paul' suggested by James Dunn.[9] According to his study on Galatians 2:16, Paul's doctrine of justification by faith is not intended to attack the idea of *earning* God's acquittal by doing meritorious *works of the law* (as understood by Luther). Paul's dismissal of the idea of being justified by *works of the law* intends to tell his readers to think of *'particular observances of the law like circumcision and the food laws which were widely regarded as characteristically and distinctively Jewish'*.[10] Thus the

---

[6] A.E. McGrath, *Iustitia Dei: A History of the Christian Doctrine of Justification* (Cambridge: 1998), 1.
[7] N.A. Dahl, 'The Doctrine of Justification: Its Social Function and Implications' in *Studies in Paul* (Minneapolis: 1977), 95–120, see especially 95–96.
[8] Dahl, 'The Doctrine of Justification', 95–120, see 108, 109.
[9] J.D.G. Dunn, 'The New Perspective on Paul' in *Paul and the Law: Studies in Mark and Galatians* (Louisville: 1990), 183–214. The genesis of this new perspective can be traced back to Stendahl's influential article, 'The Apostle Paul and the Introspective Conscience of the West' and E.P. Sanders important book, *Paul and Palestinian Judaism* (London: 1977). This new perspective has aroused a lot of discussion, e.g. P. Stuhlmacher, *Revisiting Paul's Doctrine of Justification: A Challenge to the New Perspective* (Downers Grove: 2001); S. Kim, *Paul and the New Perspective: Second Thoughts on the Origin of Paul's Gospel* (Grand Rapids: 2002). S. Westerholm, *Perspectives Old and New*, 400–445, suggests that a balanced understanding of the 'Lutheran' Paul and his critics should be maintained. However, Stanton, 'Paul's Gospel', 179, and D.A. Carson, 'Introduction' in idem., P.T. O'Brien, M.A. Seifrid (eds.), *Justification and Variegated Nomism* (Grand Rapids: 2001), 1.4, point out that the broad outlines of the approach of the new perspective on Paul have been widely accepted and are very influential among NT scholars.
[10] Dunn, 'The New Perspective', 191, original emphasis.

social (national and racial) function of circumcision and food laws in Galatians 2:1–14 is to provide the *identity* and *boundary markers* for Jews to mark out themselves from the gentiles as chosen people of God.[11] In other words, Paul's gospel to the gentiles is that the gentiles are free from observing circumcision and food laws (and other requirements of Jewish law, such as Sabbath as well, which function as identity and boundary markers of Jews), but that they are equally justified by faith and thus become members of the people of God.[12]

In this essay, I would argue that this understanding of Paul's gospel has profound implications for Christian mission to Chinese.

The Evidence of Romans 14:1 – 15:13

The above discussion of the social (national and racial) and cultural implications of Paul's law-free gospel has been mainly from the evidence of Galatians, especially the incident of Antioch.[13] The issue of compelling the (Christian) gentiles to observe the Jewish food laws at the table fellowship held in the church of Antioch was in fact to put the identity of gentiles at risk and seriously implied that 'Christ died to no purpose' (Gal. 2:21).[14]

There is a passage recording occasions of table fellowship in Romans which is also significant to this discussion. It is Romans 14:1 – 15:13, which is indeed an important passage overlooked for the discussion of the social and cultural implications of Paul's law-free gospel.[15] This passage has drawn the attention of many scholars from various perspectives since the publication of a lengthy study by Rauer (1923).[16] The main issues are as follows.

---

[11] See J.D.G. Dunn, 'Works of the Law and the Curse of the Law (Gal. 3:10–14)' in *Jesus, Paul and the Law* (Louisville: 1990), 215–241, emphasis added.

[12] Dunn, 'Works of the Law', 230–32. Also Chae, *Paul as Apostle*.

[13] J.D.G. Dunn, 'The Incident at Antioch (Gal. 2:11–18)', *JSNT* 18 (1983), 3–57. See also, idem. *The Theology of Paul's Letter to the Galatians* (Cambridge: 1993). Also, E.H.S. Kok, *The Truth of the Gospel: A Study in Galatians 2:15–21* (Hong Kong: 2000).

[14] See J.D.G. Dunn, *The Epistle to the Galatians* (London: 1993), 148–149.

[15] P.S. Minear, *The Obedience of Faith: The Purpose of Paul in the Epistle to the Romans* (London: 1971), starts his study from Romans 14 – 15 as the key passage to determine the situation of Roman Christians and to interpret the whole letter. Also, F. Watson, *Paul*; L.-k. Lo, *Paul's Purpose in Writing Romans: The Upbuilding of a Jewish and Gentile Christian Community in Rome* (Hong Kong: 1998).

[16] M. Rauer, 'Die "Schwachen" in Korinth und Rom', *BibSt* 21 (1923), 1–192. For recent discussions, see A.E.S. Nababan, *Bekenntnis und Mission in Roemer 14 und 15: Eine exegetische Untesuchung* (unpublished doctoral dissertation: Heidelberg, 1962); Minear, *The Obedience of Faith*; R.J. Karris, 'Romans 14:1 – 15:13 and the Occasion of Romans', *CBQ* 25 (1973), 155–178; Watson, *Paul*, 88–98; N. Schneider, *Die 'Schwachen' in der christlichen Gemeinde Roms: Eine historisch-exegetische Untersuchung zu Roem 14:1 – 15:13* (unpublished doctoral dissertation: Kirchilche Hochschule Wuppertal, 1989); J.M.G. Barclay, '"Do We Undermine the Law?": A

1. The *Sitz im leben* of Romans in general and the context of the controversy of Romans 14:1 – 15:13 in particular.
2. The identities of the 'strong' and the 'weak'.
3. The issues of controversy.
4. Paul's solution to the controversy.

THE *SITZ IM LEBEN* OF ROMANS AND THE CONTEXT OF ROMANS 14:1 – 15:13[17]

It is quite possible that the Roman Christians belonged to different house churches organized according to their background, without substantial inter-relationship. Paul's use of household language, such as *proslambanō* (14:1,3; 15:7) and *oiketēs* (14:4) support the hypothesis that the setting of house churches is the *Sitz im Leben* of 14:1 – 15:13. In view of Paul's use of liturgical language in Romans 14:10c–12[18] and 15:9b–12[19] it is quite probable that the specific context of Romans 14:1 – 15:13 is related to settings of corporate worship in house churches.

THE IDENTITY OF THE 'STRONG' AND THE 'WEAK'

The evidence that the issue involves clean and unclean foods (*koinos* in 14:14, *katharos* in 14:20) strongly supports the view that the 'weak' were Christians who observed the Mosaic law.[20] It is probable that most of them would have been ethnically Jewish but may have included some gentiles. The 'strong' were mostly gentile Christians who did not follow the Mosaic law, among whom

---

Study of Romans 14:1 – 15:6' in J.D.G. Dunn (ed.), *Paul and the Mosaic Law*, (Tübingen: 1996), 287–308; M.D. Nanos, *The Mystery of Romans: The Jewish Context of Paul's Letter* (Minneapolis: 1996), 85–165; Lo, *Paul's Purpose*, 117–158; J.D.G. Dunn, *The Theology of Paul the Apostle* (Grand Rapids: 1998), 680–89; M. Reasoner, *The Strong and the Weak: Romans 14:1 – 15:13 in Context* (Cambridge: 1999).

[17] Lo, *Paul's Purpose*, 117–58; and on the website {http://www.vanderbilt.edu/AnS/religious_studies/SBL2002/home2002.htm}

[18] Paul's argument in 14.10c–12 includes an Old Testament quotation from the latter Isaiah 45:23 LXX and an introductory formula *legei kurios* which is probably from Isaiah 49:18 (cf. Num. 14:28; Jer. 22:24; Ezek. 5:11). See E.E. Ellis, *Paul's Use of the Old Testament* (Edinburgh: 1957), 151; E. Käsemann, *Commentary on Romans* (London: 1982), 373.

[19] Paul uses four Old Testament quotations in 15:9b–12 which come from the Law, the Prophets and the Writings (LXX Ps. 17:50; Deut. 32:43; Ps. 116:1; Is. 11:10). Among these quotations, the one in 15:9b (which follows closely the text of Ps. 17:50 LXX) indicates an individual Jew praising God among the gentiles.

[20] The use of the word *koinos* to denote 'unclean' in the religious sense is almost exclusively Jewish. Reasoner, *The Strong and the Weak*, 17f., suggests that there were other reasons why people abstained from meat and wine in first century Rome. See also, 102–38.

there may have been some ethnic Jews who acted like Paul.[21] For convenience, these two groups of Christians are designated 'Jewish Christians' and 'gentile Christians', respectively. In other words, these designations are religio-cultural-ethnic in nature rather than strictly ethnic. This way of identifying the 'strong' and the 'weak' has been a point of growing consensus among many scholars.[22] The most significant difficulty of this interpretation is the evidence that the 'weak' were vegetarians (14:2) who not only abstained from meat but also from wine (14:21). However, the evidence found in Daniel 1:8–16; Esther 14:17 (LXX); Judges 12:1–4; Josephus *Vitae* 14, indicates that there were cases of Jews who abstained from both meat and wine when they were in a situation which was controlled by gentiles.[23]

THE ISSUES OF CONTROVERSY

The *Sitz im Leben* of the controversy between the 'weak' and the 'strong' is probably more specific than many scholars have thought. Minear rightly, in our opinion, suggests that the controversy happened on the specific occasion when the Jewish Christians and the gentile Christians worshipped and had communal meals together.[24] The 'weak' (Jewish Christians) did not abstain from meat or wine in general, they were vegetarian only when eating with the 'strong' (gentile Christians).[25] The crucial issue to concern a Jew when eating a meal with gentiles was probably how to keep the Jewish food laws in such a situation, vis-à-vis Jewish identity.[26] The controversy in Romans 14:1 – 15:13 probably reflects the issues related to an *identity crisis* faced by Jewish Christians in Rome. This is different from the incident of Antioch which reflects the issue related to an *identity crisis* faced by gentile Christians (or Christian gentiles). In Rome, the Christian community was predominantly

---

[21] For detailed discussion on the possible interpretations of the identities of the 'strong' and the 'weak', see C.E.B. Cranfield, *A Critical and Exegetical Commentary on the Epistle to the Romans* (Edinburgh: 1979), 2.690–97; U Wilckens, *Der Brief an die Roemer* (Zurich: 1982), 3.109–115; D.J. Moo, *The Epistle to the Romans* (Grand Rapids: 1996), 828–32; Reasoner, *The Strong and the Weak*, 1–23.

[22] See the bibliographical reference in Karris, 'Romans 14:1 – 15:13', 76n.6; Reasoner, *The Strong and the Weak*, 6–16. See also, P.F. Esler, *Conflict and Identity in Romans: The Social Setting of Paul's Letter* (Minneapolis: 2003), 341–344.

[23] Watson, *Paul*, 95.

[24] See Minear, *The Obedience of Faith*, 9. In early Christian times, worship and a communal meal were probably inseparable. See I Cor. 11:17–22; cf. O. Cullmann, *Early Christian Worship* (London: 1953), 14f..

[25] Minear, *The Obedience of Faith*, 10.

[26] See discussion on Tacitus, *Historiae*, V, 5:1; *Letter of Aristeas, Joseph and Asenath* in Lo, *Paul's Purpose*, 85–88.

gentile (the 'strong').²⁷ While in Antioch, the 'church' was part of a predominantly Jewish movement. Gentile members were a weak minority.²⁸

PAUL'S SOLUTION TO THE CONTROVERSY

From a detailed *personae analysis*²⁹ of this passage,³⁰ we gather the following relevant points

- Paul emphasized the importance of the *unity* between the Jewish and the gentile Christians but did not try to persuade the Jewish Christians to separate from the Jewish community. *They could be a Jew and a Christian at the same time.*
- Paul admonished the gentile Christians not to make the Jewish Christians become Jewish apostates in pursuit of Christian unity, but to support the Jewish Christians in their effort to preserve their Jewish identity.
- Paul asked the gentile Christians to exercise their freedom to choose to follow the Jewish way of eating a meal at the *specific occasion* when they participate in the communal meal held at a Jewish Christian house church. However, he affirmed their correct understanding that the Jewish practice had nothing to do with their identity as people of God. *They could maintain their non-Jewish (gentile) identity according to the gospel.*
- Paul *differentiated* between *soteriological* and *social-cultural*, *essential* and *situational*. He stood firm on the former issues without any room to compromise in his letter to Galatians, but suggested actions to please those who are wrong in their convictions and compromised on the latter issues in Romans.

The above findings are most significant in our discussion of the Christian mission to Chinese.

---

[27] So C.K. Barrett, *A Commentary on the Epistle to the Romans* (London: 1971), 22; W.G. Kümmel, *Introduction to the New Testament* (London: 1984), 309–11; Käsemann, *Commentary on Romans*, 15, 366; R.E. Brown, 'Rome' in idem. and J.P. Meir (eds.), *Antioch and Rome* (London: 1983), 109. For discussion of the composition of Roman Christians, see Cranfield, *A Critical and Exegetical Commentary*, 1.16–22.
[28] J.L. Martyn, *Galatians* (New York: 1997), 245.
[29] This phrase is borrowed from D.J.A. Cline, *I, He, We & They: A Literary Approach to Isaiah 53* (Sheffield: 1976), 37ff.. However, the meaning of this phrase here is different from Cline, see L-k. Lo, 'Identity Crisis Reflected in Romans 14:1 – 15:13 and the Implications for the Chinese Christians' Controversy on Ancestral Worship', *Ching Feng: A Journal on Christianity and Chinese Religion and Culture* 3 (2002), 30–32. For detailed discussion of this methodology in my study of Romans, see Lo, *Paul's Purpose*, 14–19.
[30] Lo, *Paul's Purpose*, 123–165.

Christian Mission to Chinese

According to the stone stele found near Xi'an[31], which is today the most reliable evidence of the arrival of the first Christian missionary and the development of Christian faith in China, it was the Nestorain monk Alopen who arrived at the then capital in 635 CE, during the period of the T'ang dynasty. If we trust the inscription of the monument (erected in 781 CE), Alopen was well received with honour by the Emperor T'ai Tsung. Translations of the 'sacred books' of the new faith were made in the imperial library, and the Emperor himself studied the religion and gave orders for its dissemination.[32] According to the inscription, Christian faith gained the favour of the succeeding Emperor, Kao Tsung (650-681), as well. Monasteries were built in cities throughout the country.[33]

From the inscription and other Nestorian texts, we find that Nestorian Christianity took up the languages of Buddhism to express its faith. It is quite obvious that Christianity was regarded by the Chinese authorities as a sect that was similar to Buddhism. This identification no doubt facilitated the Christians' entry into China during this earliest period. But Christianity was also persecuted (together with Buddhism) during the 840s CE by the Emperor Wu Tsung, aided by many of the leading Confucian scholars. The Emperor presided over a nationalistic revival of religious ideologies against Buddhism, seen as an influential foreign religion.[34] An imperial decree was issued to reduce the total number of monasteries throughout China. Over 250,000 Chinese Buddhist monks and nuns, together with more than 3,000 Christian and Zoroastrian monks and priests were forcibly returned to secular life and abandoned their vocations.[35] So, the first entry of Christianity is regarded as a failure. According to an Arabic chronicler who reports having a conversation with a Christian monk in Baghdad in 987, the monk reported that he could not find one Christian left in China.[36]

---

[31] Named as Ch'ang-an in ancient China.

[32] The English translation of the inscription can be found in P.Y. Saeki, *The Nestorian Documents and Relics in China* (Tokyo: 1951). For discussion on the monument, see idem., *The Nestorian Monument in China* (London: 1966). For discussion on Nestorian Christianity, see K.S. Latourette, *A History of Christian Missions in China* (London: 1929), 51–4; S.K. Lee, *The Cross and the Lotus* (Hong Kong: 1971); C.S. Wu, *Nestorian in Tang China and Central Asia: A Cultural Studies* (unpublished Masters dissertation, Hong Kong: 1998).

[33] However, historical evidence shows that the number appears to have been no more than a dozen, most of them in the proximity of Xi'an. For discussion of the other findings about the development of Nestorian Christianity in China, see D.T. Irvin and S.W. Sunquist, *History of the World Christian Movement* (New York: 2001), 1.316–319.

[34] See discussion in Latourette, *A History*, 54; Irvin and Sunquist, *History*, 1.318–321.

[35] See Irvin and Sunquist, *History*, 1.321.

[36] See Latourette, *A History*, 54.

The reasons behind the failure are difficult to discern. However, the identification of Christianity with Buddhism had been a strength, but also a weakness for the development of Christianity in China. Another issue was the identity of Christianity among various Chinese traditions. Furthermore, the disappearance of Christians after more than two hundred years of existence also arouses the question of the identity of Christians among Chinese people. Irvin and Sunquist suggest that

> despite the remarkable work in translation and even composition of new theological work in Chinese, for the most part the Christian church in China from the seventh through tenth centuries remained a community of resident foreigners. ... [T]he churches for the most part remained dependent on foreign clergy ... for their leadership.[37]

In other words, according to the experiences gained from the first entry of Christianity into China, the issues related to Christian mission to Chinese are

- the relationship between Christian faith, Chinese religions and cultures;
- the identity of Christianity and Chinese Christians among Chinese people.

After the first entry of Nestorian Christianity into China, there were at least four more entries of Christianity into the country. The Nestorians returned to China in the wake of the Mongol conquest of North China in 1260. The first Catholic missionary sent by the Pope reached China in 1294. However, the Catholics together with Nestorians disappeared after the fall of the Mongolians in 1368 caused by the uprisings of the native Chinese. It seems that the Nestorians and Catholics were supported by the Mongolian rulers – they perished together under an anti-foreign reaction. The effect of Nestorians and Catholics upon Chinese was very little.[38] One of the possible reasons is that the Christian community in China was foreign in its membership.[39]

A new dynasty of Ming (1368–1644) was started in the fourteenth century after the Mongolians were expelled. Almost two hundred years later, the

---

[37] Irvin and Sunquist, *History*, 1.321–2. Nevertheless, S.H. Moffett, *A History of Christianity in Asia* (San Francisco: 1991), 1.313, suggests that the decisive factor which caused the collapse of the Chinese Church 'was neither religious persecution, nor theological compromise, nor even its foreignness, but rather the fall of the imperial house on which the Church had too long relied for its patronage and protection'. Moffett's comment could be valid from a historical point of view, but it does not exclude the importance of the issues related to the identity of Christianity and of Christians among Chinese people.

[38] See Latourette, *A History*, 73–77.

[39] See Latourete, *A History*, 76.

famous Catholic missionary movement led by the Jesuit, Ricci Matteo (1552-1610) was inaugurated. This movement became the first permanent Catholic mission in China.[40]

During their occupation (c.1624–1662) of Taiwan (named as Formosa by the Dutch), the Dutch carried on missions among the aboriginal people of the island, this represents the first Protestant mission to China. However, when the Dutch were driven out, the church collapsed, leaving no permanent traces of its existence.[41]

The first Protestant missionary who arrived in the China Mainland was Robert Morrison (1807). He was sent by the London Missionary Society and started the permanent Protestant missionary movement in China.[42]

In the history of the Catholic and Protestant missions to Chinese, the main issues related to Christian mission to Chinese were similar to the past: i.e. relationship between Christian faith, Chinese religions and cultures, as well as the identity of Christianity and Chinese Christians among Chinese people. The issues can be seen most clearly in the case of the Rites Controversy with the focus on ancestral worship among Chinese Christians.

THE CHINESE CHRISTIAN CONTROVERSY ON ANCESTRAL WORSHIP

Chinese Christianity has long been labelled as a foreign religion. The criticism is that to be a Christian is not to be a Chinese. The conflict of being a Chinese and being a Christian has been an issue reflected in the well-known Rites Controversy (1615–1742) which arose among Catholic missionaries regarding how they should deal with 'Chinese rites'.[43] The issue at stake was whether Christian converts be permitted to continue the practice of the ancestral cult which was so central to the entire family and clan system, as well as the veneration of Confucius in the temples dedicated to his name which were attached to every school in the country.

The controversy was considered by eight popes and involved leading universities in Europe.[44] In the end, Rome was to support those who opposed the rites. Rome's judgement was

- that the ancient Chinese were idolaters and the modern Chinese atheists;

---

[40] For a detailed discussion of the Jesuit led missionary movement to China, see Latourette, *A History*, 78–130.
[41] See Latourette, *A History*, 209.
[42] See Latourette, *A History*, 211–215.
[43] Although this controversy started in the seventeenth century, the issue of ancestral worship has not been settled among Chinese Christians even until today.
[44] The Protestant philosopher Leibnitz published a defense of the Jesuits, but in 1700 the theological faculty of the University of Paris formally disapproved the Jesuit position. See Latourette, *A History*, 139f..

- that the Confucian classics themselves, and even the Jesuit works published in Chinese, taught doctrine contrary to the Christian faith;
- that ancestral rites were illicit because they were offered to spirits of ancestors and so involved idolatry and superstition;
- that Confucius himself was a public idolater and a private atheist, and should not be honoured by Christians as a saint.[45]

In a decree of 1704, reinforced by the bull *Ex illa die* of 1715, Pope Clement XI banned the rites.[46] Another envoy of the pope, Jean Ambrose Charles Mezzabarba, was sent to China in 1720. He was more tactful than his predecessor and presented to the famous Chinese Emperor K'ang-hsi a concession in the form of eight 'permissions' which were mainly an interpretation of the clauses that permitted ceremonies of a purely civil or political character.[47] However these concessions were far from satisfactory to the Chinese Emperor, who was in the early days very sympathetic to the Jesuit mission in China, and were annulled by Pope Benedict XIV, the successor of Clement XI.[48] On July 11, 1742, Pope Benedict XIV decided in favour of those opposing the rites. His decree, *Ex quo singulari*, condemned the Chinese rites and imposed an oath on all Catholic missionaries in China to oppose them.

The decision had incalculable consequences. The Catholic missionaries were expelled from China and an imperial edict to ban Christianity was issued. A golden opportunity of planting the gospel on Chinese soil was lost.[49] Cynically, almost two centuries after *Ex quo singulari*, during the Second World War (in 1939), Pope Pius XII reversed the decision of 1742, authorizing Christians to take part in ceremonies honouring Confucius and to observe the ancestral rites. By then, however, the veneration of Confucius was largely discontinued since China had put in a modern school system to replace the traditional Confucian-oriented 'temple-related' institutions. Besides, the Chinese were at war with Japan, and hardly had the time to spare for ancestral rites. The golden opportunity had simply gone and has not returned.

---

[45] J. Ching, *Chinese Religions* (New York: 1993), 194.
[46] Latourette, *A History*, 140ff..
[47] Latourette, *A History*, 148f..
[48] Latourette, *A History*, 148f..
[49] Latourette, *A History*, is ambivalent about the consequences of the controversy. On the one hand, he comments that the papal decision had 'established a tradition for making the Church inadaptable to Chinese conditions and beliefs. It tended and still tends to keep the Roman Catholic Church a foreign institution, one to which China must conform but which refuses to conform to China' (154). On the other hand, he suggests that 'the papal decisions made the winning of nominal adherents more difficult, but they tended to keep high the standards of the Church'. Again, 'Numbers were sacrificed for vitality' (155). However, Latourette has to answer the question (154; cf. 132), 'Whether it can win to its fold a highly cultured people like the Chinese without again making a similar adaptation remains an unanswered question.'

While Catholics have an official position on the issue of ancestral rites, Protestants can hardly come to any consensus even today.[50] Robert Morrison (the first Protestant missionary who arrived China, 1807), had studied the problem and expressed his opposition in 1832.[51] While the missionary activities expanded after the opium war (1840), the conflicts on the issue between missionaries and Chinese society, became a burning one among the missionaries. In the nineteenth century there were two missionary conferences held in China (1877, 1890) which paid a great deal of attention to the controversy.

In the first conference, almost all participants condemned Chinese ancestral worship as an act of idolatry which must not be participated in by Chinese Christians.[52] Only a few had raised questions: had missionaries the right to compel Chinese to give up their way of honouring the dead, should Chinese Christians refuse to participate in the rite if it meant losing their right of inheritance. The most positive response was proposed by T.P. Crawford and C. Goodrich, that an effort of developing Christian rites to replace ancestral worship should be pursued.[53]

In the second conference, a report on W.A.P. Martin's thorough study on the issue aroused a hot debate.[54] Martin agreed that there were some idolatrous and superstitious elements involved in Chinese ancestral worship, but suggested that there were positive elements as well. The origin of the rite comes from some best principles of humanity which include a wish to communicate with deceased parents. The three levels in the rite which include 'posture', 'invocation' and 'offering' are not necessarily equivalent to idol-worship, but rather reflect a pattern of Chinese daily living. He suggested that the Westerners' offering of flowers to remember those dead has the same meaning as the Chinese offering meats and vegetables.[55] Thus it would be

---

[50] See discussions in Church Renewal Research Development Centre (ed.), *Christian Alternatives to Ancestor Practices* (Taipei: 1985); P-h. Huang, et. al., *Christian and Ancestor Worship* (Taipei: 1994); K-k. Yeo, *Ancestor Worship: Rhetorical and Cross-Cultural Hermeneutical Response* (Hong Kong: 1996); F-t. Ying 'Christianity and Chinese Ancestor Worship – A Historical Survey' in idem. (ed.), *Chinese Ancestor Worship* (Hong Kong: 1997); K-l. Leung, 'Christianity and Chinese Ancestor Worship – Response from a Pastoral Perspective' in F-t. Ying (ed.), *Chinese Ancestor Worship*, (Hong Kong: 1997).
[51] R. Morrison, 'Worshipping at the tombs', *Chinese Repository* 1.5 (1832), 202; idem., 'Tombs of Ancestors', *Chinese Repository* 1.12 (1833), 502.
[52] Ying, 'Christianity and Chinese Ancestor Worship', 11–13.
[53] *Records of the General Conference of the Protestant Missionaries of China,* held at Shanghai, 1877 (Taipei: 1973), 396–7, 401, cited by Ying, 'Christianity and Chinese Ancestor Worship', 13n.24.
[54] *Records of the General Conference*, 620–31.
[55] *Records of the General Conference of the Protestant Missionaries of China,* held at Shanghai (Shanghai: 1890), 627.

better to work to preserve the good elements and to clear those unacceptable, so that the rite might be modified to the extent that it is in harmony with the Christian faith.

However, his accommodating approach was not welcomed by most participants. Nevertheless, the situation was not as one-sided as in 1877. Some prominent missionaries did express their support of Martin. They suggested that missionaries must learn how to differentiate *religious* and *non-religious* elements involved in the rite.[56] It was unfair to identify ancestral worship simply as idolatry. The opponents proposed a strong resolution against Martin's report. For them, *non-western cultures such as the Chinese were simply pagan cultures*. The issue at stake was not '*gospel* and *cultures* of other people', but '*gospel* and other *religious traditions*'[57] which were not compatible with Christianity, and must be totally rejected.

The debate among missionaries was reflected among Chinese converts. Strong reaction from Chinese society arose because of the absolute opposition to Chinese Christian involvement in the rite and the requirement to destroy the family ancestor tablets as a pre-requisite for baptism. Many of the anti-Christian publications focusing on the issue were condemnatory of Christianity as an immoral religion which did not honour parents and ancestors.[58]

Martin rekindled the debate in 1902 by publishing an essay, "How Shall We Deal with the worship of Ancestors?" He further expressed his view that the rite is *not religious* in nature but an ancient Chinese *social order*. A committee chaired by James Jackson of the Methodist Episcopal Mission was formed to give a report on ancestral worship to the China Centenary Missionary Conference (1907). In the report, the issue of whether ancestral worship was idolatrous was avoided. The most obvious reason against the rite was the problem of replacing the Creator by human creatures.[59] Nevertheless, the positive elements of expressing filial piety and the differentiation between the nature and practice of the rite were emphasized.[60]

Nevertheless, the main concern of the Chinese on ancestral worship, vis-à-vis the participation of a Chinese Christian in the rite, was rejected. The position was reiterated: ancestral worship was incompatible with Christian faith

---

[56] For discussion on Chinese culture's understanding of 'religion' (which is different from the west), see L-k. Lo, 'The Nature of the Issue of Ancestral Worship among Chinese Christians', *SWC* 9 (2003), 35–36.

[57] S.W. Ariarajah, *Gospel and Culture: An ongoing Discussion within the Ecumenical Movement* (Geneva: 1994), 2–4 (emphasis added).

[58] See Ying, 'Christianity and Chinese Ancestor Worship', 20n.42.

[59] Ying, 'Christianity and Chinese Ancestor Worship', 233.

[60] J. Jackson, 'Ancestral Worship' in *China Centenary Missionary Conference Records: Report of the Great Conference held at Shanghai, April 5–May 8, 1907* (New York: 1907), 239–244.

and could not be tolerated as a practice in the Christian church.⁶¹ The most significant change was from a totally negative attitude reflected in the resolutions of the two previous conferences to a more sympathetic one. The report advocated a constructive, rather than a destructive attitude, towards the rite.⁶² This change had opened up space for more positive discussion by Chinese Christians. A few of them even openly supported the stance of Christian participation in the rite which was against the basic position of the missionaries.⁶³

The Main Issues

In the debate among Chinese Christians on the rite, the main issues were:⁶⁴

1. The mixed superstitious element in the present ancestral worship was criticized, but the original meaning of filial piety was confirmed.
2. The rite of ancestral worship should be reformed rather than destroyed. Filial piety embedded in the rite was regarded as the foundation of morality in Chinese culture. The most urgent issue was to introduce a rite which would be compatible to both Christian faith and Chinese culture.
3. The most critical concern of the rite should be that people not regard ancestors as gods. Even though some had distorted the original meaning of ancestral worship, it would not be legitimate to reject the rite completely. Chinese Christians could accept the rite after some adjustments.

Nevertheless, although the above understanding of the rite as an expression of filial piety were generally accepted, the opinion of the rite as heretical idolatry propounded by missionaries still prevailed among most Chinese Christians.

The position toward the rite among most of the Protestant churches is almost the same as the Catholics in the eighteenth century. This stance has not only become a stumbling block for Chinese in becoming Christians but also indicates that a basic issue of the relationship between the gospel and the Chinese culture has not been thoroughly understood. The crux of the matter of ancestral rites is very much related to the *identity of the Chinese*.⁶⁵ As a matter of fact, ancestral rites have different stages of development in Chinese history

---

⁶¹ See Jackson, 'Ancestral Worship', 604–624.
⁶² Jackson, 'Ancestral Worship', 239.
⁶³ Ying, 'Christianity and Chinese Ancestor Worship', 55–64.
⁶⁴ Ying, 'Christianity and Chinese Ancestor Worship', 76–82.
⁶⁵ See J.W. Rawski, and S. Evelyn (ed.), *Death Ritual in Late and Modern China* (Berkeley: 1990); F-t. Ying, 'A Retrospect on Research of Chinese Ancestor Worship' in idem. (ed.), *Chinese Ancestor Worship* (Hong Kong: 1997), 218, 224.

and possess multi-layers of meaning.[66] The question of how to differentiate, especially the *religious* meanings and the *social, moral* and *cultural*, and the *implied significance* of these to Chinese and Christian identities, is vital to the development of Christianity among the Chinese.

A Christian Interpretation of the Rite of Ancestral Worship

The position of the Vatican in the eighteenth century as well as that of most Protestant missionaries and churches today is based on an interpretation of the Christian faith which focuses on the first two of the ten commandments.[67] However, the Chinese perspective on ancestral worship has to be taken into account.[68]

Furthermore, in the discussion among missionaries at the 1907 conference, the issue of 'individual conscience' was raised in relation to the Ancestral Tablet. This was a real breakthrough in the discussion of ancestral worship.[69] 'Each one must be fully persuaded in his own mind.'[70] 'A decision of the Emperor ... might make it easier for a *weak* Christian to disobey the voice of conscience. For the *strong* Christian it might only make him realize that he must oppose the Imperial decision both as to Imperial and as to the Confucian worship.'[71] These surely echo I Corinthians 8 – 10 and Romans. 14:1 – 15:13 (especially 14:5b).

I Corinthians, chapters 8 – 10 have been commonly used in the discussion of ancestral worship.[72] The issue of eating the foods offered in ancestral worship is understood as a similar case of eating the idol meat. In this sense, the issue is understood in the context of idol worship, vis-à-vis from the perspective of *gospel and religions*. Thus, ancestors are assumed to be identified as idols, and the food offered to ancestors is identified as food offered to idols. Idol worship should surely be totally prohibited and Paul admonishes the Corinthians that 'food will not commend us to God. ... We are not worse off if we do not eat, and no better off if we do' (I Cor. 8:8). He concludes that 'if food is a cause of my brother's falling, I will never eat meat, lest I cause my brother to fall' (v. 13). According to this point of view, it seems that Chinese Christians should not participate in the rite of ancestral worship

---

[66] See C.K. Yang, *Religion in Chinese Society* (Berkeley: 1961), especially 29–31, 44–48, 60ff., 253–255.

[67] For other biblical texts related to the discussion of ancestral worship, see Yeo, *Ancestor Worship*, 135–41.

[68] See Lo, 'The Nature of the Issue', 35–36.

[69] See note 50 above.

[70] Jackson, 'Ancestral Worship', 244.

[71] *China Centenary Missionary Conference Records*, 621–22; emphasis added.

[72] See Yeo, *Ancestor Worship*; Leung, 'Christianity and Chinese Ancestor Worship', 160, 204.

and should not eat the food offered to ancestors, even though the food itself is not wrong. This stance affects many Chinese Christians, they think it is better to refuse eating food offered to ancestors, so as not to participate in ancestral worship.

However, the above interpretation is problematic. It is not only that for Chinese, ancestors should not simply be identified as idols, nor the ancestral worship as simply a religious practice, but also for Paul, the issue of eating the idol meat is a non-issue. What he was concerned with is not to cause 'my brother's falling'. The issue at stake is who will be falling if we eat the foods offered to our ancestors? Are they Christians who object to the practice, such as those western missionaries in China? Or those Chinese who are attracted by Christianity but refuse to become Christians because they want to continue to participate in ancestral worship and to eat the food offered to ancestors? It is surely not the former; for they think that it is those Christians who eat the food offered to ancestors who have fallen. If we apply Paul's principle to the case, we should not put off those Chinese who prefer to continue their practice of ancestral worship after they become Christians.

Since the use of I Corinthians 8 – 10 in the discussion of ancestral worship is problematic because it moves from the perspective of gospel and religions, I would like to propose that Paul's messages in the incident of Antioch (Gal. 2:12–21) and Romans 14:1 – 15:13 are more relevant to the discussion.

As has been shown above, the main issue of the incident of Antioch and of Romans 14:1 – 15:13 is the identity crisis faced by the gentile and Jewish Christians. The relevance of Romans 14:1 – 15:13 is very significant. The issue is whether the Jewish Christians could maintain their Jewish identity and also be followers of Christ.[73] Under the pressure of the 'strong', the 'weak' have to face a choice, which Paul does not think necessary or proper. Even though the 'strong' are right in their understanding of the relation between faith and eating and drinking, they should understand the implications from the view of the 'weak'. Though the 'strong' enjoy more freedom in their daily practice, they should please the 'weak' rather than judge the 'weak' in their practices which are essential in maintaining their Jewish identity. Thus, if only the 'strong' could see from the perspective of the 'weak', they would not agree to give up their 'right' practice which is supported by their 'right' understanding.

Concluding Remarks

In the Chinese Christian controversy on ancestral worship, the popes and their delegates in the seventeenth and eighteenth centuries as well as the Protestant missionaries in the nineteenth and early twentieth centuries did not view the issue from the Chinese Christian perspective and context. They did not see that Chinese are turned away from Christianity because of the missionaries'

---

[73] See Lo, *Paul's Purpose*, 117–158.

objection to participation in ancestral worship. In the relationship between missionaries and the Chinese Christians, those missionaries are the 'strong' who forced the 'weak' (Chinese Christians) to face the identity crisis of being Chinese *and* Christian. Many Chinese, attracted by the Christian gospel, had to face the choice of whether to become Christians or to maintain their Chinese identity. For Paul, this dichotomy is totally unnecessary. It destroys the work of God (Rom. 14:20).

If we could understand the social, national, racial and cultural implications of Paul's gospel to the gentiles, and view the nature of the issue of Chinese ancestral worship from the perspective of g*ospel and cultures* (not g*ospel and religions*) the controversy between Chinese and western Christians could be very different. And the missionary history in China would also have been very different.

Bibliography

Ariarajah, S.W., *Gospel and Culture: An ongoing Discussion within the Ecumenical Movement* (Geneva: WCC, 1994).

Barclay, J.M.G., '"Do We Undermine the Law?": A Study of Romans 14:1 – 15:6' in J.D.G. Dunn (ed.), *Paul and the Mosaic Law* (Tübingen: Mohr, 1996).

Barrett, C.K., *A Commentary on the Epistle to the Romans* (London: A. & C. Black, 1971).

Becker, J., *Paul: Apostle to the Gentiles* (Louisville: Westminster John Knox Press, 1993).

Brown, R.E., 'Rome' in R.E. Brown and J.P. Meir (eds.), *Antioch and Rome* (London: Geoffrey Chapman, 1983).

Carson, D.A., 'Introduction' in D.A. Carson, P.T. O'Brien, M.A. Seifrid (eds.), *Justification and Variegated Nomism*, vol. 1: 'The Complexities of Second Temple Judaism' (Grand Rapids, Michigan: Baker, 2001).

Chae, D.J-S., *Paul as Apostle to the Gentiles* (Carlisle: Paternoster, 1997).

China Centenary Missionary Conference Records: Report of the Great Conference held at Shanghai, April 5th to May 8th, 1907 (New York: American Tract Society, 1907).

Ching, J., *Chinese Religions* (New York: Orbis, 1993).

Church Renewal Research Development Centre (ed.), *Christian Alternatives to Ancestor Practices* (in Chinese) (Taipei: China Ministries International, 1985).

Cline, D.J.A., *I, He, We & They: A Literary Approach to Isaiah 53* (Sheffield: JSOT Press, 1976).

Cranfield, C.E.B., *A Critical and Exegetical Commentary on the Epistle to the Romans*, 2 volumes (Edinburgh: T. & T. Clark, 1979).

Cullmann, O., *Early Christian Worship* (London: SCM, 1953).

Dahl, N.A., 'The Doctrine of Justification: Its Social Function and Implications', *Norsk teologisk tidsskrift* 65 (1964). Reprinted in idem., *Studies in Paul* (Minneapolis: Augsburg Press, 1977), 95–120.

Dunn, J.D.G., 'A Fresh Look at the Biblical Emphases' in J.D.G. Dunn and A.M. Suggate, *The Justice of God: A Fresh Look at the Old Doctrine of Justification by Faith* (Carlisle: Paternoster, 1993), 5–29.

— *The Epistle to the Galatians* (London: A. & C. Black, 1993).
— 'The Incident at Antioch (Gal. 2:11–18)', *Journal for the Study of the New Testament* 18 (1983), 3–57. Reprinted in idem., *Jesus, Paul and the Law: Studies in Mark and Galatians* (Louisville: Westminster John Knox Press, 1990), 129–182.
— 'The New Perspective on Paul', *BJRL* 65 (1983), 95–122. Reprinted in idem., *Jesus, Paul and the Law: Studies in Mark and Galatians* (Louisville: Westminster John Knox Press, 1990), 183–214.
— *The Theology of Paul's Letter to the Galatians* (Cambridge: Cambridge University Press, 1993).
— *The Theology of Paul the Apostle* (Edinburgh: T. & T. Clark, 1998).
— 'Works of the Law and the Curse of the Law (Gal. 3:10–14)', *New Testament Studies* 31 (1985), 523–542. Reprinted in idem., *Jesus, Paul and the Law: Studies in Mark and Galatians* (Louisville: Westminster John Knox Press, 1990), 215–241.
Ellis E.E., *Paul's Use of the Old Testament* (Edinburgh: Oliver and Boyd, 1957).
Esler, P.F., *Conflict and Identity in Romans: The Social Setting of Paul's Letter* (Minneapolis: Fortress Press, 2003).
Fung, R.Y.K., 'The Status of Justification by Faith in Paul's Thought: A Brief Survey of a Modern Debate', *Themelios* 6 (1980–81), 4–11.
Huang, P-h., et al., *Christian and Ancestor Worship* (in Chinese) (Taipei: Yah-ge, 1994).
Irvin, D.T. and S.W. Sunquist, *History of the World Christian Movement*, Vol. 1, 'Earliest Christianity to 1453' (New York: Orbis, 2001).
Jackson, J., 'Ancestral Worship' in *China Centenary Missionary Conference Records: Report of the Great Conference held at Shanghai, April 5th to May 8th, 1907*. Printed in Shanghai under the direction of the Conference Committee (New York: American Tract Society, 1907), 239–244.
Karris, R.J., 'Romans 14:1 – 15:13 and the Occasion of Romans', *Catholic Biblical Quarterly* 25 (1973), 155–178.
Käsemann, E., *Commentary on Romans* (London: SCM, 1982).
Kim, S., *Paul and the New Perspective: Second Thoughts on the Origin of Paul's Gospel* (Grand Rapids, Michigan: Eerdmans, 2002).
Kok, E.H.S., *The Truth of the Gospel: A Study in Galatians 2:15–21* (Hong Kong: Alliance Bible Seminary, 2000).
Kümmel, W.G., *Introduction to the New Testament* (London: SCM 1984).
Latourette, K.S., *A History of Christian Missions in China* (London: SPCK, 1929).
Lee, S.K., *The Cross and the Lotus* (Hong Kong: The Christian Study Centre on Chinese Religion and Culture, 1971).
Leung, K.-l., "Christianity and Chinese Ancestor Worship — Response from a Pastoral Perspective," (in Chinese) in F.-t. Ying (ed.), *Chinese Ancestor Worship*, (Hong Kong: Alliance Bible Seminary, 1997).
Lo, L.-k., 'Identity Crisis Reflected in Romans 14:1 – 15:13 and the Implications for the Chinese Christians' Controversy on Ancestral Worship', *Ching Feng: A Journal on Christianity and Chinese Religion and Culture* 3 (Fall, 2002), 23–59. Also, {http://www.vanderbilt.edu/AnS/religious_studies/SBL2002/home2002.htm}.
— *Paul's Purpose in Writing Romans: The Upbuilding of a Jewish and Gentile Christian Community in Rome* (Hong Kong: Alliance Bible Seminary, 1998).
— 'The Nature the Issue of Ancestral Worship among Chinese Christians', *Studies in World Christianity* 9.1 (2003), 30–42.
Martyn, J.L., *Galatians* (New York: Doubleday, 1997).

McGrath, A.E., *Iustitia Dei: A History of the Christian Doctrine of Justification* (Cambridge: Cambridge University Press, 1998).
Minear, P.S., *The Obedience of Faith: The Purpose of Paul in the Epistle to the Romans* (London: SCM, 1971).
Moffett, S.H., *A History of Christianity in Asia*, Vol. 1, 'Beginnings to 1500' (San Francisco: HarperCollins, 1991).
Moo, D.J., *The Epistle to the Romans* (Grand Rapids, Michigan: Eerdmans, 1996).
Morrison, R., 'Tombs of Ancestors', *Chinese Repository* 1.12 (April, 1833), 502.
— 'Worshipping at the Tombs', *Chinese Repository* 1.5 (September, 1832), 202.
Nababan, A.E.S., *Bekenntnis und Mission in Roemer 14 und 15: Eine exegetische Untesuchung* (unpublished doctoral dissertation: Heidelberg, 1962).
Nanos, M.D., *The Mystery of Romans: The Jewish Context of Paul's Letter* (Minneapolis: Fortress Press, 1996).
O'Brien, P.T., *Gospel and Mission in the Writings of Paul: An Exegetical and Theological Analysis* (Carlisle: Paternoster, 1993).
Rauer, M., 'Die "Schwachen" in Korinth und Rom', *Biblische Studien* 21 (1923), 1–192.
Rawski, J.W. and S. Evelyn (eds.), *Death Ritual in Late and Modern China* (Berkeley: University of California Press, 1990).
Reasoner, M., *The Strong and the Weak: Romans 14:1 – 15:13 in Context* (Cambridge: Cambridge University Press, 1999).
Records of the General Conference of the Protestant Missionaries of China, held at Shanghai, 1877 (Taipei: Cheng-wen, 1973 – a reprint of Shanghai: Presbyterian Mission Press, 1878).
Records of the General Conference of the Protestant Missionaries of China, held at Shanghai (Shanghai: American Presbyterian Press, 1890).
Saeki, P.Y., *The Nestorian Documents and Relics in China* (Tokyo: Maruzen, 1951).
— *The Nestorian Monument in China* (London: SPCK, 1966).
Sanders, E.P., *Paul and Palestinian Judaism* (London: SCM, 1977).
Schneider, N., *Die "Schwachen" in der christlichen Gemeinde Roms: Eine historisch-exegetische Untersuchung zu Roem 14:1 – 15:13* (unpublished doctoral dissertation: Kirchilche Hochschule Wuppertal, 1989).
Stanton, G., 'Paul's Gospel' in J.D.G. Dunn (ed.), *The Cambridge Companion to St. Paul*, (Cambridge: Cambridge University Press, 2003), 179–203).
Stendahl, K., 'The Apostle Paul and the Introspective Conscience of the West', *Harvard Theological Review* 56 (1963), 199–215. Reprinted in idem., *Paul Among Jews and Gentiles and other Essays* (Philadelphia: Fortress Press, 1983), 78–96.
Stuhlmacher, P., 'Paul: Apostate or Apostle?' in P. Lapide and P. Stuhlmacher (eds.), *Paul: Rabbi and Apostle* (Minneapolis: Augsburg Press, 1984), 11–30.
— *Revisiting Paul's Doctrine of Justification: A Challenge to the New Perspective* (Downers Grove: Inter-Varsity Press, 2001).
Watson, F., *Paul, Judaism and the Gentiles: A Sociological Approach* (Cambridge: Cambridge University Press, 1986).
Westerholm, S., *Perspectives Old and New on Paul: The 'Lutheran' Paul and His Critics* (Grand Rapids, Michigan: Eerdmans, 2004).
Wilckens, U., *Der Brief an die Roemer*, volume 3 (Zurich: Benziger Verlag, 1982).
Wu, C.S., *Nestorian in Tang China and Central Asia: A Cultural Study* (in Chinese) (unpublished Masters dissertation, Chung Chi College, Hong Kong, 1998).

Yang, C.K., *Religion in Chinese Society* (Berkeley, LA: University of California Press, 1961).
Yeo, K.-k., *Ancestor Worship: Rhetorical and Cross-Cultural Hermeneutical Response* (in Chinese) (Hong Kong: Chinese Christian Literature Council, 1996).
Ying, F.-t., 'Christianity and Chinese Ancestor Worship – A Historical Survey'(in Chinese) in F.-t. Ying (ed.), *Chinese Ancestor Worship* (Hong Kong: Alliance Bible Seminary, 1997).
— 'A Retrospect on Research of Chinese Ancestor Worship' (in Chinese) in idem. (ed.), *Chinese Ancestor Worship* (Hong Kong: Alliance Bible Seminary, 1997).

CHAPTER 10

Truth with a Mission – Reading All Scripture Missiologically

CHRISTOPHER J.H. WRIGHT

Introduction

I remember them so vividly from my childhood – the great banner texts around the walls of the missionary conventions in Northern Ireland where I would help my father at the stall of the Unevangelized Fields Mission, of which he was Irish Secretary after twenty years in Brazil. 'Go ye into all the world and preach the Gospel to every creature,' they urged me, along with other similar imperatives in glowing gothic calligraphy. By the age of twelve I could have quoted you all the key ones – 'Go ye therefore and make disciples', 'How shall they hear?', 'You shall be my witnesses ... to the ends of the earth', 'Whom shall we send? ... Here am I, send me.' I knew my missionary Bible verses. I had responded to many a rousing sermon on most of them.

By the age of twenty-one I had a degree in theology from Cambridge in which the same texts had been curiously lacking. At least, it is curious to me now. At the time there seemed to be little connection at all between theology and mission in the mind of the lecturers, or of myself, or, for all I knew, in the mind of God either. 'Theology' was all about God – what God was like, what God had said and done, and what mostly dead people had speculated on such questions. 'Mission' was about us, the living, and what we've been doing since Carey (who, of course, was the first missionary, we so erroneously thought). Or more precisely, mission is what we evangelicals do since we're the ones who know that the Bible has told us (or some of us, at least) to go and be missionaries.

'Mission is what we do.' That was the assumption, supported of course by clear biblical commands. 'Jesus sends me, this I know, for the Bible tells me so.' Many years later, including years when I was teaching theology myself as a missionary in India,[1] I found myself teaching a module called *The Biblical Basis of Mission* at All Nations Christian College – an international mission training institution. The module title itself embodies the same assumption. Mission is the noun, the given reality. It is something we do and we basically know what it is. And the reason why we know we should be doing it, the basis, foundation or grounds on which we justify it, must be found in the Bible. As good evangelicals we need a biblical basis for everything we do. What, then, is the biblical basis for mission? Roll out the texts. Add some that nobody else has thought of. Do some joined up theology. Add some motivational fervour. And the class is heart-warmingly appreciative. Now they have even more biblical support for what they already believed anyway, for these are All Nations students, after all. They only came because they are committed to doing mission.

This mild caricature is not in the least derogatory in intent. I believe passionately that mission is what we should be doing, and I believe the Bible endorses and mandates it. However, the more I taught that course, the more I used to introduce it by telling the students that I would like to rename it – from *The Biblical Basis of Mission* to *The Missional Basis of the Bible*. I wanted them to see, not just that the Bible contains a number of texts which happen to provide a rationale for missionary endeavour, but that *the whole Bible is itself a 'missional' phenomenon.*

The Bible as the Product of God's Mission

A missional hermeneutic of the Bible begins with the Bible's very existence. For those who affirm some relationship (however articulated), between these texts and the self-revelation of our creator God, the whole canon of scripture is a missional phenomenon in the sense that it witnesses to the self-giving movement of this God towards his creation and towards us, human beings in God's own image, but wayward and wanton. The writings, which now comprise our Bible, are themselves the product of, and witness to, the ultimate mission of God.

> The very existence of the Bible is incontrovertible evidence of the God who refused to forsake his rebellious creation, who refused to give up, who was and is determined to redeem and restore fallen creation to his original design for it. … The very existence of such a collection of writings testifies to a God who breaks through to human beings, who disclosed himself to them, who will not

---

[1] Another curious thought: I could have done precisely the same job in a college in England, but that would not have been considered 'mission'.

leave them unilluminated in their darkness ...who takes the initiative in re-establishing broken relationships with us.[2]

Furthermore, the processes by which these texts came to be written were often profoundly missional in nature. Many of them emerged out of events, or struggles, or crises, or conflicts, in which the people of God engaged with the constantly changing and challenging task of articulating and living out their understanding of God's revelation and redemptive action in the world. Sometimes these were struggles internal to the people of God themselves; sometimes they were highly polemical struggles with competing religious claims and worldviews that surrounded them.

So a missional reading of such texts is very definitely not a matter of, *first*, finding the 'real' meaning by objective exegesis, and only then, *secondly*, cranking up some 'missiological implications' as a homiletic supplement to the 'text itself'. Rather, it is to see how a text often has its origin in some issue, need, controversy or threat, which the people of God needed to address in the context of their mission. The text in itself is a product of mission in action.

This is easily demonstrated in the case of the New Testament.[3] Most of Paul's letters were written in the heat of his missionary efforts: wrestling with the theological basis of the inclusion of the gentiles; affirming the need for Jew and gentile to accept one another in Christ and in the church; tackling the baffling range of new problems that assailed young churches as the gospel took root in the world of Greek polytheism; confronting incipient heresies with clear affirmations of the supremacy and sufficiency of Jesus Christ, and so on.

And why were the Gospels so-called? Because they were written to explain the significance of the *evangel* – the good news about Jesus of Nazareth, especially his death and resurrection. Confidence in these things was essential to the missionary task of the expanding church. And the person to whom we owe the largest quantity of the New Testament, Luke, shapes his two volume work in such a way that the missionary mandate to the disciples to be Christ's

---

[2] C.R. Taber, 'Missiology and the Bible', *Missiology* 11 (1983), 232.

[3] Marion Soards surveys four current issues in New Testament studies (first-century Judaism, the life of Jesus, Pauline theology, and the character of the early church), and shows how they are relevant to mission studies also. But he concludes with a converse comment in line with the point being made here, 'Mission studies should remind biblical scholars that many of the writings that we study (often in painstaking and even painful detail) came to be because of the reality of mission. An awareness of, and a concern with, the key issues of mission studies may well help biblical studies find foci that will bring deeper appreciation of the meaning of the Bible' – M.L. Soards, 'Key Issues in Biblical Studies and Their Bearing on Mission Studies', *Missiology* 24 (1996), 107. With this I fully agree. Cf. also A.J. Koestenberger, 'The Place of Mission in New Testament Theology. An Attempt to Determine the Significance of Mission within the Scope of the New Testament's Message as a Whole', *Missiology* 27 (1999), and the works referred to there.

witnesses to the nations comes as the climax to volume one and the introduction to volume two.

But also in the case of the Old Testament we can see that many of these texts emerged out of the engagement of Israel with the surrounding world in the light of the God they knew in their history and in covenantal relationship. People produced texts in relation to what they believed God had done, was doing, or would do, in their world. The Torah records the exodus as an act of YHWH that comprehensively confronted and defeated the power of Pharaoh and all his rival claims to deity and allegiance. It presents a theology of creation that stands in sharp contrast to the polytheistic creation myths of Mesopotamia. The historical narratives portray the long and sorry story of Israel's struggle with the culture and religion of Canaan, a struggle reflected also in the pre-exilic prophets. Exilic and post-exilic texts emerge out of the task that the small remnant community of Israel faced to define their continuing identity as a community of faith in successive empires of varying hostility or tolerance. Wisdom texts interact with international wisdom traditions in the surrounding cultures, but do so with staunch monotheistic disinfectant. And in worship and prophecy, Israelites reflect on the relationship between their God, YHWH, and the rest of the nations – sometimes negatively, sometimes positively – and on the nature of their own role as YHWH's elect priesthood in their midst.

The Bible, then, is a missional phenomenon in itself. The writings which now comprise our Bible are themselves the product of, and witness to, the ultimate mission of God. The individual texts within it often reflect the struggles of being a people with a mission in a world of competing cultural and religious claims. And the canon eventually consolidates the recognition that it is through these texts that the people whom God has called to be his own (in both Testaments), has been shaped as a community of memory and hope, a community of mission, failure and striving.

In short, a missional hermeneutic proceeds from the assumption that the whole Bible renders to us the story of God's mission through God's people in their engagement with God's world for the sake of God's purpose for the whole of God's creation. Mission is not just one of a list of things that the Bible happens to talk about, only a bit more urgently than some. Mission is, in that much-abused phrase, 'what it's all about'.

Reading the Scriptures with the Risen Christ

Now to say, 'mission is what the Bible is all about', is a bold claim. I would not expect to be able to turn any phrase that began 'the biblical basis of...' around the other way. There is, for example, a biblical basis for marriage, but there is not, I presume, 'a marital basis for the Bible'. There is a biblical basis for work, but work is not 'what the Bible is all about'. However, I take some encouragement for my claim from an impeccable authority. It seems to me that Jesus comes very close to saying, 'This is what the Bible is all about', when he gave his disciples their final lecture in Old Testament hermeneutics. 'This is what is written,' he said. 'The Christ will suffer and rise from the dead on the third day, and repentance and forgiveness of sins will be preached in his name to all nations, beginning in Jerusalem' (Lk. 24:46–47).

Now Jesus is not quoting a specific text here, though we would love to have been able to ask which scriptures he particularly had in mind. (Doubtless, the two from Emmaus could have filled in the gaps). The point is that he includes the whole of this sentence under the heading, 'this is what is written'. He seems to be saying that the whole of the scripture (which we now know as the Old Testament) finds its focus and fulfilment *both* in the life and death and resurrection of Israel's Messiah *and* in the mission to all nations, which flows out from that event. Luke tells us that with these words Jesus 'opened their minds so they could understand the Scriptures'; or, as we might put it, he was setting their hermeneutical orientation and agenda. The proper way for disciples of Jesus of Nazareth (crucified and risen) to read their scriptures is *messianically* and *missiologically*.

Paul, though he was not present for the Old Testament hermeneutics lecture on the day of resurrection, clearly had his own way of reading his scriptures radically transformed in exactly the same way with the same double focus. Testifying before Festus he declares, 'I am saying nothing beyond what the prophets and Moses said would happen – that the Messiah would suffer and, as the first to rise from the dead, would proclaim light *to his own people and to the nations'* (Acts 26:22–23). It was this dual understanding of the scriptures which had then shaped Paul's whole CV as the apostle of the Messiah Jesus to the gentiles.

On the whole, evangelicals have been good at the former (messianic reading of the Old Testament), but inadequate with the latter (missiological reading of it). We read the Old Testament messianically in the light of Jesus, in the sense of finding in it a whole messianic theology and eschatology which we see as fulfilled in Jesus. In doing so we follow his own example, of course, and that of his first followers and the authors of the gospels. But what we have so often failed to do is to go beyond the mere satisfaction of ticking off so-called messianic predictions that have 'been fulfilled'. And we have failed to go further because we have not grasped the missiological significance of the Messiah.

The Messiah was the promised one who would embody in his own person the identity and mission of Israel, as their representative, king, leader and saviour. Through the Messiah as his anointed agent, Yahweh the God of Israel would bring about all that he intended for Israel. But what was that mission of Israel? Nothing less than to be 'a light to the nations', the means of bringing the redemptive blessing of God to all the nations of the world, as originally promised in the title deeds of the covenant with Abraham. For the God of Israel is also the creator God of all the world. Through the Messiah, therefore, the God of Israel would also bring about all that he intended for the nations. The eschatological redemption and restoration of Israel would issue in the ingathering of the nations. The full meaning of recognizing Jesus as Messiah, then, lies in recognizing also his role in relation to the mission of Israel for the sake of the nations. Hence, a messianic reading of the Old Testament has to flow on to a missiological reading – which is precisely the connection that Jesus makes in Luke 24.

However, even if we accept that Jesus offers us a messiah-focused and mission-generating hermeneutic of the scriptures, we may still query the claim that somehow there is a missional hermeneutic of the whole Bible such that 'mission is what it's all about'. This uneasiness stems from the persistent, almost subconscious paradigm that mission is fundamentally 'something we do'. This is especially so if we fall into the evangelical reductionist habit of using the word 'mission' or 'missions' as more or less synonymous with evangelism. Quite clearly the whole Bible is not just 'about evangelism', even though evangelism is certainly a fundamental part of biblical mission as entrusted to us. Evangelism *is* something we do and it *is* validated by clear biblical imperatives. The appropriateness of speaking of 'a missional basis of the Bible' becomes apparent only when we shift our paradigm of mission from *our* human agency to the ultimate purposes of *God* himself. For clearly the Bible is, in some sense, 'all about God'. What, then, does it mean to talk of the mission of God?

Whose Mission is it Anyway?

GOD WITH A MISSION

Though the phrase *Missio Dei* has been misused in some theology virtually to exclude evangelism, it does express a major biblical truth. The God revealed in the scriptures is personal, purposeful and goal orientated. The opening account of creation portrays God working towards a goal, completing it with satisfaction and resting, content with the result. And from the great promise of God to Abraham in Genesis 12:1–3 we know this God to be totally, covenantally, eternally committed to the mission of blessing the nations through the agency of the people of Abraham. From that point on, the mission of God could be summed up in the words of the hymn, 'God is working his purpose out as year succeeds to year', and as generations come and go.

The Bible presents itself to us fundamentally as a narrative, a historical narrative at one level, but a grand, meta-narrative at another. It begins with a God of purpose in creation; moves on to the conflict and problem generated by human rebellion against that purpose; spends most of its narrative journey in the story of God's redemptive purposes being worked out on the stage of human history and finishes beyond the horizon of its own history with the eschatological hope of a new creation. This has often been presented as a four-point narrative – creation, fall, redemption and future hope. This world-view is predicated on teleological monotheism – that is, there is one God at work in the universe and in human history, and that God has a goal, a purpose, a mission which will ultimately be accomplished by the power of his word and for the glory of his name. This is the mission of the biblical God.

To read the whole Bible in the light of this great over-arching perspective of the mission of God is to read 'with the grain' of this whole collection of scriptures that constitute our canon. This foundational point is a key assumption of 'a missiological hermeneutic' of the Bible. It is nothing more than to accept that the biblical worldview locates us in the midst of a narrative of the universe behind which stands the mission of the living God. All creation will render 'glory to the Father and to the Son and to the Holy Spirit, as it was in the beginning, is now, and ever shall be'. That is a missional perspective.

HUMANITY WITH A MISSION

On the day of their creation, human beings were given their mission on the planet so purposefully prepared for their arrival – the mandate to fill the earth and subdue it and to rule over the rest of creation (Gen. 1:28). This delegated authority within the created order is moderated by the parallel commands in the complementary account, 'to serve and to keep' the garden (Gen. 2:15). The care and keeping of creation is our human mission. We are on the planet with a purpose that flows from the creative purpose of God himself. Out of this understanding of our humanity (which is also teleological, like our doctrine of God) flows our ecological responsibility, our economic activity involving work, productivity, exchange and trade, and the whole cultural mandate.

To be human is to have a purposeful role in God's creation. In relation to that creational mission, Christians need to be reminded that God holds us accountable to himself for our humanity as much as for our Christianity. There is, therefore, a legitimate place for ecological concern and action, for biblical earth-keeping, within our understanding of Christian mission responsibility – on the assumption that Christians too are humans made in the image of God (indeed being restored even more fully to that humanity in Christ), who have not been given some privileged exemption from the mission God entrusted to our whole species. This ecological dimension of our mission flows not only from creation, but also reflects an eschatological perspective. The biblical vision is of a new creation, of which Christ is the heir. Our care for the earth is an expression of our understanding of its future as well as its origin (similarly to our concern for the human person).

ISRAEL WITH A MISSION

Against the background of human sin and rebellion, described in the bleak narratives of Genesis 3 – 11, running from the disobedience of Adam and Eve to the building of the tower of Babel, God initiates his redemptive mission of blessing the nations of humanity, beginning with the call of Abraham in Genesis 12. This is the essential missional purpose of God's election of Israel.

Israel came into existence as a people with a mission entrusted from God for the sake of the rest of the nations. All that Israel was, or was supposed to be – all that Yahweh their God did in them, for them and through them – was ultimately linked to this wider purpose of God for the nations.

A missiological hermeneutic of the Old Testament, in its redemptive dimension, centres around this point. Israel's election was not a rejection of other nations but was explicitly for the sake of all nations. This universality of God's purpose that embraces the particularity of God's chosen means is a recurrent theme. Though not always explicitly present, it is never far from the surface of the way in which scripture portrays Israel's intended self-understanding. We shall explore this missiological reading of the Old Testament more fully below.

JESUS WITH A MISSION

Jesus did not just arrive. He had a very clear conviction that he was sent. But even before Jesus was old enough to have clear convictions about anything, his significance was recognized. Just as Luke ends his gospel with the double significance of Jesus for Israel and for the world, so also right at the start he makes the same connection. It is there in the words of recognition spoken by Simeon as he cradled the infant Jesus, words appreciated by generations of Anglicans for their evening beauty in the *Nunc dimittis,* but rarely recognized for the missiological significance of their double messianic claim, 'Lord now let your servant depart in peace, according to your word. For my eyes have seen your salvation, which you have prepared in the sight of *all people*, to be a light for revelation to *the nations* and for glory to your people *Israel*' (Lk. 2:29–32).

It was at his baptism that Jesus receives an affirmation of his true identity and mission. The voice of his Father at his baptism combined the identity of the Servant figure in Isaiah (echoing the phraseology of Is. 42:1), and that of the Davidic messianic king (echoing the affirmation of Ps. 2:7). Both of these dimensions of his identity and role were energized with a sense of mission. The mission of the Servant was both to restore Israel to Yahweh and also to be the agent of God's salvation reaching to the ends of the earth (Is. 49:6). The mission of the Davidic messianic king was both to rule over a redeemed Israel according to the agenda of many prophetic texts, and also to receive the nations and the ends of the earth as his heritage (Ps. 2:8)

Jesus' sense of mission (the aims, motivation and self-understanding behind his recorded words and actions) has been a matter of intense scholarly discussion. What seems very clear is that Jesus built his own agenda on what he perceived to be the agenda of his Father. His will was to do his Father's will. God's mission determined his. In the obedience of Jesus, even to death, the mission of God reached its climax.

THE CHURCH WITH A MISSION

As our quotation of Luke 24 above indicated, Jesus entrusted to the church a mission which is directly rooted in his own identity, passion and victory as the crucified and risen Messiah. Jesus immediately followed the text quoted with the words, 'You are witnesses' – a mandate repeated in Acts 1:8, 'You will be my witnesses.' It is almost certain that Luke intends us to hear in this an echo of the same words spoken by Yahweh to Israel in Isaiah 43:10–12.

> You are my witnesses, declares the LORD, and my servant whom I have chosen,
> So that you may know and believe me and understand that I am he.
> Before me no god was formed nor will there be one after me.
> I, even I, am the LORD, and apart from me there is no saviour.
> I have revealed and saved and proclaimed – I, and not some foreign god among you.
> You are my witnesses, declares the LORD, that I am God.

Israel knew the identity of the true and living God; therefore they were entrusted with bearing witness to that in a world of nations and their gods. The disciples know the true identity of the crucified and risen Jesus; therefore they are entrusted with bearing witness to that to the ends of the earth. Mission flows from the identity of God and his Christ.

Paul goes further and identifies the mission of his own small band of church planters with the international mission of the Servant, quoting Isaiah 49:6 in Acts 13:47 and saying quite bluntly, '[T]his is what the Lord has commanded *us*: "I have made you a light for the nations, that you may bring salvation to the ends of the earth".'[4] So again, the mission of the church flows from the mission of God and the fulfilment of his purposes and his word. It is not so much, as someone has said, that God has a mission for his church in the world, as that God has a church for his mission in the world. Mission is not just something we do (though it certainly includes that). Mission, from the point of view of our human endeavour, means the committed participation of God's people in the purposes of God for the redemption of the whole creation. Mission, like salvation, belongs to our God and to the Lamb. We are those who are called to share in its accomplishment.

Putting these perspectives together, then, and summarizing what I have said above, a missiological hermeneutic means that we seek to read any part of the Bible,

---

[4] A missiological hermeneutic of the Old Testament if ever there was one! As the NIV footnote shows, Paul has no problem applying the singular 'you' – which was spoken to the Servant – to the plural 'us'.

- in the light of God's purpose for his whole creation, including the redemption of humanity and the creation of the new heavens and new earth;
- in the light of God's purpose for human life in general on the planet, and of all the Bible teaches about human culture, relationships, ethics and behaviour;
- in the light of God's historical election of Israel, their identity and role in relation to the nations, and the demands he made on their worship, social ethics and total value system;
- in the light of the centrality of Jesus of Nazareth, his messianic identity and mission in relation to Israel and the nations, his cross and resurrection;
- in the light of God's calling of the church, the community of believing Jews and gentiles who constitute the extended people of the Abraham covenant, to be the agent of God's blessing to the nations in the name and for the glory of the Lord Jesus Christ.

A Missiological Perspective on the Old Testament

Evangelical Christians have traditionally had less of a problem reading the New Testament from a missional angle, which is hardly surprising given the dominance within the New Testament of the apostle Paul and his missionary travels and writings. So in the rest of this essay I want to focus on how the above proposals can help us to develop a missiological reading of the Old Testament.

Certainly, *preaching* mission from the Old Testament usually rouses people's curiosity, mainly because it is unexpected. Many people, in my frequent experience, are surprised to hear a sermon on mission based on a text from the Old Testament. 'Mission' is widely viewed as a task originating from some words of Jesus on the Mount of Ascension. It seems to involve sending off somewhat peculiar but doubtless very worthy people to far-off parts of the earth to work for God in a bewildering variety of ways, and then to return from time to time to tell us about their adventures and ask for continued support. Since nothing of that sort seems to have happened in the Old Testament (not even Jonah came home on furlough to raise funds for a return trip to Nineveh), mission is deemed 'missing – presumed unborn' in that era.

A more sophisticated form of such a caricature is to be found in the way David Bosch in his magisterial survey, *Transforming Mission*, relegates the Old Testament's contribution on mission to a sub-section of a chapter entitled 'Reflections on the New Testament as a Missionary Document'.[5] The Old

---

[5] David Bosch, *Transforming Mission* (Maryknoll, 1991). The relevant words are, 'There is, in the Old Testament, no indication of the believers of the old covenant being sent by God to cross geographical, religious, and social frontiers in order to win others

Testament certainly provides essential theological preparation for the emerging mission of the New Testament church, but Bosch defines mission in terms of crossing barriers for the sake of the gospel (barriers of geography, culture, language, religion, and so on.). Since Israel received no mandate to *go to* the nations in that sense, in Bosch's view, there is no mission in the Old Testament.

Apart from observing that in fact there are many 'barrier-crossing' episodes in the grand Old Testament story of Israel's journey with Yahweh which are worthy of missiological reflection, I would argue that Bosch has defined mission too narrowly. What follows is a brief survey of some of the key Old Testament themes, which contribute to the broadening of the idea of mission which I have argued for above. This is, to be clear once again, not a search for bits of the Old Testament that might say something relevant to our narrowed concept of sending missionaries, but rather a sketch of some of the great trajectories of Israel's understanding of their God and his mission through them and for the world. We are not concerned about how the Old Testament gives incidental support to what we already do, but with the theology that under-girds the whole worldview that Christian mission assumes.

What we will merely sketch below are the missiological implications of four major pillars of Old Testament faith – monotheism, election, ethics and eschatology. A great deal more could be fruitfully explored in the same way.

THE UNIQUENESS AND UNIVERSALITY OF YAHWEH

According to the Old Testament texts, the faith of Israel made remarkable affirmations about Yahweh, affirmations which had a polemical edge in their own context and still stand as distinctive claims. Among them are the declaration that Yahweh alone is God and there is no other (e.g. Deut. 4:35,39). As sole deity, it is Yahweh, therefore, who owns the world and runs the world (Deut. 10:14,27; Ps. 24:1; Jer. 27:1–12; 1 Chron. 29:11). This ultimately means the radical displacement of all other rival gods and that Yahweh is God over the whole earth and all nations (e.g. Ps. 96; Jer. 10:1–16; Is. 43:9–13; 44:6–20). The impact of these claims is felt in such widely varying contexts as the struggle against idolatry, the language of worship, and the response to other nations, both in their own contemporary international history, and in eschatological vision.

There is no doubt that the strength of the Old Testament affirmations about the uniqueness and universality of Yahweh as God underlie, and indeed provide some of the vocabulary for, the New Testament affirmations about the uniqueness and universality of Jesus (cf. Phil. 2:9–11, based on Is. 45:23; and 1 Cor. 8:5–6, based on Deut. 6:4). It is also note-worthy that these early Christian affirmations were equally polemical in their own historical context as those of ancient Israel and in turn provided the primary rationale and motivation for

---

to faith in Yahweh. ... Even so, the Old Testament is fundamental to the understanding of mission in the New' (17).

Christian mission. We are dealing here with the missiological implications of biblical monotheism.

A fully biblical understanding of the universality and uniqueness of Yahweh and of Jesus Christ stands in the frontline of a missiological response to the relativism at the heart of religious pluralism and some forms of postmodernist philosophy.

YAHWEH'S ELECTION OF ISRAEL FOR THE PURPOSE OF BLESSING THE NATIONS

The Old Testament begins on the stage of universal history. After the accounts of creation we read the story of God's dealings with fallen humanity and the problem and challenge of the world of the nations (Gen. 1 – 11). After the stories of the flood and of the tower of Babel, could there be any future for the nations in relation to God? Or would judgement have to be God's final word?

The story of Abraham, beginning in Genesis 12, gives a clear answer. God's declared commitment is that he intends to bring blessing to the nations – 'all the families of the earth will be blessed through you' (Gen. 12:3). Repeated six times in Genesis alone, this key affirmation is the foundation of biblical mission, inasmuch as it presents the mission of God. The creator God has a purpose, a goal, and it is nothing less than blessing the nations of humanity. So fundamental is this divine agenda that Paul defines the Genesis declaration as 'the gospel in advance' (Gal. 3:8). And the concluding vision of the whole Bible signifies the fulfilment of the Abrahamic promise, as people from every nation, tribe, language and people are gathered among the redeemed in the new creation (Rev. 7:9). The gospel and mission both begin in Genesis, then, and both are located in the redemptive intention of the Creator to bless the nations. Mission is God's address to the problem of fractured humanity. And God's mission is universal in its ultimate goal and scope.

The same Genesis texts which affirm the universality of God's mission to bless the nations also, and with equal strength, affirm the particularity of God's election of Abraham and his descendants to be the vehicle of that mission. The election of Israel is assuredly one of the most fundamental pillars of the biblical worldview, and of Israel's historical sense of identity.[6] It is vital to insist that although the belief in their election could be (and was) distorted into a narrow doctrine of national superiority, that move was resisted in Israel's own literature (e.g. Deut. 7:7ff.). The affirmation is that Yahweh, the God who had chosen Israel, was also the creator, owner and Lord of the whole world (Deut. 10:14f., cf. Ex. 19:4–6). That is, he was not just 'their God' – he was God of all (as Paul hammers home in Rom. 4). Yahweh had chosen Israel in relation to his purpose for the world, not just for Israel. The election of Israel was not

---

[6] This has been shown very clearly, and in a way which underlines its importance for the whole mission of the biblical God through the people of God for the world, in the works of N.T. Wright, especially his *New Testament and the People of God* (London, 1992), 244–79, and *Jesus and the Victory of God* (London, 1996).

tantamount to a rejection of the nations, but explicitly for their ultimate benefit. If we might paraphrase John, in a way he would probably have accepted, 'God so loved the world that he chose Israel.'

Thus, rather than asking if Israel itself 'had a mission', in the sense of being 'sent' anywhere (anachronistically injecting our 'sending missionaries' paradigm again), we need to see the missional nature of Israel's existence in relation to the mission of God in the world. Israel's mission was to be something, not to go somewhere. This perspective is clearly focused in the person of the Servant of Yahweh, who both embodies the election of Israel (identical things are said about Israel and the Servant), and also is charged with the mission (like Israel's) of bringing the blessing of Yahweh's justice, salvation and glory to the ends of the earth.

THE ETHICAL DIMENSION OF ISRAEL'S 'VISIBILITY' AMONG THE NATIONS

Naturally, then, there is an enormous amount of interest in the Old Testament around the way in which Israel related to the nations. It is far from being a simple relationship. On the one hand, there is the ultimate vision of Israel being a blessing to the nations. On the other hand, there is the calling for Israel to be separate from them, to resist their idolatry, to avoid their wickedness, to reject their gods and their ways. At the same time, Israel was a nation among other nations in the broad sweep of Ancient Near Eastern macro-culture, and so there is considerable missiological interest in the variety of ways in which the faith of Israel related positively and negatively to the cultures of other nations over the centuries. For example, we could give much more missiological attention to the different responses of the patriarchal narratives to their surrounding culture; of the Deuteronomic materials to Canaanite culture; of the prophets to the relationship between Israel's experiment with royalty (king and Temple) and Canaanite parallels; of the exilic and post-exilic communities to the world of Mesopotamian and Persian religion and culture; and these are just some of the possibilities.[7]

The major point of interest here is, in its shortest expression, the missiological dimension of Israel's holiness. Israel was called to be distinctive from the surrounding world in ways that were not merely religious but also ethical. This is expressed as the very purpose of their election in relation to God's promise to bless the nations in Genesis 18:19. In the context of, and in stark contrast to, the world of Sodom and Gomorrah, Yahweh says of Abraham, 'I have chosen him so that he will direct his children and his household after him to keep the way of the LORD by doing what is right and just, so that the LORD will bring about for Abraham what he has promised him.' This verse, in

---

[7] Walter Brueggemann is one of very few Old Testament scholars who have given serious and detailed attention to the nations as a theological reality in the Old Testament. See W. Brueggemann, *Theology of the Old Testament: Testimony, Dispute, Advocacy* (Minneapolis, 1997), 492–527.

a remarkably tight syntax, binds together election, ethics and mission as three interlocking aspects of God's purpose. His choice of Abraham is for the sake of his promise (to bless the nations); but the accomplishment of that demands the ethical obedience of his community – the fulcrum in the middle of the verse.

Later, covenantal obedience is not only based on Israel's historical redemption out of Egypt, but also linked to their identity and role as a priestly and holy people in the midst of the nations in Exodus 19:4–6. As Yahweh's priesthood, Israel would be the means by which God would be known to the nations and the means of bringing them to God (performing a function analogous to the role of Israel's own priests between God and the rest of the people). As a holy people, they would be ethically (as well as ritually) distinctive from the practices of surrounding nations. The moral and practical dimensions of such holy distinctiveness are spelled out in Leviticus 18 – 19. Such visibility would be a matter of observation and comment among the nations, and that expectation in itself was a strong motivation for keeping the law (Deut. 4:6–8). The question of Israel's ethical obedience or ethical failure was not merely a matter between themselves and Yahweh, but was of major significance in relation to Yahweh's agenda for the nations (cf. Jer. 4:1–2).

This missiological perspective on Old Testament ethics seems to me a fruitful approach to the age-old hermeneutical debate over whether and how the moral teaching given to Israel in the Old Testament (especially the law), has any authority or relevance to Christians. If, as I believe, it was given in order to shape Israel to be what they were called to be – a light to the nations, a holy priesthood – then it has a paradigmatic relevance to those who, in Christ, have inherited the same role in relation to the nations. In the Old as well as the New Testament, the ethical demand on those who claim to be God's people is determined by the mission with which they have been entrusted.

ESCHATOLOGICAL VISION – THE INGATHERING OF NATIONS

Israel saw the nations (including themselves) as being subject to the sovereign rule of God in history – whether in judgement or in mercy. This is a dimension of the Old Testament faith that we need to get our minds around, since it does not sit very congenially with our tendency to a very individualistic and pietistic form of spirituality (cf. Jer. 18:1–10; Jonah). But Israel also thought of the nations as 'spectators' of all God's dealings with Israel – whether positively or negatively. That is, whether on the receiving end of God's deliverance or of the blows of his judgement, Israel lived on an open stage and the nations would draw their conclusions (Ex. 15:15; Deut. 9:28; Ezek. 36:16–23).

Eventually, however, and in a rather mysterious way, the nations could be portrayed as the beneficiaries of all that God had done in and for Israel, and even invited to rejoice, applaud and praise Yahweh the God of Israel (Ps. 47; 1 Kgs. 8:41–43; Ps. 67). And, most remarkable of all, Israel came to entertain the eschatological vision that there would be those of the nations who would not merely be joined to Israel, but would come to be identified as Israel, with the same names, privileges and responsibilities before God (Ps. 47:9; Is. 19:19–25; 56:2–8; 66:19–21; Zech. 2:10–11; Amos 9:11–12).[8]

These texts are quite breathtaking in their universal scope. This is the dimension of Israel's prophetic heritage that most profoundly influenced the theological explanation and motivation of the gentile mission in the New Testament. It certainly underlies James's interpretation of the Christ-event and the success of the gentile mission in Acts 15 (quoting Amos 9:12). And it likewise inspired Paul's efforts as a practitioner and theologian of mission (e.g. Rom. 15:7–16). And, as we saw earlier, it provided the theological shape for the gospels, all of which conclude with their various forms of the great commission – the sending of Jesus' disciples into the world of nations.

And finally, of course, we cannot omit the even wider vision that not only the nations, but also the whole creation will be included in God's purposes of redemption. For this God of Israel, of the nations, and of the world, declares himself to be creating a new heavens and a new earth, with a picture of a redeemed humanity living in safety, harmony and environmental peace within a renewed creation. Again, this is a portrait enthusiastically endorsed in the New Testament and sustains our hope today (Ps. 96:11–13; Is. 65:17–25; Rom. 8:18–21; 2 Pet. 3:13; Rev. 21:1–5).

Conclusion

Much more could be said, taking up other major themes of the Old Testament and reading them from the perspective of the missional purpose of God for his people and his world. From this angle, also, individual stories, events, persons, institutions come to have an added significance. At least I trust this sketch may have touched on some of what Jesus had in mind when he asserted that the mission of bringing the good news of repentance and forgiveness in his name to the nations is nothing less than what is written in the scriptures that pointed to himself.

It is a pleasure for me to offer this small contribution to John Olley, in recognition of his strong interest in applied and missiological reading of the Old Testament

Bibliography (for further reading on the Bible and Mission)

Ådna, J. and H. Kvalbein (eds.), *The Mission of the Early Church to Jews and Gentiles* (Tübingen: Mohr Siebeck, 2000).

Bauckham, R., *Bible and Mission: Christian Witness in a Postmodern World* (Carlisle: Paternoster / Grand Rapids: Baker, 2003).

— *God Crucified* (Carlisle: Paternoster / Grand Rapids: Eerdmans, 1999).

---

[8] See Acts 15:16–18; Eph. 2:11 – 3:6.

Beeby, H.D., 'A Missional Approach to Renewed Interpretation' in C. Bartholomew, C. Greene and K. Moeller (eds.), *Renewing Biblical Interpretation* (Carlisle: Paternoster / Grand Rapids: Zondervan, 2000), 268–283.
— *Canon and Mission* (Harrisburg, Pennsylvania: Trinity Press, 1999).
Billington, A., A.N.S. Lane, and M.M.W. Turner (eds.), *Mission and Meaning: Essays Presented to Peter Cotterell* (Carlisle: Paternoster, 1995).
Blauw, J., *The Missionary Nature of the Church* (New York: McGraw Hill, 1962).
Bosch, D.J., 'Hermeneutical Principles in the Biblical Foundation for Mission', *Evangelical Review of Theology* 17 (1993), 437–451.
— *Transforming Mission: Paradigm Shifts in the Theology of Mission* (Maryknoll, New York: Orbis, 1991).
Briggs, R.S., 'The Uses of Speech-Act Theory in Biblical Interpretation', *Currents in Theology and Mission* 9 (2001), 229–276.
Brownson, J.V., 'Speaking the Truth in Love: Elements of a Missional Hermeneutic' in G.R. Hunsberger and C. Van Gelder (eds.), *The Church between Gospel and Culture* (Grand Rapids, Michigan: Eerdmans, 1996), 228–259.
— *Speaking the Truth in Love: New Testament Resources for a Missional Hermeneutic* (Harrisburg, Pennsylvania: Trinity Press, 1998).
Brueggemann, W., *Theology of the Old Testament: Testimony, Dispute, Advocacy* (Minneapolis: Fortress, 1997).
Burnett, D., *God's Mission, Healing the Nations* (Carlisle: Paternoster, 1996).
Filbeck, D., *Yes, God of the Gentiles Too: The Missionary Message of the Old Testament* (Wheaton: Billy Graham Centre, Wheaton College, 1994).
Franks, M., 'Election, Pluralism, and the Missiology of Scripture in a Postmodern Age', *Missiology* 26 (1998), 329–343.
Goerner, H.C., *Thus It Is Written* (Nashville: Broadman Press, 1971).
Groot, A. de, 'One Bible and Many Interpretive Contexts: Hermeneutics in Missiology' in A. Camps, L.A. Hoedemaker and M.R. Spindler (eds.), *Missiology: An Ecumenical Introduction* (Grand Rapids, Michigan: Eerdmans, 1995).
Hedlund, R., *The Mission of the Church in the World* (Grand Rapids: Baker, 1991).
Hesselgrave, D.J., 'A Missionary Hermeneutic: Understanding Scripture in the Light of World Mission', *International Journal of Frontier Missions* 10 (1993), 17–20.
Hoedemaker, L.A., 'The People of God and the Ends of the Earth' in A. Camps, L.A. Hoedemaker and M.R. Spindler (eds.), *Missiology: An Ecumenical Introduction* (Grand Rapids, Michigan: Eerdmans, 1995).
Jenkins, P., *The Next Christendom: The Coming of Global Christianity* (Oxford: Oxford University Press, 2002).
Kaiser Jr., W.C., *Mission in the Old Testament: Israel as a Light to the Nations* (Grand Rapids, Michigan: Baker, 2000).
Kirk, J.A., *What Is Mission? Theological Explorations* (London: Darton, Longman and Todd / Minneapolis: Fortress Press, 1999).
Koestenberger, A.J., 'The Place of Mission in New Testament Theology: An Attempt to Determine the Significance of Mission within the Scope of the New Testament's Message as a Whole', *Missiology* 27 (1999), 347–362.
— and P.T. O'Brien, *Salvation to the Ends of the Earth: A Biblical Theology of Mission* (Leicester: Apollos, 2001).
LaGrand, J., *The Earliest Christian Mission to 'All Nations' in the Light of Matthew's Gospel* (Grand Rapids, Michigan: Eerdmans, 1995).

Le Grys, A., *Origins of the Mission of the Early Church* (London: SPCK, 1999).
Martin-Achard, R., *A Light to the Nations: A Study of the Old Testament Conception of Israel's Mission to the World* (J.P. Smith (tr.), Edinburgh and London: Oliver & Boyd, 1962).
Middleton, J. R. and B.J. Walsh, *Truth Is Stranger Than It Used to Be: Biblical Faith in a Postmodern Age* (London: SPCK / Downers Grove: Inter-Varsity Press, 1995).
Patrick, D., *The Rendering of God in the Old Testament* (Philadelphia: Fortress, 1981).
Ridder, R.R. de, *Discipling the Nations* (Grand Rapids, Michigan: Baker, 1975).
Rowley, H.H., *The Missionary Message of the Old Testament* (London: Carey Press, 1944).
Scobie, C.H.H., 'Israel and the Nations: An Essay in Biblical Theology', *Tyndale Bulletin* 43 (1992), 283–305.
Senior, D. and C. Stuhlmueller, *The Biblical Foundations for Mission* (London: SCM, 1983).
Soards, M.L., 'Key Issues in Biblical Studies and Their Bearing on Mission Studies', *Missiology* 24 (1996), 93–109.
Spindler, M.R., 'The Biblical Grounding and Orientation of Mission' in A. Camps, L.A. Hoedemaker and M.R. Spindler, *Missiology: An Ecumenical Introduction* (Grand Rapids, Michigan: Eerdmans, 1995), 123–143.
Stott, J., *The Contemporary Christian: An Urgent Plea for Double Listening* (Leicester: Inter-Varsity Press, 1992).
Taber, C.R., 'Missiology and the Bible', *Missiology* 11 (1983), 229–245.
Van Engen, C., 'The Relation of Bible and Mission in Mission Theology' in C. Van Engen, D.S. Gilliland and P. Piersonn (eds.), *The Good News of the Kingdom* (Maryknoll, New York: Orbis, 1993), 27–36.
Walls, A.F., *The Missionary Movement in Christian History: Studies in the Transmission of Faith* (Maryknoll: Orbis / Edinburgh: T. & T. Clark, 1996).
Wright, C.J.H., 'Christ and the Mosaic of Pluralisms: Challenges to Evangelical Missiology in the 21st Century' in W.D. Taylor (ed.), *Global Missiology for the 21st Century: The Iguassu Dialogue* (Grand Rapids, Michigan: Baker, 2000), 71–99.
— 'Covenant: God's Mission through God's People' in J.A. Grant and A.I Wilson (eds.), *The God of Covenant* (Leicester: Inter-Varsity Press, 2005), 54–78.
— 'Future Trends in Mission' in C. Bartholomew, R. Parry and A. West (eds.), *The Futures of Evangelicalism: Issues and Prospects* (Leicester: Inter-Varsity Press, 2003), 149–163.
— 'Mission as a Matrix for Hermeneutics and Biblical Theology' in C. Bartholomew, et al. (eds.), *Out of Egypt: Biblical Theology and Biblical Interpretation* (Carlisle: Paternoster / Grand Rapids, Michigan: Zondervan, 2004), 102–143.
— *Old Testament Ethics for the People of God* (Leicester: Inter-Varsity Press, 2004).
— *Walking in the Ways of the Lord: The Ethical Authority of the Old Testament* (Leicester: Inter-Varsity Press, 1995).
Wright, N.T., *Jesus and the Victory of God* (London: SPCK, 1996).
— *New Testament and the People of God* (London: SPCK, 1992)

CHAPTER 11

A Trinitarian Perspective on the Destiny of the Unevangelized

HAYDN D. NELSON

Introduction

It has been a privilege to be both a student and friend of John Olley and to know the extent of his interest in and passion for the Scriptures and for mission. This essay is presented both as a recognition of that interest and passion, and as a token of gratitude for John's impact upon my own life and ministry.

The destiny of the unevangelized has remained a question of perennial interest throughout the history of the Christian church and continues to be one of the most perplexing and provocative theological and missional issues facing it today.[1] Stated simply, this question concerns itself with the salvific status before God of human beings who, during their individual lifetimes and seemingly through no fault of their own, have never had the opportunity of hearing the name of Jesus Christ or of responding to the gospel (*euangelion*). Indeed, we should not be surprised at the interest this question engenders for it stands connected with the heart of Christian faith in that it is concerned with the action of the triune God in history, pre-eminently in the life, death and resurrection of Jesus Christ, and the offer of salvation that is found in him. As such, 'this question is not a piece of irrelevant theological abstraction or obscurantism'[2] but does in fact raise profound and searching questions concerning the efficacy and accessibility of this salvation and, most importantly, the nature of the God who offers it.

Although we should recognize the significant philosophical questions intrinsic to the question of the unevangelized, the intention of this essay is to approach it from a distinctively theological perspective – that of the doctrine of the Trinity. Certainly, it would not perhaps be overstating the matter to say that,

---

[1] M.J. Erickson, 'The Fate of Those Who Never Hear', *BSac* 152/605 (1995), 3–15; J. Sanders, 'The Perennial Problem', *CT* 34 (1990), 20–21.

[2] D. Strange, *The Possibility of Salvation Among the Unevangelised* (Carlisle, 2001), 20.

in recent years, there has been somewhat of a revival of interest in trinitarian theology.[3] However, what is of particular interest to our present discussion is that trinitarian concepts and images are being increasingly utilized as a way of explicating and illuminating what O'Donnell calls the 'God-world relation' and to explore the question that he himself puts, 'Is a trinitarian perspective the one which ultimately renders this relationship intelligible?'[4]

Though there are grounds for being appropriately cautious concerning the limits of trinitarian thought as a paradigm for interpreting other theological issues,[5] there would nevertheless appear to be some truth in Schwöbel's comment that 'it is difficult to point to any one area of theological reflection that is not potentially affected by being viewed from a trinitarian perspective'.[6] To that end, this essay will investigate how and to what extent a consideration of God as triune may inform or illuminate the question of the unevangelized. My fundamental thesis is that, although the destiny of the unevangelized is a question in relation to which we should remain to some extent agnostic, a consideration of it from a trinitarian perspective does provide some legitimate grounds for optimism.

The Appropriateness of Partial Agnosticism

A CONTINUUM OF POSITIONS ON THE UNEVANGELIZED

As the Christian church has addressed the question of the unevangelized, a number of broad positions have emerged, along with the inevitable positions of varying degrees between each.[7] In very general terms, each of these positions can arguably be placed on a continuum ranging from extreme exclusivism through to extreme inclusivism and, for the sake of clarity, can be briefly defined. At one end of the continuum is *Exclusivism* that affirms the exclusivity of the gospel in that salvation necessarily only comes to those who have overtly or explicitly heard the message of salvation and who have responded in faith in

---

[3] G. O'Collins, 'The Holy Trinity: The State of the Questions' in S.T. Davis, D. Kendall, and G. O'Collins (eds.), *The Trinity: An Interdisciplinary Symposium on the Trinity* (Oxford, 1999), 1; R.J. Feenstra and C. Plantinga Jr, 'Introduction' in idem. (eds.), *Trinity, Incarnation and Atonement* (Notre Dame, 1989), 3.
[4] J.J. O'Donnell, *The Mystery of the Triune God* (London, 1988), 159.
[5] R.M. Fermer, 'The Limits of Trinitarian Theology as a Methodological Paradigm', *NZSTR* 41 (1999), 158–186.
[6] C. Schwöbel, 'The Renaissance of Trinitarian Theology: Reasons, Problems and Tasks' in idem. (ed.), *Trinitarian Theology Today* (Edinburgh, 1995), 1–2.
[7] See schemas proposed in M.J. Erickson, *How Shall They Be Saved? The Destiny of Those Who Do Not Hear of Jesus* (Grand Rapids, 1997), 7; J. Sanders, 'Introduction' in J. Sanders (ed.), *What About Those Who Have Never Heard? Three Views on the Destiny of the Unevangelised* (Downers Grove, 1995), 12–15, 20; D. Strange, *The Possibility of Salvation*, 294–331.

Christ before they physically die. It often, but not always, emphasizes the object or content of faith, rather than the expression of faith itself. In other words, the emphasis is often not on belief itself but on who or what is believed. Slightly less exclusivist is a position that may be described as *Universal Opportunity Before Death*. Although similarly emphasizing the definitiveness of Christ's revelatory and salvific roles, this position widens the level of opportunity afforded to humanity by arguing that the gospel is made available to all people before they physically die. The usual means of disclosure is the preaching of the gospel but it can conceivably include visions and divine messengers, even at the moment of death. The significance of the third position, *Divine Perseverance* or *Postmortem Evangelism*, is that it encompasses humanity beyond the grave by affirming that the unevangelized receive an opportunity to respond to the gospel after physical death.

On the more inclusivist side of the continuum is the position that may be termed *Limited Inclusivism*. Although emphasizing the finality and efficacy of Christ's sacrificial death, this position affirms that salvation can come to those who, before they physically die, respond in faith to God based upon the revelation they have. Contrary to the exclusivist emphasis on the content of faith, this position places more emphasis upon faith itself – a 'faith principle'[8] or a 'direction of the heart'.[9]

Further along the increasingly inclusivist continuum is *Universalism* which affirms that salvation will ultimately come to all of humanity through the salvific work of Christ. Finally, at the extreme end of the continuum is the position that may be designated as *Pluralism*. This perspective affirms that salvation, in whichever way that concept may be understood, comes to all of humanity through all religions – that is, each religion is seen as providing a genuine encounter with what may be termed the Ultimate. In this sense, then, it encompasses the universality of the previous position but denies the exclusive claims of Christ. Consequently, it can be described as the ultimate inclusivist paradigm, for nothing is excluded.

The first three of these six views may be described as essentially exclusivist in that each affirms that overt or explicit knowledge of Jesus Christ is a prerequisite to salvation and, yet, differ somewhat concerning *when* or *how* this knowledge is appropriated. The second three, however, are more inclusivist in that each affirms that salvation may be received outside of overt or explicit knowledge of Jesus Christ. However, what unites the first five positions is the common conviction that Jesus Christ is God's *particular* and *final* revelation of himself. The particularity of Jesus affirms his uniqueness as the only Saviour of

---

[8] J. Sanders, 'Inclusivism' in J. Sanders (ed.), *What About Those Who Have Never Heard?*, 36–38.

[9] Pinnock states, 'The issue God cares about is the direction of the heart, not the content of theology.' See C.H. Pinnock, *A Wideness in God's Mercy: The Finality of Jesus Christ in a World of Religions* (Grand Rapids, 1992), 158.

humanity and the finality of Jesus affirms that he is, in some way, the definitive and authoritative revelation of God – both of who God is in himself and of his intentions toward humanity. Of course, adherents of the sixth view (that of *Pluralism*) would forcefully contest both affirmations and would view the other five positions as essentially exclusivist in that they assert *solus Christus*.

THE PRESENCE OF MYSTERY

When one considers the nature of God and his intentions, particularly toward the unevangelized, we would be wise to recognize the presence of both a sense of revealedness and a sense of hiddenness. That is, although God has revealed himself sufficiently (*Deus revelatus*) so that we might be reconciled to him, God nevertheless remains hidden behind or within his revelation (*Deus absconditus*). Of course, this is not to suggest that God's hiddenness means that he is absent – as Baelz observes, 'A hidden God he may be, an absent God never.'[10] Nor is it to suggest that some form of ontological disjunction exists between the divine hiddenness and the divine revealedness. Rather, it is simply to recognize that despite the reality, reliability and sufficiency of divine revelation and the illumination this brings of God's nature and actions, the essential *mysterion* of God remains. Jewett expresses it well, saying, 'God remains free in his revelation, transcendent in his condescension. …God has revealed himself and consequently we know him; but though we know him truly, we do not know him fully, as he knows us.'[11]

In light of this, rather than perceiving theological enquiry as a problem-solving enterprise, it is perhaps preferable that it be understood as a mystery-discerning endeavour.[12] To follow the dictum of Anselm, it is 'faith seeking understanding'.[13] Hence, when we consider the destiny of the unevangelized, it should perhaps not surprise us to find echoes of both revelation and continuing mystery. For example, we may note the explicit exclusivity that revelation accords to Jesus Christ (Jn. 14:6; Acts 4:12); the divine intention that desires all to be saved (1 Tim. 2:4); the recognition that not all are saved (Mt. 7:14[14]) and, the continuing clear command for mission – to go and make disciples of all nations (Mt. 28:19).

However, although there appears to be some clarity concerning these aspects of salvation, many would argue that the destiny of the unevangelized is

---

[10] P.R. Baelz, *Prayer and Providence* (New York, 1968), 60.
[11] P.K. Jewett, *God, Creation and Revelation: A Neo-Evangelical Theology* (Grand Rapids, 1991), 86.
[12] T.G. Weinandy, *Does God Suffer?* (Edinburgh, 2000), 30–36.
[13] Anselm, 'Proslogium' in S.N. Deane (ed.), *St Anselm: Proslogium; Monologium; An Appendix in Behalf of the Fool by Gaunilon; and Cur Deus Homo* (Chicago, 1930), 1.
[14] We should note, however, that the word 'few' here should not be pushed too far for Jesus also speaks of 'many' who are saved (Mt. 8:11; 20:28). See L. Morris, *The Gospel According to Matthew* (Grand Rapids, 1992), 175.

not addressed so directly. Of course, this is not to suggest that some perspectives on the question cannot be legitimately inferred from scripture, but it is to invite caution concerning according dogmatic certainty to statements that are in fact inferential and tentative – whether it be toward portraying God as more benevolent (inclusive) or more restrictive (exclusive) than he has explicitly revealed himself to be.

To that end, it is perhaps significant that the only time a person asks a question of Jesus concerning the number of those saved (Lk. 13:23–30), he does not directly answer the question but instead redirects it back to the inquirer's own salvific standing before God and exhorts those listening to 'make every effort to enter through the narrow door' (Lk. 13:24a). In other words, Jesus' answer would appear to evidence a desire that his followers not focus on speculation concerning the destiny of the unevangelized, but rather concentrate their efforts toward the salvation of themselves and then, following from the Great Commission, toward others with whom they come into contact. To draw from sporting parlance, it is the theological equivalent of being told to keep our eyes on the ball. Indeed, from a purely pragmatic point of view, it would appear to be pointless for God to reveal the destiny of the unevangelized to people who, by definition, they will never meet. There is, therefore, some truth in Ghanakan's comment that

> It is God's prerogative to save, not our's. Our preoccupation with criteria for salvation has led us to rigid claims rather than to discover the dynamism of the biblical understanding of God's relationship with his created world. If God has created the world, he is certainly concerned for its redemption. How this will be accomplished has been revealed to us to a great extent in the Biblical accounts of God's dealings with his people. But there are questions still confronting us and they are for God to answer.[15]

Therefore, in my view, it is entirely appropriate to be *partially agnostic* concerning the destiny of the unevangelized. Rather than embracing the escapism of total agnosticism or the dogmatism of total certainty, this position seeks to hold a discerning middle ground by recognizing that although God has revealed himself to an extent sufficient for salvation and mission, he has still left some questions unanswered. Hence, contrary to Küng who labels "supercilious" those who would express some caution concerning authoritative pronouncements on who will and will not be saved,[16] this perspective humbly recognizes the presence of both revelation and mystery. In the words of

---

[15] K. Gnanakan, 'Salvation Outside Christ?', *ATAJ* 4 (1996): 83. See also, J.I Packer, *Celebrating the Saving Work of God: The Collected Shorter Writings of J.I. Packer* (Carlisle, 1988), 1.168.

[16] H. Küng, *On Being A Christian* (London, 1977), 99.

Newbigin, 'To refuse to answer the question that our Lord himself refused to answer (Lk. 13:23–30) is not "supercilious"; it is simply honest.'[17]

Yet, though I am arguing for a sense of partial or limited agnosticism regarding the destiny of the unevangelized, it is not necessary to construe this agnosticism as pessimistic in nature.[18] Indeed, scholars have noted the optimism that can be found, for example, in the writings of Justin Martyr through his development of the concept of the seminal Logos (*spermatikos logos*) who universally mediates true knowledge of God to humanity.[19] Though some suspect a Greek philosophical influence in Justin's thought, it remains largely uncontested that he sought to base his Logos understanding primarily upon the Christian scriptures – particularly the writings of John.[20] In Origen we find his utilization of the *apokatastasis* (the restoration of all things) of Acts 3:21 leading him to an optimistic universalism, though characteristically inconsistent and therefore arguable.[21] In the Reformation period we note Zwingli's view. He affirms that salvation can come to all those with a 'pious heart'[22] and contends that only those who *have heard and refused the gospel* may be condemned.[23] He does so while still affirming the pre-eminence of Christ. As Timothy George expresses it, 'No one preached *solus Christus* more strongly than he.'[24]

In more contemporary times, we see optimism in the limited inclusivism of the Catholic scholar Rahner, with his concept of 'anonymous Christians',[25] and

---

[17] L. Newbigin, *The Open Secret: An Introduction to the Theology of Mission* (Grand Rapids, 1995), 173.

[18] Although Okholm and Phillips acknowledge that one can be pessimistically agnostic toward the unevangelized, they nevertheless recognize that 'this agnostic stance toward the unevangelized can also be construed optimistically'. See D.L. Okholm and T.R. Phillips, *More Than One Way? Four Views on Salvation in a Pluralistic World* (Grand Rapids, 1995), 20.

[19] J. Martyr, 'First Apology' in A. Roberts and J. Donaldson (eds.), *The Ante-Nicene Fathers* (Grand Rapids, 1885), 1.178 (46).

[20] L.W. Barnard, *Justin Martyr: His Life and Thought* (Cambridge, 1967), 88, 99–100.

[21] H. Crouzel, *Origen* (Edinburgh, 1989), 265.

[22] M. Schuler and J. Schultess (eds.), *Huldreich Zwinglis Werke* (Zurich, 1828-1842), 4.65.

[23] Zwingli believed we should see every person as a candidate for salvation, as one of the elect, until proved otherwise. See Schuler and Schultess (eds.), *Huldreich Zwinglis Werke*, 123. See also, U. Zwingli, *Ulrich Zwingli: Selected Works* (Philadelphia, 1972), 244, 'And this is my reason, because when I find no unfaith in any one I have no reason to condemn him.'

[24] T. George, *Theology of the Reformers* (Nashville, 1988), 125.

[25] K. Rahner, *Theological Investigations* (London, 1976), 14.283. Küng counters by saying that what Rahner means by 'anonymous Christians' is really 'anonymous Roman Catholics' and asks, 'What would Christians say if they were graciously recognized by Buddhists as "anonymous Buddhists"?' – Küng, *On Being a Christian*, 98.

in Küng, with his 'ordinary and extraordinary ways'.[26] Alongside these are evangelicals, such as Clark Pinnock, with his 'hermeneutic of hopefulness',[27] and John Sanders, with his 'faith principle', 'wider hope' and so on,[28] who find significant scriptural support for a more optimistic outlook.

While the debate will no doubt continue as to how substantial and cogent are arguments for a more inclusivist optimism, I would suggest that a consideration of the question from the perspective of God as a triune being provides a significant additional reason for drawing an inference of optimism, rather than pessimism, concerning God's intentions toward the unevangelized.

The Possibility of Optimism

THE NATURE OF GOD

Earlier, I made note of a range of positions that have been advocated in answer to the question of the destiny of the unevangelized and it is important to recognize that much of their differentiation derives directly from theological divergence concerning their conceptions of the nature of God. For example, Hick's pluralistic perspective on divinity leads him to advocate nothing less than a 'Copernican revolution in theology'.[29] He argues that there have been developmental phases in orthodoxy – what he terms 'epicycles'[30] – and sees it as inevitable that the church ultimately embraces a theological and epistemological universe in which the centre is not the church, and not even the Christian God, but rather the 'Absolute'.[31]

Similarly, Robinson's universalism derives partially from his conception of how a loving God should act. In his view, a God who is love necessitates a future that cannot include a hell[32] and, consequently, we are faced with 'two doctrines of God, and between them there can be no peace'.[33] Basing much of his argument upon what may be described as an over-realized eschatology, he argues that such is the magnitude of God's restoration of all things in Christ

---

[26] Essentially, Küng argues that Christianity is not exclusive but unique. There are 'ordinary' and 'extraordinary' avenues of salvation – that is, non-Christian ('the paths') and Christian ('the way'). H. Küng, *Christianity and the World Religions* (London, 1987), 24.

[27] Pinnock, *A Wideness in God's Mercy*, 20–35.

[28] J. Sanders, *No Other Name: An Investigation into the Destiny of the Unevangelised* (Grand Rapids, 1992), 217–24 and idem., 'Inclusivism', 22–51.

[29] J. Hick, *God and the Universe of Faiths: Essays in the Philosophy of Religion* (London, 1977), 131.

[30] Hick, *God and the Universe of Faiths*, 124, 131–132.

[31] Hick, *God and the Universe of Faiths*, 131–132.

[32] A.J. Nicholls, 'The Exclusiveness and Inclusiveness of the Gospel', *Themelios* 4 (1979), 63.

[33] J.A.T. Robinson, *In the End, God* (London, 1950), 102.

that all future blessings are realized now. Hence, he writes, 'The New Testament asserts the final *apokatastasis*, the restoration of all things, not as a daring speculation, nor as a possibility, but as a reality – a reality that shall be and must be, because it already is.'[34] In other words, such is the universal efficacy, definitiveness and finality of the *apokatastasis* in Christ, that universalism is the only position that makes sense of this New Testament trajectory.

What is important to note from these perspectives is that to significant and sometimes even definitive extents particular conceptions of God guide particular perspectives on God's intentions toward the unevangelized. Indeed, particular conceptions of God and therefore of how he acts toward the unevangelized sometimes derive some of their tone from scriptural statements that are interpreted as being decisively determinative in relation to God's nature – for example, 'God is love' (1 Jn. 4:16). Such interpretative choices can be found, for example, in trinitarian theologians such as Zizioulas who argues that love is the 'supreme ontological predicate' and is 'constitutive of His substance, i.e. it is that which makes God what he *is*".[35] Open theists such as Rice and Pinnock similarly argue that, 'The statement *God is love* is as close as the Bible comes to giving us a definition of the divine reality'[36] and that, 'love is the very essence of his being'.[37] Yet, though it is indeed true that God is love, if one wishes to work from explicit 'God is…' statements, then statements such as 'God is light' (1 Jn. 1:5) and 'God is spirit' (Jn. 4:24) should presumably also be taken into account. Indeed, if one were to give priority to the statement 'God is light' then one could argue that such a statement, particularly in its context, supports the contention that 'holiness' and not 'love' is central or constitutive of the divine character.[38]

My point is simply to urge caution that we do not advance one aspect of God's revelation of himself, as important as it is, without recourse to other revealed aspects and attributes and the context they provide. As Collins argues, '[A] balanced view of God recognizes that a single attribute is not adequate to

---

[34] Robinson, *In the End, God*, 99.
[35] J.D. Zizioulas, *Being as Communion: Studies in Personhood and the Church* (Crestwood, 1985), 46, original emphasis.
[36] R. Rice, 'Biblical Support for a New Perspective' in C.H. Pinnock, et al., *The Openness of God: A Biblical Challenge to the Traditional Understanding of God* (Downers Grove, 1994), 18, original emphasis.
[37] C.H. Pinnock, *Most Moved Mover: A Theology of God's Openness* (Carlisle, 2001), 81.
[38] For example, Strong believes that holiness is the 'fundamental attribute in God'. See A.H. Strong, *Systematic Theology* (Philadelphia, 1907), 295–6. Alternatively, more recently, Grenz argues that 'love is the fundamental "attribute" of God'. See S.J. Grenz, *Theology for the Community of God* (Carlisle, 1994), 93.

describe him.'³⁹ Rather than seeing holiness and love, or any other divine attribute, standing in apparent if not actual contradiction with each other, it would be preferable to follow the advice of John Webster when he writes, 'Holiness and love, that is, are mutually conditioning and mutually illuminative terms, which can only be expounded in relation to each other, and which both serve as conceptual indicators of the being and ways of the triune God.'⁴⁰ The danger of not ensuring such balance and, on occasion, holding affirmations in theological tension, is that we may end up with a skewed understanding of the nature of God and, by implication, a skewed and therefore impoverished understanding of his intentions toward the unevangelized. Accordingly, opting for a trinitarian perspective is a distinctive way of keeping our conceptions of the nature of God appropriately at the centre of our discussion.

TRINITARIAN DISTINCTIVES

In what has become something of a guiding principle in trinitarian theology, Rahner's Rule states that, *'The "economic" Trinity is the "immanent" Trinity and the "immanent" Trinity is the "economic" Trinity.'*⁴¹ Although much dissected,⁴² the primary point that Rahner appears to be making is that there is a fundamental correlation between the immanent and economic Trinity or, as Jüngel puts it, 'God corresponds to himself.'⁴³ As such, it makes the constructive and helpful point that our conceptions of triune ontology (immanent Trinity) ought to be guided and informed by God's revelation to us in the economy of salvation (economic Trinity). Our conceptions ought not 'to float free from the God who becomes present to history in his Son and Spirit'.⁴⁴ Although it may be argued that in the economy God has not revealed *all* that he is (that is, the *mysterion* mentioned previously remains) I would nevertheless still contend that he has not revealed *other* than he is. Consequently, we must guard our conceptions of triune ontology from being separated or even divorced from the scriptural narrative that raises these questions in the first place.⁴⁵ With these parameters in mind, then, what aspects of trinitarian theology are suggestive of optimism in regard to God's intentions toward the unevangelized?

---

³⁹ C.J. Collins, *The God of Miracles: An Exegetical Examination of God's Action in the World* (Leicester, 2001), 49.

⁴⁰ J. Webster, 'The holiness and love of God', *SJT* 57 (2004), 258.

⁴¹ K. Rahner, *The Trinity* (London, 1970), 62, original emphasis.

⁴² E.g. see discussion in C.M. LaCugna, *God For Us: The Trinity and Christian Life* (Chicago, 1991), 216–217.

⁴³ E. Jüngel, *The Doctrine of the Trinity: God's Being is in Becoming* (Edinburgh, 1976), 24.

⁴⁴ C.E. Gunton, *The Christian Faith: An Introduction to Christian Doctrine* (Oxford, 2002), 184.

⁴⁵ G.D. Fee, 'Paul and the Trinity: The Experience of Christ and the Spirit for Paul's Understanding of God' in Davis, Kendall and O'Collins (eds.), *The Trinity*, 72.

The first and fundamental affirmation that derives from God's triunity is that *God is essentially relational*. As God's revelation of himself progressed from the *Shema* of the Old Testament (Deut. 6:4) and defined itself ultimately in the person of Jesus Christ, the early church began to struggle with describing an experience of multiplicity. Although they still worshipped the one God of the Old Testament, they knew him now as God the Father, God the Son and God the Holy Spirit. Indeed, the writings of the apostles in the New Testament evidence a unity and multiplicity in which distinctions are drawn between the persons, which are often reflected by the roles thought more *appropriate* to each, whilst maintaining their fundamental unity (Eph. 1:3–14; 2:18; 4:4–6).

As the Fathers sought to articulate this trinitarian faith of the early church, they moved from a Greek to a Christian conception of ontology by utilizing existing philosophical words and modifying their meanings, sometimes to a radical extent, to better reflect a scripturally informed conception of God's triunity. In particular, and in very general terms, the word *hypostasis*, which had formally referred to 'being' and had been almost synonymous with *ousia*, began to take on relational dimensions when it was conjoined with *prosopon* – a distinctly relational term. The result of this development was that *relationality had entered the realm of ontology*. Zizioulas describes this development as philosophically revolutionary and summarizes it in the statement, '*To be* and *to be in relation* becomes identical.'[46] In the view of Gunton, this was nothing less than the establishment of a 'new ontological principle'.[47]

Indeed, such is the relationality of the divine ontology that Fiddes argues that God's triunity – as Father, Son and Holy Spirit – should be conceived not as three persons *in* relationship but as three persons *as* relationships. In other words, 'there are no persons "at each end of a relation," but the "persons" are simply the relations'.[48] Though a distinctive approach to articulating triune relationality, its antecedent can be found in the trinitarianism of Aquinas who also argues that 'relation is necessarily the same as person' and that it is precisely this relationality that distinguishes the divine persons – whether it be fatherhood, sonship or procession (*paternitas, filiatio* or *processio*).[49]

Although I would argue that conceiving persons as relations is potentially problematic, recognizing the dimensions of relationship that distinguish the divine persons illuminates the essential divine relationality. Indeed, Augustine's answer to the Arian challenge in his *De Trinitate* follows a similar line of thinking in pointing out that the difference between the Father and Son

---

[46] Zizioulas, *Being as Communion*, 88, original emphasis.
[47] C.E. Gunton, *The Promise of Trinitarian Theology* (Edinburgh, 1991), 8.
[48] P.S. Fiddes, *Participating in God: A Pastoral Doctrine of the Trinity* (London, 2000), 34.
[49] T. Aquinas, *Summa Theologiæ* (London, 1976), 7.142–3 (40.1).

is not a matter of *substance* nor of *accident*, but of *relation*.[50] Furthermore, since the Father is named the Father since he is the Father of the Son; and the Son since he is the Son of the Father; and the Spirit since he is the Spirit of both the Father and Son, we recognize that God's triune nature is one that is disposed toward those who are 'other'. He is indeed an essentially relational being. As Jewett puts it, God is the 'One-who-is-for-Others in himself'.[51]

But, secondly, the essential relationality of the triune God leads us to state that *God is perfectly relational*. In a robust defense of the doctrine of divine impassibility, Weinandy draws upon Aquinas' philosophical argument that God is *actus purus* (pure act) – that is, God's nature is 'to be' or *ipsum esse* (to-be itself). In the trinitarian context, then, Weinandy argues that since the divine persons are subsistent relations fully or purely in act, there is no intrinsic relational potential in God for there can be no potential in that which is pure.[52] Consequently, the triune God is *perfect* relationality. Furthermore, since there is no intrinsic relationality in God that is yet to be actualized, since God is perfectly relational, God is able to reflect his perfect relationality in extrinsic relational potential. That is, his *ad intra* perfect triune relationality overflows and is reflected *ad extra* toward persons who are other.[53]

Although principally a philosophical argument, it receives its primary historical articulation in the event of the incarnation. That is, the decisive historical culmination of this *ad extra* dimension of divine triune relationality is the incarnation when the transcendent God (God *over* us) became, in a climactic and defining way, God *for* us and *with* us. Jewett, who earlier characterized God as the 'One-who-is-for-Others in himself', likewise recognizes this extrinsic relational potential by stating that he is also the 'One-who-is-for-others-outside-himself' (creation) and, in particular, the 'One-who-is-for-sinful-others' (redemption).[54]

In relation to the destiny of the unevangelized, this conception of perfect triune relationality which is reflected or overflows outwardly illuminates the fact that the very core of God's being – the very essence of his triunity – is one that is positively disposed toward persons who are other from him. This is not to suggest that God, to be God, is in *need* of relationship – as in the finite God of Process theism, for example – but that God's perfection as a triune being, expressed as it is in the birth, life, death and resurrection of Jesus Christ, is one that is definitively and positively inclined toward others. Indeed, such is the potency of the triune relationality that some scholars ponder whether,

---

[50] Augustine, 'On the Trinity' in P. Schaff (ed.), *A Select Library of Nicene and Post-Nicene Fathers of the Christian Church* (Grand Rapids, 1956), 3.89 (5.6).
[51] Jewett, *God, Creation and Revelation*, 299.
[52] Weinandy, *Does God Suffer?*, 119.
[53] Weinandy, *Does God Suffer?*, 128.
[54] Jewett, *God, Creation and Revelation*, 299.

irrespective of the Fall, God always intended to become incarnate.[55] Although some may find this a likely proposal (for among other things it has in its favour a grounding in the essential and perfect relationality of the triune God) it nevertheless labours under the fact that it is inherently speculative because the Fall *did* occur and the incarnation took place in the light of that premise. Yet, such a proposal does highlight the divine relational inclination toward others. Furthermore, the perfection of God's relationality means that his relationships are both intimate and enduring. The doctrine of trinitarian *perichoresis* – the 'permeation of each person by the other, their coinherence without confusion'[56] – is one reflection of the intimate and abiding nature of such *ad intra* perfect relationality.

Finally, the essential and perfect triune relationality leads us to state that God's *relationality is both defined and regulated by his revelation of himself in the economy of salvation*. In other words, our conception of God's triunity, and by implication our inferences concerning his intentions toward the unevangelized, is guided by the fact that God has reached out to us in Christ. This means, therefore, that our deliberations are to be thoroughly christological. Such a posture does not mean that we are no longer being theocentric in our thinking, but is simply a recognition that to be accurately theocentric we need to be primarily christocentric – for it is in Christ's face that we see 'the light of the knowledge of the glory of God' (2 Cor. 4:6b).

As we discussed earlier, illumination of the immanent Trinity derives from the economic Trinity, and what can be known about the economic Trinity revolves around and receives its defining expression in the person and work of Jesus Christ. Having this christological focus means that we are afforded insight into the other-centredness (the ex-centredness) that defines the inner triune life. For example, we see Paul's realization of the fact that the triune God is fundamentally *for him* in his recognition that the Son 'loved me and gave himself for me' (Gal. 2:20b). Yet, this christological focus also ensures that we remain thoroughly trinitarian for we also recognize that the giving of the Son came out of the magnitude of the love the Father has for the world (Jn. 3:16) and that the sending of the Holy Spirit as the *parakletos* (our helper, encourager and advocate – Jn. 14:26; 15:26; Rom. 8:26) came from both the Father and the Son.

---

[55] W. Pannenberg, *Systematic Theology* (Grand Rapids, 1994), 2.64; Zizioulas, *Being as Communion*, 97; T.F. Torrance, *The Christian Doctrine of God, One Being Three Persons* (Edinburgh, 1996), 210; C.E. Gunton, *Christ and Creation* (Grand Rapids, 1992), 94, 96; L.E. Wilkinson, 'Emmanuel and the Purpose of Creation' in D. Lewis and A.E. McGrath (eds.), *Doing Theology for the People of God: Studies in Honor of J. I. Packer* (Downers Grove, 1996), 245–261.
[56] Fiddes, *Participating in God*, 71.

Conclusion

The trinitarianism that is evident in the economy of salvation both expresses and informs the essential and perfect relationality that is intrinsic to the triune divine life. In other words, the extrinsic relationality of the triune God – as evidenced by the Father's love of us, the sacrifice of the Son for us and the sending of the Spirit to us – illuminates a divine life that is fundamentally inclined *toward* rather than *away* from persons who are other. God's very nature (as reflected in his triunity) has as its default position the benefit and not the detriment of those who stand distinct from him. The very realities of creation and redemption – that we were created to walk in relationship with him and that he has reached out to us in Christ to restore that relationship – derive from the relational other-centredness of the triune divine life. Consequently, though I would argue that the presence of both revelation and continuing mystery means that we should adopt a posture of partial agnosticism concerning the destiny of the unevangelized, the nature of God as a triune being is nevertheless sufficiently suggestive for such agnosticism to be formulated optimistically. As Gnanakan notes, 'If God has created the world, he is certainly concerned for its redemption.'[57] The nature of God's triunity is one of benevolence, not austerity.

Bibliography

Anselm, 'Proslogium' in S.N. Deane (ed.), *St Anselm: Proslogium; Monologium; An Appendix in Behalf of the Fool by Gaunilon; and Cur Deus Homo* (Chicago: Open Court, 1930), 1–34.

Augustine, 'On the Trinity' in P. Schaff (ed.), *A Select Library of Nicene and Post-Nicene Fathers of the Christian Church*, series 1, vol. 3 (Grand Rapids, Michigan: Eerdmans, 1956), 17–228.

Aquinas, T., *Summa Theologiæ*, vol. 7 (London: Blackfriars, 1976).

Baelz, P.R., *Prayer and Providence* (New York: The Seabury Press, 1968).

Barnard, L.W., *Justin Martyr: His Life and Thought* (Cambridge: Cambridge University Press, 1967).

Collins, C.J., *The God of Miracles: An Exegetical Examination of God's Action in the World* (Leicester: Inter-Varsity Press, 2001).

Crouzel, H., *Origen* (Edinburgh: T. & T. Clark, 1989).

Davis, S.T., D. Kendall and G. O'Collins (eds.), *The Trinity: An Interdisciplinary Symposium on the Trinity* (Oxford: Oxford University Press, 1999).

Erickson, M.J., *How Shall They Be Saved? The Destiny of Those Who Do Not Hear of Jesus* (Grand Rapids, Michigan: Baker, 1997).

— 'The Fate of Those Who Never Hear', *Bibliotheca Sacra* 152/605 (1995), 3–15.

Fee, G.D., 'Paul and the Trinity: The Experience of Christ and the Spirit for Paul's Understanding of God' in S.T. Davis, D. Kendall and G. O'Collins (eds.), *The*

---

[57] Gnanakan, 'Salvation Outside Christ?', 83.

Trinity: An Interdisciplinary Symposium on the Trinity (Oxford: Oxford University Press, 1999), 49–72.

Feenstra, R.J. and C. Plantinga Jr., 'Introduction' in idem. (eds.), *Trinity, Incarnation and Atonement* (Notre Dame, Indiana: University of Notre Dame Press, 1989), 1–20.

Fermer, R.M., 'The Limits of Trinitarian Theology as a Methodological Paradigm', *Neue Zeitschrift Für Systematische Theologie und Religionsphilosophie* 41 (1999), 158–186.

Fiddes, P.S., *Participating in God: A Pastoral Doctrine of the Trinity* (London: Darton, Longman and Todd, 2000).

George, T., *Theology of the Reformers* (Nashville: Broadman Press, 1988).

Gnanakan, K., 'Salvation Outside Christ?', *Asia Theological Association Journal* 4 (1996), 69–84.

Grenz, S.J., *Theology for the Community of God* (Carlisle: Broadman and Holman, 1994).

Gunton, C.E., *Christ and Creation* (Grand Rapids, Michigan: Eerdmans, 1992).

— *The Christian Faith: An Introduction to Christian Doctrine* (Oxford: Blackwell, 2002).

— *The Promise of Trinitarian Theology* (Edinburgh: T. & T. Clark, 1991).

Hick, J., *God and the Universe of Faiths: Essays in the Philosophy of Religion* (London: Collins Fount, 1977).

Jewett, P.K., *God, Creation and Revelation: A Neo-Evangelical Theology* (Grand Rapids, Michigan: Eerdmans, 1991).

Jüngel, E., *The Doctrine of the Trinity: God's Being is in Becoming* (Edinburgh: Scottish Academic Press, 1976).

Küng, H., *Christianity and the World Religions* (London: Collins, 1987[2]).

— *On Being A Christian* (London: Collins, 1977).

LaCugna, C.M., *God For Us: The Trinity and Christian Life* (Chicago: Harper Collins, 1991).

Martyr, J., 'First Apology' in A. Roberts and J. Donaldson (eds.), *The Ante-Nicene Fathers*, vol. 1 (Grand Rapids, Michigan: Eerdmans, 1885), 163–187.

Morris, L., *The Gospel According to Matthew* (Grand Rapids, Michigan: Eerdmans, 1992).

Newbigin, L., *The Open Secret: An Introduction to the Theology of Mission* (Grand Rapids, Michigan: Eerdmans, 1995).

Nicholls, B.J., 'The Exclusiveness and Inclusiveness of the Gospel', *Themelios* 4 (1979), 62–69.

O'Collins, G., 'The Holy Trinity: The State of the Questions' in S.T. Davis, D. Kendall and G. O'Collins (eds.), *The Trinity: An Interdisciplinary Symposium on the Trinity* (Oxford: Oxford University Press, 1999), 1–25.

O'Donnell, J.J., *The Mystery of the Triune God* (London: Sheed and Ward, 1988).

Okholm, D.L. and T.R. Phillips, *More Than One Way? Four Views on Salvation in a Pluralistic World* (Grand Rapids, Michigan: Zondervan, 1995).

Packer, J.I, *Celebrating the Saving Work of God: The Collected Shorter Writings of J.I. Packer*, vol. 1 (Carlisle: Paternoster, 1988).

Pannenberg, W., *Systematic Theology*, vol. 2 (Grand Rapids, Michigan: Eerdmans, 1994).

Pinnock, C.H., *A Wideness in God's Mercy: The Finality of Jesus Christ in a World of Religions* (Grand Rapids, Michigan: Zondervan, 1992).

— *Most Moved Mover: A Theology of God's Openness* (Carlisle: Paternoster, 2001).
Rahner, K., *The Trinity* (London: Burns & Oates, 1970).
— *Theological Investigations*, vol. 14 (London: Darton, Longman & Todd, 1976).
Rice, R., 'Biblical Support for a New Perspective' in C.H. Pinnock, et al., *The Openness of God: A Biblical Challenge to the Traditional Understanding of God* (Downers Grove: Inter-Varsity Press, 1994), 11–58.
Robinson, J.A.T., *In the End, God* (London: James Clarke, 1950).
Sanders, J., *No Other Name: An Investigation into the Destiny of the Unevangelised* (Grand Rapids, Michigan: Eerdmans, 1992).
— 'Inclusivism' in idem. (ed.), *What About Those Who Have Never Heard? Three Views on the Destiny of the Unevangelised* (Downers Grove: Inter-Varsity Press, 1995), 21–55.
— 'Introduction' in idem. (ed.), *What About Those Who Have Never Heard? Three Views on the Destiny of the Unevangelised* (Downers Grove: Inter-Varsity Press, 1995), 7–20.
— 'The Perennial Problem', *Christianity Today* 34 (1990), 20–21.
— (ed.), *What About Those Who Have Never Heard? Three Views on the Destiny of the Unevangelised* (Downers Grove: Inter-Varsity Press, 1995).
Schuler, M. and J. Schultess (eds.), *Huldreich Zwinglis Werke. Erste vollstandige Ausgabe,* vol. 4 (Zurich, 1828–1842).
Schwöbel, C., 'The Renaissance of Trinitarian Theology: Reasons, Problems and Tasks' in idem. (ed.), *Trinitarian Theology Today* (Edinburgh: T. & T. Clark, 1995), 1–30.
Strange, D., *The Possibility of Salvation Among the Unevangelised* (Carlisle: Paternoster, 2001).
Strong, A.H., *Systematic Theology* (Philadelphia: Judson Press, 1907).
Torrance, T.F., *The Christian Doctrine of God, One Being Three Persons* (Edinburgh: T. & T. Clark, 1996).
Webster, J., 'The holiness and love of God', *Scottish Journal of Theology* 57 (2004), 249–268.
Weinandy, T.G., *Does God Suffer?* (Edinburgh: T. & T. Clark, 2000).
Wilkinson, L.E., 'Emmanuel and the Purpose of Creation' in D. Lewis and A.E. McGrath (eds.), *Doing Theology for the People of God: Studies in Honor of J.I. Packer* (Downers Grove: Inter-Varsity Press, 1996), 245–261.
Zizioulas, J.D., *Being as Communion: Studies in Personhood and the Church* (Crestwood, New York: St Vladimir's Seminary Press, 1985).
Zwingli, U., *Ulrich Zwingli: Selected Works* (Philadelphia: University of Pennsylvania Press, 1972).

CHAPTER 12

Communities of Witness.
The Concept of Election in the Old Testament and in the Theology of Karl Barth

MICHAEL O'NEIL

Introduction

In many respects this essay has its genesis in the kind and genuine interest shown by John Olley towards my work during the latter days of his term as principal of the Baptist Theological College of Western Australia. During my honours programme in which I examined various aspects of Karl Barth's doctrine of election, John opined more than once that this doctrine had suffered in the history of theology as a result of its being considered in abstraction from its Old Testament roots. John referred me to Rowley's thesis that the 'fundamental conception of Israel's election' was that 'it was election for service; and the rendering of that service was the supreme honour for which she was chosen'.[1] In this essay, then, I would like to express my appreciation for John's academic leadership and support by taking up in a more detailed manner his suggestion for my research. The structure of the essay is straightforward. It commences with an overview of the major contours of the concept of election as it is developed in the Old Testament, followed by a similar treatment of the concept in Barth's proposal. A brief concluding section notes several observations and reflections arising from the study.

Election and the Old Testament

Zimmerli, examining the linguistic data which is descriptive of election in the Old Testament, notes that 'the theology of election first takes on its full significance in the period of Deuteronomy, where it is developed with great

---

[1] H.H. Rowley, *The Biblical Doctrine of Election* (London, 1950), 53–4. See also, 39, where Rowley indicates another purpose of Israel's election, namely, that of revelation.

emphasis'.² This is not surprising. The concept of election functions as an interpretive mechanism which seeks to understand the often mysterious patterns of divine activity. In this case, says Zimmerli, it arose as a theological reflection regarding why Yahweh, given the array of possibilities open to him, should so concern himself in such a special way with Israel.³

J.W. Wright, in a recent essay, arrives at a similar conclusion. He observes that the terminology of election is never employed in the narrative of Genesis through Numbers as a rationale for Yahweh's call of Abram, his deliverance of Israel in the exodus, or the theophany and gift of the Law at Sinai.⁴ Nevertheless, the use of the concept in Deuteronomy provides an interpretive 'narrative summary of the main storyline of the Torah that points to the vocation of Israel'.⁵ In addition, the concept also functions to incorporate the hearers of the story narrated by the character Moses, and, importantly, to incorporate the Deuteronomist's hearers and readers as well, into the grand narrative of Yahweh's saving activity, thereby constituting them also as Yahweh's elect.⁶

Analysis of those passages where election is prominent indicates several primary aspects of the Old Testament presentation of this concept. Of first importance is recognition of its wholly gracious character. Eichrodt, for example, insists that 'there can be no escaping the fact that in the Old Testament *divine love is absolutely free and unconditioned in its choices*'.⁷ So, too, Zimmerli asserts that behind Yahweh's election stands 'an irrational, free decision of love ... which cannot be examined further'.⁸

Second, this election is historical in character. According to Preuss, Israel's election is grounded in the historical deeds of salvation by which God called the nation into existence and constituted them a worshipping community. It refers 'not to some kind of supratemporal or primeval divine decree but rather to a historical action of YHWH'.⁹ Further, because it is historical, election is also descriptive of the continuing activity of Yahweh in the history of his relation with his people.

---

² W. Zimmerli, *Old Testament Theology in Outline* (Edinburgh, 1978), 44.
³ Zimmerli, *Old Testament Theology*, 44.
⁴ J.W. Wright, 'Election' in T.D. Alexander and D.W. Baker (eds.), *Dictionary of the Old Testament Pentateuch* (Downers Grove, 2003), 216.
⁵ Wright, 'Election', 216.
⁶ Wright, 'Election', 217.
⁷ W. Eichrodt, *Theology of the Old Testament* (London, 1961), 1.286, emphasis original.
⁸ Zimmerli, *Old Testament Theology*, 45.
⁹ H.D. Preuss, *Old Testament Theology* (Louisville, 1995), 1.30–33, 35–7. See also, Preuss, *Old Testament Theology* (Louisville, 1996), 2.284. Preuss' work is especially significant in that he has identified Israel's election as the organizing centre of his Old Testament theological project.

Third, Zimmerli speaks of 'the "dialogical" nature of election'.[10] Yahweh's election of Israel must find its echo in Israel's election of Yahweh. Those whom Yahweh has chosen are thus charged to 'choose life' by living in accordance with covenant stipulations set forth by Moses (Deut. 30:19–20). Wright concurs, 'Election runs both ways between God and God's people, though God's election of Israel has a narrative, theological and logical priority over Israel's election of Yahweh.'[11]

Fourth, although God can and does elect particular individuals for special tasks, the concept is generally communal rather than individualistic, and is utilized as a call to Israel to live faithfully in accordance with its particular vocation as the people of God.[12] Klein argues that 'the dominant use of election terminology applies to the people as a body or nation' and that the Old Testament writers 'make a distinction between God's choice of a corporate people and his choice of individuals who may or may not ultimately benefit from that corporate choice'.[13] Individuals find 'their election' within the broader compass of this people that God has chosen for himself.[14]

The previous two observations indicate that, fifth, election in the Old Testament is not to be understood in an absolute or static sense. Election can be forfeited if those whom God has chosen refuse to live in accordance with their election. This is seen clearly with respect to elect individuals such as Eli and Saul, but may also be observed on a larger scale as almost entire generations fall under divine judgement on account of their failure to trust and to obey God.[15]

Finally, these various aspects of the Old Testament presentation of the concept of election are likely to be misunderstood unless they are set within the broader context of the purpose of election. Such misunderstanding evidently arose within ancient Israel itself. It is notable that the prophets of the pre-exilic and exilic period only rarely mention the election of Israel. When they do the

---

[10] Zimmerli, *Old Testament Theology*, 46.
[11] Wright, 'Election', 218.
[12] Wright, 'Election', 218.
[13] W.W. Klein, *The New Chosen People: A Corporate View of Election* (Grand Rapids, 1990), 28, 35. See also, Preuss, *Old Testament Theology*, 1.30, who says that 'statements about the election of individuals are of secondary importance to the election of the people' which is of 'decisive importance'.
[14] Klein, *The New Chosen People*, 35.
[15] See 1 Sam. 2:27–31; 13:11–14; 15:17–28. Note that while almost the entire generation which came forth from Egypt fell under divine judgement, God's election of Israel per se, was not forfeited. Just as belonging to the corporate people did not in itself guarantee divine salvation or blessing, so also the faithlessness of the people did not overthrow the faithfulness of God.

context indicates that they are critical of 'all self-satisfied claims on the part of Israel to be a "chosen people"'.[16]

Contemporary misunderstanding of election also occurs, particularly when its purpose is understood primarily in soteriological terms, as has often been the case in the history of theology, particularly in the Augustinian-Calvinist tradition. The notion that election refers to the selection of particular persons as the sole recipients of saving grace and eternal blessedness not only appears arbitrary, but morally suspect as well. An example of a modern reading of the Old Testament data through the lens of a prior dogmatic conviction about election is seen in the work of Snaith. In an attempt to emphasize the sovereign freedom of God in his election, Snaith speaks of an exclusivity of God's love which 'has been part of "the offence of the Gospel" since almost the first days. .... Either we must accept this idea of choice on the part of God with its necessary accompaniment of exclusiveness, or we have to hold to a doctrine of the Love of God other than that which is Biblical. The alternative is clear, and we do not see how it can be avoided.'[17]

Perhaps another alternative is available, however, which will enable contemporary presentations of the doctrine of election to avoid the offence which has continually plagued them. This, of course, is to understand the purpose of election in terms of service, as suggested by Rowley.[18]

The question regarding the character of this service naturally arises. In what was this service to consist? Perhaps the first word to be spoken in this regard is one of caution. In an eagerness to avoid the pitfalls of particularism it is too easy, perhaps, to latch onto key biblical statements which seem to provide the proof of Israel's calling as a missionary nation.[19] While such texts clearly indicate that Israel's election was to have a salutary effect on the surrounding nations, a more carefully nuanced statement is required if the precise nature of its service is not to be overstated.

Israel's service, first and foremost, was a service of *God*, a service arising out of the special honours accruing to it as a result of its election. Israel's awareness that it was God's treasured possession in distinction from the surrounding nations was both ancient and fundamental.[20] Chosen and redeemed by Yahweh, Israel was placed under particular obligations of obedience and worship by which it would indeed be a holy and priestly kingdom.

---

[16] Zimmerli, *Old Testament Theology*, 47. See, e.g. Amos 3:2 and Ezek. 20:5–8. While he does not use the language of election, it is evident that Micah also confronted a complacent people who misunderstood the ground of their relation with Yahweh (e.g. Mich. 2:6; 3:9–11).

[17] N.H. Snaith, *The Distinctive Ideas of the Old Testament* (Carlisle, 1944), 139.

[18] See also, R.L. Smith, *Old Testament Theology: Its History, Method, and Message* (Nashville, 1993), 125, 137.

[19] See, e.g. texts such as Gen. 12:3; Ex. 19:6; Deut. 4:6–8; Is. 49:3–6 and Jonah.

[20] Zimmerli, *Old Testament Theology*, 45–46.

By the time of the Deuteronomist the theology of election was a conscious attempt to relate the special bond between Yahweh and Israel to the existence of the surrounding nations, an attempt carried out in a period characterized by crisis and threat.[21] According to Clements, what is intriguing in Deuteronomy is that 'although it consciously considers Israel's position in relation to the nations, it does not develop from this any role or service that Israel is to play in regard to them'.[22] Preuss concurs, saying, 'any possible significance attributed to the chosen people's responsibility toward the foreign nations is passed by in silence. *Israel, first of all, must and ought to discover itself again.*'[23] According to Preuss, then, the first responsibility Israel has is to live in accordance with its own identity and purpose as the elect of God.

Nonetheless, Preuss can also affirm that Israel's election was not only a gift, but also a mission for God's people, and rejects the view that election is restrictive or concerned solely with Israel's exclusive well-being.[24] To the contrary, Yahweh's redemptive activity on Israel's behalf has the purpose 'of other nations coming to know and acknowledge him as God. Thus YHWH's activity on his people's behalf is exemplary of his intention for his world.'[25] In effect, Preuss wants to maintain a distinction between active and passive mission as the nature of Israel's calling. Israel is not called as an active missioner toward the nations, even in the case of Deutero-Isaiah's Servant, or the book of Jonah. Rather, Yahweh's 'activity on behalf of his people shall possess the power of attraction that works outwardly in an enticing fashion to demonstrate the truth of YHWH before the rest of the world'.[26] Israel mediates by what it is and what it experiences, that is, passively, a wider participation in its own community with God.[27]

In sum, election in the Old Testament was the gracious work of Yahweh in history by which he called the nation of Israel into existence and into community with himself. Although this election bequeathed special privileges

---

[21] R.E. Clements, *Old Testament Theology: A Fresh Approach* (London, 1978), 89.

[22] Clements, *Old Testament Theology*, 95.

[23] Preuss, *Old Testament Theology*, 1.33 (emphasis added).

[24] Preuss, *Old Testament Theology*, 2.285.

[25] Preuss, *Old Testament Theology*, 2.300.

[26] Preuss, *Old Testament Theology*, 2.292. For Preuss' comments on the book of Jonah specifically, see 2.303.

[27] Preuss, *Old Testament Theology*, 2.302. Preuss goes on to comment, 'The servant *was not to be* a light to the nations, and this is not mentioned as his mission, but rather he *is* this light; that is, his influence consists in the fact that "light", that is, salvation, is to be transmitted to the nations', 2.305 (original emphasis). See also Clements, *Old Testament Theology*, 96, who arrives at a similar conclusion, stating that 'the light that God had given to Israel would become a light by which other nations also might live. ... The picture is not that of a "mission" in the strict sense of a going out to the nations, but rather that, when Israel returns to its homeland, it will bring the faithful of other nations in its train.'

upon Israel, it also charged it with special responsibilities to the end that Israel's corporate existence would become a revelatory vehicle of Yahweh's person and purpose for the nations. Israel, therefore, was elected to be a priestly kingdom offering acceptable service to God in life and worship, and testifying to his righteousness and grace to the nations surrounding it. In no sense can it be understood that its election spelt the rejection of the other nations. Rather, as Vriezen insists,

> Israel was only elected in order to serve God in the task of leading those other nations to God. In Israel God sought the world. Israel was God's point of attack on the world. When from the knowledge that it is God's people Israel derived the certainty of its special election, and because of that considered itself to be superior to the other nations, the prophets must contradict this and recall the people to the living God, whose mercy is great for Israel but also for the world. For in His mercy He called Israel to the service of His kingdom among the nations of the earth.[28]

Karl Barth's Doctrine of Election[29]

McCormack suggests that history will declare that Karl Barth's greatest contribution to the development of church doctrine will be located in his treatment of election.[30] Certainly the doctrine is a central pillar in Barth's theological architecture. In the opening pages of his treatment Barth refers to the doctrine of election as 'the sum of the Gospel because of all the words that can be said or heard it is the best. ... But more, the election of grace is the whole of the Gospel, the Gospel *in nuce*. It is the very essence of all good news.'[31] Barth's extensive deliberations over this doctrine – some 500 pages of densely argued material – are his attempt to maintain the sovereign freedom of divine grace, while avoiding the loss of the character of the doctrine as *grace*, as *gospel*. Barth's complaint is that the traditional grounding of election in an obscure pre-temporal divine decree which divides humanity into those elect and those passed over casts a shadow of darkness over the doctrine because in this formulation the bad news overshadows the good.[32]

What, then, are the major contours of Barth's understanding of election? The first and primary feature of Barth's presentation is his christological

---

[28] T.C. Vriezen, *An Outline of Old Testament Theology* (Oxford, 1970²), 88.

[29] For a fuller discussion of material presented in this section, see M.D. O'Neil, 'Karl Barth's Doctrine of Election', *EQ* 76 (2004), 311–326.

[30] B.L. McCormack, 'Grace and Being: The Role of God's Gracious Election in Karl Barth's Theological Ontology' in J. Webster (ed.), *The Cambridge Companion to Karl Barth* (Cambridge, 2000), 92.

[31] K. Barth, *Church Dogmatics*, II/2, 'The Doctrine of God' (Edinburgh, 1957), 3, 13–14.

[32] See, e.g. Barth's comments on the divine decree – *CD* II/2, 25, 103–4, 134, 146, 158.

ordering of the doctrine. Simply put, Barth's doctrine of election consists 'in the assertion that the divine predestination is the election of Jesus Christ'.[33] From this simple phrase, however, Barth draws significant implications. First, he is making a statement about divine ontology. Before election has a human referent, it refers to God's eternal and unconditional act of self-determination, in which he ordained himself to be God-for-humanity in the person and under the name of Jesus Christ. It is in this way that Barth's theology finds its ontic ground. Neither the incarnation nor the crucifixion represent or effect a change in the divine being because God had already and eternally determined himself to be God in this relationship of oneness with humanity in and through the person of the Son, and to be God *only* in this form and this relation.[34]

Second, Barth identifies Jesus Christ as both electing God and elected person. Barth identifies Jesus Christ as electing God in order to assert that the electing God is not an unknown quantity, but the very God we encounter in Jesus Christ, and that we can go no further back with regard to the mystery of election.[35] Because this is so, it is possible to have complete confidence that God will never prove to be anything other than the God of electing grace, for it is *this* Jesus, who 'for us and for our salvation' suffered and died, who is also the electing God.[36] As elect person, Jesus Christ is not simply one of the elect, nor only the means of the election of all other elect persons, but he is himself *the* elect of God *in* whom all humanity are likewise elected. Jesus Christ, as electing God, elects all humanity in his own humanity and his own election, so that his election carries with it the election of all others. God chose Jesus Christ, and in so doing chose also all humanity and determined that he would be gracious to it.[37] The election of all humanity in Jesus Christ signals their non-rejection – there is no double decree, no decreed rejection, no 'Book of Life' which is simultaneously a Book of Death.[38]

---

[33] *CD* II/2, 103. Barth's entire section on the election of Jesus Christ (CD II/2, 94–194) greatly repays careful study and provides crucial insight into the outlines of his thought.
[34] Clearly, Barth's formulation intends the continued assertion of divine immutability, the incarnation and crucifixion notwithstanding. See J.D. Godsey (ed.), *Karl Barth's Table Talk*, vol 10, *SJT Occasional Papers* (Edinburgh, 1963), 49.
[35] G.W. Bromiley, *Introduction to the Theology of Karl Barth* (Edinburgh, 1979), 87.
[36] Barth, *CD* II/2, 123, 'He is the Lamb slain, and the Lamb slain from the foundation of the world. For this reason, the *crucified* Jesus is the "image of the invisible God".' See also, B.L. McCormack, 'The Sum of the Gospel: The Doctrine of Election in the Theologies of Alexander Schweizer and Karl Barth' in D. Willis and M. Welker (eds.), *Toward the Future of Reformed Theology: Tasks, Topics, Traditions* (Grand Rapids, 1999), 489. He comments, 'This decision – in which God ordains himself to have his being only in the gracious movement which reaches its climax in the cross and resurrection – is election.'
[37] Barth, *CD* II/2, 116–17.
[38] Barth, *CD* II/2, 16, 167–8, 349, 453.

The second feature of Barth's presentation of election is its dialogical character. This is seen firstly in the election of Jesus Christ himself. The basis of the election of Jesus Christ as the elect person lies in the primal obedience of the Son of God in which he willed to be obedient to the determination willed for him by the Father. According to Barth, 'The obedience which He renders as the Son of God is, as genuine obedience, His own decision and electing ... the fact that He is elected corresponds as closely as possible to His own electing.'[39] As the eternal Son, then, he chose his being chosen, a decision affirmed and ratified by his obedience as the incarnate Son. In similar manner all those who are included in the primal election of Jesus Christ must also receive, actualize and make their election concrete by genuine faith, decision and obedience.[40]

The third feature of Barth's presentation concerns the manner in which he orders the election of the community and the individual. Barth deplores the privatization of election that has occurred in the history of theology,[41] and therefore seeks to correct this by positing a 'mediate and mediating' election of the community, between the election of Jesus Christ and that of the individual.[42] According to Barth,

> the one community is *mediate* in that it is the middle point between the election of Jesus Christ and (included in this) the election of those who have believed, and do and will believe, in Him. It is *mediating* in so far as ... all the election that has taken place and takes place in Jesus Christ is mediated, conditioned and bounded by the election of the community.[43]

As already noted, Jesus Christ is the proper and primary focus of election. However, in this election he is not alone, but is with a people whom he represents as king and head.[44] Barth employs the image of the circle to present his understanding of election. Those called and gathered around Jesus Christ constitute an 'inner' circle of the election which has taken place in and with the election of Jesus Christ. Beyond this there exists a wider circle which includes the rest of humanity, and which is labeled by Barth as 'the outer circle of the election which has taken place (and takes place) in Jesus Christ'.[45] When Barth

---

[39] *CD* II/2, 105.
[40] Numerous passages speak of this requirement. See, e.g. *CD* II/2, 177, 236, 320–324.
[41] *CD* II/2, 306.
[42] *CD* II/2, 195–196.
[43] *CD* II/2, 196–197.
[44] *CD* II/2, 8.
[45] *CD* II/2, 196–7. Also, note Barth's parenthetical comment in this sentence. This indicates that Barth considers election an event which occurs in time, as well as in pre-temporal eternity. It is crucial to recognize that for Barth election has two 'moments' and that those in the outer circle are in one sense elect, and in another, yet to be elected, or better, to have their election actualized and made a concrete reality.

speaks of the elect individual he asserts that they are elect only in and with the community, 'elect through its mediacy and elect to its membership ... an election to participation in the ministry of the community'.[46] This inner circle is a circle of proclamation and faith, and those outside of it live lives that are 'lost,' bearing the rejection of those who are apart from Jesus Christ.[47] Barth says further that

> Election means faith. And since those who believe are the Church, election means to be in the Church. We have here a closed circle which cannot be penetrated. There is no election to anything else or to any other situation. There is no election of an individual man on the basis of which he is not led by the Word into faith, and therefore into the fellowship of believers, and therefore into the Church. ... Election and the Church are coinciding circles.[48]

The fourth feature of Barth's presentation has been hinted at already. It is the notion that the election of God is a dynamic rather than a static reality. God is not a prisoner of an unalterable decree uttered in pre-temporal eternity which simply requires an outworking in time. God is a living God and his decree of election is likewise a living decree, an 'act of divine life in the spirit, an act which affects us, an act which occurs in the very midst of time no less than in that far distant pre-temporal eternity'.[49] Election takes the form of the history, encounter and decision between God and humanity which begins in the primal election of Jesus Christ, but which also requires fulfillment in the 'second moment' of election wherein the elected human person, in response to the awakening activity of God, activates him or herself as an elected person and actually elects God.[50] The dynamic quality of election is also displayed in the fact that

---

[46] *CD* II/2, 410.

[47] *CD* II/2, 415.

[48] *CD* II/2, 427–8. Yet this circle is not so closed or predetermined that it cannot expand: 'The election of each individual involves, and his calling completes, an opening up and enlargement of the (in itself) closed circle of the election of Jesus Christ and His community in relation to the world – or (from the standpoint of the world) an invasion of the dark kingdom of the lies which rule in the world. ... The existence of each elect means a hidden but real crossing of frontiers, to the gain of the Kingdom of God' (*CD* II/2, 417. See also, *CD* II/2, 419).

[49] *CD* II/2, 180–85; specifically 185. For a full discussion of the role of the Spirit in Barth's doctrine of election, see M.D. O'Neil, 'The Mission of the Spirit in the Election of God' (unpublished Masters thesis, Murdoch University, 2001).

[50] Barth, *CD* II/2, 177, 180. In this important section Barth wrestles with the intricate dynamic of divine and human autonomy, seeking to establish a comprehensive human autonomy within an overarching divine autonomy. It is also worth noting that this section provides a thorough and effective rebuttal to the notion that Barth's doctrine of election is a 'divine monologue' conducted in pre-temporal eternity in which the entire

in the course of God's eternal deciding we have constantly to reckon with new decisions in time. As the Bible itself presents the matter, there is no election which cannot be followed by rejection, no rejection which cannot be followed by election. ... (God) is always the living God. And since His life is the dynamic of that order, developments and alterations in it are always possible and do in fact take place. Neither in the history of Israel and the Church, nor in the life of the individual can we dismiss these as mere appearance.[51]

The final aspect of Barth's presentation of election to be considered here is his understanding of the purpose of election. Already we have noted that election represents the divine self-determination to be gracious to humanity in Jesus Christ. We have further noted that the election of all humanity in Jesus Christ represents their non-rejection, or what might be termed their election to the promise of election, which must be actualized and confirmed in their own decision so that they then live the life of the elect, and no longer the life of one rejected by God, and threatened by actual rejection.[52] We have also noted the correspondence between election and participation in the life and ministry of the community.

It is evident, then, that Barth conceives of the purpose of election in terms of vocation. As the mediate and mediating community 'it has been chosen out of the world for the very purpose of performing for the world the service which it most needs and which consists simply in giving it the testimony of Jesus Christ and summoning it to faith in Him'. Should the community cease this mediatorial service it has 'forgotten and forfeited' its election.[53] The community exists for the service and witness of Jesus Christ. 'Under this name God Himself established and equipped the people which bears the name to be "a light of the Gentiles", the hope, the promise, the invitation and the summoning of all peoples and at the same time, of course, the question, the demand and the judgment set over the whole of humanity and every individual man.'[54]

Election to vocation is true also of the individual. Barth insists that election not only distinguishes the person of the elect but also determines the life-content to which those so distinguished are called, a life-content which is

---

encounter between God and humanity is dehistoricized and rendered meaningless. For such criticisms of Barth, see A.E. McGrath, *The Making of Modern Christology* (Oxford, 1986), 105–6; H. Thielicke, *Theological Ethics* (Grand Rapids, 1966), 1.98–117. For an important discussion of this theme in Barth, see J. Webster, 'Rescuing the Subject: Barth and Postmodern Anthropology' in G. Thompson and C. Mostert (eds.), *Karl Barth: A Future for Postmodern Theology?* (Adelaide, 2000), 49–69.

[51] Barth, *CD* II/2, 186–187.
[52] See *CD* II/2, 320–324.
[53] *CD* II/2, 196–197.
[54] *CD* II/2, 53.

nothing other than Jesus Christ, who is himself 'the reality and revelation of the life-content of the elect man'.[55] He argues that, 'inwardly and inseparably bound up with that which God is for him, is that which he may be for God; with his deliverance, his employment; with his faith in the promise of God, his responsibility for its further proclamation; with his blessedness, his obedience in his service and commission as a witness of the divine election of grace'.[56]

Jesus Christ, therefore, as elect person, is not only the ground and means of election, but also its pattern. Election is to authentic human existence as that is determined in Jesus Christ the elect person from all eternity, and as it was demonstrated in the earthly existence of Jesus of Nazareth, the incarnate Son of God and Son of Man. True creaturely existence, or authentic humanity, is that which echoes the 'Yes' which is uttered by the Son to the Father from all eternity, and is humanity-for-others in their creaturely existence. It is this form of existence, this life-content which is the *telos* of election, both for the elect individual and the elect community, and which is then blessed and crowned with the gift of eternal participation in the divine life of the triune God. Thus John Webster is able to say of Barth's doctrine that election 'is not fate but form ... election is to that form of human life which Jesus Christ himself establishes'.[57]

Concluding Reflections

Although much more could be written about election both in the Old Testament and in Karl Barth, enough has been said to allow us to make several observations before concluding this essay. First, this brief study has indicated the broad correspondence that exists between Barth's proposal and the Old Testament contours of the concept of election. This correspondence is evident in the manner in which election is grounded in the sovereign freedom of divine grace, is dialogical in character and is dynamic rather than static in nature. It is also evident in both sources that election is primarily a corporate reality with instances of individual election being oriented toward the community. Finally, the correspondence is evident in the teleological nature of election, in which the elect community finds the purpose of its election in the witness it provides to the surrounding world of the word and work of God.

Several differences are also clear. Most apparent, of course, is the christological ordering of the doctrine provided by Barth. However, it is hardly surprising that the Old Testament is silent at this point. Associated with this difference is the view of Preuss that election in the Old Testament is understood as the concrete action of Yahweh in history, and as such does not refer to a supra-temporal decree or activity of God. Barth retains the dynamic aspect of

---

[55] *CD* II/2, 419, 421.
[56] *CD* II/2, 414, cf. 343, 345.
[57] J. Webster, *Karl Barth* (New York, 2000), 191–192.

election as an event which occurs in history, although this 'second moment' of election is grounded in an eternal primal decision of election. Barth's motive for making this move, as already noted, is grounded in dogmatic reflection on the immutability of God in light of the New Testament exposition of the incarnation, and the subsequent death and resurrection of Jesus Christ. These differences, then, may be accounted for by the fact that Barth's reflections include the witness of the New Testament in addition to that of the Old Testament.

This remarkable degree of correspondence provides significant material for a reconsideration of common criticisms directed against Barth's doctrine on the grounds that it is less than biblical.[58] In a sense, it casts the criticisms back onto some of the more Calvinist critics, for in light of election in the Old Testament, it is now they who must examine whether the dogmatic proposal of a pre-temporally fixed decree of election and reprobation is biblically sustainable. Barth himself asks, 'When it is a question of the understanding and exposition of what the Bible calls predestination or election, why and on what authority are we suddenly to formulate a statement which leaves out all mention of Jesus Christ?'[59] He continues, '[O]nly in some other context than that of Holy Scripture can the concept of election, of foreordination, of the eternal divine decree, refer elsewhere, to the twofold mystery of an unknown God and unknown man.'[60]

This leads to a second observation which can only be superficially raised here, but which has to do with theological interpretation of scripture. It is evident that Barth's doctrine does not rest on any particular text of scripture, including Ephesians 1:4 which Barth only rarely mentions in the 500 pages of his exposition. Rather, the form of Barth's doctrine derives from a method of realist theological-canonical exegesis in which he attempts to understand the entirety of the being and purpose of God on the basis of his revelatory activity in Jesus Christ as witnessed in the Old and New Testaments. Barth's method, then, is to use scripture to construct an overarching narrative of the eternal purpose of God, and then to interpret individual texts in light of this narrative.

How adequate is this method? Barth's theological exegesis allows him to interpret the peripheral in light of that which is central, the hidden – in this case, God's eternal election – in light of that which is revealed. As we have seen in this study, this method of reading scripture has yielded profound theological insight, which in many respects is faithful to the contours of the Old Testament presentation of the concept. Nevertheless, it is also true that it leads him at times to strained interpretations of scripture – as in his exposition of Judas or the identification of various 'elect pairs' in the Old Testament which

---

[58] See, e.g. the concerns in D.A. Carson, *Divine Sovereignty and Human Responsibility: Biblical Perspectives in Tension* (London, 1981), 216.
[59] Barth, *CD* II/2, 153.
[60] *CD* II/2, 153.

testify to the duality of election and reprobation – in which he draws conclusions beyond the explicit witness of the text as a whole. As might be anticipated, then, Barth's method exhibits both strength and weakness, which indicates that it is possible to appreciate Barth's construction without being committed to following him entirely.[61]

Third, and in accordance with the matter raised in the introduction of this paper, it has become apparent that John Olley's supposition has been judged accurate, namely, that election in the testimony of the Old Testament is particularly oriented towards the category of service or vocation rather than eternal salvation, and consequently, that the doctrine has suffered in theological history as a result of the neglect of this testimony.

Fourth, the pastoral implications of this study are also very significant. The dynamic and dialogical nature of election as portrayed in the Old Testament and in Barth, as well as its primarily corporate nature has much to contribute to contemporary reflection on the nature of Christian conversion and discipleship. Election, as viewed in this study, forges an inseparable link between Christian confession and Christian life, and so helps counter the widespread vapidity in contemporary Christian commitment. It is not by accident that Barth follows his chapter on 'The Election of God' with another on 'The Command of God' for, as he insists, the two concepts belong together. Nor is it accidental that there is forged an inseparable link between election and obedience in such seminal texts as Exodus 19:4–6. As was the case with Christ (that his being elected corresponded 'as closely as possible to His own electing') so also the confirmation of our own election consists in our choosing to live in obedience to it.[62]

Finally, the ecclesial ramifications of this study also bear reflection. In a profoundly illuminating insight Preuss noted that *'Israel, first of all, must and ought to discover itself again'*.[63] The fundamental requirement of Israel as the elect community was that it live with integrity in accordance with its identity as God's chosen people. By so doing, and only by so doing, could it fulfill its calling to be a priestly kingdom, a light to the gentiles, and a community of witness to the surrounding nations.

Another difference between Barth and the Old Testament emerges here, however. As noted in the discussion above, the mission of Old Testament Israel as a community of witness vis-à-vis the nations is understood in a more passive sense. In Barth's presentation the mission of the church as a community of witness is far more active, and its election must not be understood as an end in itself. No doubt Barth, too, was convinced that the church must live with

---

[61] For a landmark examination of Barth's hermeneutical principles, see R.E. Burnett, *Karl Barth's Theological Exegesis: The Hermeneutical Principles of the Römerbrief Period* (Tübingen, 2001).

[62] *CD* II/2, 105. See also, 2 Pet. 1:10.

[63] Preuss, *Old Testament Theology*, 1.33 (emphasis added).

integrity in accordance with its particular identity,[64] but that is not the focus of his doctrine of election. For Barth, the elect community is essentially an apostolic or missionary church. Indeed, apart from its witness to Jesus Christ it does not exist,[65] for the mission of the church 'is not secondary to its being; the church exists in being sent and in building up itself for the sake of its mission'.[66]

Once more the essential reason for this difference may be traced to the New Testament.[67] Here Barth finds in the existence of the apostles the *telos* of election. Their calling, appointment and mission is paradigmatic for the meaning and purpose of election in every age.[68] In light of the commission given to them and through them to the whole church, it is unthinkable that election could be reduced to a private matter. Rather, says Barth,

> If we ask about the meaning and direction of the life of the elect ... we have to reply that the elect lives as such in so far as he is there on behalf of others, i.e. in so far as it is grounded in him and happens through him that the omnipotent loving-kindness of God is at all events directed and opened up to the world. ... [H]e is saved and blessed on the basis of his election, and is therefore already elected, in order that he may share actively, and not merely passively, in the work and way of the omnipotent loving-kindness of God.[69]

Bibliography

Barth, K., *Church Dogmatics* II/2, 'The Doctrine of God' (G.W. Bromiley (tr.), Edinburgh: T. & T. Clark, 1957).

Bosch, D.J., *Transforming Mission: Paradigm Shifts in Theology of Mission* (Maryknoll, New York: Orbis, 1991).

Bromiley, G.W., *Introduction to the Theology of Karl Barth* (Edinburgh: T. & T. Clark, 1979).

Burnett, R.E., *Karl Barth's Theological Exegesis: The Hermeneutical Principles of the Römerbrief Period*, Wissenschaftliche Untersuchungen zum Neuen Testament 2 Reihe (Tübingen: Mohr Siebeck, 2001).

Carson, D.A., *Divine Sovereignty and Human Responsibility: Biblical Perspectives in Tension* (London: Marshall, Morgan and Scott, 1981).

---

[64] Nowhere is this more evident than in the theses of the Barmen declaration. In being bound to one Lord the church is set free from all lesser allegiances and commitments.

[65] C. O'Grady, *The Church in the Theology of Karl Barth* (London, 1968), 107.

[66] D.J. Bosch, *Transforming Mission: Paradigm Shifts in Theology of Mission* (Maryknoll, 1991), 372. In light of what he regards as Barth's 'magnificent and consistent missionary ecclesiology', Bosch goes on to affirm the assessment of Johannes Aagaard that Barth may be 'the decisive Protestant missiologist in this generation' (373). See also, W. Scott, *Karl Barth's Theology of Mission* (Downers Grove, 1978), 31.

[67] See Barth's exposition of various New Testament passages in *CD* II/2, 423–449.

[68] *CD* II/2, 449.

[69] *CD* II/2, 423.

Clements, R.E., *Old Testament Theology: A Fresh Approach* (London: Marshall, Morgan and Scott, 1978).
Eichrodt, W., *Theology of the Old Testament*, vol. 1 (J.A. Baker (tr.), London: SCM, 1961).
Godsey, J.D. (ed.), *Karl Barth's Table Talk*, vol. 10, Scottish Journal of Theology Occasional Papers (Edinburgh: Oliver and Boyd, 1963).
Klein, W.W., *The New Chosen People: A Corporate View of Election* (Grand Rapids, Michigan: Academie, 1990).
McCormack, B.L., 'Grace and Being: The Role of God's Gracious Election in Karl Barth's Theological Ontology' in J. Webster (ed.), *The Cambridge Companion to Karl Barth* (Cambridge: Cambridge University Press, 2000), 92–110.
— 'The Sum of the Gospel: The Doctrine of Election in the Theologies of Alexander Schweizer and Karl Barth' in D. Willis and M. Welker (eds.), *Toward the Future of Reformed Theology: Tasks, Topics, Traditions* (Grand Rapids, 1999), 489–493.
McGrath, A.E., *The Making of Modern Christology* (Oxford: Blackwell, 1986).
O'Grady, C., *The Church in the Theology of Karl Barth* (London: Geoffrey Chapman, 1968).
O'Neil, M.D., 'Karl Barth's Doctrine of Election', *Evangelical Quarterly* 76 (2004), 311–326.
— 'The Mission of the Spirit in the Election of God' (unpublished Master's thesis, Murdoch University, Perth, Western Australia).
Preuss, H.D., *Old Testament Theology*, 2 vols (L.G. Perdue (tr.), Louisville, Kentucky: Westminster John Knox Press, 1995, 1996).
Rowley, H.H., *The Biblical Doctrine of Election* (London: Lutterworth Press, 1950).
Scott, W., *Karl Barth's Theology of Mission* (Downers Grove, Illinois: Inter-Varsity Press, 1978).
Snaith, N.H., *The Distinctive Ideas of the Old Testament* (Carlisle: Paternoster, 1997 – original, 1944).
Thielicke, H., *Theological Ethics*, vol. 1, 'Foundations' (Grand Rapids, Michigan: Eerdmans, 1966).
Vriezen, T.C., *An Outline of Old Testament Theology* (S. Neuijen (tr.), Oxford: Blackwell, 1970^2).
Webster, J., *Karl Barth* (New York: Continuum, 2000).
— 'Rescuing the Subject: Barth and Postmodern Anthropology' in G. Thompson and C. Mostert (eds.), *Karl Barth: A Future for Postmodern Theology?* (Adelaide: Australian Theological Forum, 2000).
Wright, J.W., 'Election' in D. Alexander and D.W. Baker (eds.), *Dictionary of the Old Testament Pentateuch* (Downer's Grove: Inter-Varsity Press, 2003), 216–219.
Zimmerli, W., *Old Testament Theology in Outline* (D.E. Green (tr.), Edinburgh: T. & T. Clark, 1978).

CHAPTER 13

Repristination. The Recovery of the Gospel in Post-Secular Australia

STUART DEVENISH

Introduction

By any statistical, anecdotal or influence measure the decline of the Australian church is incontestable, such that many evangelical, charismatic and Pentecostal Christians have called for the re-missionalization of Australia. But the question of *how* the re-missionalization task might be achieved is problematic. For most people the primary goal is the recovery or *aggiornamento* of the church itself.[1] But renewal focused on the church encounters particular difficulties which will not be discussed here. My approach in this essay will be to propose that the renewal of the church in our time is dependent on the recovery of the gospel. By 'recovery' I mean the recognition on the part of Christians and non-Christians alike that the message of Jesus represents 'good news' for their lives, contributing positively to each dimension of human existence – physical, social, cultural and spiritual. This alternative approach proceeds on the assumption that the apostolic *kerygma* laid the foundations on which the primitive church was established, and the primary task of the church in our time (as in every time) is the embodiment and proclamation of that *kerygma*. But, following the gutting of the gospel in Bultmann's demythologization programme, the question has become, '*How* can the gospel be renewed?'

Spiritual Exile

In his imaginative 'Faith at the *Nullpunkt*,[2] the Old Testament scholar Walter Brueggemann describes the exile as providing a creative opportunity for Israel

---

[1] Vatican II, for example, called for the renewal of the church. For contemporary examples, see A. Nichols, *Christendom Awake: on Re-energizing the Church in Culture* (Edinburgh, 1999); W.J. Abraham, *The Logic of Renewal* (London, 2003).

[2] 'Nullpunkt' is a term used by Walter Zimmerli in 'Plans for Rebuilding After the Catastrophe of 587' in idem., *I Am Yahweh* (Atlanta, 1982), 11 – cited by W. Brueggemann, 'Faith at the *Nullpunkt*' in J. Polkinghorne and M. Welker (eds.), *The End of the World and the Ends of God: Science and Theology on Eschatology* (Harrisburg, 2000), 145n.9.

to repent and return to God, precisely at the point of its experience of abandonment. Out of this painful spiritual end-point or *Nullpunkt* came Israel's realization that it must relinquish its nostalgia for the past and choose instead to embrace the possibility that God had in mind a unique provision for the new day ahead. Part of that provision was an imaginative new 'algebra' or attitude which would equip Israel for future restoration and obedience. What Israel finds in the 'fissure' of exile is the re-discovery that Yahweh is never at the *nullpunkt* and that exile is a gracious provision of a 'corrective' time-out where the people of God are forced to recover their perspective of faith and hope in the largesse of God's redemptive purposes. Brueggemann observes that Israel's belated embracing of obedience leads to Yahweh's coming to the rescue at three levels: first, at the *communal level* it leads from exile to a purposeful homecoming; second, at the *cosmic level* it leads from shadowy images of chaos to images of a renewed creation; third, at the *personal level* the spectre of death is replaced by God's rescue which results in an outbreak of victorious worship and praise.

There have been moments in history when western Christianity has reached its own *nullpunkt,* but perhaps none have been as critical as the present moment. Since the Enlightenment the church has undergone its own 'Babylonian Captivity' to the hegemonic cultural forces of modernity. The modern period of history is 'less a time than a conceptual place, an ideological tone. It is less a distinct period than an attitude.'[3] At its heart the cultural phenomenon of modernity is the modification of tradition,[4] the commodification of nature, the prioritization of reason and the elevation of ego. Socially, the outcome of modernity has been the fragmentation of beliefs and values, to such an extent that Robert Pippin can state that 'modernity promised us a culture of unintimidated, curious, rational, self-reliant individuals, and it produced ... a herd society, a race of anxious, timid, conformist "sheep", and a culture of utter banality'.[5] Philosophically, modernity has been a season of unremitting scepticism towards religion under Kant's idealism, Hume's naturalism, Comte's positivism, Marx's materialism, Freud's pan-psychism and Nietzsche's pessimism. The theological outcome of modernity's elevation to the dominant *zeitgeist* has not only been the 'displacement of God',[6] but the imposition of an ideological meta-discourse which required theology to adopt the language and thought-forms of modernity in order to express itself and to

---

[3] T.C. Oden, *After Modernity... What? Agenda for Theology* (Grand Rapids, 1992), 44.
[4] J. Deely, *Four Ages of Understanding: The First Postmodern Survey of Philosophy from Ancient Times to the Turn of the Twenty-first Century* (Toronto, 2001), 458.
[5] Cited by C.E. Gunton, *The One, the Three and the Many: God, Creation and the Culture of Modernity* (Cambridge, 1993), 28.
[6] Gunton, *The One, the Three and the Many*, 13.

justify its very existence. The hermeneutics of modernity[7] forcefully legitimates itself by rewarding those who function by its 'rules', and by marginalizing those people and movements who make any form of truth-claims counter to its own. Thus all theology (including evangelical theology in its various forms) has been forced to worship at the altar of modernity.

> The fundamental eros of the leading contemporary theological traditions of Bultmann, Tillich, Bonhoeffer, Whitehead, and Rahner is accommodation to modernity. This is the underlying motif that unites the seemingly vast differences between the many forms of existential theology, process theology, liberation theology, and demythologization – all are searching for some more compatible adjustment to modernity.[8]

On one hand, the result has been the development of an elite cohort of sophisticated and well-read theologians committed to the paradigm of modernity, whose liberal theological constructs have pervaded the thought-forms and power-structures of entire movements within Christian history. And, on the other hand, there have developed at the level of the local Christian church tendencies which have contrived to destroy the *elan vital* (life-force) of experiential Christianity and replace the biblical gospel with a culturally relative belief-system which has proven to be a faulty compass in changing times. The beliefs and convictions which derive from the gospel have been eroded from within by the Trojan horse of an accommodationist theology. This is the bitter-root which has led to the phenomenon of the *nullpunkt* of the gospel and brought about the decline in the western church, including the church in Australia.

Rudolf Bultmann and Demythologization

At the heart of this cultural captivity of the Christian church and its gospel is the person and thought of Rudolf Bultmann (1884–1976). Bultmann was an encyclopaedic scholar and renowned theologian, a graduate of the Tübingen School who became Professor of New Testament at Marburg from 1921 until his retirement in 1951. A range of confluences flow through Bultmann's scholarship. Most pertinent for our purposes here are his commitment to Neo-Kantian idealism and the existentialist philosophy of Martin Heidegger, both of which drank deeply from the wells of modernity and resulted in an intense scepticism concerning the historicity of the biblical record and the plausibility of Christianity's supernaturalist gospel. Bultmann's use of 'world picture' was a direct loan of Heidegger's concept. In his chapter, 'The age of the world

---

[7] J.-F. Lyotard, *The Postmodern Condition: a Report on Knowledge* (Minneapolis, 1993), xix.
[8] Oden, *After Modernity,* 33.

picture', Heidegger contrasts the world picture of the modern world with that of the medieval world and the result is what he calls 'degodisation'.[9] A quotation will assist our discussion.

> The loss of the gods is the situation of indecision regarding God and the gods. Christendom has the greatest share in bringing this about. But the loss of the gods is so far from excluding religiosity that rather only through that loss is the relation of the gods changed into mere 'religious experience'. When this occurs, then the gods have fled. The resultant void is compensated for by means of historiographical and psychological investigation of myth.[10]

And it is precisely this investigation of myth which Bultmann decides to take as central to his theological project in the task of demythologization. For Bultmann, demythologization is predicated on the world picture of the New Testament being 'mythical'. It was Bultmann's conviction that the message of the New Testament was inaccessible to residents of the twentieth century on the basis that the primitive cosmology and supernaturalist epistemology found in its pages lay out of reach of their scientific and rational world-picture.

Positively, the rationale for the demythologization programme was to recover the central *kerygma* of the biblical message by eliminating the 'husk' of its first-century metaphysical thought-forms, so that scientifically-minded twentieth-century citizens could appreciate the intrinsic 'seed' of its redemptive message. Bultmann states,

> Contemporary Christian proclamation is faced with the question whether, when it demands faith from men and women, it expects them to acknowledge [the] mythical world picture of the past. If this is impossible, it then has to face the question whether the New Testament proclamation has a truth that is *independent* of the mythical world picture, in which case it would be the task of theology to demythologise the Christian proclamation.[11]

Negatively, the project of demythologization relied on scientifically-derived methods which called history into question (looking back), which removed the possibility of any form of eschatology (looking forward), which addressed scripture through the sceptical disciplines of textual and source criticism (looking down), and which called into question the transcendent occurrences of the virgin birth, Jesus' miracles and his resurrection (looking up). While Bultmann's intention may have been to bring the gospel of Jesus Christ to the

---

[9] M. Heidegger, *The Question Concerning Technology* (New York, 1997), 115–54, specifically 116. *Entgotterung* means 'loss of the gods' but a direct transliteration is 'degodisation'.
[10] Heidegger, *The Question Concerning Technology*, 116–117.
[11] R. Bultmann, *New Testament & Mythology* (London, 1984), 3 (emphasis added).

cultural foreground by objectifying the gospel through the removal of its mythological components, the exact opposite effect has occurred. As a result, the gospel of redemption through Christ has been brought to its own *nullpunkt*. If it was Nietzsche's 'madman' who announced the 'death of God', it is Bultmann who has effectively conducted the experiment which brought about the death of the Christian gospel in our time.

Christianity Captive to Modernity

As justification for the programme of demythologization, Bultmann states that it is 'impossible to repristinate a past world picture by sheer resolve, especially a mythical world picture, now that all of our thinking is irrevocably formed by science'.[12] So committed was Bultmann to the idea of mankind's progression towards a form of social utopianism (the goal of both Marxist eschatology and Darwinian social-evolution) that he makes no allowance for so-called 'primitive' mythology to re-emerge into the social and psychological development of a later (and therefore supposedly higher) cohort of humanity. It is interesting to note that Bultmann's programme of demythologization exhibits an inordinate 'faith' in science and an extremity of 'doubt' concerning religion and its place in modern society.

Dostoyevsky's question, 'Can civilised men believe?'[13] is more than a rhetorical question. It challenges the assumption that only the religious person lives by faith with the assertion that all people operate out of epistemological presuppositions, the ontological foundations of which have no possibility of empirical proof. This is also true of the truth-claims of modernity (e.g., rationalism, immanence and materialism) something which is now becoming evident. Huston Smith states that 'Modernity's coming to see the gods it worshipped for what they were – idols that failed – was the most important religious event of the twentieth century. With the ground cleared of these illusions, we can now inspect the scorched earth to see if it shows signs of new life.'[14]

The secularization thesis (so popular amongst sociologists and, indeed, some theologians) has turned out to be an embarrassing debacle for humanist scholarship. Nancy Ammerman suggests that the picture of religion painted by many sociologists was one of 'a shrunken, emasculated apparition at the periphery of modern society'.[15] It is ironic then that the world picture of modernity (the harbinger of Cartesian doubt and the well from which almost all

---

[12] Bultmann, *New Testament & Mythology*, 3.
[13] Cited by H. Smith, *Why Religion Matters: the Fate of the Human Spirit in an Age of Disbelief* (New York, 2001), 155.
[14] Smith, *Why Religion Matters*, 153.
[15] N.T. Ammerman, *Bible Believers: Fundamentalists in the Modern World* (New Brunswick, 1987), 2.

critics of religion have liberally imbibed) is itself in a state of demise. From the 'scorched earth' of modernity's demise there has now arisen the 'post'-modern world picture which has awakened a veritable avalanche of 'pre-modern' manifestations of the spiritual. Those manifestations include western articulations of the pseudo-religious New Age, the ancient forms of pre-Christian paganism or 'perennial philosophy', and the emergence of the monolithic phenomenon of Islam onto the world's stage. Religion has simply refused to 'go away'. And Christianity itself (unlikely as it might appear from its present weakened state in the western world) is undergoing a revolution in the so-called two-thirds world. The African theologian John Mbiti urges that the signs of the 'church's universality [are] no longer in Geneva, Rome, Athens, Paris, London, New York, but Kinshasa, Buenos Aires, Addis Ababa and Manila'.[16]

But it would be too simplistic to argue that Bultmann's demythologization project can now be safely consigned to the annals of history. On the contrary, this essay takes as its point of departure the fact that Bultmann's demythologizing project continues to exert considerable influence on western Christian theology, and that this represents the most significant point of resistance to Christian mission in the contemporary world, including Australia. Liberal theology's vocal champion John Shelby Spong (Bultmann's theological grandchild) continues to forcefully articulate a disembowelled gospel fashioned more from the substance of modern epistemology than from biblical content. This impulse finds ready support from secular and humanist proponents in the fields of philosophy, sociology and literary theory. The impression given to interested onlookers is that liberal Christianity has sold its birthright for a mess of pottage, and what remains is a devitalized movement whose truth-claims are implausible and irrelevant. This betrayal of the gospel represents a major source of anxiety to biblically-grounded Christians and *the* primary disincentive to those 'carriers'[17] of the gospel who by reason of their office or calling within the Christian community have been charged with the proclamation of the gospel to the world.

Bultmann's Critics

From the beginning there have been strong critics of Bultmann's approach. Karl Barth tried to sympathetically 'understand' Bultmann saying (with irony), 'I know of no contemporary theologian who has so much to say about understanding, or one which has so much cause to complain of being

---

[16] J. Mbiti, *Christianity in Africa* (Edinburgh, 1995), 154, cited by P. Jenkins, *The Next Christendom: the Coming of Global Christianity* (Oxford, 2002), 2.

[17] A term used by C.S. Lewis of evangelists and missionaries whose task is to 'infect' people with the message of Christ. See C.S. Lewis, *Mere Christianity* (London, 1970), 159.

misunderstood.'[18] Helmut Thielicke says there is no escaping Bultmann's challenge, it represents a *status confessionis*[19] which expresses the 'spirit' of the modern age and as such represents 'the most serious challenge theologians have had to face for many a day'.[20] For Thielicke the result of Bultmann's demythologizing project is the inversion of the outward, objective historical and theological significance of the 'Christ event' to become an internal, subjective psychological and existential 'personal awakening' for so-called 'modern' humanity. In this scenario Bultmann's demythologized ('degodized'?) theology is little more than 'an imminentist philosophy of consciousness',[21] and either we follow its trajectory towards an end-point which is anything but Christian, or we undertake a radical re-examination of the concept of myth from within orthodox theology in order to win a new freedom of the truth as we know it in Christ.[22]

Likewise David Cairns was concerned with the question of pastoral application of Bultmann's theology when he asked the question, 'Will this preach?'[23] In simple terms his answer is 'No!' on the basis that the internal tensions generated by Bultmann's theology render a disastrous assault on his own project which ultimately 'sinks' the vessel he seeks to launch.[24] From these critics we learn that today's Christians should be suspicious of Bultmann's demythologization project on the grounds that within it lie the seeds of the destruction of the gospel. In being reinterpreted from God's historic call to repentance into the language and philosophy of twentieth century modernity the gospel is subjected to a negative alchemy through which it loses its saving genius. As Athanasius foresaw, Athens has encamped around Jerusalem and overrun it.

The Concept of 'Myth'

Bultmann's assertion that it is 'impossible to repristinate a past world picture'[25] begs the question of what it is that requires repristination – culture, epistemology or the gospel? Again, it is important to note Bultmann's deep dependence on Heidegger's concept of 'world picture'. The logical place to

---

[18] Cited by J. Schneiwind, 'A Reply to Bultmann' in H.-W. Bartsch (ed.), *Kerygma and Myth: a Theological Debate* (London, 1972), 83.
[19] H. Thielicke, 'The Restatement of New Testament Mythology' in Bartsch (ed.), *Kerygma and Myth*, 138.
[20] Thielicke, 'The Restatement', 140
[21] Thielicke, 'The Restatement', 153.
[22] Thielicke, 'The Restatement', 173–174.
[23] D. Cairns, *A Gospel Without Myth? Bultmann's Challenge to the Preacher* (London, 1960).
[24] Cairns, *A Gospel Without Myth?*, 218.
[25] Bultmann, *New Testament & Mythology*, 3.

begin is by observing that the 'pristine' state of which Bultmann speaks is the first century world picture which he imagines is a three-story structure, 'with earth in the middle, heaven above it, and hell below it'.[26] Bultmann appears to pit the gospel against culture, mistakenly assuming that the gospel can stand apart from culture as something hermetically distinct. This is in deep contrast to the Christological doctrine of the incarnation and to basic missiological anthropology, both of which presuppose that the gospel must always be embedded within the particularity of a given time, place and culture. Barth sharpens the question when he asks, 'Who is it, or what is it, in the New Testament which before all else calls for constant new understanding and exposition? Is it the 'cradle' of the language, the thought-forms ... in which the message is enshrined? Or is it not before all else the message itself?'[27]

Granted, Bultmann is seeking to carry out a missiological task when he seeks to interpret the gospel across the divide of language and culture *without* the missiological tools of contextualization and enculturation which only became available in the late 1970s. Nonetheless he makes the mistake of associating too closely Jesus' message of redemption with the contours of first century thought-forms and culture. As Barth points out, it is not culture which must be in any sense 'restored', but the relevance and potency of the gospel. It is the gospel which has been lost in transmission across generational and linguistic divides – not culture.

The times and circumstances in which we find ourselves in twenty-first century Australia, for example, are clearly different from those in which Bultmann formulated his disastrous demythologizing project. These are times in which the hegemony of modernity has given way to the cultural tribalism of postmodernity and times in which Australians are now asking questions of meaning as a matter of course – often mediated through spirituality. Therefore the questions today's Australian Christian must ask are, first, 'What is the relevance of the Christian gospel in contemporary Australia?' and, second, 'Can the gospel be repristinated so as to provide answers to the spiritual seeking of contemporary Australians?'

In seeking to answer these questions there is good reason for putting forward an argument which runs directly counter to Bultmann's project of demythologization. While that project sought to reinterpret the supposed primitive and mythological world picture of the New Testament into the scientific world picture of twentieth century humanity; the counter-argument I will now put forward seeks not to de-mythologize the gospel but to re-mythologize it. Understandably contemporary readers may be wary of the concept of myth, but careful attention to its meaning will offer surprising results.

---

[26] S. Ogden, *New Testament & Mythology* (London, 1984), 1.
[27] In Bartsch (ed.), *Kerygma and Myth*, 2.87.

It is routine for dictionaries to provide multiple definitions for a concept, indicating that more than one meaning can be found for most words or concepts. Myth is no exception. The *Macquarie Dictionary*[28] provides the following definitions of 'myth' (abbreviated): (1) A traditional story, usually concerning some superhuman being or person; a traditional story about deities and the creation of the world. (2) Any invented story; an imaginary or fictitious thing or person. The first definition can be referred to as the 'classical' understanding of myth in the sense that it refers to the 'founding stories' of a tribe, people, religious group or culture. In this classical definition, myth refers to the defining story from which the identity and reason-for-being of the community which owns it is derived.

Every social, ethnic and religious grouping requires a set of central 'facticities' from which it derives its history, identity, traditions and reasons-for-being. This is as true of scientists, philosophers and agnostics as it is for Hindus, Buddhists and Christians. This statement reveals the fact that myth is not simply an out-moded vestige from the past (as Comte asserted), but is a continuing necessity for the health and wellbeing of all peoples and cultures in all places at all times. Anthropologists such as Charles Kraft take myth seriously, knowing that central to the proper functioning of a society's maze-ways and patterns of social meaning is a healthy mythology – including the components of religion and worldview.[29] Examples of 'myths' which function in contemporary Australian culture are the 'ANZAC myth', the prevailing myth of the Australian outback, the stories of bushrangers such as Ned Kelly, the picnic at Hanging Rock, and mythical creatures such as the yowie. In each case these myths provide a deep and abiding sense of 'texture' and 'feel' to the Australian identity.

The second definition of myth can be referred to as the 'popular' understanding of myth; something which is nothing more than fairy-tale, blatantly untrue and has no apparent basis in fact. This is the realm of the 'urban myth' where stories which purport to be true on the grounds of some level of plausibility circulate through popular culture, but have no enduring basis in truth. The early Church, for good reason, was anxious about this 'popular' form of myth. Paul wrote to Timothy and Titus warning them to 'have nothing to do with godless myths and old wives' tales' (1 Tim. 4:7).[30] The practical nature of these minor epistles implies that Paul's protreptic injunctions are not statements of philosophical apologetic, but of differentiation between the emerging Christian church and the received Jewish, Greek and

---

[28] A. Delbridge, J.R.L. Bernard, D. Blair, et al. (eds.), *The Macquarie Dictionary* (Sydney, 1981), 1133.

[29] See C. Kraft, *Christianity in Culture: a Study in Dynamic Biblical Theologizing in Cross-Cultural Perspective* (Maryknoll, 1990).

[30] See 1 Tim. 1:4; 4:7; 2 Tim. 4:4; Tit. 1:14.

Roman religious beliefs with their accompanying superstitions and folk-traditions.

The Gospel as Myth

The task before us is to provide the outlines for the resuscitation or 'repristination' of the Christian gospel in Australia and beyond. I propose to provide such an outline by establishing three immovable points.

(1) THE GOSPEL AT THE CORE OF CHRISTIANITY IS 'MYTHICAL' IN FORM

The gospel is the underlying story which has provided the Christian community with its legitimating story from its inception, and as such assumes a function which is mythic in character. The New Testament scholar N.T. Wright refers to the Gospels as 'myth' in the sense that 'they are the foundational stories for the early Christian worldview'.[31] Therefore the Gospels can be understood as 'myth' in the 'classical' sense referred to above, as narrativized accounts of the historic Christ-event from which the *kerygma* or gospel of redemption is to be found. The 'mythic' element of the Christian gospel is 'true' only if one is a Christian and has undergone the crisis of conversion and come to reside 'within' the meaning structure it provides. George Lindbeck calls this 'intratextuality', a process whereby one is delivered 'inside' the truth of the Christian confession. He says, 'Becom[ing] a Christian involves learning the story of Israel and of Jesus well enough to interpret and experience oneself and one's world in its terms.'[32]

Two scholars in particular have contributed to a contemporary understanding of myth insofar as it relates to the Christian message. The first is Catholic theologian Urs von Balthasar, in his *Theodramatik* (1973–1983) and his volume, *The Glory of the Lord: a Theological Aesthetics* (1982). After establishing a similarity between the themes of the Old Testament and ancient Egyptian, Sumerian and Babylonian mythologies, Balthasar identifies in Jesus – the central focus of the New Testament – someone who fulfils the categories of myth in a surprising way. Citing Bentzen,[33] Balthasar writes, 'Jesus ... unifies all the aspects of the primal man and, in the story of his humiliation and exaltation, again brings to bear the whole mythology of the ancient East. .... [Therefore] not all myth can be cast on the rubbish heap of theology.'[34] For Balthasar Christ so fulfilled the type and anti-type of classical myth that he

---

[31] N.T. Wright, *The New Testament and the People of God* (London, 1992) 426.
[32] G. Lindbeck, *The Nature of Doctrine: Religion and Theology in a Postliberal Age* (Philadelphia, 1984), 34.
[33] A. Bentzen, *Messias, Moses redivivus, Menschensohn* (Zurich, 1948), 56.
[34] H.U. von Balthasar, *The Glory of the Lord, a Theological Aesthetics* (Edinburgh, 1982), 1.633.

elevates it; indeed, he transposes 'mythical existence into Christian existence'.³⁵ In this case

> The Biblical and Christian history of salvation was such a totally new beginning over against the mythical theater that it was simply impossible to effect a transposition and assimilation, at least in the early stages. The mystery of God's stepping into the world had to be clearly distinguished from everything mythological. Only at a later stage of reflection, if at all, could this mystery be understood ... as the true drama.³⁶

Balthasar argues for the continued use of myth as applied to the way in which the Christian gospel functions for the Christian faith community (the 'classical' definition), but is careful to distinguish it from other mythologies which were predominant in the early centuries of the developing Christian self-awareness (the 'popular' definition).

The second writer who has contributed to a Christian understanding of myth is C.S. Lewis who converted to Christianity in 1929 during the early stages of Bultmann's career. Lewis describes Christianity as a 'true myth'. Because of the clarity of Lewis's writing it is best to allow him to speak for himself.

> [T]he heart of Christianity is a myth which is also a fact. The old myth of the Dying God, *without ceasing to be myth*, comes down from the heaven of legend and imagination to the earth of history. It *happens* – at a particular date, in a particular time, followed by definable historical consequences. We pass from a Balder or an Osirir, dying nobody knows when or where, to a historical Person crucified ... *under Pontius Pilate*. By becoming fact it does not cease to be myth: that is the miracle. ... God is more than god, not less: Christ is more than Balder, not less. We must not be ashamed of the mythical radiance resting on our theology. We must not be nervous about 'parallels' and 'pagan Christs': they *ought* to be there – it would be a stumbling block if they weren't. We must not, in false spirituality, withhold our imaginative welcome. If God chooses to be mythopoeic – and is not the sky itself a myth – shall we refuse to be *mythopathetic*?³⁷

> Now the story of Christ is simply a true myth: a myth working on us in the same way as [any] other, but with this tremendous difference that it *really happened* and one must be content to accept it in the same way, remembering that it is God's myth where the other myths are men's myths; i.e. the Pagan stories are

---

[35] Balthasar, *The Glory of the Lord*, 634.
[36] Balthasar, *Theo-Dramatic Theory. 1. Prolegomena* (1988), 91-2, cited by A. Nichols, *No Bloodless Myth; a Guide through Balthasar's Dramatics* (Edinburgh; 2000), 22.
[37] C.S. Lewis, cited by Louis A. Marcos, 'Myth Matters' in *Christianity Today*, at {http://www.christianitytoday.com/ct/2001/006/1.32.html}, accessed 20.10.04.

God expressing Himself through the minds of poets, using such images He found there while Christianity is God expressing Himself through what we call 'real things'. Therefore it is true, not in the sense of being a 'description' of God (that no finite mind would take in) but in the sense of being the way in which God chooses to (or can) appear to our faculties.[38]

It should not surprise us that both authors are working in the field of aesthetics, and both discover the reality that Christ fulfils and exceeds the archetype of the mythical hero, the truth-claims about whom are trans-rational and universally applicable.

(2) IT IS POSSIBLE TO 'REPRISTINATE' THE GOSPEL

Despite having been demythologized it *is* possible for the gospel to be 'repristinated'. Arguably the result of the 'demythologization' project has been something other than that which Bultmann himself expected. It would have surprised him to discover that the result of his demythologization project has not been to demythologize the *kerygma* but to dekerygmatize the church.[39] Our task now is to deconstruct the demythologizing project and to 'repristinate' the Christian gospel in order to allow it to do its work of spiritual enlivening in the world in which we live today. How can this be done?

First, there are precedents in the biblical drama which strengthen the case for the possibility of repristination. The account of Josiah's reform is found in 2 Kings 22 – 23 and 2 Chronicles 34 – 35. Josiah ascended the throne of Judah as a young vassal king under Sennacherib of Assyria. His reign came at a time when idolatry was rampant in Judah and Israel, the Book of the Law had been lost, the Temple worship had become degraded by the inclusion of altars to the Baals and the Asherah, and the Passover as Israel's primary cultic-celebration had been discontinued. Josiah began seeking God, and as he began defiling the images and altars of the pagan deities, a number of things happened. The Book of the Law was found, the Passover was re-instituted, and the covenant between Judah and Yahweh was renewed. But despite Josiah's best efforts, the reform appears to have been a top-down affair with little participation from the people as a whole, and the result was an abortive attempt to recover the covenantal relationship between the Israelite nation and its God Yahweh. The failure of the reform is recorded in 2 Kings 23:26–27.

> Nevertheless, the Lord did not turn away from the heat of his fierce anger, which burned against Judah because of all that Manasseh had done to provoke him to anger. So the Lord said, 'I will remove Judah also from before my presence as I

---

[38] R.L. Green and W. Hooper, *A Biography of C.S. Lewis* (London, 1974), 116–118.
[39] The insight is provided by the Swiss theologian Fritz Buri, cited by H. Ott, 'Objectification and Existentialism' in Bartsch (ed.), *Kerygma and Myth*, 307.

removed Israel, and I will reject Jerusalem, the city I chose, and this Temple, about which I said, 'There shall my Name be.'

The reform instituted by Josiah was not enough to forestall Yahweh's judgement as is evident in the fall of Jerusalem under Nebuchadnezzar (king of Babylon) some twenty-five years later. Following Israel's exile to Babylon, Jeremiah composed a lament for Josiah (2 Chr. 35:25 and Jer. 22:10) to mark the end of the short-lived attempt to restore the covenant.

The fact remains however that during the seventy years of captivity a *nullpunkt* was arrived at where a new 'algebra' of faith was rediscovered, and the certainty of restoration was prophesied. Jeremiah foretold the time when Yahweh himself would renew the covenant, saying, 'I will put my law in their minds and write it on their hearts. I will be their God and they will be my people' (Jer. 31:33). Isaiah too spoke of renewal of the kingship (Is. 32:1), of the covenant (55:3 and 59:21), of God's favour towards his people (61:1-2), and of Jerusalem (the centre of Israel's worship) which would now become a 'city no longer deserted' (62:12). In these passages God himself is the originator and source of a form of renewal which goes beyond that imagined by the Old Testament. In Christ, God was reconciling the world to himself (2 Cor. 5:19) and signalling the prospect of the renewal not only of his free offer of salvation to all those who came near through faith in Christ, but of history and the cosmos itself.

Second, the world has moved on from the false idealism of modernity upon which Bultmann stood as he undertook his demythologization project. No longer can we be certain of the ubiquitous acceptance of the so-called scientific world picture – on the contrary, there is a spiritual renaissance erupting beneath our very feet. Huston Smith makes the statement that 'the traditional [religious] worldview is transparently intelligible, the scientific worldview is not'.[40] According to David Tacy, spirituality is on the rise in Australia and finds expression in such diverse fields as the theory of culture and society, theoretical physics, anthropology, Australian theology, feminist theology, postmodern theory, nursing and health studies, and Aboriginal cultural studies.[41] Tacy's work represents an important contribution to studies of spirituality and religion in Australia. He states that 'spirituality is not a marginal experience, but is pivotal and central to human experience; it is only our embarrassment or arrogance (or a mixture of both) that relegates it to the margins'.[42] According to Tacy, the problem with established religion (e.g. Christianity) is that it has 'rejected the truth of *mythos* (story) for the truth of *logos* (reason)'.[43] Again, according to Tacy,

---

[40] Smith, *Why Religion Matters*, 233.
[41] D. Tacy, *Re-enchantment: the New Australian Spirituality* (Sydney, 2000), 3.
[42] Tacy, *Re-enchantment*, 22.
[43] Tacy, *Re-enchantment*, 30.

> Our [Australian] tastes and attitudes clear away all unnecessary encumbrances, paving the way for a direct and often shattering experience of the divine. In this light, the Australian anti-religious temperament can be viewed almost as a kind of radical Protestantism, an attack on religious orthodoxy, a resistance to authority, a clearing away of icons, not to get rid of God but to know God more directly. Australians have unwittingly set the scene for a dramatic inclusion of the sacred into their lives.[44]

However the unfolding spiritual renaissance in Australia is not matched by the preparedness of the churches to offer a living spirituality based upon the teachings of the 'way' of Jesus. Watts and Williams make the statement that

> Many people assum[e] that the Christian churches have little serious interest in helping people to follow a path of personal religious transformation, and that for this it is necessary to turn to Oriental traditions. There are many who have turned to transcendental meditation on the assumption that nothing similar was available in Christianity. .... We are disappointed that Christianity has kept its own contemplative tradition so hidden that most 'outsiders', and perhaps quite a few 'insiders' are wholly unaware of it.[45]

I believe that this unpreparedness on the part of the churches is directly accountable to the churches having lost any form of gospel to preach to those who are lost and who seek spiritual meaning in order to replenish their souls. In real terms the west – including Australia – is now undergoing a spiritual revolution. Australia is now a mission field[46] but the spiritual 'responsiveness' of the average Australian is not matched by the missional 'readiness' of the churches. I believe that readiness will be recovered when the gospel is renewed or 'repristinated'.

Third, nature and the outward objects of human observation might well be the proper objects of scientific attention, but spirituality and religious experience do not properly belong to that realm. As Max Scheler states,

> The God of religious consciousness 'is' and lives exclusively in the religious act, not in metaphysical thinking extraneous to religion. ... The God of religion is the god of the saints and the god of the people, not the cerebral god of the 'intellectuals.' The fount of all religious truth is not scientific utterance but *faith* in the words of the *homo religiosus*, the 'holy man.'[47]

---

[44] Tacy, *Re-enchantment*, 62.
[45] F. Watts and M. Williams, *The Psychology of Religious Knowing* (London, 1988), 3.
[46] R.W. Jenson, 'What is a Post-Christian?' in C.E. Braaten and R.W. Jenson (eds.), *The Strange New Word of the Gospel* (Grand Rapids, 2002), 29.
[47] M. Scheler, *On the Eternal in Man* (New York, 1960), 134.

If repristination of the Christian gospel is to take place in the contemporary world, then it must mean above all that people of faith participate in the realities of the gospel *as if it were fundamentally true*. One of the difficulties western Christians have had to engage is the notion of 'true' and 'false'. In a world of scientific language where the criteria for establishing truth are closely monitored, religious truth-claims have suffered exhaustive interrogation. But, as Polkinghorne asserts, a myth is neither 'true nor false, it is either living or dead'.[48]

If a myth has become degraded, as the Christian gospel has become during the reign of modernity, it can only be renewed and restored by those who receive it as true as a spiritual artifact in the 'doing of faith' in the wider world. The conditions for the re-actualization of myth revolve around two things. The first is the wholistic participation of the community for whom the myth is determinative, and the second is the changes in cultural circumstances which cause the wider culture to adopt the truth-claims inherent within the myth as an innovation which is relevant to its deepest concerns. Both of these are occurring in our day as a kind of involuntary, self-correcting removal of Cartesian dualism which works to re-integrate human consciousness in a re-enchanted spiritual world where myth once again 'actualizes' the human spirit.

(3) A REPRISTINATED GOSPEL PROVIDES A SUPERNATURAL HOPE

Finally, only when repristinated can the gospel be presented as the 'good news' of Jesus Christ; the supernatural intervention of God into his world which has the potential to breathe life back into the Christian community, to meet the spiritual needs of 'seekers', and to provide a fresh spiritual resource for culture-building in an age of fragmentation and decline. It is in this sense that the stanza from T.S Eliot's 'Four Quartets' finds its application, 'We shall not cease from exploration, and the end of all our exploring will be to arrive where we started, and to know the place for the first time.'[49]

Summary

The task of this essay has been to offer an alternative to Bultmann's misguided and mistaken demythologization programme, the outcome of which has been the disempowerment of the church's mission in our day. As we have seen, Bultmann's criticism of the New Testament writers for their entrapment in the worldview of first century Palestine was characterized by his own blindness to his own cultural entrapment to the worldview of twentieth century Germany.

On the rising tide of spiritual re-enchantment in the twenty-first century, it is now possible to speak of the repristination of the gospel of Christ, on the

---

[48] Cited by R. Miller, *Arguments Against Secular Culture* (London, 1995), 165.
[49] Cited by O. Guiness, *The Journey; our Quest for Faith and Meaning* (Colorado Springs, 2001), 219.

basis of its re-mythologization. Christ, the dying and rising hero of faith, comes to 'save' his wayward people precisely at their *nullpunkt* or moment of greatest need. The humanist scholar Erasmus made the comment that 'to restore great things is sometimes a harder and nobler task than to have introduced them'.[50] While our task *has* been difficult, nonetheless it has cleared the way for the reinvigoration of Christian mission in the contemporary western world, Australia included.

It is a pleasure to have written this essay for Dr. John Olley: friend, pastor, leader, teacher, scholar and missionary extraordinaire!

Bibliography

Abraham, W.J., *The Logic of Renewal* (London: SPCK, 2003).
Ammerman, N.T., *Bible Believers: Fundamentalists in the Modern World* (New Brunswick: Rutgers University Press, 1987).
Bartsch, H.-W. (ed.), *Kerygma and Myth: a Theological Debate* (London: SPCK, 1972).
Bentzen, A., *Messias, Moses redivivus* (Zurich: Menschensohn, 1948).
Brueggemann, W., 'Faith at the *Nullpunkt*' in J. Polkinghorne and M. Welker (eds.), *The End of the World and the Ends of God: Science and Theology on Eschatology* (Harrisburg, Philadelphia: Trinity Press, 2000), 143–154.
Bultmann, R., *New Testament and Mythology and Other Basic Writings* (London: SCM, 1984).
Cairns, D., *A Gospel Without Myth? Bultmann's Challenge to the Preacher* (London: SCM, 1960).
Deely, J., *Four Ages of Understanding: The First Postmodern Survey of Philosophy from Ancient Times to the Turn of the Twenty-first Century* (Toronto: University of Toronto Press, 2001).
Delbridge, A., J.R.L. Bernard, D. Blair, et al. (eds.), *Macquarie Dictionary* (Sydney: Macquarie Library, 1981).
Green, R.L. and W. Hooper, *A Biography of C.S. Lewis* (London: Souvenir Press, 1974).
Guiness, O., *The Journey; Our Quest for Faith and Meaning* (Colorado Springs, Colorado: Navpress, 2001).
Gunton, C.E., *The One, the Three and the Many: God, Creation and the Culture of Modernity* (Cambridge: Cambridge University Press, 1993).
Heidegger, M., *The Question Concerning Technology* (New York: Harper & Rowe, 1997).
Jenkins, P., *The Next Christendom: the Coming of Global Christianity* (Oxford: Oxford University Press, 2002).
Jenson, R.W., 'What is a Post-Christian?' in C.E. Braaten and R.W. Jenson (eds.), *The Strange New Word of the Gospel* (Grand Rapids, Michigan: Eerdmans, 2002).
Kraft, C., *Christianity in Culture: a Study in Dynamic Biblical Theologizing in Cross-Cultural Perspective* (Maryknoll, New York: Orbis, 1990).
Lewis, C.S., *Mere Christianity* (London: Collins Fontana, 1970).

---

[50] Cited by W.J. Abraham, *The Logic of Renewal* (London, 2003), 144.

Lindbeck, G., *The Nature of Doctrine: Religion and Theology in a Postliberal Age* (Philadelphia: Westminster Press, 1984).
Lyotard, J.-F., *The Postmodern Condition: a Report on Knowledge* (Minneapolis: University of Minnesota Press, 1993).
Marcos, L.A., 'Myth Matters', *Christianity Today*, {http://www.christianitytoday.com/ct/2001/006/1.32html}
Mbiti, J., *Christianity in Africa* (Edinburgh: Edinburgh University Press, 1995).
Miller, R., *Arguments Against Secular Culture* (London: SCM, 1995).
Nichols, A., *Christendom Awake: on Re-energizing the Church in Culture* (Edinburgh: T & T Clark, 1999).
— *No Bloodless Myth; a Guide through Balthasar's Dramatics* (Edinburgh; T. & T. Clark, 2000).
Oden, T., *After Modernity... What? Agenda for Theology* (Grand Rapids, Michigan: Zondervan, 1992).
Ogden, S., *New Testament & Mythology* (London: SCM, 1984).
Polkinghorne, J. and M. Welker (eds.), *The End of the World and the Ends of God: Science and Theology on Eschatology* (Harrisburg, Philadelphia: Trinity Press, 2000).
Scheler, M., *On the Eternal in Man* (New York: Harper, 1960).
Schneiwind, J., 'A Reply to Bultmann' in H.-W. Bartsch (ed.), *Kerygma and Myth: A Theological Debate* (London: SPCK, 1972), 45–101.
Smith, H., *Why Religion Matters: the Fate of the Human Spirit in an Age of Disbelief* (New York: Harper San Francisco, 2001).
Tacy, D., *Re-enchantment: the New Australian spirituality* (Sydney: HarperCollins, 2000).
Thielicke, H., 'The Restatement of New Testament Mythology' in H.-W. Bartsch (ed.), *Kerygma and Myth: A Theological Debate* (London: SPCK, 1972), 138–174.
Turner, P., 'The powerlessness of talking heads: re-evangelization in a postmodern world – the place of ethics' in C.E. Braaten and R.W. Jenson (eds.), *The Strange New Word of the Gospel: Re-Evangelizing in the Postmodern World* (Grand Rapids, Michigan: Eerdmans, 2002).
Urs von Balthasar, Hans, *The Glory of the Lord, a Theological Aesthetics,* (Edinburgh; T. & T. Clark, 1982).
Watts, F. and M. Williams, *The Psychology of Religious Knowing*, (London: Geoffrey Chapman, 1988).
Wilder, A., 'A Hard Death', *Poetry* 107 (1965–66), 168–169.
Wright, N.T., *The New Testament and the People of God* (London: SPCK, 1992).
Zimmerli, W., 'Plans for Rebuilding after the Catastrophe of 587' in idem., *I Am YAHWEH* (Atlanta: John Knox Press, 1982).

CHAPTER 14

From 'Behave, Believe, Belong' to 'Belong, Believe, Behave' – A Missional Journey for the 21st Century

BRIAN S. HARRIS

Introduction

It was a throw away comment made by Craig Vernall at the *Mission to New Zealand* Conference, June, 2003.[1] Talking about the changes that had seen his congregation grow from a weekly attendance of around one hundred and fifty to seven hundred, he said that a key ethos change had been from 'behave, believe, belong' to 'belong, believe, behave'. The implication was that in the past you would only feel welcome in the church if your behaviour was consistent with certain sub-cultural expectations of what was acceptable for church-goers. Having met the implied ethical requirements of church attendance, you would imbibe the setting and doctrine so that you came to a place of belief which in turn would lead to formally belonging to the church community. But now, Vernall suggested, his church community had found a way to welcome and embrace the wider community in such a way that they belonged before they either believed or behaved in a manner consistent with Christian faith.

I thought it a comment worth pondering. And did so. It was reinforced when reading Webber's *The Younger Evangelicals*. Again it was an incidental comment. Webber attributes it to an email he received from Dawn Haglund where speaking of paradigm shifts she suggests that the old paradigm was 'behave, believe, belong' but the new is 'belong, believe, behave'.[2]

I thought back to some of my pastoral experiences. I remembered the outcry when one of the young students on our welcoming team arrived to fulfil her duty barefooted and wearing Bermuda shorts. She had come straight from the

---

[1] C. Vernall, 'Bethlehem's Journey', *Mission to New Zealand* Conference (Auckland: Carey Baptist College, 2003).
[2] R. Webber, *The Younger Evangelicals: Facing the Challenges of the New World* (Grand Rapids, 2002), 48.

beach. Several members of the congregation approached me and asked me to give her a talk on the importance of appropriate dress. 'After all,' as some of them said, 'if you were going to visit the Queen you'd wear your smartest clothes. And worship is entry into the presence of one greater than royalty.'

I also recollected the delightfully eccentric academic who had come to faith through the ministry of the church. Post-conversion he was as eccentric as before. For some this was offensive. I remember one regular at the church prayer meeting routinely praying that he would *really* be converted. I always wondered what that prayer meant.

Another memory was of the longhaired young man who had formerly struggled with drug abuse. In an era when church expectations were for short hair, he left his locks intact. A few days after giving the moving story of his journey to faith he received a letter thanking him for what he had said. Enclosed was some money to enable him to get a haircut, the donor being anxious that he should now 'look like a Christian'.

Fortunately my pastoral experience was usually loftier than these examples might suggest, but each served as a reminder that acceptance into the Christian community is often via conformity to a set of unscripted but powerful sub-cultural expectations of behaviour. In other words, 'behave' dominates the trio of behave, believe, belong.

Two questions immediately spring to mind. Is a paradigm shift to 'belong, believe, behave' possible?[3] If so, is it desirable? To quote Stanley Hauerwas' memorable insight, our concern should be 'not only for the church that does exist but for the church that should exist'.[4]

EMBRACING THE PARADIGM

Initially the desirability question seemed self-evident. Surely the church is nothing if not a community of welcome and embrace? Christ's incarnation was not delayed until such time as the planet engaged in impeccable behaviour. Both Bethlehem's cradle and Calvary's cross speak of the divine 'yes' to humanity in spite of its indifference, cruelty and fallen-ness. Tax collector Zacchaeus, the five time married and now co-habiting woman at the well and the Christ-denying Peter, have life narratives where the journey of faith is characterized by welcome rather than a promising behavioural record. Add to this that the first divine 'no' is to human aloneness ('It is not good that the man should be alone,' Gen. 2:18) and the case seems pretty compelling.

---

[3] The question might not be, 'Is it possible?' but, 'Has it already happened?' In *The Practicing Congregation* Bass makes the perceptive comment that, 'This book does not argue that mainline churches should change. Rather, it argues that mainline churches are changing and have already changed' – D.B. Bass, *The Practicing Congregation: Imagining a New Old Church* (Herndon, 2004), 3.

[4] S. Hauerwas, *A Community of Character: Toward a Constructive Christian Social Ethic* (Notre Dame, 1986), 6.

In addition, the postmodern context sees community (and thus belonging) as an ideal. So taken is he with the concept that North American theologian Stanley Grenz chooses 'community' as the integrating theme for his theology.[5] Grenz attributes part of his adopting the theme of community to his reading of *Habits of the Heart*, a seminal sociological work which explores the tension between individualism and the need for community in the USA.[6] One of the issues highlighted in *Habits of the Heart* is the link between religion and individualism. The privatization of faith, whether the plea from evangelicals to come into a personal (individual) relationship with God, or the more liberal invitation to worship God in whatever shape or form the individual chooses to conceive the Divine, tends to see the emphasis fall back to individual response rather than to community mediation. While individualism might lead to ownership of decisions taken, it can also lead to a sense of isolation and alienation. Against a pendulum that has swung too far in its emphasis on the individual, Grenz suggests community as a correcting and integrating motif.

One could also explore the biblical theme of hospitality. From the record of Abraham's welcome to the three visitors in Genesis 18 to the affirmation in Hebrews 13:2 that in welcoming the stranger one might entertain angels without being aware of it, or the great multitude in Revelation 19 delighted to be invited to the wedding feast of the Lamb, the Bible extols the virtue of hospitality. By contrast, the shameful and sordid events of Judges 19 include, amongst other significant wrongs, a failure of hospitality. Ewing notes, 'In the desert, every tent, however poor its owner, offers welcome to the traveler. ... It is the master's pride to be known as a generous man; any lack of civility or of kindness to a guest meets severe reprobation. In the guest's presence he calls neither his tent, nor anything it contains his own. During his sojourn, the visitor is owner.'[7] It could be argued that the welcome of hospitality is a different matter to the conferring of the status of one who belongs, but that misses the point that the first stage in the trio under investigation is of an ethos that notices, reaches out, includes and incorporates the other.

It could be that the motivation behind belong-believe-behave is not essentially theological but pragmatic. Simply put, the welcome of belonging creates an openness to explore new systems of belief and new models of behaviour.

---

[5] See, e.g. S. Grenz, *Theology for the Community of God* (Nashville, 1994) or S. Grenz, and J. Franke, *Beyond Foundationalism: Shaping Theology in a Postmodern Context* (Louisville, 2001).

[6] R.N. Bellah, W.M. Sullivan, et al. (eds.), *Habits of the Heart: Individualism and Commitment in American Life* (New York, 1985). See e.g. Grenz' use of Bellah in S. Grenz, *Revisioning Evangelical Theology: A Fresh Agenda for the 21st Century* (Downers Grove, 1993), 148–149.

[7] W. Ewing, 'Hospitality' in F.C. Grant and H.H. Rowley (eds.), *Dictionary of the Bible* (Edinburgh, 1963²), 400.

Similarly, one could argue that creating an atmosphere of acceptance and belonging is psychologically sound. Psychologist Carl Rogers is well known for his insight that unconditional positive regard is key to individuals being freed to embrace constructive and life-serving change. In a helpful summary of the therapeutic importance of unconditional positive regard Rogers writes,

> The reactions of the client who experiences for a time the kind of therapeutic relationship which I have described are reciprocal of the therapist's attitudes. In the first place, as he finds someone else listening acceptantly to his feelings, he little by little becomes able to listen to himself. He begins to receive the communications from within himself – to realize that he *is* angry, to recognize when he is frightened, even to realize when he is feeling courageous. As he becomes more open to what is going on within him he becomes able to listen to feelings which he has always denied and repressed. He can listen to feelings which have always seemed so terrible, or so disorganizing, or so abnormal, or so shameful, that he has never been able to recognize their existence in himself. ... While he is learning to listen to himself he also becomes more acceptant of himself. As he expresses more and more of the hidden and awful aspects of himself, he finds the therapist showing a consistent and unconditional positive regard for him and his feelings. Slowly he moves toward the same attitude toward himself, accepting himself as he is, and therefore ready to move forward in the process of becoming.[8]

Presumably, theologically, this would translate into a shift away from an emphasis on sin and the fall, to one on grace and hope.[9]

QUESTIONING THE PARADIGM

Significant though these arguments are, the paradigm should not be accepted without question. Five issues spring to mind:

- Is the journey to faith really linear? Linked to this, isn't the model too static? When, for example, does one get the tick of approval affirming that one is now behaving as a Christian?
- Is it possible to 'belong' to something that one does not yet believe in or whose ethics do not guide one's behaviour?
- In both paradigms, 'believe' is placed in the middle. Is the role of belief really secondary?

---

[8] C. Rogers, *On Becoming a Person: A Therapist's View of Psychotherapy* (London, 1961), 63.

[9] Evangelicals usually critique Rogers for his optimistic view of human nature and the absence of a category for human sinfulness. See e.g. S.L. Jones and R.E. Butman, *Modern Psychotherapies: A Comprehensive Christian Appraisal* (Downers Grove, 1991), 255–277.

- Does the model imply that we are all really 'anonymous Christians'[10] and that the invitation to belong is therefore appropriate regardless of personal belief or behaviour?
- By placing behaviour at the end of the trio, do we run the risk of endorsing what Bonhoeffer classifies as 'cheap grace'?[11]

Is the journey to faith really linear?

In older evangelical understandings of Christian conversion, the journey to faith went through clear and predictable stages. All people started at the comparable point of being sinful from birth[12] and in need of a saviour from sin. On recognizing one's sinfulness and accepting Christ's substitutionary death on the cross, by inviting him to forgive one's sin and enter one's life, one was 'saved' or 'justified'. Justification occurred at the moment of conversion and ensured a person an eternal future as a child of God. Post-justification one embarked on the journey of sanctification, most simply understood as becoming more Christ-like. On Christ's return or at the end of one's life (whichever came first) one had the expectation of glorification when one would live with God forever.[13] An example given was that of the thief on the cross who on the basis of his reaching out to Jesus was assured that on that very day he would be together with Jesus in paradise (Lk. 23:43). Justification was instant and sufficient to guarantee that thief a place in heaven, even though his imminent death was to

---

[10] The term is associated with Karl Rahner. It should be noted that Rahner did not suggest that all are automatically Christians, but rather that those who do not consciously reject God are believers. He writes, 'It is true that it would be wrong to go so far as to declare every man, whether he accepts the grace or not, an "anonymous Christian". Anyone who in his basic decision were to really deny and reject his being ordered to God, who were to place himself decisively in opposition to his own concrete being, should not be designated a "theist", even an anonymous "theist"; only someone who gives – even if it be ever so confusedly – the glory to God should be thus designated. Therefore no matter what a man states in his conceptual, theoretical and religious reflection, anyone who does not say in his heart, "there is no God" (like the "fool" in the psalm) but testifies to him by the radical acceptance of his being, is a believer' – quoted in G. McCool (ed.), *A Rahner Reader* (London, 1975), 213–214.

[11] Bonhoeffer's words at the start of *The Cost of Discipleship* (London, 1959), 35, remain as startling and relevant today as they were in the 1930s: 'Cheap grace is the deadly enemy of our Church. We are fighting today for costly grace.'

[12] Augustine's doctrine of original sin was usually accepted. Original sin was understood to mean the dimension of sin with which we begin life, or the effect which the sin of Adam has upon us as a precondition of our lives. See e.g. M.J. Erickson, *Christian Theology* (Grand Rapids, 1985), 627–639.

[13] The exact sequence and process of glorification has always been a source of controversy amongst evangelicals. Debates include the absence or otherwise of 'soul sleep' as well as the absence or otherwise of the millennium. If accepted, the actual sequence of the millennium (pre- or post-, with a range of qualifications and understandings) has been contested.

prevent any significant progress on the route of sanctification. The most important step was therefore that of justification, as this ensured an eternity in the presence of Christ.

While this understanding of Christian conversion remains amongst evangelicals, the neat division into tidy stages is increasingly questioned, as is the precise nature of conversion. The validity of simply making a decision for Jesus is challenged. Robert Webber writes, '[T]he postmodern world is fertile ground for the Christian message, but it must be the full message and not a reductionism to a decision without an in-depth follow up to Christian thought and practice. If we are to evangelise effectively, we must set about building community and providing healing to the hurts of life.'[14]

Linked to this is the growing claim that the felt need in communities is no longer for a release from guilt and sin, but rather revolves around finding meaning and purpose. Richard Harries writes,

> During the late medieval and Reformation period people were gnawed by a sense of guilt, and in our time it is predominantly a feeling of meaningless which oppresses us. What this historical analysis brings out is that whereas in the late medieval and Reformation period the Christian faith could be powerfully preached as deliverance from sin and a sense of guilt, it is much more difficult to do that today when there has been a widespread loss of a sense of sin.[15]

A more holistic understanding of conversion is thus being called for. A problem with the shift from 'behave, believe, belong' to 'belong, believe, behave' is that it retains a sense of stages to be passed and ticked off the list. The more likely trajectory is one of simultaneously feeling a sense of identification with and acceptance by a Christian community while increasingly understanding and accepting traditional Christian teaching and, where required, making gradual ethical course corrections. Dictating the precise order serves no useful function, nor is it likely to be accurate. The biblical image of growing toward maturity is probably both more accurate and more helpful.

Is it possible to 'belong' to something that one does not yet believe in or whose ethics do not guide one's behaviour?

At another level of query one has to ask if it is possible to 'belong' to something that one does not yet believe in or whose ethics do not guide one's behaviour. Underneath is the question of what it means to 'belong'.

Certainly if 'belong' implies 'having been formally accepted into membership of' the model has little likelihood of success in a postmodern era.

---

[14] R.E. Webber, *Ancient-Future Faith: Rethinking Evangelicalism for a Postmodern World* (Grand Rapids, 1999), 150.

[15] R. Harries, *God Outside the Box: Why Spiritual People Object to Christianity* (London, 2002), 105.

A common concern expressed by many church leaders is that while they can get people to attend and participate in the ministry of the local church, they find it hard to get them to join the church officially. The experience of the Baptist Churches of Western Australia is probably representative where in 2003 the combined average Sunday service attendance for all churches in the Union was 10,904 compared to a membership of 5,419.[16] The numbers attending church are far greater than of those who are formally church members.

However, to think of 'belong' in the narrow terms of church membership is probably not what was intended by Vernall's or Haglund's comments.[17] More probable is that they envision a community where one feels one has found a 'place' in the sense used by Paul Tournier in his classic *A Place for You*. The book opens with this account.

> The words were those of a young student with whom I had formed a deep friendship. He was sitting by my fireside, telling me of his difficulties, of the anxiety that never left him, and which at times turned to panic and to flight. He was trying to look objectively at what was going on inside himself and to understand it. Then, as if summing up his thoughts, he looked up at me and said: 'Basically, I'm always looking for a place – for somewhere to be.'[18]

Though the incident was recounted back in the 1960s it has a strikingly contemporary ring. Perhaps the longing for 'a place – for somewhere to be' is universal. It could be argued that the psalmist expresses a similar sentiment in Psalm 84:10, 'Better is one day in your courts than a thousand elsewhere.'[19] It sees other images of church spring to mind such as church as community, or church as family.

Church as family brings us back to the heart of the question being looked at. When told that his mother and brothers were waiting for him, Jesus turned to his disciples and declared that 'whoever does the will of my Father in heaven is my brother and sister and mother' (Mt. 12:46–50). The behavioural component of doing 'the will of my Father in heaven' was a necessary companion to the declaration of being part of Christ's family. We need to return to the question of whether it is possible to 'belong' to something that one does not yet believe in or whose ethics do not guide one's behaviour. Or can the sequence really be 'belong, believe behave'?

---

[16] From *Special Report, Background Information* for Dr Paul Borden for Consultancy 2004 (Perth, 2004), 45.

[17] It is interesting to note that when Vernall spoke of the rapid growth of his church it was attendance figures rather than membership figures to which he referred.

[18] P. Tournier, *A Place for You* (Crowborough, 1968), 9.

[19] Ps 27:4 also expresses a comparable emotion.

Is the role of belief really secondary?

A third issue is over the place of belief. In both the new and old paradigm the suggestion is that belief comes in the middle. While a welcome invitation to humility for those who struggle for theological precision, the validity of the claim must be questioned.

One could argue that the sentiment is correct. Jesus urged his listeners to have the faith of little children. It was their intuitive and spontaneous faith that seemed to impress him, rather than their doctrinal orthodoxy (See e.g. Mt. 18:1–6). In more critical vein, James 2:19 notes that even demons hold some accurate beliefs. However, to dismiss the importance of sound doctrine on such a basis would be trite. Much of the New Testament explores the struggle for accurate and sound teaching.

Perhaps what is called for is a chastened view of doctrinal formulations. Certainly the multitude of books being published on effective apologetics for a postmodern era stress that if apologetics is to have a future it will need to be more relational and more willing to listen.[20]

In addition, the call for a post-foundational basis for theology is becoming widespread. Images for doctrinal orthodoxy now revolve around webs of coherence rather than undisputed foundations and for truth to be seen as a centred rather than a boundaried set.[21] While some worry about the demise of traditional understandings of truth,[22] others argue that a contextual, relational view of truth is both more accurate and appropriate for a postmodern context.

The implication that belief now flows from belonging rather than from behaving should probably be modified to acknowledge that belief is usually related to multiple factors. Certainly, belief cannot be divorced from one's community of reference. Openness to a community of faith would usually lead to a greater openness to its belief system. It is debatable if the two can be separated. Uneasiness with the beliefs of a community would make identification with (belonging to) the community improbable. In the sense that one might identify with a community (belong), accept its beliefs but only aspire to its behaviour (behave as a goal rather than as a reality) the progression might well be belong, believe behave. If belief is not seen as a stand-alone category, it

---

[20] Compare the titles of books on apologetics over a period of time. For example, in 1949, G.F. Robinson and S.F. Winward entitled their work on apologetics, *Here is the Answer* (London, 1949). By 1992 Alister McGrath entitled his book on apologetics, *Bridge Building* (Leicester, 1992). In 2002 Richard Harries published *God Outside the Box: Why Spiritual People Object to Christianity* (London, 2002). The difference in ethos implied by each title is striking.

[21] Helpful works include Grenz and Franke, *Beyond Foundationalism* and S. Grenz, '*Die Begrenzte Gemeinschaft* ('The Boundaried People') and the Character of Evangelical Theology', *JETS* 45 (2002), 301–316.

[22] See, e.g. R.J. Middleton and B.J. Walsh, *Truth is Stranger Than it Used to Be: Biblical Faith in a Postmodern Age* (Downers Grove, 1995).

is probably best placed at the centre of the trio. Certainly, the emphasis that beliefs are communal rather than individual is consistent with postmodern thinking. Thus belief would not head the trio, as there can be no understanding of what the Christian faith is apart from the community of faith who uphold the faith.

Does the model imply that we are all really 'anonymous Christians'?

The fourth reservation around a shift to 'belong, believe behave' revolves around the issue of whether the affirmation of belonging before any requirement to believe or behave might imply that people are already 'anonymous Christians' waiting to be included into the family they are part of – albeit without their knowledge. In this view, the acknowledgment of belonging without other pre-requisites is an affirmation of the person's true, though previously unknown, status. The willingness to have the status of belonging conferred is probably enough to meet the prerequisite of not being actively opposed to theism.[23]

The stance is not without merit. Those who stumble into the faith community, no matter how tentatively, have arrived at their true home. Made to reflect the image of the Creator God, we discover our humanity the moment we recognize that the voice calling to Adam in Eden's garden, 'Where are you?' calls our name as well. Hearing that voice is the start of hearing our true identity and finding the place of belonging. However, of necessity, discovering where we most truly belong will be accompanied by a realization that all other allegiances were, at best, a pale shadow of this new allegiance that sets us free to discover who we have been made to be.

Do we run the risk of endorsing what Bonhoeffer classifies as 'cheap grace'?

A fifth objection is that a stress on belonging without prerequisites of belief or behaviour could imply that cheap rather than costly grace is operative. While the danger exists, it is worth noting that it was a risk Jesus was prepared to take. In accompanying Zacchaeus to his home before the tree-climbing tax collector had offered to relinquish his ill gotten gains, Jesus appears to have affirmed the importance of acceptance prior to moral change (Lk. 19:1–10). Add to this Jesus' reputation of associating with drunkards and people with questionable morals and the earlier paradigm of 'behave, believe, belong' appears to be inconsistent with the model of ministry engaged in by Jesus. In the end we have to have the gospel's confidence that a genuine experience of grace leads to transformation.

While the detailed scrutiny of 'belong, believe, behave' leaves some significant questions, rather than treating the statement as one of absolute truth it is probably more fruitful to view it as indicative of an ethos change. It is an ethos change that affirms that core Christian images revolve around inclusion,

---

[23] See footnote 10.

community and open-heartedness. At this level, the model is hard to fault. One of the major missiological barriers faced by the church is that it is perceived to be self-righteous, judgemental and hypocritical. It is this perception that raises another, perhaps more compelling, missiological question. Indeed, it could be another paradigm shift that we need.

ANOTHER PARADIGM SHIFT

Thus far we have been working from the assumption that if the church were to be a community of welcome and embrace it would find a steady stream of people grateful for the ethos change and waiting to swell its ranks. This assumption is almost certainly flawed. Suspicion of and even hostility toward the church has increased. While not facing religious persecution, churches in the West are in serious danger of being marginalized. On the basis of current trends, Peter Brierly predicts that whereas in 1970 80% of those living in the 'first world' claimed some kind of allegiance to the Christian faith (however nominal), by 2050 the percentage is likely to have declined to 57%.[24]

The irony is thus that while we debate if we are willing to accept people whose belief or behaviour might not conform to our standards, the line of those waiting to belong has dwindled. Perhaps it has completely disappeared or more probably, perhaps it never existed. It could be that the paradigm shift from 'behave, belong, believe' to 'belong, believe, behave' is too late. Has this therefore been an exercise in futility, comparable to debating the number of angels who can fit on a pinhead?

The model can be salvaged if an additional paradigm shift takes place. It depends on how one interprets 'belong' and on how one answers the question, 'who belongs to who?' In traditional models, conversion marked the leaving of one's former lifestyle and adopting the lifestyle of the new community. While certain aspects of this model are valid, perhaps discontinuity with the past was over-stressed. In short, perhaps the queue to belong to the church does not exist because the church is perceived to criticize and critique the world it seeks to win.

In other words, the believing community requires others to 'belong' to it, but the community it seeks to win is not sure that those who make the call have ever belonged to their world in a constructive way. Put differently, incarnation must precede any invitation to belong to a new community.

We could look at the dilemma by placing ourselves in the shoes of the average 17 year old.[25] She probably hasn't been to church before, and if she has, is likely to have felt out of place. But she would have been fed information

---

[24] P. Brierley, 'Evangelicals in the World of the 21st Century', Occasional Paper for the 2004 Forum for World Evangelization, Pattaya (2004), 4.

[25] This section is a modified version of part of a paper I presented at the *Mission to New Zealand* Conference in 2003. See B. Harris, 'The Need for a Double Conversion' (Auckland, 2003).

about the church. The media have portrayed it as an uncomfortable relic from the past. That could be acceptable if it weren't a relic with an opinion. But it is enormously opinionated! Apparently it believes that sex and fun are distasteful. Its leaders are invariably hypocrites and paedophiles. It condemns homosexuals to hell while its clergy can't keep their hands off young boys. And though not exactly the flat-earth society, it insists that the world is around six thousand years old.

True, much of what she would believe about the church would be stereotypical and unfair. But she is part of a generation for whom image is reality. So if you put yourself into those shoes, it's not so hard to understand that though 99.4% of young people believe in God, the majority rate Christianity as irrelevant to a genuine spiritual quest.[26] No matter how welcoming the church might attempt to be, the likelihood of her ever coming within its embrace is slight. Even if she did, she is unlikely to want to 'belong' to a group associated with such images. However, the paradoxical dilemma is that this generation's values are probably closer to Christian values than any previous generation.

In contrasting modern to postmodern values, Jones suggests that both modern and postmodern audiences value relational approaches and that there has been a shift from the

- rational to the experiential
- scientific to the spiritual
- unanimous (or the homogenous) to the pluralistic
- exclusive to the relative
- egocentric to the altruistic
- individualistic to the communal
- functional to the creative
- industrial to the environmental
- local to the global
- compartmentalized/ dichotomized to the holistic
- relevant to the authentic.[27]

Most striking is the positive nature of most of these shifts. While many Christians are anxious about the shift to a postmodern ethos, Jones' analysis suggests that the emerging values are closer to core Christian values than those held during the modern era.[28] To a desire for greater community, altruism,

---

[26] MTV poll, 2002.
[27] T. Jones, *Postmodern Youth Ministry: Exploring Cultural Shift, Creating Holistic Connections, Cultivating Authentic Communities* (Grand Rapids, 2001), 30–37.
[28] Millard Erickson provides a helpful summary of some evangelical responses in M. Erickson, *Postmodernizing the Faith: Evangelical Responses to the Challenge of*

creativity and indeed most of the contemporary values Jones outlines, the gospel gives loud agreement. While it takes more than the overlap of some values to make someone a Christian, a key missiological principle is that one examines a culture and its values for both lines of continuity and discontinuity with the Christian gospel. The more the lines of continuity and the fewer the lines of discontinuity the easier the missiological task. On this basis, we could conclude that the postmodern ethos is more consistent with the Christian message than the modern ethos had been. As was said at the *Mission to New Zealand Conference*, in Auckland,

> If we were trying to recruit a new missionary and told them, '99.4% of the people you have to reach already believe in God and they value the experiential, spiritual, communal, creative, holistic, authentic and relational, and are altruistic and global in their concern and ecologically responsible' it could be that our potential recruit would turn around and say, 'That's not enough of a challenge. Send me to a more difficult group!'[29]

The implication is that while historically the church has felt that it holds the moral high ground in calling people to faith, the ethical superiority of the church is no longer self-evident. Indeed, the very notion of requiring people prior to belief or belonging to 'behave' as Christians behave seems increasingly absurd. Mission to the western world takes place in a setting that sometimes shows a kinder and more charitable face than 'the average face'[30] shown by the church in its 2000 year history.

Missiologically, we have created significant hurdles for ourselves and they are not the hurdles posed by the cross. While clearly needing an ethos shift from 'behave, believe, belong' to 'belong, believe, behave', on its own, this will accomplish little. Repentance for past and present wrongs, as well as a willingness to affirm and embrace the positive change that has taken place in society is also needed.

FOR 'BOTTOM LINE' THINKERS

In summary then, while applauding an ethos change from 'behave, believe, belong' to 'belong, believe behave' a more dramatic paradigm shift is required.

Postmodernism (Grand Rapids, 1998). Particular concerns tend to centre around two of the shifts highlighted by Jones, viz. those towards pluralism and relativism.

[29] Harris, 'The Need for a Double Conversion', 2.

[30] While it is impossible to give precise content to the notion of the 'average face' of the church over its 2000 year history, it is an unsettling concept and one worth pondering. To counteract some of the negative images, an increasing number of apologetic works are drawing attention to the more positive aspects of the church's history. See, e.g. A.J. Schmidt, *Under the Influence: How Christianity Transformed Civilization* (Grand Rapids, 2001).

In the book of Jonah, the prophet turns out to be harder to reach than the Ninevites. It could be that the scenario has not changed significantly. Missiological obstacles in the West are not limited to a failure to welcome and embrace, but a failure to convince that the Christian message leads to a life-affirming transformation of both individuals and communities. Seeing such transformation incarnated in communities of care and embrace could prove a powerful apologetic for the Christian faith in the twenty-first century.

The image of Jonah is a suitable one with which to end. Thomas Carlisle's poem, 'You Jonah', captures the essence of the missiological task for the twenty-first century.

And Jonah stalked
to his shaded seat
and waited for God
to come around
to his way of thinking.

And God is still waiting for a host of Jonahs
in their comfortable houses
to come around
to his way of loving.[31]

Bibliography

Baptist Union of Western Australia, *Special Report*, Background Information for Dr Paul Borden for church consultancy *2004* (Perth, 2004).

Bass, D.B., *The Practicing Congregation: Imagining a New Old Church* (Herndon: The Alban Institute, 2004).

Bellah, R.N., W.M. Sullivan, et al. (eds.), *Habits of the Heart: Individualism and Commitment in American Life* (New York: Harper and Row, 1985).

Bonhoeffer, D., *The Cost of Discipleship* (R.H. Fuller (tr.), London: SCM, 1959).

Brierley, P., 'Evangelicals in the World of the 21st Century', Occasional Paper for the 2004 Forum for World Evangelization, Pattaya (2004).

Erickson, M.J., *Christian Theology* (Grand Rapids, Michigan: Baker, 1985).

— *Postmodernizing the Faith: Evangelical Responses to the Challenge of Postmodernism* (Grand Rapids, Michigan: Baker, 1998).

Ewing, W., 'Hospitality' in F.C. Grant and H.H. Rowley (eds.), *Dictionary of the Bible* (Edinburgh: T. & T. Clark, 1963^2).

Grenz, S., '*Die Begrenzte Gemeinschaft* ("The Boundaried People") and the Character of Evangelical Theology', *Journal of the Evangelical Theological Society*, 45 (2002), 301–316.

— *Revisioning Evangelical Theology: A Fresh Agenda for the 21st Century* (Downers Grove: Inter-Varsity Press, 1993).

---

[31] Quoted in J. Verkul, *Contemporary Missiology: An Introduction* (Grand Rapids, 1978), 100.

— *Theology for the Community of God* (Nashville: Broadman and Holman, 1994).
— (and J. Franke), *Beyond Foundationalism: Shaping Theology in a Postmodern Context* (Louisville: Westminster John Knox Press, 2001).
Harries, R., *God Outside the Box: Why Spiritual People Object to Christianity* (London: SPCK, 2002).
Harris, B., 'The Need for a Double Conversion' a paper from *Mission to New Zealand* Conference (Auckland: Carey Baptist College, 2003).
Hauerwas, S., *A Community of Character: Toward a Constructive Christian Social Ethic* (Notre Dame, Indiana: University of Notre Dame Press, 1986).
Jones, T., *Postmodern Youth Ministry: Exploring Cultural Shift, Creating Holistic Connections, Cultivating Authentic Communities* (Grand Rapids, Michigan: Zondervan, 2001).
Jones, S.L. and R.E. Butman, *Modern Psychotherapies: A Comprehensive Christian Appraisal* (Downers Grove: Inter-Varsity Press, 1991).
McCool, G. (ed.), *A Rahner Reader* (London: Darton, Longman & Todd, 1975).
McGrath, A.E., *Bridge Building* (Leicester: Inter-Varsity Press, 1992).
Middleton, R.J. and B.J. Walsh, *Truth is Stranger Than it Used to Be: Biblical Faith in a Postmodern Age* (Downers Grove: Inter-Varsity Press, 1995).
Robinson, G.F. and S.F. Winward, *Here is the Answer* (London: Marshall, Morgan and Scott, 1949).
Rogers, C., *On Becoming a Person: A Therapist's View of Psychotherapy* (London: Constable, 1961).
Schmidt, A.J., *Under the Influence: How Christianity Transformed Civilization* (Grand Rapids, Michigan: Zondervan, 2001).
Tournier, P., *A Place for You* (E. Hudson (tr.), Crowborough: Highland Books, 1968).
Verkul, J., *Contemporary Missiology: An Introduction* (Grand Rapids, Michigan: Eerdmans, 1978).
Vernall, C., 'Bethlehem's Journey', a paper from *Mission to New Zealand* Conference (Auckland: Carey Baptist College, 2003).
Webber, R.E., *Ancient-Future Faith: Rethinking Evangelicalism for a Postmodern World* (Grand Rapids, Michigan: Baker, 1999).
— *The Younger Evangelicals: Facing the Challenges of the New World* (Grand Rapids, Michigan: Baker, 2002).

CHAPTER 15

Prophetic Preaching for a Missional Church

MICHAEL J. QUICKE

Introduction

As its title suggests, this chapter explores a connection from within two of John Olley's great interests – Old Testament and mission. Prophetic preaching owes its origins to the Old Testament and language about 'missional church' has emerged out of insights from The Gospel and Our Culture Network.[1]

Both these terms can be used with passion: 'Oh for more prophetic preaching! Oh for a more missional church!' I confess that I *do* write with some passion because, as a preacher and teacher of preachers, I have become increasingly alarmed at what I perceive to be preaching's failure of nerve and loss of missionary perspective. Undeniably, preaching has become increasingly marginalized in a declining western mainstream church.[2]

This chapter, with broad-brush strokes, explores some of the issues involved. First, we need to identify some characteristics of so-called 'prophetic preaching' looking at its Old Testament roots and especially considering its role of confronting worldly culture by offering a counter-story. Second, a brief overview of issues within culture change will introduce insights from The Gospel and Our Culture Network concerning the 'missional church'. Third, a missiological model offers one way of integrating preaching's prophetic role into the life of today's church. Finally, some preliminary challenges flowing from this model will be outlined.

---

[1] The Gospel and Our Culture Network emerged out of Lesslie Newbigin's call for 'the missionary encounter of the gospel with our Western culture'. See G.R. Hunsberger and C. van Gelder (eds.), *Church between Gospel and Culture* (Grand Rapids, 1996), xiii–xix.

[2] See the analysis in M. Quicke, *360degree preaching; hearing, speaking and living the Word* (Grand Rapids, 2003).

Prophetic Preaching

What does it mean to describe Christian preaching as 'prophetic'? Several key characteristics of prophetic preaching are rooted in its Old Testament background: its authority, its transformational power and the nature of its societal challenge.

First, the *authority* of 'prophetic preaching' is grounded in biblical understanding of how God speaks through his messengers. The authoritative Old Testament refrain 'Thus says the Lord' expressed the source of the prophet's task. 'The Lord God has spoken; who can but prophesy?' (Amos 3:8). 'If I say, "I will not mention him, or speak any more in his name" then within me there is something like a burning fire shut up in my bones; I am weary with holding it in, and I cannot' (Jer. 20:9). Sidney Greidanus argues for continuity between prophets and apostles and today's preachers. He claims that as Old Testament prophets and apostles spoke God's word, and understood God's word to be God's deed, so preachers share these two characteristics.[3] When Christian preachers respond to scripture, as Old Testament prophets did when they heard the word of the Lord, they stand under God's authority speaking God's word that it might be God's deed. 'Whoever speaks must do so as one speaking the very words of God' (1 Pet. 4:11).

Second, and closely linked with its authority, is the *transformational power* of prophetic preaching. God's word does not return empty (Is. 55:11). God's words are God's deeds. The Hebrew word *dabar* can be translated as either 'word' or 'deed' – 'word-event' or 'event-word'. Proclaiming God's word therefore creates new possibilities with boldness, immediacy and razor-edged relevance. Old Testament prophets both forth-tell and foretell because God has already decided to act on his word. Sometimes prophetic symbols visualized this (such as Is. 20; Jer. 19; Ezek. 4:1–3). Prophetic preaching creates new people in community.

Third, and perhaps the most obvious characteristic of prophetic preaching, is its *content and style* as it confronts people with social justice issues. Whenever contemporary preachers pronounce fiery moral judgments, as though the mantle of eighth century Amos or Micah has fallen upon their shoulders, they are deemed to be 'prophetic'. Actually few current practitioners seem evident in the evangelical wing of the church. Sounding out political, social and economic implications of God's righteousness and justice always marks prophetic preaching. Never limited to private personal concerns, prophetic preachers dare to deal with issues having wider societal repercussions beyond the individual and congregational.

Old Testament prophets present a distinctively subversive challenge for the people of God. 'They join together the holiness of God, the moral quality of

---

[3] S. Greidanus, *The Modern Preacher and the Ancient Text: Interpreting and Preaching Biblical Literature* (Grand Rapids, 1988), 8.

historical reality and a counter-future for the world.'⁴ They read the signs of the times and address them in the light of God's revealed will. They speak of God's alternative community, a people belonging to the Holy God of Israel, warning complacent people about false successes and offering exiled people 'a new thing' (Is. 43:19–21). Evocative hope is never far away but neither is God's judgement. They speak of peace but rigorously reject false substitutes (Jer. 23:9–40). With passion and boldness, theirs is an uncomfortably disturbing role recalling the community of faith to God's will. They are God's disturbers of human status quo. Skylba says, 'Like poets of all ages, they see reality at its deepest level. They take a long loving look at that reality and either they see God or the absence of God. From that divine epicenter moved waves of tenderness or anger as yet not experienced by the merchants and farmers of Israel or Judah. Prophets knew the vitality of God and speak accordingly.'⁵ Discerning God's character and purpose, Old Testament prophets declare how God's people should live within current events and culture.

Jesus' synagogue sermon (Lk. 4:16–21) forms the bridge between Old Testament prophets and New Testament preaching. In *A Brief History of Preaching*, Yngve Brilioth claims that by this sermon Jesus reveals how Christian preaching is rooted in Jewish proclamation with three primary elements: liturgical (its worship context), exegetical (its textual authority) and prophetic (its empowering by the Spirit – Lk. 4:14,18).⁶ When Jesus declared, 'Today this scripture has been fulfilled in your hearing' (v. 21) he embodied Isaiah 61:1,2 and provoked both amazement (v. 22) and fury (vv. 28,29). His preaching powerfully confronted people with God's character and purpose, once revealed by Isaiah in the past tense and now applied in Nazareth in the present tense. Note how the three characteristics of prophetic preaching are all present: authority, transformational power and the societal dimensions of God's righteousness and justice.

Arguably, part of Jesus' complex role as Word made flesh includes being understood as a 'prophet of the justice of the reign of God'. Combining elements of prophetic roles he 'subverted the temple and reinterpreted the Torah so that once again it could bear witness to the justice of the covenant, God's promise to the people of the land. Recognizing the powerful presence of God in Jesus' work as broker and prophet, the people of Galilee willingly and gladly proclaimed: "A great prophet has arisen among us"' (Lk. 7:16).⁷

---

⁴ W. Brueggemann, 'Prophets, Old Testament' in W.H. Willimon and R. Lischer (eds.), *Concise Encyclopedia of Preaching* (Louisville, 1995), 389.
⁵ R.J. Skylba, quoted in S.V. DeLeers, *Sunday Prophecy* (Papers of the Annual Meeting of the Academy of Homiletics, Memphis Theological Seminary, Memphis, Tennessee, 2004) 106.
⁶ Y. Brilioth, *A Brief History of Preaching* (Philadelphia, 1965), 10.
⁷ W.R. Herzog II, quoted in D. Neville (ed.), *Prophecy and Passion* (Hindmarsh, 2002), 63.

When Timothy is charged to preach the word (2 Tim. 4:2) he stands within the new order of Christian preaching in continuity with Old Testament prophets, Jesus Christ and apostles. Klaas Runia and others argue that Paul's words in 2 Corinthians 5:18–20 embrace all Christian preachers.[8] 'So we are ambassadors for Christ, since God is making his appeal through us' (v. 20). Elsewhere I have argued that sermons are therefore events with complex dynamics that are empowered by our trinitarian God. God the Father initiates revelation through scripture and supremely the Word made flesh (Jn. 1:14); Jesus Christ, reigning Lord of the Church, is central to its continuing life and ministry and the Holy Spirit continues to speak and convict today. 'Christian preaching, at its best, is a biblical speaking/listening/seeing/doing event that God empowers to form Christ-shaped people and communities.'[9] Because preaching is empowered by God – Father, Son and Holy Spirit – it can be termed 'prophetic' whenever it is biblically authoritative, divinely transformational and when it declares God's truth for believers in society.

Arguing that prophetic preaching should not be 'reduced to moral denunciations on the whole', Stephen Long helpfully defines prophetic preaching as 'a charisma, divinely inspired, which either seeks to recover a faithful word from within the Christian tradition or seeks to discover a necessary word in new situations that threaten the rule of God'.[10] Its positive role proclaims all that God's loving and just kingdom stands for but its negative role discerns and confronts all that threatens God's love and justice. It is the apparent absence of this discerning and confronting that should particularly concern us today.

By God's power, prophetic ministry probes, disturbs and energizes people to be different. To borrow from Walter Brueggemann, it is the 'evoking of an alternative community that knows it is about different things in different ways ... prophetic ministry seeks to penetrate despair so that new futures can be believed in and embraced by us'.[11]

Sadly, many examples of past preaching failed to 'evoke' an alternative community and speak the 'necessary word'. Illustrating Jeroboam's political compromise (1 Kgs. 14:1–16), John Olley provides an infamous twentieth century example.

> It is easier to move with dominant cultural trends than to oppose. Perhaps none has been as extreme as the situation in Germany where on 13 November, 1933, twenty thousand German Christians had attended a mass meeting in the Berlin Sports Palace ... complete with swastikas, flaming torches, brass bands, *Sieg*

---

[8] Quoted in Greidanus, *The Modern Preacher*, 8.
[9] Quicke, *360degree preaching*, 27.
[10] D.S. Long, 'Prophetic Preaching' in Willimon and Lischer (eds.), *Concise Encyclopedia*, 386.
[11] W. Brueggemann, *The Prophetic Imagination* (Philadelphia, 1978), 111.

Heils, and Nazi hymns. The Old Testament was denounced for 'its Jewish morality' ... a heroic Aryan Jesus, whom one bishop had triumphantly claimed as an archetypical Storm Trooper, was to take the place of the Jewish Preacher from Nazareth.[12]

Such monumental failures of preaching's prophetic role in the past are easy targets. Compliance with Nazism in Germany or with racism in the USA can be universally condemned now. However, the present challenge for the mainstream western church is subtler, where contemporary preachers are finding it 'easier to move with dominant cultural trends than to oppose'. 'The natural inclination of the Christian community, like all religious communities, is to adapt its witness of faith to its most immediate human needs. In doing this the community always runs the risk of obscuring the wider dimension of the gospel.'[13]

Some preaching can claim to have impacted culture positively. Henry Mitchell, for example, argues the importance of black preaching's role in black culture.[14] However, we are likely to agree with Walter Brueggemann's assessment that the church has largely accommodated to modern culture's understanding of knowledge and power which has left it privatized and powerless. He states that the Bible world invites us into a contrasting reality, into a counterstory about God, world, neighbor and self. It has counterpoint – the subversive process of unlearning and disengaging from a story we find no longer to be credible or adequate.[15] Too much twenty-first century evangelical preaching is silent on this counterstory. It offers good news with minimal disturbance to lifestyle and community life beyond the church's front doors. Evangelical pulpits are full of bold talk about sin and repentance in private morality and yet are often mute about how those who repent are called to live together differently in society. The standard US accolade given after a sermon – 'Good job pastor' – sounds suspiciously like congratulating some kind of in-house performance. Preaching to please people seems prevalent, rather than preaching God's word that discerns and confronts.

Of course, preaching has always been tempted to please hearers. A sociological study of pastors' theological understanding and position on social issues since the 1960s in six Protestant denominations in Oregon showed how pastors' choices of social issues were selective and how later these same choices were often abandoned or neglected. For example, preachers did not

---

[12] J.W. Olley, *First and Second Kings* (Eastwood, 2001), 53.
[13] J. Ward and C. Ward, *Preaching from the Prophets* (Nashville, 1995), 11.
[14] H.H. Mitchell, *Black Preaching – the Recovery of a Powerful Art* (Nashville, 1990), 12–16.
[15] See W. Brueggemann, *Texts Under Negotiation: The Bible and Postmodern Imagination* (Minneapolis, 1993).

choose certain major issues in the last thirty years: divorce (with a 'puzzling' silence on divorce laws), legalized gambling and Sunday closing laws.

> Why do the leaders of the new Christian right choose to fight some threats to their traditional culture and to ignore others? A major part of the answer lies ... in what these leaders believe their constituency will wholeheartedly support. That constituency is mainly white, well integrated into the major structures of workaday society and moderately well off.[16]

Overall, 'many evangelicals have been quietly accommodating themselves to the cultural changes around them'.[17] In other words, there has been a loss of prophetic preaching. However, it is important to place such general tendencies within the specific context of western culture and its recent complex transition.

Culture Change

The western church, with its preaching, is set within culture that has been undergoing a profound shift from modernity to post-modernity, beginning in the latter part of the twentieth century. Three issues should be noted: the decline of the western mainstream church, the separation of personal values from societal norms in modernity and the fresh challenges of postmodernity.

The Gospel and Our Culture Network, flowing out of Lesslie Newbigin's seminal work, has focused attention on mission issues facing the western church.[18] With humility it has recognized how many parts of the western church wallow in crisis. Increasing materialism, pluralism, relativism and, ironically, spirituality are sidelining mainstream churches into irrelevancy. Gibbs frames its challenge dramatically, '[A]ny church is potentially just one generation away from extinction. Now we are faced with a generation of under thirty-five-year-olds who are turning away from institutional expressions of Christianity, opting to define their own spiritual journey.'[19] Some researchers predict that if present trends continue in the US 60% of all existing Christian congregations will disappear before the year 2050.[20] Recent UK research shows only 7.9% of the population now attends church, down from 11% twenty years ago. It claims that non-Christian spirituality will eclipse Christianity within the next twenty to thirty years. 'Many people believe that this "New Romantics" movement will prove more significant than the Protestant Reformation of the sixteenth

---

[16] B. Johnson, 'Theology and the position of pastors on social issues: continuity and change since the 1960s', *RRR* 39 (1998), 11.
[17] Johnson, 'Theology and the position of pastors', 12.
[18] See, especially, L. Newbigin, *Foolishness to the Greeks* (Grand Rapids, 1986).
[19] E. Gibbs, *Church Next* (Downers Grove, 2000), 11.
[20] Gibbs, *Church Next*, 16.

century.'[21] However pessimistic such analyses may be, global statistical surveys confirm dramatic growth in the so-called majority church of Latin America, Africa and Asia but continual serious decline in North America, Western Europe and Australasia.

This serious decline has occurred largely in the western church that has coexisted with 'modern' culture for the previous two hundred and fifty years. Modernity's certitude grounded in absolute truth, reinforced by science and technology, made room for Christian doctrine with emphasis on the veracity of scripture texts, endorsement of historical textual criticism and the teaching of sound doctrine. During modernity the Christian church's values largely overlapped those of western culture. It was assumed that church and world both adhered to the same Christian worldview.

However, though these cultural assumptions gave the church a unique role, modernity also encouraged the rise of secularism that increasingly separated spiritual from material. Christian truth was viewed as a private matter between individuals and God as compared with social, political and economic facts of the 'public square.' As a result too many churches have become private clubs with minimal impact on society.

> The church's former privileged position in western societies under the Christendom model is now gone and will not be regained. The church as a faith community is relegated by the culture's frame of understanding to the private world of personal values, beliefs and opinions. By and large the church has willingly (if sometimes unknowingly) accommodated itself to that relegation and become a privatized, voluntary association for perpetuating its set of faith opinions.[22]

Newbigin challenged the western church to see contemporary western culture not as a secular society but as a pagan society and suggests that its paganism, having been born out of the rejection of Christianity, is far more resistant to the gospel than the pre-Christian paganism with which cross-cultural missions have been familiar. In an influential essay, Hunsberger describes Newbigin's missiological critique as a 'gauntlet' thrown down to challenge the western church for its failure to develop a domestic missiology.[23] He claims that for many churches the term 'mission' has been downgraded to something functional and superficial, defined largely as growing larger churches or merely

---

[21] C. Midgley, 'Spirited away: why the end is near for religion' (*The Times*, Nov. 4, 2004).

[22] G.R. Hunsberger, 'The Newbigin gauntlet; developing a domestic missiology for N. America' in Hunsberger and Van Gelder (eds.), *The Church between Gospel and Culture*, 6–7.

[23] Hunsberger, 'The Newbigin gauntlet', 3–25.

surviving as small ones. This privatizing tendency has muzzled prophetic preaching so that it no longer tells out a counterstory for the people of God.

Provocatively, Walter C. Hobbs has described North American Christianity as having 'a faith *twisted* by culture', uncritically making presumptions and taking values derived from culture instead of testing them by biblical standards. The gospel is 'too often shot through with Western sentiments such as individualism, consumerism, security, personal happiness and corporate success'.[24] He contrasts how Amos preached, first railing against the gross evils of surrounding peoples (Amos 1:3 – 2:3) but then, in the same tone, speaking directly to the people of God (Amos 2:4, onwards).

In addition, the western church is roiling from the impact of culture shift in a complex transition, broadly termed – from modernity to postmodernity ('after modernity'). The influence of philosophers such as Derrida has helped erode basic modernist convictions about authoritative answers and absolute truths. Instead of one meta-narrative which is true for everyone, postmodernity claims that anything can be true for anyone – truth is what you make it. With Descartes, modernity claimed, 'I think therefore I am'; with postmodernity the claim is, 'I feel therefore I am.' Yet, in spite of this relativism, unacceptable to Christian conviction, there have come positive opportunities for the gospel. There seems to be fresh openness to mystery, wonder and transcendence. Intuition and imagination have gained currency, as has the desire for authentic relationships. Instead of being satisfied by cerebral certainties, postmodern people yearn for experience, authenticity in relationships, holism in worship and life, awe in personal spirituality and local stories that help make sense of their own stories.

In this context the challenge of developing the missional church has arisen. The term 'missional' emphasizes 'the essential nature and vocation of the church as God's called and sent people'.[25] Each church community should embody God's claims and promises by its worship and witness in its own context. Every relationship should speak authentically of disciples seeking to learn and grow together for the sake and by the grace of Christ. Instead of generic congregations repeating standard formulae, they need to become communities of missionaries for the gospel living it out to a suspicious and sometimes hostile world. Such a missional church has many characteristics. Gibbs describes twelve empirical indicators: it proclaims the gospel, with the Bible as normative, and its members as committed learners in their discipleship; it understands itself to be different from the world because it belongs to Christ, and the entire community shares in missional vocation; its members live Christianity to one another, practice reconciliation, hold themselves accountable to one another in love and practice hospitality; joyful,

---

[24] W.C. Hobbs, 'Faith twisted by Culture' in C. van Gelder (ed.), *Confident Witness-Changing World* (Grand Rapids, 1999), 96–7.

[25] Gibbs, *Church Next*, 51.

thankful worship is central to its life and as a community it has a vital public witness. Importantly, 'there is a recognition that the church itself is an incomplete expression of the reign of God'.[26] 'Missional' means 'the church *being* in the world as a transforming presence'.[27]

Preaching for a Missional Church

Preaching in this context, the missional church needs to rediscover its prophetic dimensions. No longer can it focus only on personal values and beliefs and avoid challenging whole church communities to live out God's counterstory.

Sadly, there is evidence that even in churches adopting missional criteria preachers can miss the prophetic task. Some recent doctoral research conducted in the suburban mid-west US focused on preaching's impact upon developing the character of eighteen churches committed to missional characteristics, as New Church Developments (NCDs). While recognizing that there are other influences on church ethos, one project looked for evidence that preaching had developed a congregation's self-understanding as a missional church.[28] The six chosen characteristics of 'missional practice' were: the Bible normative for the church's life and discipleship, practicing hospitality, joyful worship, discerning God's vocational calling for the church, vital public witness and living counter-culturally. It found considerable positive evidence with regard to all these characteristics except the last. To the issue, 'Are these churches risking their corporate lives in any meaningful ways that would show they are God's people and not merely nice people?' there was minimal response. One pastor rightly recognized that he was being asked about preaching with a prophetic voice.

> For years I think I lied to myself about being prophetic about culture. First we would get on our legs organizationally, then we would grow in our passion for following Jesus, then we would proclaim the scandal of the gospel with full throat. What does that strategy accomplish? It attracts and assimilates those who become used to hearing whispers on the area of social transformation instead of shouts. Would our church have grown and developed as it did if I had gone another way? I cannot know. I am beginning to shout in my teaching, and my homiletic whispers are giving way to a clear proclamation of destroying the idols which bind and compromise us. Amazingly the congregation has come to me and said, 'It's about time! Don't let me off the hook in this area of my life.'[29]

---

[26] Gibbs, *Church Next*, 52.
[27] Gibbs, *Church Next*, 53
[28] See C. Williams, 'The impact of preaching on the development of the character of New Church Developments' (unpublished doctoral thesis, Columbia Theological Seminary, 2003).
[29] Williams, 'The impact of preaching', 33.

Another survey found a failure of preachers to ask, 'How might they seek to practice both the culture-affirming Jesus who builds bridges to seekers, along with the counter-cultural Jesus who calls disciples to share in his suffering...to transcend privatizing tendencies of suburbia.'[30] There seems much anecdotal experience in evangelical churches that people have been 'let off the hook' by practicing only the 'culture-affirming Jesus.'

For preaching to be prophetic today it must learn the skills of *inculturation*, 'by which profound faith is given richness of local expression'.[31] For authentic local inculturation the preacher needs *theologically* to be faithful to gospel revelation, *culturally* to communicate without 'colonizing' others but rather by allowing them full participation, and *missiologically*, 'we must learn how to cross cultural boundaries in ways that develop genuine biblical identities which reflect their distinctive local circumstances'.[32]

A MODEL FOR PROPHETIC PREACHING

How best can preachers respond to this challenge? One possibility visualizes their responsibilities within a missiological model. Hunsberger has usefully summarized Newbigin's theology of culture by the model below.[33] Though not designed for preachers, the backwards and forwards flowing dynamics within its three cornered relationships have profound implications for the recovery of prophetic preaching.[34]

GOSPEL:	"challenging relevance" in the culture "hermeneutical circle" with the church
CULTURE:	radical discontinuity regarding the gospel radical independence regarding the church
CHURCH:	adherence to the given tradition dialogue with the varied cultures

---

[30] D. Boumgarden, 'Discerning some leadership factors needed for starting up strong, missionally faithful congregations' (unpublished doctoral thesis, Columbia Theological Seminary, 2003).
[31] Hobbs, 'Faith twisted by Culture', quoted in van Gelder, *Confident Witness*, 95–6.
[32] Van Gelder, *Confident Witness*, 96.
[33] Hunsberger, 'The Newbigin Gauntlet', 9.
[34] A triangular model of gospel-culture relationships, reproduced by permission from *Missiology: An International Review* 19 (1991), 395.

First, the *conversion-encounter axis* lies between gospel and culture. The gospel encounters a particular culture with 'challenging relevance' for its message of Jesus Christ and his kingdom is utterly new – 'Jesus is introduced as one who bursts open the culture's models with the power of a wholly new fact.'[35] Those who respond to the gospel undergo the paradigm shift of conversion. This is the classic *kerysso* ('I herald') and *euangelizimaio* ('I bring good news') preaching of the New Testament. Preaching's core message of repentance from sin and of faith in Christ confronts hearers in culture and changes their lives. 'God decided, through the foolishness of our proclamation, to save those who believe. ... God's foolishness is wiser than human wisdom' (1 Cor. 1:21,25). This means a 'radical discontinuity regarding the gospel' for those living in any particular culture. However, new life in Christ cannot be totally disconnected from culture because 'the gospel and a person's response to it of necessity remain embodied in a particular culture's way of seeing, feeling and acting'.[36]

In the majority of evangelical churches this axis dominates the preaching scene. Preaching is primarily evangelistic, offered in many styles, but with one desired outcome – the winning of new converts. Emphasis is placed on individual spiritual responses. This has well-suited modernity's assumption that matters of Christian belief are private and have no role in the 'public square'. However, it avoids the challenge of prophetic preaching that calls individuals into conversion within God's new community, with social responsibilities as they live out God's counterstory together.

Second, the *reciprocal relationship axis* lies between the gospel and church. Assuming conversion, this challenges believers to embody the outcomes of 'hearing/seeing/doing God's word so that they are formed as Christ-shaped individuals and community'. The relationship is reciprocal between gospel and church because every church, no matter how short its history, inevitably reads scripture out of its traditions. Each church interprets scripture in the light of its experience, and its experience in the light of scripture. This is the so-called 'hermeneutical circle'. 'The community's tradition shapes its reading of the Bible, while its reading and rereading of the book further shapes its self-understanding.'[37]

Preachers have critical responsibility along this axis. Recognizing a church's given tradition, preachers have to emphasize scriptural distinctives to help believers grow in community for the sake of those around. In New Testament preaching terms this is typically *didasko* ('I teach'), with the application of doctrine so that believers might grow into maturity for works of ministry (Eph. 4:11). As with the conversion axis, preachers can avoid the prophetic challenge by applying teaching in an individualistic way.

---

[35] Hunsberger, 'The Newbigin Gauntlet', 8.
[36] Hunsberger, 'The Newbigin Gauntlet', 9.
[37] Hunsberger, 'The Newbigin Gauntlet', 10.

Third, is the *missionary dialogue axis* between church and its local culture. This axis assumes that a church community has been formed so that it can live out the gospel challenge in its own particular missionary context. Newbigin called for a relationship of true dialogue – a process of new converts (in community) being open to living out the unique implications of the gospel within the particularities of human cultures. Because of these dynamics, the missionary church is always in the *process* of becoming an appropriate inculturated form of the body of Christ. This means that new converts (in community) have a relationship with local culture(s) that is not only in 'radical discontinuity regarding the gospel' but also 'radical independence regarding the church'. Every church engaged in missionary dialogue is changing into something new in a continuing process.

Particularly along this axis, prophetic preachers need to discern and confront. For the New Testament context this axis was long. In a pluralistic pagan society the missionary church modeled new ways of love and purity in relationships and behavior. The communal emphasis on a called-out people sounds out through the epistles.[38] However, with the 'Christianizing' of society, most recently seen in modernity, society was assumed to share the same values as the church. In modern western culture the gap between society and church was deemed to be short. Stanley Hauerwas and William Willimon claim that modernity actually 'tamed' the church, 'as it went about congratulating itself for transforming the world, not noticing, that in fact the world has tamed the church'.[39]

However, if the church in modernity could mistakenly shorten the third axis, it should not doubt its length in postmodernity, as a wide gap has opened up between churches and their local culture's values and practice. Preaching today must engage in the corporate dimensions of being a missional church daring to dialogue with local cultures, fleshing out what it means to belong to Christ. It means a re-imaging of the church by defining its mission.

> The basic reality is the creation of a new being through the presence of the Holy Spirit. This new being is the common life (*koinonia*) in the Church. 'It is out of this new creation that both service and evangelism spring, and from it they receive their value. ... These different acts have their relation to one another not in any logical scheme, but in the fact that they spring out of the one new reality.'[40]

Preachers need to rediscover the power of prophetic preaching to discern and confront. To disturb the world by the radical discontinuity of the gospel

---

[38] E.g. 1 Pet. 1.
[39] S. Hauerwas and W.H. Willimon, *Resident Aliens: Life in the Christian Colony* (Nashville, 1989), 41.
[40] Newbigin, quoted in Hunsberger, 'The Newbigin Gauntlet', 15.

message, disturb the church lest it accommodate too easily to the world and disturb the particular culture in which a church lives by the witness of its common life.

Some urgent challenges

For preachers there are urgent challenges. Elsewhere I have described the preacher's spirituality by the 'three circles model' – overlapping circles of knowledge, skills and character.[41] Several issues from Hunsberger's missiological model should impact preachers today in these three areas.

In terms of knowledge, preachers should recognize that they face in three directions with the gospel. First, they face culture and second, the church. 'The gospel invites conversation with both the culture and church simultaneously. It confronts culture about godlessness and church about its worldliness.'[42] Yet, in a third direction preachers challenge the church to live counter-culturally, modeling a new identity as a missional people for its cultural context. Preachers have to identify 'those attitudes and values prevalent in the church through the permeation of culture that are a contradiction of the values inherent in the gospel'[43] in order to 'untwist faith'. The gospel's 'challenging relevance' presents new life in the kingdom of God that runs counter to worldly culture and causes believers to grow together, finding maturity and identity in Christ. An authoritative, transformational prophetic word sounds out gospel to world, to church and to the world through the church.

Preachers should therefore understand and practice the corporate implications of the gospel. Its challenge should never be limited to individual responses (whether devotional or life-style) that avoid the corporate social dimensions of being in community, 'in Christ'. The formation of a missional community involves preacher and hearers together entering missionary dialogue to live God's counterstory, with its radical critique of self-centered, self-interested individualism. This seems peculiarly appropriate in postmodernity. Stanley Grenz urges that postmodernity should move us from focusing on the individual to recognizing the role of the community of faith; from rational certainty alone to an intellectual encounter within human experience; from the dualism of mind and matter to a holistic approach to life and the gospel; from an emphasis on uniformity to a celebration of diversity that focuses on local stories and particulars rather than general principles.[44]

---

[41] Quicke, *360degree preaching*, 89–97.
[42] L. Bryant in Van Gelder (ed.), *Confident Witness*, 159.
[43] Gibbs, *Church Next*, 64.
[44] See S.J. Grenz, 'The Missional Church in a Postmodern World', an address at the conference on 'Worship, Evangelism, and Mission of the Church', Northern Theological Seminary, Lombard, Ill. (Nov. 5, 2001).

These three directions require fresh skills from preachers. In particular, preachers need to develop missionary methodology and sensitivities. Richard Mouw challenges us to develop missionary seriousness and carefulness in analysis of culture. He advocates four aspects of the apostle Paul's strategy in Acts 17: he studied the Athenian perspective on reality, discerned an underlying spiritual motif, looked for positive points of contact within the worldview and invited them to find fulfillment in Christ. Similarly, missionary empathy needs to find commonalities with people immersed in their culture. Mouw defines missionary vision as 'an insightful awareness of how the Spirit of God is already at work in a culture before we go there'.[45] As missionaries live with people, listen to them, identify with them and build bridges with them, so should preachers.

Identifying with the church community in its missionary task also requires pastoral skills. Some have argued that prophetic preachers, by definition, are lonely charismatic figures who are in continual opposition to institutions.[46] However, this missiological model brings prophetic preachers within the community of faith in missionary dialogue with local culture. Stephen Long contends that 'prophetic preaching is the most pastoral of activities' that 'is never discontinuous with the past but finds resources internal ... to call that community to its true identity'.[47] Such preaching requires commitment of preachers to focus on community rather than on programmes and issues. Dan Devadatta criticizes many churches that have 'tended to reduce the mission of the church to issues' – whether winning people to Christ or addressing social issues. Rather, he calls for prophetic preaching that recalls the church to self-understanding based on 1 Peter 1:1–2,17–25. He says that 'normal Christian life and community is that we have been chosen to live our days as strangers whose citizenship is not on earth'.[48]

Such preaching sounds different in its missionary dialogue. Without compromising gospel truth there are fresh questions about how best to preach in postmodernity. Brueggemann argues for realistic life-changing preaching that recognizes how supple and open lives are.

> People do not change, or change much, because of doctrinal argument or sheer cognitive appeal. ... People do not change, or change much, because of moral appeal. People in fact change by the offer of new models, images and pictures of how the pieces of life fit together. Transformation is the slow, steady process of

---

[45] R.J. Mouw, 'The Missionary Location of the North American Churches' in van Gelder, *Confident Witness*, 13.
[46] This view was advanced by Max Weber and Adolf Von Harnack as they set the roles of prophet against priest, charismatic loners against institutions. See S. Long, 'Prophetic Preaching' in Willimon and Lischer (eds.), *Concise Encyclopedia*, 387.
[47] Long, 'Prophetic Preaching', 388.
[48] D. Devadatta in Van Gelder (ed.), *Confident Witness*, 115.

inviting each other into a counterstory about God, world, neighbor and self. ... [T]his process has as counterpoint the subversive process of unlearning and disengaging from a story we find no longer to be credible or adequate.[49]

Preaching is '*funding* postmodern imagination'. The biblical text provides 'the pieces, materials and resources out of which a new world can be imagined. Our responsibility, then, is not a grand scheme or a coherent system, but the voicing of a lot of little pieces out of which people can put life together in fresh configurations.'[50]

In one of the few published attempts that relates preaching directly to Hunsberger's model, Lee Bryant calls for 'agonistic preaching' that struggles to live the questions of our time 'questioning the text from where we are, and then reshaping or counter-questioning those questions in response to God's word'. He stresses the role of biblical narrative which needs to be retold with a forth-telling that identifies key moments in the life of our people and even fore-tells 'the dynamics that will impact us, the nature of the struggle in that new time and place'.[51]

For preachers prophetic preaching involves significant issues of character – a need for humility and courage. People-pleasing preaching should not remain an option. Reflecting on the difficulties of this prophetic task Gordon McDonald states some principles that have emerged out of his experience. They include being aware of the priority themes of the Bible and their practical or political implications and staying free from ideological entrapment. He describes how he carefully selected three issues with which he could identify over a long period of time: famine-related issues in Africa, racial reconciliation and environmental matters. He models the humility and courage needed to speak a prophetic word. 'Every once in a while, a word well-spoken because it is immersed in prayer, clothed in humility, backed with solid thought and the fullness of God's Spirit breaks through and people see something different.'[52]

The church in western culture is greatly in need of such 'breaking through' words as prophetic preaching, marked by biblical authority. God's power to transform and its societal content challenges God's people to live his counterstory. This is the urgent task facing preachers today.

Bibliography

Brilioth, Y., *A Brief History of Preaching* (Philadelphia: Fortress Press, 1965).
Brueggemann, W., *Texts Under Negotiation: The Bible and Postmodern Imagination* (Minneapolis: Fortress Press, 1993).
— *The Prophetic Imagination*, (Philadelphia: Fortress, 1978).

---

[49] Brueggemann, *Texts Under Negotiation*, 24,25.
[50] Brueggemann, *Texts Under Negotiation*, 25.
[51] Bryant in van Gelder, *Confident Witness*, 60,61.
[52] G. Macdonald, 'Body Politics', *Leadership* 25 (Fall, 2004), 108.

Gelder, C. van (ed.), *The Church between Gospel and Culture* (Grand Rapids, Michigan: Eerdmans, 1996).
Gibbs, E., *ChurchNext – Quantum Changes in How we do Ministry* (Downers Grove, Illinois: Inter-Varsity Press, 2000).
Greidanus, S. *The Modern Preacher and the Ancient Text: Interpreting and Preaching Biblical Literature* (Grand Rapids, Michigan: Eerdmans, 1988).
Grenz, S., *A Primer on Postmodernism* (Grand Rapids, Michigan: Eerdmans, 1996).
Hauerwas, S. and W.H. Willimon, *Resident Aliens: Life in the Christian Colony* (Nashville: Abingdon Press, 1989).
Hunsberger, G.R. and C. van Gelder (eds.), *Church between Gospel and Culture* (Grand Rapids, Michigan: Eerdmans, 1996).
Neville, D. (ed.), *Prophecy and Passion* (Hindmarsh, SA; Australian Theological Forum, 2002).
Mitchell, H.H., *Black Preaching – the Recovery of a Powerful Art* (Nashville: Abingdon Press, 1990).
Newbigin, L., *Foolishness to the Greeks* (Grand Rapids, Michigan: Eerdmans, 1986).
Olley, J.W., *First and Second Kings – Then and Now* (Eastwood, NSW: Morling Press, 2001).
Quicke, M.J., *360degree preaching: hearing, speaking and living the word* (Grand Rapids, Michigan: Baker 2003).
Ward, J. and C. Ward, *Preaching from the Prophets* (Nashville: Abingdon Press, 1995).
Willimon, W.H. and R. Lischer (eds.), *Concise Encyclopedia of Preaching* (Louisville: Westminster John Knox Press, 1995).

AUTHOR INDEX

Alter, R., 23, 52
Ammerman, N., 191
Augustine, 166–167

Baelz, P.R., 160
Balthasar, U. von, 196
Barth, K., 172, 177–186, 192–193, 194
Bediako, K., 14–15
Bloch-Smith, E., 6
Bonhoeffer, D., 189, 208
Bosch, D., 64, 65–66, 149–150
Brecht, M., 66
Brett, M.G., 1
Brierly, P., 213
Brilioth, Y., 220
Brueggemann, W., 62, 187–188, 221, 222, 231
Brichto, H.C., 8–9
Bryant, L., 232
Buber, M., 57
Bultmann, R., 187, 189–191, 201–202

Cairns, D., 193
Campbell, A.F., 26
Charleston, S., 13–14
Christensen, D., 106
Clements, R.E., 176
Cohen, D.J., 50
Collins, C.J., 165
Cooper, A., 6, 7

Dahl, N.A., 122
Davey, C.J., 46
Davis, E.F., 58
Devadatta, D., 231
Devenish, S., 187
DeWaard, H., 65

Edelman, D.V., 26
Eichrodt, W., 173
Endres, J., 37
Erasmus, 202

Ewing, W., 206

Farmer, K.D., 55
Fiddes, P.S., 166
Firth, D.G., 20
Fokkelmann, J.P., 23
Freedman, D.N., 108, 109, 118
Frisch, A., 40, 43, 46
Fritz, V., 36

Gauchet, M., 2
George, T., 162
Gerrish, B., 75
Gerstenberger, E.S., 56
Ghanakan, K., 169
Gibbs, E., 223, 225
Goertz, H., 75
Goldstein, B., 6, 7
Gondarra, D., 13
Greidanus, S., 219
Grenz, S., 206, 230
Gunton, C.E., 166

Halpern, B., 3, 3n.7
Harries, R., 209
Harris, B.S., 204
Hauerwas, S., 205, 229
Hendrix, S., 66–67, 68, 76
Hick, J., 163
Hobbs, W.C., 225
Hoerth, A.J., 36
Hunsberger, G.R., 224, 227, 230, 232
Hurowitz, V., 34, 46

Jewett, P.K., 160, 167
Jones, T., 214–215
Jordan, I., 2
Jüngel, E., 165

Klein, W.W., 174
Korpel, M.C.A., 79
Kraft, C., 195

Author Index

Kraus, H-J., 58
Kugel, J., 52
Küng, H., 161, 163

Labuschagne, C.J., 118
Lewis, C.S., 197
Lightstone, J.N., 107
Lindbeck, G., 196
Lo, L-K., 121
Lohse, B., 70, 72
Long, S., 221, 231
Luther, M., 64–78

Martin, W.A.P., 131–132
Martin-Achard, R., 80
Martyr, J., 162
Mbiti, J., 192
McCormack, B.L., 177
McDonald, G., 232
Miller, P.D., 56
Minear, P., 125
Mitchell, H., 222
Moberly, W., 9, 10
Moltmann, J., 72
Mouw, R., 231

Nelson, H., 157
Newbigin, L., 162, 223, 224, 227, 229

O'Donnell, J.J., 158
Olley, J., 1, 20, 33, 41–42, 43, 44, 48, 50, 64, 88, 91, 106, 154, 157, 172, 184, 202, 218, 221
O'Neil, M., 172
Origen, 162
Otto, E., 4

Parker, K.I., 46–47
Parsons, M., 64
Pattel-Gray, A., 2
Peskett, H., 76
Pinnock, C., 163, 164
Pippin, R., 188
Polkinghorne, J., 201
Preuss, H.D., 173, 176, 182, 184

Quicke, M.J., 218

Rahner, K., 162, 165, 189, 208n.10
Ramachandra, V., 76
Rauer, M., 123
Rice, R., 164
Roberts, C.H., 112
Robinson, J.A.T., 163
Rogers, C., 207
Rose, D.B., 2
Rowley, H.H., 1, 1n.1, 2, 8, 172, 175
Runia, K., 221

Sanders, J., 163
Sanneh, L., 15
Schreiner, S., 71
Schwöbel, C., 158
Shenk, W., 67
Skeat, T.C., 112
Skylba, R.J., 220
Smith, H., 191, 199
Snaith, N.N., 175

Tacey, D., 2, 199–200
Thielicke, H., 193
Tillich, P., 189
Tomes, R., 45–46
Toorn, K. van der, 5
Tournier, P., 210
Turner, D., 13

Verkuyl, J., 65
Vitringa, K., 79
Vriezen, T.C., 177

Wacholder, B.Z., 113
Wagner, C.P., 116
Wan, S.-k., 13
Webster, J., 165, 182
Wenham, G., 10
Westermann, C., 54
Willimon, W., 229
Wright, C., 8–9, 11, 140
Wright, J.W., 173, 174
Wright, N.T., 196

Yeo, K.-K., 12

Zimmerli, W., 172–173, 174
Zizioulas, J.D., 164, 166

SCRIPTURE INDEX

Genesis
1:28 *146*
2:15 *146*
2:18 *205*
3–11 *146*
10:4 *84*
10:5 *84*
12 *146, 151*
12:1–3 *145*
12:3 *31, 151, 175*
12:6–7 *10*
13:18 *10*
14:18–20 *10*
14:18–22 *1*
15:6 *94, 95*
15:15 *95*
17:5 *95*
18 *206*
18:10 *97*
18:14 *97*
18:19 *152*
21:12 *96*
25:3 *97*
33:9–11 *40*
35:14 *13*
35:20 *5, 13*
40:34–35 *38, 39*

Exodus
6:2 *1n.1*
9:16 *97*
15:15 *153*
19:4–6 *151, 153, 184*
19:6 *175*
20:24–25 *5*
20:28 *35n.13*
23 *7*
23:14–17 *5*
23:20–24:11 *7*
23:24 *7*
24:26–27 *7*
32 *109*

33:19 *97*
34:11–16 *8*

Numbers
25 *8*

Leviticus
17–26 *8*
18–19 *153*
18:5 *98*
18:28 *7*
19:23 *7*
25:10 *9*
25:13 *9*
25:23 *11*
25:23–24 *9*

Deuteronomy
4:6–8 *153, 175*
4:35 *150*
4:39 *150*
6:4 *150, 166*
7:1–4 *8*
7:7 *151*
7:7–8 *11*
8:17–18 *11*
9:5 *11*
9:28 *153*
10:14 *150, 151*
10:27 *150*
12 *45*
12–25 *118*
12:5 *35n.13*
12:9–10 *39*
13 *4*
13:7–10 *4*
16:5–6 *5*
16:22 *5*
17:1–7 *45*
17:16–17 *45*
18:11 *6*
19:14 *1, 8*

20:16–18 *7*
23:3 *82*
26:14 *9*
27:5 *35n.13*
29:4 *100*
30 *98*
30:12–14 *98*
32:21 *100*
32:43 *102, 124n.19*

Joshua
24 *7*
24:14–15 *7*

Judges
12:1–4 *125*
19 *206*

1 Samuel
2:27–30 *174n.15*
5:1–4 *30*
8:20 *30*
9 *27*
9:12–13 *5*
10:1 *5, 27*
10:17 *27*
11 *27*
13–14 *22*
13–15 *26*
13:11–14 *174n.15*
13:14 *27*
15:17–28 *174n.15*
16–17 *20–32*
16:1–13 *21, 26*
16:5 *21*
16:7 *48*
16:11 *27*
16:14–23 *21, 22, 26, 28*
16:18 *21n.2, 22, 28*
17:1–11 *25, 29*
17:8–10 *29*

Scripture Index

17:11 *29*
17:12–23 *29*
17:12–32 *25*
17:15 *27*
17:17 *22*
17:17–18 *29*
17:23 *29*
17:24–26 *28–31*
17:24–30 *30*
17:28 *27n.20*
17:32–36 *28*
17:32–37 *22*
17:33 *26*
17:34–36 *27*
17:43–44 *30*
17:45–47 *30*
17:49 *29*
17:50–51 *29*
17:52–53 *29*
17:55 *22*
17:55–58 *23*
20:6 *5*
28:3 *6n.17*
49:8 *103*
65:2 *100*

2 Samuel
5–8 *23–24*
5:6–10 *24*
5:11 *24, 38n.27*
5:17–8:14 *24*
14:16 *6*
16:1 *27*
18:4 *5*
18:6–9 *27*
21–24 *23, 24*
22:50 *102*
24:25 *34n.11*
28:14 *6*

1 Kings
1–11 *33–49*
1:1–2:46 *41, 43*
3:1–3 *41, 42, 42n.42, 43*
3:1–15 *41*
3:1–5:14 *41*
3:3 *47*

3:4–4:34 *43*
3:5–14 *44, 43*
3:10–14 *38*
5:1 *38*
5:1–6:38 *43*
5:3 *39*
5:4 *39*
5:5 *39*
5:15–32 *41*
6 *36*
6:1 *38, 38n.25*
6:1–10 *34*
6:1–9:9 *41*
6:2 *35, 36, 39*
6:3 *35, 36*
6:4 *35*
6:5–6 *35*
6:7 *35*
6:8 *35*
6:9 *35*
6:11–13 *38, 43, 44*
6:18 *36*
6:19 *35*
6:21–28 *37*
6:31 *35*
6:31–32 *37*
6:38 *38, 39*
6:39 *35*
7:1 *39*
7:1–12 *43*
7:7–8 *39n.30*
7:8–9 *39, 41*
7:9–12 *35*
7:13–14 *37, 43*
7:15–51 *36*
7:23–26 *36*
7:27–37 *36*
7:37 *37*
7:38–39 *36*
7:40–51 *36*
8 *39, 44, 46*
8:9–11 *40*
8:10–11 *38*
8:13 *40, 46*
8:22– 53 *37*
8:22–66 *38*
8:24–26 *39*
8:41–43 *153*

8:53 *47*
8:56 *39*
9:1 *47*
9:1–9 *43, 44, 47n.62*
9:3–9 *38*
9:4 *47*
9:10 *38n.28*
9:10–23 *43*
9:10–25 *41*
9:15–19 *39*
9:20–22 *45*
9:24 *41, 43, 44*
9:25 *45, 48*
9:26–10:29 *41*
9:26–11:43 *43*
10 *47*
10:14 *45*
10:27 *45*
10:28 *45*
11:1 *43*
11:1–8 *41n.36*
11:1–13 *41*
11:3 *45*
11:6 *47*
11:7 *42n.42*
11:9–13 *43*
11:11–13 *38, 43*
11:14–12:24 *41*
14:1–16 *221*
19:10 *100*
21 *109*
21:3 *6*
21:17–24 *8*

2 Kings
22–23 *198*
23:26–27 *198–199*

1 Chronicles
21 *34n.11*
22 *34n.11*
29:11 *150*

2 Chronicles
2:3 *38n.26*
3:1 *34n.11*
22 *38*
22:4 *38n.27*

34–35 *198*
35:25 *199*

Ezra
9–10 *82*

Nehemiah
13:1 *82*
13:26 *45*

Esther
10:1 *84*
14:17 *125*

Psalms
1 68n.23
2:7 *147*
2:8 *147*
17:1–5 *54*
17:50 *124n.19*
19:4 *99*
22 *58–61*
22:1 *54*
22:1–2 *59*
22:3–5 *59*
22:6–8 *59–60*
22:9–10 *60*
22:11 *60*
22:11–18 *60*
22:15 *60*
22:19–21 *60*
22:21 *60*
22:22-26 *60-61*
22:27–31 *61*
24:1 *150*
27:4 *210n.19*
32:1–2 *94*
47 *153*
47:9 *154*
67 *153*
69:22–23 *100*
72:10 *86*
84:10 *210*
96 *150*
96:11–13 *154*
116:1 *124n.19*
117:1 *102*

Isaiah
1:9 *97*
4:14 *220*
8:4 *98*
8:19 6n.17
10:22–23 *97*
11:10 *102, 124n.19*
14:9 6n.17
17:9 *101*
19:19–25 *154*
20 *219*
20:6 *83*
23:2 *84*
23:6 *84, 86*
24:15 *86*
28:11 *98*
28:16 *99*
29:10 *100*
29:16 *97*
32:1 *199*
35 *11*
40 *64, 68*
40–55 *79*
40:2 *73*
40:3 *73, 74*
40:9 *72*
40:10 *75*
40:18–20 *69*
40:21–31 *69*
41:1 *79, 147*
41:1–5 *84*
41:5 *79, 83*
41:25 *85*
42:4 *79, 80, 84, 87*
42:10 *79, 83, 84*
42:12 *79, 84*
42:15 *79*
43:4 *85*
43:5–6 *85*
43:9–13 *150*
43:10–12 *148*
43:19–21 *220*
44:6–20 *150*
45:9 *97*
45:14 *85*
45:22 *83*
45:23 *150*
46:11 *85*
49:1 *79, 84*
49:3–6 *175*
49:6 *103, 147, 148*
49:12 *85*
49:18 *103*
51:4–5 *87*
51:5 *79, 84*
52:7 *99*
52:15 *102*
53:1 *99*
54 *11*
55:3 *199*
55:11 *219*
56:2–8 *154*
59:20–21 *101*
59:21 *199*
60:9 *86, 87*
60:19–20 *87*
61:1 *220*
61:1–2 *199*
61:2 *220*
62:12 *199*
65:1 *100*
65:17–25 *154*
66:19 *86*
66:19–21 *154*

Jeremiah
2:10 *84*
4:1–2 *153*
10:1–16 *150*
18:1–10 *153*
19 *219*
20:9 *219*
22:10 *199*
22:13–17 *39n.31*
23:9–40 *220*
25:22 *84*
27:1–12 *150*
31:33 *199*
32:12 *109*
45:1–5 *109*
47:4 *84*
51:59–64 *109*

Ezekiel
4:1–3 *219*
27:6–7 *83*
36–37 *11*
36:16 *153*

Scripture Index

Daniel
1:8–16 *125*
2 *115*
8:26–27 *114*

Hosea
1:10 *97*
2:1 *97*
2:23 *97*

Joel
3:5 *99*

Amos
1:3–2:3 *225*
2:4 *225*
3:8 *219*
9:11–12 *154*
9:12 *154*

Jonah
1:3 *87*

Nahum
2:1 *99*

Habakkuk
2:4 *103*
2:14 *94*

Zechariah
2:10–11 *154*

Malachi
1:2 *97*

Matthew
6:2 *70*
7:14 *160*
12:21 *80*
12:46–50 *210*
15:27–28 *114*
18:1–6 *211*
24:6–7 *115*
24:34 *114*
28:19 *160*

Luke
2:29–32 *147*
4:16–21 *220*
4:18 *220*
4:21 *220*
4:22 *220*
4:28 *220*
4:29 *220*
7:16 *220*
13:23–30 *161, 162*
13:24 *161*
19:1–10 *212*
23:43 *208*
24 *145, 148*

John
1:14 *221*
3:16 *168*
14:6 *160*
14:26 *168*
15:26 *168*

Acts
4:12 *160*
13:47 *148*
15 *154*
16:1–3 *13*
16:8–9 *116*
16:11–12 *116*
17 *231*
20:5 *116, 117*
28:30 *111*

Romans
1:5 *121*
1:16–17 *93, 99*
3:21–26 *93*
3:21–31 *93*
3:27–31 *93, 94*
3:29–30 *93, 122*
3:31 *94*
4 *92, 93, 94–95, 151*
4:1 *94*
4:3 *94, 95*
4:4–5 *94*
4:6 *94*
4:7–8 *94*
4:9 *95*
4:10–11 *95*
4:12 *95*
4:15 *95*
4:16 *95*
4:18 *95*
4:19 *95*
8:18–21 *154*
8:26 *168*
9–11 *92, 93, 96–101*
9:1–5 *92, 96*
9:6 *96*
9:6–7 *96*
9:6–13 *96*
9:7 *96*
9:9 *97*
9:11 *96*
9:12 *97*
9:13 *97*
9:14 *97*
9:15 *97*
9:16 *97*
9:17 *97*
9:18 *97*
9:20 *97*
9:22–24 *97*
9:23 *97*
9:24 *97*
9:29 *97*
9:32–33 *98*
9:33 *98*
10:1–4 *96*
10:4 *98*
10:5 *98*
10:9–10 *99*
10:11 *99*
10:12 *122*
10:13 *99*
10:14–15 *99*
10:15 *99*
10:16 *99*
10:17 *99*
10:18 *99*
10:19 *100*
10:20 *100*
10:21 *100*
11:1 *100*
11:1–6 *96*
11:5 *100*
11:7 *100, 101*

11:13 *92, 121*
11:13–32 *96*
11:25 *101*
11:26 *101*
11:28 *101*
11:29 *101*
11:31 *101*
11:32 *101*
14:1 *101, 124*
14:1–15:13 *123–126, 134, 135*
14:2 *125*
14:3 *101, 124*
14:4 *124*
14:5 *134*
14:10–12 *124*
14:11 *103*
14:14 *124*
14:20 *124, 136*
14:21 *125*
15 *92*
15:7 *124*
15:7–16 *154*
15:7–21 *93, 101–102*
15:9–12 *124*
15:16 *92, 121*
15:18 *92*
16:20 *114*

1 Corinthians
1:21 *228*
1:25 *228*
8 *12*
8–10 *134, 135*
8:5–6 *150*
8:13 *134*
14:25 *48*
15:23–28 *114*

2 Corinthians
3:13–18 *92*
4:6 *168*
5:18–20 *221*
5:19 *199*
5:20 *221*
6:2 *103*

Galatians
1:6–9 *91*
1:12 *91, 92*
1:13–14 *91*
1:16 *121*
2:1–14 *123*
2:7–9 *92, 121*
2:11–14 *92*
2:12–21 *135*
2:16 *122*
2:20 *168*
2:21 *123, 162*
3:28 *14n.47, 122*
3:28–29 *12*
5:6 *122*
6:15 *122*

Ephesians
1:3–14 *166*
1:4 *183*
2:18 *166*
3:1–13 *121*
3:6 *12*
4:4–6 *166*
4:11 *228*

Philippians
2:9–11 *150*

Colossians
1:25–27 *121*
4:10 *112*
4:11 *112*
4:12 *112*
4:14 *112*

1 Thessalonians
4:13–5:11 *113*
4:16–17 *114*

2 Thessalonians
1:5–10 *113*
2:1–12 *113*
2:15–3:16 *113*

1 Timothy
2:4 *160*
4:7 *195*

2 Timothy
4:2 *221*
4:9–13 *112*
4:10 *112*
4:11 *113*
4:11–13 *116, 117*
4:13 *110, 111, 112*
4:21 *111*

Philemon
24 *112*

Hebrews
1:2 *114*
9:26 *114*
10:25 *114*
10:37 *114*
13:2 *206*
13:22–23 *117*

James
2:19 *211*
5:3 *114*
5:7 *114*
5:8 *114*

1 Peter
1:1–2 *231*
1:17–25 *231*
4:11 *219*

2 Peter
3:13 *154*

1 John
1:5 *164*
2:18 *114*
4:16 *164*
4:24 *164*

Revelation
7:9 *151*
19 *206*
21:1–5 *154*

SUBJECT INDEX

Abram (Abraham), 1, 1n.1, 10, 11, 94, 95, 101, 144, 145, 146, 149, 151, 152–153, 173
ancestors (divinized), 6
ancestor veneration, 9, 12; worship, 9, 129–131, 131, 133, 134–135
ancestral cultural practices, 1–19 religion, 1–19, 2, 3, 4, 6n.19, 7, 8, 9–10, 11, 13; rites, 130, 131, 133–134
'anonymous Christian', 162, 208, 212
Ark, 40, 46, 47
asserting, 52, 56, 57–58, 61
Assyria, 3, 4
Australia, 2, 10, 12, 13, 15, 187, 189, 192, 194, 196, 199, 200, 202, 210

Babylon, 11, 80, 85, 199
Baruch, 109, 118, 119
behaviour, 204–217
belief, 204–217
belonging, 204–217
body of Christ (the church), 13, 229
Buddhism, 127, 128

calling, 91–105, 226
chiasm, 24, 40
Chinese, 129–139
Christ, 66, 67, 68, 69, 70, 71, 72, 73, 74, 75, 76, 91, 92, 98, 99, 114, 115, 135, 142, 144, 145, 146, 147, 148–149, 151, 154, 157, 158, 159, 160, 162, 163–164, 166–167, 168, 169, 177–180, 181, 182, 184, 185, 190, 193, 196–197, 199, 200, 201–202, 208, 212, 220, 221, 225, 228, 229, 231
church, 180, 210, 225, 227, 228, 229, 230
coastlands, 79
community, 56, 60, 62, 68, 107, 115, 125, 126, 143, 173, 176, 179–180, 181, 182, 184, 185, 192, 196, 204, 205, 206, 209, 210, 211, 212, 213, 214, 219, 220, 222, 225, 226, 228, 230, 231

control, 55, 57, 60, 61
coram Deo, 74
cultural transformation, 8

Dagon, 30
Daniel, 113–115
David, 20–32, 44, 48, 82, 85
'degodisation', 189–193, 194, 198
Demas, 112–113
Deus abscondus, 160
Deus revelatus, 160
Deuteronomic canon, 108, 119; theology, 3
dischronologized narrative, 23–24, 26
disenchantment, 2, 3, 4
distress, 51, 52, 53, 54, 55, 56, 57, 58, 59, 60, 61, 62

Egypt, 45, 83, 85
election, 96, 97, 101, 146, 149, 151–152, 153, 172–186
elohim, 5–7, 6n.17
enemy, 55–56, 57, 59, 60
Enlightenment, the, 188
eschatological expectation, 80
eschatology, 113, 144, 153–154, 163, 190
evangelism, 145
evangelist, 74, 112
exclusivism, 158
exile, 11, 48, 109, 188
expressing, 52, 56–57, 61
Ezra, 109–110, 119

faith, 123, 132, 153, 159, 191, 204, 206, 207, 212, 213, 215, 222, 228
food laws, 125
forgiveness, 73, 94

Germany, 201
God: alienation from, 54, 57, 58; anger of, 97; authority of, 21; centrality of, 72; confidence in, 59; Creator, 13,

132, 141, 144, 151; dependence upon, 60; Father, 166–167, 168, 169, 179, 221; holiness of, 219, 220; immutability of, 183; impotence of, 57; jealous, 82; judgement of, 153, 174, 181, 199, 220; love of, 164–165; mercy of, 91–105, 153; mission of (*mission Dei*), 72, 76, 141–143, 145–146, 148, 151; mystery of, 160; name of, 1–2; nature of, 163–165; personal, 145; prerogative of, 97–98, 101; power of, 21, 31, 54, 58, 75, 76, 80, 97, 221; presence of, 54; reality of, 31, 48; relational, 166; transcendent, 167; triune, 158, 163, 165–168; unfaithfulness of, 54; unicity of, 80, 150, 151; Yahweh, 1, 3, 110, 118, 150–151
Goliath, 20–32
gospel, 48, 66, 67–76, 91–105, 121–139, 142, 150, 151, 157, 158, 159, 162, 175, 177, 187, 189, 191, 192, 193–194, 196–201, 207, 222, 225, 227, 228, 229, 230
Gott an sich, 73
grace, 68, 69, 70, 71, 72, 73, 74, 94, 95, 175, 177, 178, 182, 225
Great Commission, the, 161

Hagiographa, the, 109
Hezekiah, 4, 5
Hiram, 38, 41
History of David's Rise (HDR), 22
Holiness Code, the, 4, 5
Holy of Holies, the, 35, 36, 47
Holy Spirit, 72, 74, 146, 165, 166–167, 169, 221, 229, 231, 232
hypostasis, 166
hospitality, 206, 225, 226

identity crisis, 125
idolatry, 70, 71, 133, 134, 150, 152, 198
imagining, 52, 56, 58, 61
indigenous community, 2, 3; religion, 2; rites, 7–8
inner sanctuary, 36n.18, 37
intrapsychic dynamics, 54–56
investing, 52, 56, 61

islands, 79–90
Israel, 96, 98, 100, 109, 114, 143, 144, 147, 148, 149, 150, 151–153, 173–177, 181, 184, 187–188, 196; missiological significance of, 31; missional existence of, 31; visibility of, 152–153, 176

Jerusalem, 3, 23, 114, 116, 117, 199
Josephus, 106, 108, 109, 117, 125
Jesse, 21, 26, 29
Jesus Christ, 12, 14
Joshua, 7
Josiah, 5
Jubilee Year, 9
justification ('rectification'), 94, 103, 121–122, 208–209

kerygma, 187, 190, 196, 198
kingdom of God, 113, 114, 177, 221, 228, 230

land, 4, 6, 7–9, 11, 13, 15; tenure, 3, 4
law, 73, 73n.58, 74, 94, 95, 98, 122, 124, 153, 173
limited inclusivism, 159
liturgy, 51
Logos, 162
Luke, 110, 115, 116, 117, 119, 142–153, 144, 147

master editor(s), 106, 108, 109, 110, 118–119
materialism, 48, 191, 223
Messiah, 144–145, 148
modernity, 188–189, 191–192, 194, 199, 223, 224, 225, 229
missio Dei (see 'God')
mission, 1, 20, 64, 64n.2, 65, 68, 71, 72–76, 106, 127–133, 140–156, 176, 184, 185, 192, 214, 229
missional reading, 140–156
missionary, 1, 231; activity, 80, 81, 127, 128, 129, 131; dialogue, 229, 230; methodology, 230
missiological framework, 31; hermeneutic, 146, 147, 148
missiology, 2, 3, 10, 11–15, 224

Subject Index 243

monotheism, 151
Moses, 40, 44, 47, 98, 110, 173, 174
mystery, 101, 160, 161, 165, 169, 173, 197, 225
myth, 190, 193–198, 201

Naboth, 6, 8
narrative sequence, 21–24
Nestorian Christianity, 127, 128
New Age, 192
new creation, 146
nullpunkt, 187–188, 189, 191, 199, 202
numerical compositions, 118

ousia, 166

paganism, 192
pagan influence, 37–38
paradigm, 205; shift, 204, 213–215, 228
particularism, 80, 81–83, 175
Paul, 13, 90–104, 111, 112, 113, 114, 115, 116, 119, 121–139, 142, 144, 149, 151, 195
perichoresis, 168
performance, 52, 53, 62
Peter, 115
Pharaoh's daughter, 33, 34, 39, 41, 42, 44, 45, 46, 47
Phoenician influence, 37, 37n.22, 46
pluralism, 151, 159, 160, 214, 223, 229
poetics, 28–31
polytheism, 81
Portico of Judgement, the, 39, 39n.30
postmodernity, 194, 206, 209, 211, 215, 223, 225, 229, 230
post-mortem evangelism, 159
prayer of dedication, 37, 38, 40, 41, 44, 46
preachers, 72, 74, 76, 219, 221, 222, 227, 228, 229, 230, 232
preaching, 72, 74, 159, 218–233; authority of, 219, 220, 221, 230; challenge of, 219, 220, 221; evangelical, 66; prophetic, 218, 219–223; transformative, 219, 220, 221, 230, 231–232
Process theism, 167

prophets, 107; former, 107, 108, 109, 115; latter, 107, 108, 109, 115
psalms: cultic function of, 51; form of, 51–52; lament, 50–63; mythic narrative, 53; narrative, 53–54; parabolic narrative, 53; penitential, 55, 56; poetic narrative, 53, 60, 61; poetry of, 52–53

redemption, 9, 11, 15
remnant, 100, 143
repristination, 187–203
'rites controversy', 129

salvation, 94; 'mechanics' of, 99
Samuel, 5, 6, 6n.17
Saul, 20–32
Self-centredness, 69
Sennacherib, 3, 4, 198
Servant of the Lord, 81, 84, 103, 147, 148, 152, 176
Solomon, 33–49
speech, 28–31
strong, the, 124–125, 135

tabernacle, the, 44, 47
table fellowship, 123
Tanakh, the, 106–120
Temple, the, 33–49, 109, 114, 198
Ten Commandments, the, 109, 118, 134
Timothy, 13, 111, 117, 195
Torah (see 'law'), 11, 48, 92, 106, 107, 108; new, 116, 117, 143, 220
Trinitarian theology, 157–158

Ugarit, 5, 82, 84
unevangelized, the, 157–171
universal applicability, 91–105
universalism, 81–83, 159, 162, 163

Vorlage, 25–26

Warlpiri people, 2, 15; translation, 14
weak, the, 124–125, 135
Word Count Project, the, 106
worship, 48, 50, 51, 64, 69, 80, 82, 150, 166, 175, 199, 206, 220, 225, 226
Writings, the, 108, 109, 115, 124n.19

www.ingramcontent.com/pod-product-compliance
Lightning Source LLC
Chambersburg PA
CBHW070304230426
43664CB00014B/2633